women in
popular culture

Recent Titles in
American Popular Culture
Series Editor: *M. Thomas Inge*

Film: A Reference Guide
Robert A. Armour

Women's Gothic and Romantic Fiction: A Reference Guide
Kay Mussell

Animation: A Reference Guide
Thomas W. Hoffer

Variety Entertainment and Outdoor Amusements: A Reference Guide
Don B. Wilmeth

women in
popular culture

A REFERENCE GUIDE

Katherine Fishburn

American Popular Culture

Greenwood Press
Westport, Connecticut • London, England

Library of Congress Cataloging in Publication Data

Fishburn, Katherine, 1944-
    Women in popular culture.

    (American popular culture, ISSN 0193-6859)
    Bibliography: p.
    Includes index.
    1. Women in popular culture—United States—History.
I. Title. II. Series.
HQ1426.F685   305.4'0973   81-13421
ISBN 0-313-22152-9 (lib. bdg.)   AACR2

Library of Congress Catalog Card Number: 81-13421
ISBN: 0-313-22152-9
ISSN: 0193-6859

First published in 1982

Greenwood Press
A division of Congressional Information Service, Inc.
88 Post Road West, Westport, Connecticut 06881

Printed in the United States of America

10   9   8   7   6   5   4   3   2   1

This book is lovingly dedicated
to my parents,
Ruth Owen Richards
and
John W. Richards,
who taught me
that there is always more to learn.

Contents

	ACKNOWLEDGMENTS	ix
	INTRODUCTION	3
Chapter 1	Histories of Women in Popular Culture	25
Chapter 2	Women in Popular Literature	86
Chapter 3	Women in Magazines and Magazine Fiction	125
Chapter 4	Women in Film	136
Chapter 5	Women in Television	154
Chapter 6	Women in Advertising, Fashion, Sports, and Comics	161
Chapter 7	Theories of Women in Popular Culture	196
Appendix 1	Selected Periodicals	211
Appendix 2	Special Issues and Sections of Periodicals	213
Appendix 3	A Selected List of Bibliographies, Biographies, and Information Guides Relevant to Women in Popular Culture	215
Appendix 4	Chronology of Important Dates	219
Appendix 5	Important Research Centers and Institutions	227
	INDEX	231

Acknowledgments

For their contributions to this work, I would like to thank the following: the Michigan State University Reference Librarians, especially Walter Burinski, Agnes F. Haigh, and Emma Jane Arnold; the Michigan State University Special Collection Librarians, especially Anne Tracy; Russel B. Nye, who introduced me to this subject; Donald Lewsader, who expertly typed the text of this manuscript; and my husband, Drew H. Fishburn, who edited the manuscript and otherwise showed he loves me.

For their professional encouragement and emotional support, I would like to give special thanks to my colleagues and friends: Wendy K. Neininger, formerly of Michigan State University, now with Michigan Bell Telephone; Nellie Y. McKay, University of Wisconsin, Madison; and Janet E. Samuelson, Michigan State University.

Without the preliminary work of all the scholars whom I cite below, my own work would not have had a reason for being. Therefore, for their thousands of hours of labor and the thousands of pages that they have written—and I have read—I thank them.

women in
popular culture

Introduction

Although women have always played central roles in the creation and consumption of America's popular culture, their most significant role has been the largely passive one of providing popular culture with its major images. That is, the images of women, far more than those of men, pervade the various forms of popular culture through which we manifest our national identity and signify our national intentions. In short, women as a group— a class, a sex—have been used for over two hundred years to represent most of the social mythology that is expressed in popular culture.

In studying the role and image of women in popular culture, we find that, in general, women have been used to symbolize both this country's desires and its fears. The image of women, therefore, has ranged anywhere from the idealized lady of exemplary tastes and behavior to the terrible mother who would destroy us all. The image of women in popular culture, in other words, takes both a positive and a negative valence, with the positive image expressing our dreams and the negative image our night-mares. At the same time that popular culture projects these fantasies of our collective imagination, individual women have balked at accepting these artificial images as their own. In rejecting the content of popular culture, these women, in effect, have rejected the prevailing social mythol-ogy itself. What they have embraced in its stead is the tenet that women should decide for themselves, on an individual basis, who they are going to be and what they are going to become. Rather than allowing society to determine their identity as a group, they insist on their right to determine their own identities on a personal level. The study of women in popular culture, therefore, follows two concurrent and dialectical streams that converge only to clash and not to join—with the forces of popular culture taking the reactionary or conservative position and the foes of popular culture the radical or revolutionary position. Given this historical pattern of conflict, it almost goes without saying that the study of women in popular culture is a study of political process whereby individual women attempt to subvert the group mentality that would keep their identities subject to the desires and fears of the collective imagination.

Regardless of the fact that individual women historically have fought the idea, the myth that there is such a creature as the quintessentially American woman is an enduring one that has permeated our popular culture since its inception. Although the presence of a myth has been a constant, the myth itself has not remained unchanged. In fact, in the course of our history, the image of the ideal woman has undergone various transmutations that closely correspond to major social and political upheavals. In the colonial and prerevolutionary period, for example, when women were at a premium and hard work was needed from everyone, the ideal American woman was a helpmeet; in the nineteenth century, with the rise of capitalism and the middle class, she was a lady; in the twentieth, with its wars and future shock, she has been wife, mother, and companion. The fact of these changes suggests that the image of the American woman, as pictured in popular culture, is a phenomenon directly related to issues of public policy—whether this policy be constituted formally, as law or propaganda in times of war or national emergency, or agreed upon informally, as ongoing social mythology. In either case, the image of the ideal woman has been implicitly—and often explicitly—expressive of the national interest.

Correspondingly, the negative image of woman has expressed the national fears and insecurities. Thus, in the seventeenth century we had witches, women who were blamed for corrupting otherwise decent people: in the eighteenth and nineteenth centuries we had loose and fallen women, who were blamed for destroying the family; in the twentieth we have had "suffragettes" and "bra-burners" who were accused of wanting to ruin the home and the country and, in the case of the latter, wanting sexually integrated public bathrooms. We have also seen, in the twentieth century, the transformation of the "mother"—the ideal image of the nineteenth century—into the "mom" or the "terrible mother," the witch of the family and the scourge of the country.

The fact that popular culture relies upon and reinforces sexual stereotypes of its women says less about women than it says about America and our national psyche. Since at least the nineteenth century, this country has relied upon a complex iconography of women to express its social mythology. Sometimes women have been used to express the country's genuine mythology, but more often they have been used to express its affected mythology. By the latter phrase, I mean the mythology that Americans pretend they believe in while behaving to the contrary. For example, what Americans really believe in is getting ahead—the business ethic where success is measured by income. Americans also believe in individuality, independence, freedom of speech, and free enterprise. Women—with few exceptions—have never been used to represent these beliefs. Women have been used—in some instances continue to be used—to represent the qualities opposite to these. Thus, women, according to popular myth, belong in the home where they will best serve their country's interest by being good wives and mothers. In the home women do not get ahead; do not achieve recognition in the form of pay for their work. Women at home lose their individuality to the roles expected of them as wives and mothers; do not enjoy independence. And while they may have freedom of speech, they do not engage in free enterprise in the home—in fact the notion of domestic free enterprise seems to suggest illicit sexual activity. Women, while being touted as the exemplars of what is best about America, as a class have been denied the American dream and the American experience. They have been denied, in other words, the opportunity to participate on an equal footing with the men of this country. This has been denied them because the social mythology on which this country runs is a male-dominated mythology that relegates women to second-class status.

As Elizabeth Janeway observes in *Man's World, Woman's Place*, social mythology is difficult to combat and finally impossible to eradicate. Mythology resists attack because it ultimately is not a logical construct that can be discredited and dislodged by rational arguments. It is a projection of emotional needs (and fears) and so ingrained in our collective imagination, our popular culture, our very identity as a people, that it is rendered virtually invisible by its omnipresence. It is also the vital bonding agent that holds us together as a culture; without it we would be too fragmented to be a people. But as necessary as a social mythology is, and as stubbornly resistant to change as it can be, it is nothing less than substantive change in our social mythology that today's feminists are calling for. One of the most important contributions of the early consciousness-raising groups of the 1960s and 1970s—and what made them so politically effective, and dangerous—was their ability to help people (primarily women) see the social myths that surround us and control our thinking and behavior. Once women could see the myths, they could set about modifying or getting rid of them— or at the very least developing strategies for circumventing them. Many of the earliest studies of women in American popular culture were especially helpful in this finger-pointing. Although some of the papers presented at conferences were nothing more than lists of images and litanies of injustices—and were therefore painful to sit through for several reasons, not the least of which was that at first they seemed to have no point—they did serve a purpose. They literally showed us something about ourselves; or, more precisely perhaps, something about how writers, filmmakers, and advertisers saw us. They identified our mythology. It is a mythology that has its immediate roots in the nineteenth-century cult of true womanhood, to use Barbara Welter's famous phrase. But it is a mythology that goes back to our very origins as a people.

Although seventeenth-century colonial society was clearly paternalistic in structure and nature, based as it was on the British class system and a male-dominated religious hierarchy, women did enjoy a measure of equality with their men. Economically speaking at least, colonial women enjoyed more status than their successors in the nineteenth century. In the first place, women were in short supply in the colonies; there just weren't very many of them to go around, a situation that gave those who were here a certain legitimate value. In addition, because most of a family's essential needs were provided by its own labor, a woman's abilities to card, weave, and sew, to make candles and soap, and to prepare and preserve food were crucial to her family's well-being and survival as an economic unit. Her abilities in these areas were also essential to the survival of the colonies themselves. It was not a question of whether or not the woman's place was in the home; the fruits of a woman's labor were required, so women worked with their men. Because of their indispensable status as workers, there was at this time, at least from the vantage of economics, no need to mythologize or otherwise transform them into decorative possessions.

Under the law and within the church, however, women were subordinate to their men. Although there were exceptions among the well-to-do, most women of colonial America did not own property. They did not because, under most circumstances, they were not permitted to do so by law. Even those women of property held no public office. Although the Quakers did permit women to witness as the spirit moved them during meetings, the Puritans, while offering women an equal chance for salvation, accepted in full the teachings of Saint Paul (found in his Epistle to the Ephesians, 5:22-23) that required wives to submit to their husbands. Because of this hierarchy, women had no formal positions of responsibility or authority within the all-powerful Puritan churches of the time.

In the colonial and prerevolutionary period of American history, therefore, women were in a bizarre situation that would become paradigmatic of the woman's experience in America. On the one hand, they were lauded and respected because of the work they contributed to the colonies. On the other, they were legally subordinate to men—as daughters to their fathers, as wives to their husbands, as churchwomen to their ministers, as citizens to their governors.

Although the seventeenth century is not known for the popular culture that it generated, one form of writing, the Indian captivity tales, was widely read. One of the most popular of these was Mrs. Mary Rowlandson's *The Soveraignty and Goodness of God ... Being a Narrative of the Captivity of Mrs. Mary Rowlandson* (1682), which appeared in no fewer than thirty-one editions. Although its narrator-protagonist is a woman, its subject, as were the other tales of the time, is really God. Believing that the Indian was the devil's disciple, the American colonists interpreted capture by the savages from a religious perspective, seeing the captivity itself as an opportunity for God to test their faith. In these stories, therefore, the conflict of good versus evil took center stage, with the Grace of God overshadowing any human heroes or heroines. Other, less positive examples of how women were tested by the religious rigors of the colonial period can be found in the 1637 trial of Anne Hutchinson for the heresy of antinomianism. Put on trial for assuming the role of religious teacher, a role reserved for men, Hutchinson defended her right to testify publicly based on her divine revelations. Although she defended herself stoutly at first, she soon gave way to exhaustion and in the end was banished for her heretical behavior. When later she gave birth to a "monster" (a hydatiform mole; that is, a benign cluster of tumors that had grown in her placenta), this was taken as a sign of God's displeasure and her fall from Grace. Other, more famous, examples are the 1692 Salem witchcraft trials, during which it was mostly women who were implicated and burned as witches.

Although church governance remained patriarchal in spirit and structure, women in the eighteenth century began to participate more fully in the activities of their churches, especially in the charities and other benevolent societies. By the nineteenth century, they had infiltrated this former male bastion completely. If they could not hold church office or be ordained, they could control the social activities of the church—and they did. In part this desire to work for the church was an expression of women's need for something to do after their contributions to the economy during the revolutionary war. This war, as the other three major wars that Americans have fought, brought considerable—if only temporary—change to women's lives. During the war, women, who organized as Liberty's Daughters, staged effective boycotts of British goods and provided much of the colonies' goods and services by making cloth and running the farms and households in their husbands' absence. After the war, however, women found themselves gradually shouldered out of the American commercial system. The goods that they had been manufacturing at home were slowly but surely becoming the province of factories. Although young women found work in the first of these factories, the New England textile mills, their wages were less than those paid men and the working conditions themselves were far from tolerable. By the close of the eighteenth century, therefore, middle-class white women had lost much of their previous economic importance as productive members of society; as a consequence of this, they also lost a measure of real power and status.

Black women of this time had even less status than white women. Unable, in most instances, to find work in the factories because of the white women's unwillingness to work beside them, black women were primarily domestic servants—either hired as cheap labor in the homes of the north or bought for cheap labor in the south. With the abolition of the slave trade in 1808, the condition of black women could be said to have deteriorated, as owners ad to look to their own slave women to increase the slave population. That is, black women were valued as prize livestock might be—for their breeding capacities. If white women lost economic ground by the close of the century, black women continued, with few exceptions, to experience the more desperate and degrading conditions of real or putative slavery.

Although black women of the eighteenth and nineteenth centuries were— as Alice Walker writes in her poignant essay "In Search of Our Mothers' Gardens" (*Ms.*, May 1974)—deprived of the right to artistic expression, one woman out of all the thousands of slaves and against all odds became a poet. Phillis Wheatley, who was sold at a slave auction in Boston in 1759, became in 1773 the first black woman in America to have a book of poetry published. Achieving minor celebrity status in England, this young woman died virtually unnoticed in her own land. And her poetry, while of acceptable merit as classical poetry goes, does not speak of the dreams and desires of Phillis Wheatley. Instead, even more so than Mrs. Rowlandson's captivity tale, Phillis Wheatley's poetry speaks of God and religion.

In contrast to Phillis Wheatley's obscure works, the major women's voices to have come out of the eighteenth century are those of Abigail Adams and Susanna Haswell Rowson. Abigail Adams, wife of John Adams and mother of John Quincy Adams, wrote voluminous letters to her husband and is perhaps today best known for having admonished him and the other men who were building this new country to "remember the ladies and be more generous and favorable to them than your ancestors" (quoted in Eleanor Flexner, *Century of Struggle*, 15). Rowson is best remembered for her sentimental tear-jerker, *Charlotte Temple: A Tale of Truth* (1791), that was a best-selling novel in England and the United States. A Britisher by birth, Susanna Haswell visited the colonies with her parents before moving here permanently with her husband William Rowson in 1797. As so frequently occurs in the strange history of women in American popular culture, the very women whose writings encourage mindless passivity in females have themselves been highly businesslike professionals. Not only was Rowson a notable author, but she also founded a girls' school in Boston and participated in numerous business and intellectual ventures.

Her heroine, Charlotte Temple, however, seems to be Rowson's antithesis. Taking her cue from and riding the crest of Samuel Richardson's international popularity of the time, Mrs. Rowson constructed a sentimental tale of seduction that became an archetype in its own right. Calling her novel "A Tale of Truth," she sought to disarm those critics who still considered fiction immoral. (In fact, *Charlotte Temple* is apparently based on events in Rowson's own family history.) Through her heavy-handed didacticism, she used her story to convince readers that the wages of sin is death. Charlotte's sin is that of losing her virginity, a fall that would provide the plots of many forms of American popular culture in the years to come. The punishment she receives for her moment of folly is to die while giving birth. Like other writers who followed her, Rowson makes it clear that any marriage at all is to be preferred to this ignominious ending.

With this stand, Susanna Rowson planted the seeds of what would become the literature of the feminine mystique, in which women are identified solely in terms of their relationship to men. Nor was Rowson alone in setting the stage for these developments. She had considerable support in the popular press, especially the magazines, which had always been sensitive to the tastes of their female readers. In 1787, for example, when Noah Webster founded the *American Magazine* in New York, he assured the women in his first issue that he would provide them with suitable entertainment. Toward this end, he published Gothic and sentimental fiction and began the "how-to" columns that would later provide the substance of the specialty magazines of the twentieth century. In 1821, the *Saturday Evening Post* tried to attract women readers through its department "The Ladies' Friend," which featured poetry and articles appropriate for the gentle sex. Other magazines that were established at about the same time that Rowson was writing were the *Ladies' Magazine and Repository of Entertaining Knowledge* (1792), the *Ladies' Monitor* (1801), and the *Weekly Visitor or Ladies' Miscellany* (1804). The purpose of these early magazines, as ostensibly that of eighteenth-century novels, was to instruct their readers. Because there were no more glamorous forms of entertainment to compete with these magazines, they held a virtual monopoly on their readers' attentions. Therefore, they can be given substantial credit for popularizing the cult of domesticity in the nineteenth century.

The late eighteenth and early nineteenth centuries saw the importation from England and Europe of technological developments that would, by mid-century, become the American version of the Industrial Revolution. Although this revolution itself did not really take hold in America until after the Civil War, its preliminary effect was to change quite radically the lives of certain American women. In response to the social upheaval occasioned by the advent of a market economy—the corollary of the Industrial Revolution itself—the newly expanding middle class evolved the myth of the lady, whereby American women would remain the repositories of all that was chaste, unworldly, and moral in American culture. By the mid-nineteenth century, the cult of domesticity, which had achieved a mere toehold in the country in the waning years of the eighteenth century, finally established a firm grasp over the popular imagination. The cult of domesticity, which promulgated the lady as the ideal type of American woman, seems to be the first case of a coherent and comprehensive perceptual paradigm to have come out of the history of American women. Although women of the seventeenth and eighteenth centuries had been labelled variously, it wasn't until the nineteenth century that this labelling took the form of a truly prescriptive (and proscriptive) formula for American womanhood. Perhaps most importantly, the social mythology of the lady lodged in the popular imagination. Once secured in the national psyche, the myth of the lady enjoyed a new status of permanence and respectability. In short, the myth became reified. Heralding and assisting its establishment as objective truth, was the popular culture of the day, especially the popular ladies' magazines, which dispensed editorial advice about behavior befitting ladies. Although the new social requirements for American women were couched in positive images of influence, nurturing, and domesticity, becoming a lady was hardly a fair exchange for what women lost at this time. Stated most baldly, in accepting the role of lady, women lost the right to their own individual identities. With all its trappings of glory, the myth of the lady on her pedestal wasn't much more than a glorified trap that, ultimately, tended to dehumanize women. That is, a woman who is a "lady" is no longer an individual human being; she is an idea, a concept. Among the most serious consequences attendant upon this dehumanization was the fact that women lost the right to their own bodies.

Perhaps the most egregious example of this dehumanization that accompanied the cult of domesticity is the case of the black woman. Clearly the southern states could ill afford—psychologically or economically—to see their slave women as ladies, since ladies were characterized by their delicate constitutions, sexual purity, and moral superiority to men. In order to circumvent this potential problem, the mythology developed that black women were subhuman creatures, who, by nature, were strong and sexual. This mythology had the double advantage of exempting the black woman from the myth of the lady and highlighting the qualities of the white woman, whose frailty and purity stood out in vivid contrast to the strength and sexuality of her black women slaves. The human toll on the black woman is another matter altogether. Not only did she lose her humanity, but she lost her femininity under this mythology. By identifying standards of femininity and beauty in white terms, the dominant culture insured that no black woman would be identified with the myth of the lady. In terms of popular literature, the only possible type of black heroine wouldn't be black at all, but white—a mulatta, a woman with skin light enough for her to pass as a white person. In terms of personal experience, we have only hints of what these white standards have meant in the lives of black women. But evidence of their influence can be found in such cosmetic items as hair-straighteners and skin-lighteners. Even though a nineteenth-century black woman couldn't, by white standards, be beautiful, she could be sexually desirable—as the number of people born of mixed blood attests. But like the lady, the sexual black woman was a myth, an object. She was the whore, the loose woman who was always available to satisfy the needs of a man. Like the lady, the black whore had no right to her own body.

But whereas the lady was deprived of her sexuality, the black woman was identified with hers.

If the black slave was considered sexual but not beautiful, the white lady was beautiful but not sexual. The question of the white woman's sexual nature, in fact, is one of the greatest—and bitterest—ironies to come out of the nineteenth century's cult of the lady. On the one hand, white women were identified by their sexual organs (they were even called "the sex"); on the other, white women were reputed to have no sexual drives or needs at all. In 1848, the same year as the Seneca Falls Convention, Charles Meigs published *Females and Their Diseases* in which he argued, for example, that women were controlled so thoroughly by their sex organs that any female disorder could be attributed to a malfunctioning of one or more of these organs. If Meigs overstated the influence of women's sexual organs on their physical (and mental) health, he was not alone. But he also shared the podium with authors of sex-in-life manuals who often advised couples to forego sex altogether and with those who taught that women (contrary to the information of the previous century) had no sexual desires. This was also the time, however, during which J. Marion Sims, the "father of American gynecology," briefly popularized the barbaric practice of clitoridectomy in the United States.

Although Sims mutilated women, he also advanced the science of surgical gynecology. It was Sims, for example, who originated the technique for repairing the fistulae (the tears in the tissue between the bladder and the vagina) that often accompany difficult childbirth. The problem is that Sims perfected his technique by performing the same operation over and over on the same black women, whom he fed and sheltered in order to have available a constant supply of experimental subjects. On the one hand, therefore, Sims healed women, saving them from the putrification caused by torn bladders; on the other, he brutalized women, often crippling them for life.

Another famous nineteenth-century physician whose treatment of women is difficult to evaluate is Silas Weir Mitchell. Mitchell is best known today for inventing the "rest cure," a treatment for neurasthenic men and women that was intended to rehabilitate them by total immobility. Thus, patients undergoing the rest cure were virtually isolated from the rest of the world, restrained from physical activity, and encouraged to overeat in order to induce a sort of false pregnancy. Although this was a cure intended for both sexes, not unexpectedly it was prescribed far more for women than men. One famous nineteenth-century feminist who had to fight back insanity because of her rest cure was Charlotte Perkins Gilman, who attacked the cure in her story, "The Yellow Wallpaper," in which a woman author is imprisoned in a nursery by her physician-husband and forbidden to do any writing. Just before she is driven insane by the lack of activity and her husband's insistence that she not excite herself, the woman remarks that getting back to her writing would do her good, would give her something constructive to do. She also notes, quite perceptively, that it is her own husband, himself a doctor, who is preventing her from getting well.

Two other areas of medicine that suggest that women in the nineteenth century had lost the right to their very bodies are obstetrics and birth control. Until the eighteenth century, women traditionally had been attended at their lying-in by female midwives who assisted the birth. With the rise of professionalization in medicine came the phenomenon of the male midwife, the nineteenth-century physician who encouraged women to seek his services and to do so in lying-in hospitals. One of the most tragic consequences of the doctors' success in replacing midwives was the fact that they, unlike the "ignorant" and "untrained" women whom they had supplanted, were themselves responsible for a dramatic increase in the incidence of puerperal (or childbed) fever. Unaware of what they were doing, these professional men transmitted this often-fatal disease from one woman to another, sometimes causing an epidemic among their patients. Having complete confidence in themselves as gentlemen in whose hands a lady was safe and having no understanding of germs, these men not only failed to sterilize their hands and clothes, but they often moved directly from dissecting corpses to assisting childbirth—thus, practically insuring the death of the women they attended. In the matter of birth control, although clearly many women in the nineteenth century practiced it—as woman had been doing for centuries—in 1873 it fell under the jurisdiction of the government. It was in this year that the moralist crusader Anthony Comstock secured congressional passage of the Comstock Law; under the terms of this law it became illegal to transmit obscene material—including information on birth control—through the U.S. mail.

Not only were women of the nineteenth century denied information about their bodies, but they were also bombarded with misinformation. In 1866, for example, Dr. A. W. Chase published the thirty-eighth edition of *Dr. Chase's Recipes; or, Information for Everybody: An Invaluable Collection of About Eight Hundred Practical Recipes*, in which he attributes menstrual distress and discomfort to the fact that young girls read too many novels. He also cites a case history of a young woman who, ashamed of the blood stains on her clothing, immersed herself in a cold stream while she was menstruating and, one presumes as a consequence, became insane. This clearly was a time during which women were ill a great deal of the time—a situation that can be explained in large measure by the fact that women were wearing incredibly restrictive undergarments like the corset that inevitably must have made even breathing difficult. Sensing that a virtual epidemic of female complaints was ravaging the country, Catharine E. Beecher set out to gather statistics on the state of women's health. She published the results of her survey in her 1855 *Letters to the People on*

Health and Happiness, in which she reported that women as a group were indeed more prone to become ill than men. In 1873, the same year that Congress passed the Comstock Law, Dr. Edward H. Clarke published *Sex in Education* in which he took as his premise the fact that education harmed women physically, that too much education would prevent women from conceiving children.

If women were discouraged from becoming educated as late as 1873, it was contrary to the efforts of early reformers like Emma Willard who, in 1821, had founded the Troy Female Seminary; or Catharine Beecher who, in 1824, had founded the Hartford Female Seminary. Although these seminaries provided little more than domestic education, they were a step in the right direction. Willard and Beecher were followed by Mary Lyon who, in 1837, founded what was to become in 1893 Mount Holyoke College. In fact several colleges—including Swarthmore, Vassar, Smith, and Wellesley—were founded in the period 1864-1875.

Catharine Beecher, sister of Harriet Beecher Stowe, not only founded a seminary for young women but also published several works in which she expressed her concern that these young women were not being educated in the art and science of running a home. Unlike the more radical feminist reformers who called for an abolition of the concept of separate spheres for women and men, Beecher was convinced that it was in the best interests of women to have a sphere of their own. In her 1841 manual, *A Treatise on Domestic Economy For the Use of Young Ladies At Home and At School* (reprinted as *A Treatise on Domestic Economy* with an introduction by Kathryn Kish Sklar, New York: Schocken Books, 1977), for example, she writes that in a democracy, in order to secure both individual and general good, it is necessary to have a system of subordination, whereby husbands are superior to their wives. To establish support for her position on this issue, she quotes from Alexis de Tocqueville. Of the status of American women, de Tocqueville writes, "'I have nowhere seen women occupying a loftier position; and if I were asked...to what the singular prosperity and growing strength of that people ought mainly to be attributed, I should reply, —*to the superiority of their women*'" (quoted in Beecher, 8-9). Although Beecher clearly agrees with de Tocqueville, she expresses her concerns in this treatise that women are losing their sphere of influence by failing to keep their end of the bargain. That is, if, by nature, women belong in the home, they must take this responsibility seriously by running the home efficiently, smoothly, and economically. Beecher's purpose in this and her other manuals, such as *The American Woman's Home* (1869) which she wrote with her sister Harriet, is to teach women precisely how they can become better homemakers. Her *Treatise* and other manuals are, in other words, textbooks on domestic science, in which she treats the work of women at home as analogous and equally important to the work of men outside the home.

Another of the most influential and outspoken advocates of women's education was Sarah Josepha Hale, who edited *Godey's Lady's Book* from 1837 until 1877. As editor of this popular woman's magazine, Hale enjoyed power and prestige known to few women of her time. Hale came to the magazine after Louis Antoine Godey bought out the *Ladies' Magazine*, which Hale herself had founded in 1828, and merged it with his own *Lady's Book*, which he had founded in 1830. During her forty-year reign as editor of *Godey's*, Hale increased the magazine's circulation, encouraged her contributors to sign their names instead of just using initials as they had been wont to do, and, in general, dominated the magazine publishing industry with her authoritative presence. Her editorial policy was to promote women's education; by this, she meant, as Catharine Beecher meant, primarily training in the domestic arts. Her persuasive powers were great enough in the field of education that she convinced Matthew Vassar to remove the word *female* from the name of the college for women he founded; in 1867, at Hale's urging, he renamed Vassar Female College, calling it simply Vassar College. Although Hale supported women's education, she virtually ignored politics—including the entire Civil War. Instead of politics, her magazine featured sentimental literature, information on health and beauty aids, embroidery patterns, recipes, and embellishments. (Embellishments are those ornate illustrations and hand-painted fashion-plates for which *Godey's* is so famous.) But even with these attractive features, the magazine couldn't survive without the leadership of Sarah Hale. A mere nineteen years after her death in 1879, *Godey's Lady's Book* followed its remarkable editor to the grave. In her lifetime, however, Sarah Josepha Hale, by combining traditional mores and contemporary advice with appealing illustrations, had designed the popular format which, to this day, has remained the archetypal woman's magazine.

A form of nineteenth-century popular culture that played the dual role of perpetuating the cult of domesticity and undermining it at the same time, was popular woman's fiction. Identified variously as "sentimental," "domestic," or "sentimental domestic" fiction, this genre enjoyed such success among readers that Nathaniel Hawthorne was moved to refer to its authors as a "mob of scribbling women." Interpretations of this fiction vary, but the most commonly held idea today is that nineteenth-century woman's fiction was a tribute to women's ability to survive—and even thrive—in situations inimical to their well-being and happiness. While it is true that much nineteenth-century woman's fiction idealized the home, much also described the reality behind the myth. Moreover, those women who supported the concept that a woman's place was in the home did so in the conviction that it was in the domestic sphere that women could enjoy real status and power.

Woman's fiction emerged as a significant new form in 1822 with the publication of Catharine Maria Sedgwick's *A New-England Tale*, moved to new heights of popularity with the 1850 publication of Susan Warner's *The Wide, Wide World*, and died out as a form sometime after the end of the Civil War. Between its meteoric rise and subsequent fall, literally hundreds of examples of the woman's novel were published in the United States—none of which are read today by anyone other than students of women's literature, a situation that could be said to avenge Hawthorne and the other Romanticists who were proportionately neglected by their public. If the magazine industry saw only one female star in the nineteenth century, the publishing industry that specialized in fiction and poetry saw a veritable constellation of women authors. In addition to Sedgwick and Warner were Mrs. E. D. E. N. Southworth, author of *Capitola; or, The Hidden Hand, Ishmael; or, In the Depths*, and *Self-Raised; or, From the Depths*; Caroline Lee Hentz, author of *Ernest Linwood, The Inner Life of the Author*; Maria Cummins, author of *The Lamplighter*; Marion Harland (pseudonym for Mary Virginia Hawes Terhune), author of *Alone*; and Augusta Jane Evans, author of *St. Elmo*.

Partially in response to the sentimentalism rife in the poetry of authors like Lydia Huntley Sigourney and the cult of domesticity itself, but most particularly in an effort to win political equality for themselves, women like Elizabeth Cady Stanton and Susan B. Anthony joined together in the fight for woman's suffrage. In 1848, when Stanton and Lucretia Mott convened the Seneca Falls Convention, they set into motion a struggle that would be waged on several fronts until the vote for women finally was approved by Congress in 1919 and ratified by the states in 1920. Accompanying the fight for suffrage—and often complicating it—were other reform movements. The most famous of these is abolition, the antislavery movement that gave many of the women who would become active feminists their initial exposure to organizing and public speaking. Another was the reform movement in fashion, led most dramatically—if not successfully—by Amelia Jenks Bloomer who advocated the infamous loose trousers that to this day bear her name, the Bloomer costume. Although Stanton was attracted to the bloomers and other forms of less restrictive clothing, she only wore them a few times before realizing that public ridicule was interfering with the major issue of winning the vote for women. Whereas Stanton showed good political sense in eschewing the Bloomer costume and the Reform Dress, she was not to be swayed from another area of reform, that of pointing out the antifemale passages in the Bible. In 1895 and 1898, to the chagrin of the National American Woman Suffrage Association, she published her attacks on the Old Testament in *The Woman's Bible*. Another area of embarrassment to the suffrage movement was the free love campaign waged by Victoria Woodhull. Yet another delicate issue was temperance. With Frances Willard's election in 1879 as president of the Women's Christian Temperance Union (which had been founded in 1874),

the question of temperance became intertwined with that of suffrage—
a relationship not altogether to the liking of the more pragmatic feminists
who understood that they would need male support for woman's suffrage.

If white middle-class women were active in numerous reform movements
and in woman's clubs in the nineteenth century, black women were equally
active after the Civil War. Even before the Civil War, two ex-slave women
had captured a measure of national attention with their exploits. In 1843,
a former slave named Isabella, heeding a message from God, adopted the
descriptive name of Sojourner Truth and became an itinerant preacher.
Eight years later, in 1851, this powerful orator addressed a women's rights
convention in Akron, Ohio, and transfixed the audience by delivering an
impromptu speech that is remembered as "Ain't I a Woman?" In this speech
she identified her experiences and trials as a black slave as relevant to the
question of women's rights—and did so with such emotional effect that she
silenced the hecklers in the crowd who had been unwilling to let the white
women organizers speak at their own convention. Although this ex-slave
could neither read nor write, she told her story to Olive Gilbert who
published it in 1878 as *The Narrative of Sojourner Truth*. The other major
black woman of the mid-nineteenth century was Harriet Tubman, who in
1849 escaped from slavery and subsequently spent the next few years of
her life in the Underground Railroad risking her own life to help other
slaves to escape to freedom. In 1862 this diminutive black woman served
as a scout with the Union Army during the Civil War. Although the passage
of the Thirteenth Amendment in 1865 brought slavery to an end and passage
of the Fourteenth in 1868 brought equal protection under the law, by the
1880s Jim Crow statutes were being enacted that severely restricted the
lives and rights of blacks living in the south. In 1896 the Supreme Court
declared that separate facilities for blacks and whites were legal (a decision
not overturned until 1954). During this time, probably in response to the
narrowing opportunities for blacks, black women became active proponents of education and active participants in women's clubs and federations.
In 1895, for example, they established the National Federation of Afro-
American Women and convened the National Colored Women's Congress
in Atlanta, Georgia. Three years earlier, in 1892, the black feminist and
abolitionist Frances E. W. Harper had published *Iola Leroy; or, Shadows
Uplifted*, the first novel published by a black woman in the United States.
In this novel Harper, whose heroine is a beautiful fair-skinned mulatta
woman, set about revealing to her readers the dreadful truths behind the
southern mythology. After describing the degrading effects of slavery on
blacks and whites, Harper, in the second half of her novel, shows how
the black middle class can uplift the race as a whole.

The thing to remember about women like Sojourner Truth, Harriet
Tubman, and Frances E. W. Harper is that they, like Elizabeth Cady
Stanton, Susan B. Anthony, and Lucretia Mott were remarkable exceptions

to the myth of the lady. In contrast to the lady, the black women activists and the white feminists were not myths, but very real political persons who rose in rebellion against the restrictive mythology of the time that characterized black women as subhuman and all women as subordinate to men. Whereas the lady and her negative print, the loose black woman, were products of the popular imagination—ideas, in other words, that had been imposed upon women as a group—the black activists and the suffragists originated among women themselves. Both groups of women were early feminists, women who were determined to fight for their rights as citizens. Although they shared many of the same concerns, they were not always in accord in terms of either goals or strategies. (Moreover, they were not always in accord within their respective groups, let alone between them.) These groups were, properly speaking, collations of individuals. But the popular conception of the white feminists, however, was that they all could be characterized by—or caricatured as—the "suffragette," a term used to stereotype and denigrate women activists. The popular imagination, in other words, unable to accept the feminists on their own terms, had to make of them a negative myth, by which they represented a threat to the country's welfare. The middle-class black women, of course, were dealt with in the popular imagination by invoking the antebellum stereotypes of the loose woman or the mammy. In other words, these women, who were not products of popular culture or molded by nineteenth-century social mythology, nonetheless had to contend with the effects of the myth in their public and private lives.

As the above suggests, the nineteenth century is the source of much of the social mythology and many of the images that characterize the popular culture of the twentieth century. Although the nineteenth century did not invent the concept of separate spheres for women and men, it solidified it in the image of the lady and the cult of domesticity. It also gave visual form to the concept in the restrictive, cumbersome, and weighty clothes women were expected to wear. More than in any previous era in the United States, women became appendages to their men. Rather than the hard-working helpmeets of the colonial period, women in the nineteenth century became ladies of leisure—a status that gave proof of their husbands' wealth and their own superfluousness. Rather than functioning as producers of goods, women, in the nineteenth century, became consumers. The need for consumption stimulated the rapid growth of the advertising industry, which from the very beginning addressed its messages primarily—and often exclusively—to women. If the nineteenth century is at least partially responsible for current popular images of women, it is also responsible for the political uprising among women that was intended, at least on some level, to counter the deleterious effects of the dominant social mythology of the time. But the woman's movement, which was highly visible from 1848 to 1920, all but disappeared from the granting of suffrage to the publication of Betty Friedan's *The Feminine Mystique* in 1963. During this time few women's voices were raised in protest against the essentially negative female stereotypes that originated in the popular imagination and found expression in its creations.

Perhaps because of the brutalizing effects of two world wars, the overriding threat of nuclear destruction, and the trauma of Vietnam, the mid-twentieth century has been especially vicious in its negative stereotyping of women. Unable to cope with the horrors of modern warfare and the prospects of imminent devastation on a global scale, the century has sought to project its fears in the image of what Harold Schechter calls "Kali on Main Street"—the ravening jaws of the terrible mother (*Journal of Popular Culture* 7, no. 2 [Fall 1973]: 251-63). Another invention of twentieth-century social mythology has been the bitch—the brittle, selfish, castrating woman of male nightmares. But if the popular imagination has turned an ugly face on its women in response to its own dread, it expressed a far different attitude at the beginning of the century.

In 1914, for example, seven years after Anna Jarvis had waged an extensive campaign in its favor, Mother's Day was instituted by a joint resolution of Congress, under the presidential eye of Woodrow Wilson. In 1915, David Wark Griffith premiered his infamous *Birth of a Nation*, in which he introduced to the country his child-heroine, Lillian Gish—who, with her sister Dorothy and the other child actresses in Griffith's stable, epitomized the Victorian ideal of the chaste and delicate woman. Even in the vamp, the screen's counterimage to the virgin played by Gish and Mary Pickford, there was a certain Victorian innocence. Theda Bara, perhaps the best known of these vamps, made her first appearance in film also in 1915, starring in *A Fool There Was*. In 1921, the same year that Congress passed the progressive Sheppard-Towner Act which provided federal assistance for infant and prenatal care, the "Miss America" Beauty Pageant was inaugurated in Atlantic City, New Jersey. By the late 1920s, a reemerging awareness of women's sexuality was evident in such publications as Margaret Sanger's sex manual, *Happiness in Marriage*; Clara Bow's appearance as the "It" girl in Elinor Glyn's *It*, which was a euphemism for an innocent sex appeal; and the less innocent play, *Sex*, which opened on Broadway in 1926 and starred none other than the author herself, the inimitable Mae West. But Mae West proved too much for the American public. For using the word *sex* as the title of this play, she was sentenced to ten days in jail on Welfare Island. Because of the suggestive dialogue of her movies, most of which she wrote herself, and her image on screen West is credited with inciting the film industry to implement, in 1934, its self-censoring Production Code.

With the introduction of the code, which specifically prohibited any form of on-screen sexuality or obscene language, the film industry ushered in a period where women, if they were sexual, were somehow less than human. The code itself consisted of twelve paragraphs of prohibitions that included guidelines for crime, sex, and obscenity. The general operating principles of the code were to prevent the production of films that somehow would "lower the standards" of those who saw them; in addition, neither natural nor human law could be mocked nor sympathy allowed for the transgression of these laws. The sanctity of marriage, therefore, had to be honored; adultery was not an acceptable subject. Sexual perversion, white slavery, miscegenation (which was explicitly defined as sex between the white and black races), sex hygiene, childbirth, children's sex organs— all were forbidden on screen. The industry, in other words, capitulated to the dictates of the Catholic Legion of Decency and other pressure groups that demanded that Hollywood clean up its act. The consequences for women were twofold.

On the one hand, the Production Code certainly spelled the doom of one of the screen's greatest originals, the self-sufficient and outrageously funny Mae West, who was unable professionally to survive a climate inimical to her brand of sexuality and humor. And if the code ruined Mae West, it also put a damper on other sex goddesses of the 1920s. After the complexities and mysteries of the almost-androgynous Greta Garbo and Marlene Dietrich and the tough sexuality of Jean Harlow—all three precode figures—audiences of the 1930s were presented with the more wholesome images of Katharine Hepburn, Jean Arthur, and the young Shirley Temple. By removing sex from the screen, on the other hand, the code did force writers and directors to invent more realistic roles for women. Although the men in the audience may have been disappointed by the new image, this transformation did have its compensations for women. The women in the comedies of the 1930s and 1940s may not have been smoldering sensualists, but they were clever and witty companions to their men. Or, like Katharine Hepburn and Spencer Tracy in the 1949 classic *Adam's Rib*, they were feisty competitors, engaged in what had become a more cerebral battle of the sexes.

In areas other than film, the 1920s and 1930s witnessed such events as the founding in 1920 of the Women's Council of the Commission on Interracial Cooperation, which was followed in 1922 by the founding by black women of the Anti-Lynching Crusaders and in 1930 by the founding of the Association of Southern Women for the Prevention of Lynching. In 1923 the National Women's Party proposed the passage of an Equal Rights Amendment—an amendment that remains unratified to this day. Jane Addams became the first woman to win the Nobel Peace Prize in 1931. Women's sports had a star at the 1932 Los Angeles Olympics in the person of Mildred ("Babe") Didrikson, who won gold medals in the javelin throw, the hurdles, and the high jump. In 1921 Kotex sanitary napkins were introduced to the public through advertisements, and in 1936 Tampax tampons were first marketed. In response to the more relaxed social atmosphere of the 1920s, skirts had risen and the flapper had become the symbol of the new woman. Even though the flapper's liberation was largely a façade, women did enjoy more freedom and professional opportunities than they had in the nineteenth century. But skirts came down again during the depression and women were by and large discouraged from taking jobs from men.

The war years of the 1940s were perhaps the most complex yet of the twentieth century. In the same year that the United States entered the war on Japan, the concept of "Woman of the Year" was introduced. The next year, 1942, Philip Wylie lashed out at what he called momism in *Generation of Vipers*. Although women were encouraged by all forms of popular culture to join the war effort by taking factory jobs, once the shortage in the work force had been overcome and the end of the war was in sight, women were urged—again by popular culture—to return to the home, where, they were assured, they were needed most.

With this effort to redomesticate women was born what Betty Friedan was to call the feminine mystique. From all appearances it was an all-out effort on the part of the country to use its popular culture as propaganda. In this proselytizing, movies and magazines led the way, supported by the efforts of such pop psychologists as Ferdinand Lundberg and Marynia Farnham who claimed in their 1947 *Modern Woman: The Lost Sex* that women were unhappy and sexually maladjusted because they had betrayed their femininity. Another view of women that contributed to the widespread notion that they do not belong in the man's world of art and business is that offered by Waverley Root in his 1949 essay, "Women Are Intellectually Inferior" (*American Mercury* 69 [October 1949]: 407-14). In this essay Root provides what he considers to be a scientific answer to the old-age question of why there have been no women geniuses. His answer is that genius, like other recessive characteristics more common in men than women—like color blindness and hemophilia—is tied to the X-chromosome and results from the same degenerative pattern as that leading to insanity. Not only is Root to be marveled at for his convoluted reasoning, but also for the way he so readily discounts and disparages those women of genius that he does mention. Women who by "lenient standards" are geniuses, he writes, are remarkably masculine in their characteristics (Root, 410). Perhaps his most amusing example of this is the fact that Amy Lowell smoked "large black cigars" (Root, 410). Given the conflicting messages of pre- and postwar popular culture, it is no wonder that women were confused about what their proper place should be. The war office urged them into the factories when the men were on the lines; when the men came home, it was actually the women who went home—and many went home to stay.

And stay they did where—if we are to believe the popular culture of the 1950s and 1960s—they lived happily ever after in their well-furnished suburban homes while their husbands commuted to work each day. But just as in the nineteenth century, during the height of the cult of domesticity, real women of the mid-twentieth were enjoying real success in the real world while popular culture encouraged women to stay at home. Two events that span the 1950s indicate the disjunction of the decade. In 1950 Gwendolyn Brooks won the Pulitzer Prize for poetry with her collection *Annie Allen*; in 1959 the Barbie doll was introduced on the market. In between these years— and extremes—several events of note took place. In 1951, for example, both the "I Love Lucy" show and "Search for Tomorrow" premiered on American television. The same year that Alfred Kinsey's *Report on Sexual Behavior in the Human Female* was published, 1953, Hugh Hefner founded *Playboy* magazine. In 1954, cognizant of the virtual chasm between the woman's sphere at home and the man's sphere at work, *McCall's* magazine introduced its ill-fated "Togetherness" campaign in an effort to camouflage this difference—and increase circulation and advertising revenues. In 1955, if a woman were poor, desperate, and pitiful enough, she might get to be on "Queen for a Day," a television program in which women competed for prizes by telling the most heart-rending story to a studio audience who picked a queen by clapping for her. If a woman weren't this desperate, she could at least dye her hair and the world could only ask, "Does she...or doesn't she?" Only her hairdresser knew for sure. (This slogan was the brainchild of Shirley Polykoff, who was so successful at devising slogans for Clairol that she was able to found her own advertising firm in 1972.)

But the 1950s were more than fun and games. In 1952, for example, Charlotta A. Bass, nominated as the vice-presidential candidate on the Progressive party's ticket, became the first black woman to run on a national presidential ticket. In 1955, a woman who could not have appeared on "Queen for a Day," let alone won the title, in a single dignified gesture of rebellion refused to move to the back of the bus. When Rosa Parks was arrested in Montgomery, Alabama, for asserting her right to sit where she wanted to on a public conveyance, she inspired what was to become the economically and politically successful Montgomery Bus Boycott, led in 1956 by Martin Luther King. In sports, Tenley Albright became the first of many American women to win the world championship in figure skating.

As impressive as the accomplishments of these women were, they were exceptions to the general flight to the suburbs. Although the suburbs were touted as the objectification of the American dream, Betty Friedan showed how distorted this dream had become when she unveiled the feminine mystique in her 1963 book of that name. With the publication of this book, Friedan initiated the second woman's movement of the twentieth century. Like the 1848 Seneca Falls convention that had given nineteenth-century women a goal to rally around, Friedan's book gave her twentieth-century readers just the impetus they needed to rebel against the modern version of the cult of domesticity. The reaction was swift and the future of feminism looked bright. By 1966 Friedan had enough of a political base to found the National Organization for Women. By 1972, Gloria Steinem, Elizabeth Forsling Harris, and others had enough of an economic backing that they could publish the preview issue of *Ms.* magazine. In 1977 the National Women's Conference convened in Houston for three days, during which time the delegates—who came from racially, economically, and politically diverse backgrounds—passed a twenty-five-point National Plan of Action that called for passage of the ERA, the right to abortions, and various federally and state-supported programs.

In response to the demands of blacks and women, the federal government, since the early 1960s, has been acting to eliminate racial and sexual discrimination. In 1961, for example, the Kennedy administration set up the Citizen's Advisory Council on the Status of Women. In 1964 Congress passed Title VII of the Civil Rights Act, which forbids racial and sexual discrimination in hiring practices. In 1972 it passed Title IX of the Education Amendments Act, which forbids sexual discrimination in schools that receive federal funding. In 1974 Congress took the unprecedented step of revising the Little League baseball charter to allow females to play on formerly all-male Little League teams. And in 1978 federal Judge Carl Rubin ruled that girls cannot be forbidden to engage in contact sports.

In this same period, however, popular culture continued the myth that woman was mindless and only interested in catching a man. Helen Gurley Brown, for example, rose to instant fame with the publication in 1962 of *Sex and the Single Girl*, in which she counseled women on how to initiate and enjoy love affairs. She further institutionalized her advice to women when, in 1966, she became editor of *Cosmopolitan* magazine. It was in the mid-1960s that television contributed its own myth of the dizzy woman when it premiered in 1964 "Bewitched," starring Elizabeth Montgomery as a witch; and in 1965 "I Dream of Jeannie," starring Barbara Eden as a jinni. But if women had dominated the movie screens in the 1950s, in the form of Marilyn Monroe and her imitators Jayne Mansfield and Kim Novak, by the 1960s they were almost a forgotten idea. Instead of the sex goddesses of the 1920s or the women's films of the 1940s, we saw in the 1960s the virtual disappearance of women in film. In their place were films like *Butch Cassidy and the Sundance Kid, Lawrence of Arabia,* and *Midnight Cowboy*, in which male friendships and relationships provided the "sexual" interest.

But women struck back in print in the 1970s. In 1970 Kate Millet published *Sexual Politics* and Shulamith Firestone *The Dialectic of Sex: The Case for Feminist Revolution*—the first a radical view of male literature, the second a radical view of the family and society itself. Nor was the work of feminists limited to scholarly polemical texts. In 1970, for example, Trina Robbins edited *It Ain't Me, Babe*, the first feminist underground comic. This comic features "Breaking Out" written by the It Ain't Me Babe

Basement Collective (with artwork by Carole), in which various female characters from comic strips—including L'il Lulu, Petunia Pig, and Witch Hazel—break out of their traditional comic personae and join the feminist revolution. This was followed in 1972 by Trina Robbins's *Girl Fight Comics* and Lyn Chevli and Joyce Sutton's *Tits & Clits Comix*. Also appearing in 1972 were Marge Piercy's feminist novel, *Small Changes*; and Mary Jane Sherfey's controversial study *The Nature and Evolution of Female Sexuality*, in which she claims that female sexuality has been repressed by society because, left uncontrolled, it would be detrimental to social stability. In a belated response to *Playboy* magazine, the short-lived *Viva*, a magazine for women that featured artistic photographs of nude men, was first published in 1973. Two years later Joanna Russ published *The Female Man* and in 1976 Marge Piercy published *Woman on the Edge of Time*—both novels are feminist science fiction that posit societies in which women are not subordinate to men. In Whileaway, one of the worlds of *The Female Man*, in fact, there are no men at all—which places this novel in line with Charlotte Perkins Gilman's recently rediscovered feminist utopian novel, *Herland*, which was written in 1915.

One of the major themes that run through these feminist writings is that women, after relinquishing the rights to their own bodies in the nineteenth century, are now determined to regain control over them in the twentieth. The plots of the feminist underground comics, for example, often focus on women's natural bodily functions—such as sex and menstruation—to show how women can accept and enjoy their physical selves. The plots of much of the feminist science fiction that has been published recently focus on alternate methods of conceiving, bearing, and raising children. In Suzy McKee Charnas's *Motherlines*, for example, women conceive not by mating with men—there are none in her utopian society—but with horses. The children, all female of course since the horse's semen only acts as a catalyst to conception, raise themselves in packs until menarche, at which time the young women return to the adults for their maturation ceremony. Another example of the fact that women are reclaiming their bodies is the proliferation of self-help manuals on women's health, such as the Boston Women's Health Book Collective's *Our Bodies, Ourselves*, which was published in 1973 and reprinted in 1976. This book is a compendium of information, liberally illustrated, about the female body and how to take care of it.

Another expression of the prevailing social attitudes towards a woman's physicality can be found in how she is perceived and treated as an athlete. Although the world of sports remains a male stronghold, with many fathers still refusing to let their daughters compete with boys in contact sports, there were two significant events in 1977 that suggest that women, on an individual basis at least, are being recognized for their athletic abilities. In this year Janet Guthrie became the first woman to race in the grueling Indianapolis 500, and Chris Evert was named *Sports Illustrated*'s Athlete

of the Year. It was also the year, however, that Bowie Kuhn refused to
admit women into the locker rooms for postgame interviews during the
World Series.

The world of film was almost as unpredictable in its treatment of women
as the world of sports. If women were encouraged by a revival of interest in
women on screen in such films as *An Unmarried Woman, Julia, The Turning
Point,* and *Norma Rae,* they could not be reassured by the accompanying
resurgence of the infatuation with child-women on screen in such films
as *Pretty Baby,* the *Blue Lagoon,* and *Tess.* Nor could they be reassured
by Woody Allen's remark that eighteen-year-old Mariel Hemingway is
"probably the most beautiful woman the world has yet seen" (*Time,* 30 June
1980, p. 62). It was also during the 1970s that women began taking a serious
look at the degrading—and potentially dangerous—stereotyping of women
that occurs in pornographic films, where women are portrayed not as human
beings but as objects that long for and enjoy sadomasochistic brutality.

If feminists are distressed by what they continue to see projected in this
country's popular culture, they are also distressed by the dissension they
see among women themselves. In recent years, feminists have had to
acknowledge the indisputable fact that many women do not favor the Equal
Rights Amendment, do not favor abortion, do not favor the universal
draft—and will go to great lengths to try to prevent them. Although women
since 1963 have made great strides, socially and politically, they are faced
today with the effects of a reactionary backlash that is attempting to repeal
some of their hard-earned rights. The battle continues between the voices
of the popular imagination that would keep women subordinate to men
and in the home, and those of feminism that would free women to decide for
themselves what they want to do. It is a battle that was fought over the
vote a hundred years ago, and it is one that appears still to have a lot
of momentum. It is a battle that pits against one another two incompatible
views of women. Those who represent the popular imagination support
the view that woman is definable as a social concept. Those who represent
the feminist position contend that woman is not an idea but a person
with certain inalienable rights over her self, her body, and her life. It is
a battle that daily is being waged in the popular and the counterculture
of this country.

What makes the position expressed by the members of the feminist
counterculture so radical is that their goal is to achieve nothing less than
a total reorganization of our culture. Because they see that our social
mythology—as it is currently constructed—is built around and dependent
upon women's subordinate status, they believe that the only way to achieve
full equality is by revolutionizing society itself. In a remarkable effort to
transform our social mythology, these women are turning the weapons
of the popular imagination—its comics, magazines, and fiction—back upon
itself. Whether or not they will be successful in restructuring our world
remains—very literally—to be seen.

CHAPTER I

Histories of Women in
Popular Culture

In some respects all the works cited in this book qualify as histories of women in popular culture and, therefore, could be gathered into this first chapter. But that would have been cumbersome and would have tended to obscure the diverse nature of the subject. In an effort to make the information as accessible as possible, I have divided it into several chapters, each with a particular generic focus. The problem in doing this, as will become immediately apparent, is that the study of women in popular culture is, perhaps above all, an interdisciplinary one that does not lend itself readily to artificial divisions. Thus, many of the choices I have made in assigning a work to a particular chapter appear to be—and in some cases are—somewhat arbitrary. I have tried to compensate for this by making cross-references to material that has a similar subject.

The organizing principle in chapter one is as follows: general histories of American women (including particular time periods and geographic locations); women's rights and social policy (including suffrage); women and the professions (including women in professions and how women have been treated by male professionals—with an emphasis in both cases on medicine); interdisciplinary studies (including sociological and literary studies that overlap with histories); documentaries; and anthologies. Most of the material that appears here is part of the new social history of American women; most has been written since 1970.

One of the best examples of the new social history of women is Mary P. Ryan's *Womanhood in America: From Colonial Times to the Present*. A comprehensive study of the relationship between women and their culture, this book provides a remarkable overview of the transformation of the American woman—as she has appeared in reality and as she has been de-scribed in imaginative literature. Marshalling evidence from both primary and secondary sources, Ryan has written a model of interpretive history. Her thesis is that womanhood is a historical phenomenon and as such can be understood only in its historical context. Like other feminist historians she is disturbed by the persistence of outmoded myths of femininity and by this culture's unwillingness to let them go. In the events of the past three hundred years, she locates certain patterns that characterize the transformation of American womanhood from helpmeet in the home to coworker on the job. For Ryan, the patterns fall into three distinct time frames. The first pattern she sees is that of the seventeenth-century woman who was recognized as an indispensable worker in the colonial economy but who was virtually without legal existence. The second is that of the woman of the Industrial Revolution who lived in a distinct sphere of the home—segregated from both the marketplace and the other features of the so-called man's world. The third is that of the woman of the twentieth century who is entering the male spheres of business and politics in ever-increasing numbers. To discuss these patterns, Ryan divides her history into seven chapters, chapters that demonstrate both the changes and the continuities in American womanhood.

Chapter one, "Adam's Rib: Women in the Agricultural Settlements of the Seventeenth Century," focuses on "the contradiction between equality of function and dependency of status" faced by women during this time (Ryan, 4). To demonstrate the schizophrenic division in the situation of seventeenth-century women, Ryan establishes the central role of women in the household economy, where they were solely responsible for the manufacture of goods and the production and preservation of food used by the family. At the same time, women were subject to paternalistic laws that left them devoid of property rights and unable to participate in the government of church and state. Although women had virtually no legal existence, they did not feel especially rebellious, according to Ryan, because what they did contribute to the economy was valued highly. Moreover, because these colonial women were not isolated from the rest of their culture, they did not suffer the alienation known to today's suburban housewife. They also enjoyed active social lives and functioned as community social workers. The inherent contradictions in their way of life did lead, however, to severe frustrations that manifested themselves, according to Ryan, most obviously in the Salem witchcraft trials of 1692, in which women were—by and large—both the accusers and the accused.

In chapter two, "Patriarchy in Disarray: Women and Commercial Capitalism: 1750-1820," Ryan establishes a causal relationship between a growing economic sophistication and the transformation of the concept of womanhood. As production of goods moved out of the house, the economic responsibilities of women declined considerably, thus creating a new disparity between the sexes that had not been so evident in the seventeenth century. Not only did women lose control of most manufacturing processes, but even from the start of the factory system they were paid lower wages than men for the same work. If the factory girl was on the poor end of the new woman's continuum, her counterpart, the lady, was on the rich end. With the advent of commercial capitalism was born the notion of conspicuous consumption and with it the lady, whose sole purpose was to show off her husband's wealth and status. Thus arose the remarkably resilient concept of the division of the spheres—the cult of domesticity—which transformed women from producers to consumers. Although by 1820 the pattern had been laid, it hadn't yet set.

Ryan discusses how the pattern congealed in chapter three, "Creating Woman's Sphere: Gender in the Making of American Industrial Capitalism: 1820-1865" (Ryan, 74). According to her, much of the successful proselytizing on behalf of the concept of the woman's sphere was undertaken by the publishing industry itself which relied heavily on selling books to women. Among the most successful of these publications was *Godey's Lady's Book*, a woman's magazine that helped to create what Ryan calls the geography of the female sex—a geography in which some twentieth-century women remain confined (Ryan, 77). Although women of the nineteenth century were certainly identified primarily by their roles as wife and mother, there were other activities available to them. Two of the most popular areas that women could work in were reform movements and the church—work that gave women the experience and the confidence to engage in more overtly political activities such as the struggle for suffrage. Thus, as Ryan points out, with the arrival of the concept of domesticity was born its opposition.

One of the strengths of Ryan's book is the attention she gives to all classes. In chapter three, for example, she investigates the role of the black woman in American society; and in chapter four, "The Breadgivers: Immigrants and Reformers: 1865-1920," she discusses the role of immigrant women. She uses the term *breadgiver* to symbolize the nurturing role of women as it appeared in the marketplace, since the most frequent type of employment for immigrant women at this time was domestic work. At the same time, the educated, upper-class women joined settlement houses, where they, too, functioned more or less as professional housewives. Ryan points out that these women, and others like them, gained emotional and political strength from what she calls their homosocial bonding. In other words, they took the myth of the female sphere and made it work for themselves.

For Ryan—as others—women's history is a series of contradictions and sometimes outright paradoxes. She mentions, for example, the bizarre veneration of motherhood in a century that would simultaneously deny women their sexuality—and that witnessed a significant decline in the birthrate. She also remarks on the paradoxical effects that gaining suffrage had on women's condition. On the one hand, women gained with it a new status; on the other, they lost considerable political clout because it immediately became obvious that women were not voting as a bloc. Concurrent with this loss was a series of changes in the concept of womanhood that, once more, was not without its paradoxes and ironies. Just as women gained the freedom to enjoy sexuality, they were bombarded with scientific misinformation about their bodies, the most egregious of which was the infamous vaginal orgasm. As Ryan identifies them in "The Sexy Saleslady: Psychology, Heterosexuality, and Consumption in the Twentieth Century," the psychologists of the period were the "high priests of womanhood" (Ryan, 169). Unlike the experts who had preceded them in fashioning the ideal woman, the sexual psychologists claimed to have access to a woman's inner life. Here Ryan argues much as Betty Friedan does in *The Feminine Mystique* (discussed below, in chapters three and seven) that pop psychologists (aided by populizers of psychological theory) conspired with popular culture and advertisers to transform women into the perfect sexual companions for their husbands. The outcome of this effort, according to Ryan, is that women were sold a bill of goods that promised them a fulfilling intimacy and that delivered instead isolation and alienation.

In chapter six, "A Kaleidoscope of Roles: Twentieth-Century Women at Work and in the Home," Ryan discusses the consequences of the latest feminine mystique, one that fragments women into myriad simultaneous roles. As far as Ryan is concerned, the dramatic increase in the number and kinds of jobs open to women in the twentieth century "occasioned a more multifaceted and widespread pattern of sexual inequality" (Ryan, 195). The most obvious forms of inequality are the lower pay scales for women and the dead-end, sex-typed jobs into which they have been channeled. Ryan spends considerable space in this chapter illustrating the double binds that have trapped women into schizophrenic roles; perhaps the most obvious example of this no-win situation is the one in which the black woman has found herself where, if she is a competent, loving mother, she is condemned for being a castrating matriarch.

Ryan concludes her book with a newly revised chapter seven, "The Current Best Chance: Feminism and Family Change since 1960." She is perhaps at her feminist best in this chapter, as she recounts the efforts of the antifeminists to disrupt the women's 1977 convention in Houston, observing that they were "just a beleaguered minority" that gave evidence of the "strength and breadth of feminist consensus" (Ryan, 221). An important point that Ryan reiterates in this chapter, and one that Carl N. Degler pursues at length in *At Odds: Women and the Family in America from the Revolution to the Present* (discussed below), is the fact that the fate of women is intimately related to that of the family. Many of the issues raised by both feminists and antifeminists revolve around the problem of how to raise children in a society where both mothers and fathers have full-time outside work. One drawback to significant change in this area Ryan attributes to the relatively constant definition of masculinity in this culture; although the image of women has undergone radical transformations in the last three hundred years, it has not been accompanied by a similar transformation in the image of men. Ryan does see the possibility for this change to occur, however, and predicts that if it does it will, in effect, reshape American society as we know it. Not the least of these changes will be the dissolution of what she calls "the ersatz barricade between the family and public life" (Ryan, 244).

In summary, what Ryan has accomplished here is a comprehensive study of the relationship between women and their culture—and that between women and the cultural mythology that would define them. Her book is thoroughly researched and documented, making it an invaluable resource for scholars.

Two more recent publications on the history of American women, which build on what Ryan has accomplished, are the aforementioned Carl N. Degler's *At Odds: Women and the Family in America from the Revolution to the Present* and Mary Beth Norton's *Liberty's Daughters: The Revolutionary Experience of American Women, 1750-1800*. Degler's book is an attempt to bring together the history of women and that of the family in the United States and in so doing show that they are bound together: that to understand one it is necessary to understand the other. His methodology is based on a combination of statistical and anecdotal evidence; he provides no bibliography but does include informative footnotes. Degler takes as his premise that the family, which he defines in terms of composition and behavior patterns, "is an anti-individualistic institution" that for two hundred years has provided "the best known alternative to the individualism, competitiveness, and egoism that infuse the modern, industrial and urban world" (Degler, 472). When American women have sought their own independence, therefore, they have had to do so by fighting their traditional roles of wife and mother—by struggling against the anti-individualism inherent in the family. Degler's very readable book is a history of this struggle. In his discussion of women and the family, he draws upon the thinking of Nancy F. Cott, Anne Firor Scott, Carroll Smith-Rosenberg, and Herbert G. Gutman. Although he is often limited by the absence of written records, he makes a special effort to include the role of the black woman in the black family. Other features of the book include chapters on what he calls the "sorority of sisterhood" among nineteenth-century women; on the relationship between women's sexuality and their subordination, including chapters on fertility, abortion, and the efforts to insure social purity; on suffrage; and several on women's work patterns.

Mary Beth Norton's book focuses on the fifty-year period that surrounded the American Revolution. She takes as her premise the somewhat controversial position that even in the eighteenth century women enjoyed no sense of self-worth, no real pride in their accomplishments except as they pertained to the domestic sphere. Perhaps one of her most startling conclusions is that even women who were notable housewives—who fulfilled the domestic responsibilities assigned to them and excelled in their efforts—were often unhappy with their truncated lives. Norton argues, in other words, that there never was a golden age in America when women achieved coequal status with their men solely on the basis of their economic contributions to the family. Throughout her text, Norton includes copious material which she has gleaned from reading the papers of approximately 450 colonial families from both north and south. This material corroborates her contention that women in the eighteenth century were socially, economically, and emotionally subordinate to their men. Norton finds evidence of women's secondary status not only in letters and diaries but also in the common law of the time, which, like the eighteenth-century English law on which it is based, subordinated women's personal and property rights to those of their husbands.

Like Degler, Norton stresses the friendships among women and comments on the fact that they were perceived by men and women alike as "essential to a woman's happiness" (Norton, 108). This bonding between women is central to Norton's thesis because she takes the position that in the eighteenth century the spheres were indeed rigidly defined, that "female whites shared a universal domestic experience that differentiated their world from that of men" (Norton, 8). In other words, because of their different roles and responsibilities, men and women had little in common. As the phrase "female whites" suggests, Norton, like Degler, not only makes distinctions between the experiences of men and women, but she defines the differences between white women and black women. Because of a lack of information on their lives, Norton is not able to present as complete a picture of eighteenth-century black women as she is of their white counterparts, but she does elaborate on the kinship systems that blacks evolved in order to keep track of relatives. Norton's findings substantiate those of Degler's, that "against all odds" black men and women valued the institution of marriage and did whatever they could to keep their families intact (Norton, 66).

Although the lives of eighteenth-century women were determined largely by what men required of them, there were ways that women found to circumvent their subordination. For example, before marrying, a woman could draw up a contract with her prospective husband whereby she would retain some control of her property and the right to determine her heirs. Women also found ways of participating in activities outside the home. One way was to become active in the church. Another opportunity presented itself during the Revolutionary War when women engaged in economic boycotts of British goods. Not only did they refuse to buy British imports, but by their own handiwork they were able to replace much of the cloth that the colonies had been importing. Norton attributes to the war women's newfound ability to stand up to those who would criticize them. At the same time, women were changing because they had accepted the responsibility for raising their sons and preparing them for the duties of citizenship—a task heretofore left to the boys' fathers.

Norton's book contains copious references and footnotes, and a very useful essay on manuscript sources. Her book is also illustrated with examples of eighteenth-century paintings.

Nancy F. Cott takes as her premise, in *The Bonds of Womanhood: "Woman's Sphere" in New England, 1780-1835*, that the same bondage that confined women served also to consolidate their identity as a group. To demonstrate the dual nature of women's bonds at this time, Cott draws on documents like sermons, letters, diaries, magazine articles, and historical accounts of the period. In so doing, she illustrates the effect of economic progress and religion on the period's attitudes toward women and what they were permitted (and required) to do. The paradox she finds in the concept of a "woman's sphere" is a "simultaneous glorification and devaluation" of women, their work, and the home itself (Cott, 62). She identifies the "central convention of domesticity" as "the contrast between the home and the world," as exemplified by the kind of work women and men were engaged in (Cott, 64). The source of this contrast she lays at the feet of religion and rhetoric, saying that "New England ministers had pointed out the importance of the mother's role," while those who wrote "domestic literature, especially the female authors, denigrated business and politics as arenas of selfishness, exertion, embarrassment, and degradation of soul" (Cott, 85, 67). What Cott finds particularly ironic about the situation is that domesticity was supposed to be woman's "natural" occupation, and yet she needed continually to be reminded of it and educated for it.

If the education of the time was intended to prepare women in the domestic arts and sciences, it had a further unexpected consequence, according to Cott, who asserts that this focus on their "gender...fostered women's consciousness of themselves as a group united in purpose, duties, and interests" (Cott, 125). If ministers of religion used the cult of domesticity to keep women in their place, this too backfired, as women were brought together in religious activities and associations that gave them "vital identity and purpose that could be confirmed among their peers" (Cott, 159). In other words, women of the nineteenth century were able to make a virtue of necessity, finding positive values in what was essentially a major effort to keep them in their place.

Cott's ideas are provocative and, as I have suggested, documented by extensive references to primary materials of the time. She provides the locations of the manuscripts she cites and a complete list of the sermons and women's documents to which she refers.

Another major text on the nineteenth century is Ann Douglas's *The Feminization of American Culture*. In this remarkable—and often controversial—study of the relationship between nineteenth-century New England women and their newly disestablished Protestant ministers, Douglas (who also has published under the name Ann Douglas Wood; see, for example, discussion later in this chapter and in chapter two) argues for "the intimate

connection between critical aspects of Victorian culture and modern mass
culture" (Douglas, 3). It is in the sentimental literature of mid-nineteenth-
century America that Douglas finds the "split between elite and mass
cultures" that we recognize today (Douglas, 4). Sentimentalism itself she
contrasts to the other major ism of the time—Romanticism—arguing that
the "exaltation of the self found in the works of the romantics...was not,
like sentimentalist self-absorption, a commercialization of the inner life"
(Douglas, 308). She links the advent of sentimentalism to the "failed political
consciousness" in which the Protestant ministers lost their status, their
power, and their political clout (Douglas, 307). Concurrent with the disestablishment of the clergy, which was accomplished by 1833, was what
Douglas labels the disestablishment of women. The disestablishment of
Protestant ministers can be traced quite clearly in the changing state laws
that formally dissolved the official relationship between church and state.
The disestablishment of women is less readily observed, as, of course,
women were never legally established in the first place. But Douglas's
argument is a compelling one, as she documents the decline in real power
that both the clergy and their female parishioners experienced in the
mid-nineteenth century. It is her view that as the ministers lost their authority, which had been grounded in the financial support they had formerly
received from the state in the form of tithes, they were "pushed into
a position increasingly resembling the evolving feminine one" (Douglas,
48). The consequences to American culture of this convergence Douglas
describes as "not altogether beneficial" (Douglas, 11).

"Not altogether beneficial" is one of the few understatements that Douglas
allows herself, as she is clearly scornful of what she otherwise describes
as the "rancid writing" of the sentimental novelists and poets (Douglas, 309).
In this popular literature of the nineteenth century, Douglas finds the pro-
genitor of today's mass culture. She finds it in the literature's "fundamental
and complicated obsession with mediocrity" and in its covert hostility by
which the disestablished male clergy expressed its rage (Douglas, 201).
That is to say, although the clerical and female worlds seemed to share the
same conservative values and speak the same pious homilies, the clergymen
and the male sentimentalists despised women. According to Douglas, the
popular journalism of the time was especially rife with "sexual tension" that
reveals a mutual dislike between men and women (Douglas, 274). Apparently neither side was content with what Douglas calls the pseudoprofession
of feminine (or clerical) influence (Douglas, 51). The real crime in the
fall of Calvinism, Douglas believes, is that a masculine world of genuine
political power was replaced by an essentially powerless feminine world of
no real worth. Moreover, in Douglas's opinion, " 'Feminization' inevitably
guaranteed, not simply the loss of the finest values contained in Calvinism,
but the continuation of male hegemony in different guises" (Douglas, 13).

Douglas's book is clearly a trenchant indictment of mid-nineteenth-century sentimentalism, as it appeared in the imaginative literature of the time and in the religious and political writings. In its emotionalism and anti-intellectualism this sentimentalism espoused a simplistic view of the complexities of life and in so doing trivialized them. Examples of this trivialization abound in Douglas's book. She notes, for example, that in the new liberalized theology that followed disestablishment, pain was no longer regarded as necessary to religious conversion. Similarly, death became so camouflaged that it no longer appeared real. That is, the new rural cemeteries and the elaborate burials that originated in the 1830s seem to Douglas to have been "for the vicarious edification and stimulation of the living. The cemetery functioned not like experience but like literature; it was in several senses a sentimental reader's paradise" (Douglas, 253). Paradise itself was also domesticated and sentimentalized in the consolation literature of the time. Douglas compares the authors of consolation literature to television reporters, saying that "they purveyed news of the heavenly realm back to earthly audiences" (Douglas, 257).

Douglas concludes her study of the pernicious effects of feminization on American culture with a brief account of the lives and work of two major Romanticists of the period: Margaret Fuller and Herman Melville. Her purpose in doing so is to demonstrate the legitimacy of the Romantic vision and to document the penalties that Fuller and Melville paid by living in what was a period inimical to their genius. This book is an important one for the information it contains and the issues it raises; it is especially pertinent to a study of women and popular culture because its focus is on what the author believes to be the birth of American popular culture.

A book that should be read in conjunction with Douglas's is Susan Phinney Conrad's *Perish the Thought: Intellectual Women in Romantic America, 1830-1860*, in which she examines the women intellectuals' reaction to and interpretation of the nineteenth-century cult of domesticity. Like Douglas, Conrad is interested in the effects of sentimentalism on women; she is particularly interested in how the women intellectuals of the mid-nineteenth century tried to transform sentimentalism as a result of their contact with Romanticism. Her thesis is that Romanticism, "by seeming to offer a new and vital synthesis of womanhood and intellect, lured women into genuinely intellectual roles" (Conrad, 11). In contrast to these intellectual women were those who were attracted to and those who wrote the sentimental novels of the time; these women, according to Conrad, avoided reason in favor of sensibility and sentimentalism and championed women's "accomplishments"—embroidery, painting, singing— instead of a rigorous education. The theme of these writers, whose genre was the domestic novel, was the home; their effect was to downplay "the life of the mind" and, as a result, to reinforce "the popular notion of woman's basic anti-intellectualism" (Conrad, 26). In this context Conrad discusses Susanna Rowson, notable for the best-selling novel *Charlotte*

Temple; Susan Warner, known for what Conrad calls the most famous
domestic novel, *The Wide, Wide World;* Lydia H. Sigourney, remembered
as the "sweet singer of Hartford"; and Caroline Lee Hentz, whose work
Ernest Linwood Conrad quotes from as an example of a woman protesting
against intellectual activity: " 'Book! Am I writing a book? No indeed! This
is only a record of my heart's life, written at random and carelessly thrown
aside....' " (Conrad, 27).

On the other hand, many women, bluestockings among them, were
intent on obtaining a legitimate education and leading a life in which they
could cultivate their intellect. The time covered by Conrad's book was an
especially important one for women's education, as it saw the establishment
of many women's academies, seminaries, and colleges, such as the Georgia
Female College (1836), Mary Lyon's Mount Holyoke (1837), and New York's
Elmira College (1855). During this time several colleges admitted women
to regular courses of study, such as Oberlin College, which graduated
three women in 1841, and Antioch College, which admitted women in
1853. In the 1820s, Emma Willard had founded her Troy Female Seminary
(1821) and Catharine Beecher had founded her Hartford Female Seminary
(1824). Side by side with these advances in education, however, was the
prevailing view that women should not receive an education because it
would debilitate them physically. In this light, Conrad quotes from several
nineteenth-century sources, the writers of which were clearly threatened
by the prospects of a truly educated woman. She quotes, for example, from
the *North American Review* of 1836 in which it is stated of women that
" 'Hers be the domain of the moral affections, the empire of the heart...
leave the rude commerce of camps and the soul-hardening struggles of
political power to the harsher spirit of man, that he may still look up to
her as a purer and brighter being' " (Conrad, 38).

For those women who challenged the social conservatives of the time
and remained true to their own intellectual capabilities Conrad spares no
praise. Thus, chapter two, "The Beauty of a Stricter Method," focuses on
the life, thinking, and writing of Margaret Fuller, author of the powerful
Woman in the Nineteenth Century (1845). Chapter three, "Women's History
and Feminist Thought," focuses on the transformation of romantic thought
as expressed by Elizabeth Oakes Smith, feminist historian and author of
Woman and Her Needs (1851); Elizabeth Ellet, historian, antifeminist,
and author of *The Woman of the American Revolution* (1848); and Lydia
Maria Child, abolitionist and author of *History of Women in All Ages
and Nations*. Chapter four, "Within the 'Phalanx of Associated Inquiry,' "
focuses on the intellectual women of the American feminist movement,
such as Elizabeth Cady Stanton and Paulina Wright Davis. Davis coedited
with Caroline Healey Dall *The Una*, a periodical that provided "the forum
for intellectual women engaged in the feminist movement" (Conrad, 157).
Chapter five, "The 'Woman of Letters' in Transition," describes the life

and work of Elizabeth Palmer Peabody, translator, teacher, author, and bookshop-owner.

Not all nineteenth-century women lived in New England, of course, and several studies are available of those women who migrated west and those who lived in the southern United States. The scholars who investigate western and southern women of the nineteenth century find themselves having to cope with what are essentially false stereotypes and myths about these particular women. Much of what they attempt to do in their studies, therefore, is to break down the stereotypes and challenge the myths that would have us believe that western women were unencumbered by the cult of domesticity and southern women trapped by it.

In *Frontier Women: The Trans-Mississippi West, 1840-1880,* for example, Julie Roy Jeffrey helps lay to rest the myth that women who immigrated to the western United States in the nineteenth century enjoyed more social freedom than their eastern sisters. Although she has not footnoted her work—in an effort to keep it more accessible to the general public— the evidence for her thesis is compelling. As the bibliographical essays that follow each chapter demonstrate, Jeffrey is conversant with recent scholarship on the nineteenth century. To this scholarship, Jeffrey herself has contributed the writing of the emigrant women themselves: much of *Frontier Women* is laced with excerpts from letters and diaries written by pioneer women. Of her approach, Jeffrey admits that she had thought to find a feminist outlook in the work of these women; what she instead found was a culture very like the cult of domesticity current in the eastern United States at that time. In explanation, Jeffrey writes that the "domestic ideal was a goal toward which women could direct their efforts, the promise of a day when their lives would not be so hard, their tasks so numerous. Domesticity, with its neat definition of woman's place, helped women bear what they hoped were temporary burdens and reestablished their sense of identity and self-respect. It served as a link with the past" (Jeffrey, 72-73).

Although Jeffrey's entire book is a fascinating look at a heretofore much neglected subject, perhaps her most intriguing chapter is that on the Mormon women, " 'If Polygamy Is the Lord's Order, We Must Carry It Out.' " Jeffrey sees the Mormon experience, with its emphasis on polygamy, as being quintessentially characteristic of the ability of the cult of domesticity to survive—even flourish—in frontier conditions. Moreover, because of the lower-class origins of most nineteenth-century Mormons, Jeffrey argues that their absorption with the cult of domesticity "gives plain evidence" that this middle-class ideology indeed did spread to other classes (Jeffrey, 178).

Another look at frontier women is Beverly J. Stoeltje's " 'A Helpmate for Man Indeed': The Image of the Frontier Woman." In this essay, which appears in a special issue of *Journal of American Folklore* that focuses on women, Stoeltje investigates the three major types of female images—and their male counterparts—found in western folklore of the late nineteenth century. These types are: the refined lady; the helpmate, and the bad woman. Of the three, it was only the helpmate who truly flourished in the frontier environment, but to do so, according to Stoeltje, she gave up her sexual identity. The lady failed to adapt and either returned east or pined away and died early. The bad woman, as a threat to morality, was relegated to the very fringes of society.

An essay that is critical of the approach taken by Stoeltje and others who would type women is Glenda Riley's "Women in the West." It is Riley's contention that much of the work being done on frontier women remains locked in stereotypical perceptions of what were in fact complex situations. She is particularly critical of those studies she considers as being "riddled with generalization and misrepresentation" (Riley, 313). Her footnotes offer a substantial bibliography of the subject, and clarify exactly which studies fail to acknowledge the variables of frontier life. Because of its bibliographical analysis this is an extremely valuable essay. It is also valuable because Riley quotes from several primary sources to prove her point that the experiences of frontier women do not lend themselves to easy categorization. She concludes her essay with a series of questions that need to be addressed by historians of frontier women; two areas of neglect that she mentions are the roles of ethnic and black women in the west and the role of social class in women's history.

A comprehensive bibliography helpful in the study of frontier women is Dawn Lander Gherman's "Frontier and Wilderness: American Women Authors," which is a compilation of primary and secondary sources relating to the experiences of women in the United States. Gherman includes sources on women of color as well as white women, and such primary works as diaries, journals, slave narratives, and captivity tales. Her checklist is partially annotated. (For a collection of essays on western history and literature, see L. L. Lee and Merrill Lewis's *Women, Women Writers, and the West*, discussed below, in chapter two.)

In *The Southern Lady: From Pedestal to Politics 1830-1930*, Anne Firor Scott traces the transformation of the southern white women from the lady of the manor to a progressive political leader. Much of the material that Scott uses in her study is found in manuscript collections at various southern universities, including the University of North Carolina, Tulane, and the University of Georgia, and at the Schlesinger Library at Radcliffe. Her sources range from unpublished diaries and letters to magazine articles and novels published between 1830 and 1930. Although Scott's book is not primarily theoretical, she does analyze in some detail the experiences of the southern white woman in a social context. Her purpose, as she explains it, is to contrast the image and the reality of the southern lady, who, over a period of one hundred years, freed herself from socially determined roles.

In part one, "The Antebellum Lady," Scott describes the paradoxical situation of the southern white woman, who, before the social upheaval brought by the Civil War, was torn between the desire to conform to the image of the lady and the need to cope with the demands of everyday life. As Scott reminds us, in the nineteenth century all forms of popular culture conspired to keep woman in her place as a passive creature who lived through and for her husband. For most of the women in the south, however, this idealized lady of leisure had no place in reality because of the physical labor required to run a farm or a plantation. That the image survived—and even flourished—in the face of overwhelming contradictory evidence indicates to Scott its significance to southern people. Although the image of the lady clearly met unexpressed psychological needs of both men and women, Scott finds evidence that some women, even before the war, were chafing under the system that enslaved them while purporting to revere them.

One area of discontent was the relationship of southern white women to their slaves. Not only were women angry about the double standard that allowed their husbands free access to their female slaves, but women were angry about the fact that they themselves were responsible for the labor and welfare of all the slaves the family owned. The plantation mistress, according to Scott, felt—and rightly so—that she had no privacy. Another bone of contention for women was their lack of education, which Scott feels was the major impetus for women to join women's clubs after the Civil War.

The war itself, of course, brought change to the South and to women's role in particular. During the war years, women were forced to assume the responsibilities of their husbands in running the farms. As a consequence of the war, the patriarchy itself was weakened considerably, which permitted the expression among women of increased dissatisfaction with the traditional image of the lady. These facts, coupled with the national interest in public education, led naturally, as Scott explains in "The New Woman," to new patterns in women's roles. Like their compatriots in the northeast, the women of the postwar South gained self-confidence and political expertise by participating in the socially approved activities of missionary and church societies, in the WCTU, and in women's clubs. Eventually, the work of these women culminated in the drive for suffrage, a drive that Scott found took a particularly racist twist in the South. (On this, see also Aileen Kraditor's *Ideas of the Woman Suffrage Movement, 1890-1920*, discussed below.) Opponents of women's suffrage argued against it because it would enfranchise blacks; proponents, according to Scott, often argued for it on the grounds that white women would be able to counter the votes of the already franchised black men. Although women worked hard to earn the right to vote, Scott reports that only four southern states ratified it in 1920: Texas, Tennessee, Kentucky, and Arkansas. One of the most interesting details of Scott's study of the politically active white southern women is their comparatively progressive attitude—a fact that she attributes to the kind of woman who would be political in the first place: those who had the courage to speak out were, by definition, going against tradition and were thus not unexpectedly ideologically opposed to conservatism.

Besides the decline of the patriarchy and the increasing industrialization of the south after the war, Scott looks to better contraceptive methods and improved medical treatment for women as explanations for why and how the woman's role changed in the south. Scott considers it important that women were able to limit the size of their families and reduce the risks of childbirth because these developments freed women to pursue other activities. That they could also get an education and find work outside the home freed them from their obsession with marriage and from being economically beholden to men. In sum, Scott argues that the 1930s were more complex than the 1830s; because of the effects of two major wars and the promise of another, life in the south in the 1930s was no longer the agrarian ideal of imaginative literature. As a consequence of these social, economic, and political changes, the narrow concept of the southern belle was largely invalidated; living proof of its inaccuracy was visible in the large number of women who worked for a living and who were politically astute members of a changing society. Although the image of the lady no longer controlled women by the 1930s, its influence according to Scott could still be found in the life-styles that some women assumed in order to protect themselves from male criticism. But these vestiges of the myth could not obscure the fact that southern women, far from being stylized ideals, were leading richly various lives—lives that were different from those of the past and each other.

Scott's text is thoroughly documented and is followed by a bibliographical essay. Among the southern novelists that she mentions are Augusta Evans and Ellen Glasgow; among the abolitionists, Sarah and Angelina Grimké. Journals she recommends as resources include the *Southern Literary Messenger*, the *Southern Ladies Companion*, and the *Southern Quarterly Review*.

On the same subject, Margaret Ripley Wolfe, in "The Southern Lady: Long Suffering Counterpart of the Good Ole' Boy," argues that the southern lady has become such a stereotyped figure of literature and myth that few authors or historians do her justice. Two ways southern women are described in literature Wolfe finds especially misleading: the transformation from belle to matron and the sexual relations of the southern lady. Wolfe faults both novelists and historians for not permitting the southern lady "the same flexibility of behavior as her counterpart the southern gentleman" (Wolfe, 19).

Other works that provide additional insight to the subject of southern women are Lillian Smith's *Killers of the Dream*, which documents the effects of slavery on white women; and Irving H. Bartlett and C. Glenn Cambor's "The History and Psychodynamics of Southern Womanhood."

Taking a psychoanalytical approach to the history of southern women, Bartlett and Cambor contend that the idealized southern lady was different from her national counterpart because of the social conditions surrounding slavery. The practice of having black women raise white children, according to these authors, led to several unforeseen and largely unnoticed consequences for both races and both sexes. One result was to allow white males to act out their oedipal fantasies through black women; another, related result was the adulation of white women at the expense of their sexuality. Yet another was to provide multiple and paradoxical female roles for white girls, whose real mothers were revered but childlike themselves and whose surrogate black mothers were strong but submissive. Besides shedding new light on an old myth, Bartlett and Cambor's essay offers a comprehensive review of scholarship on the subject.

Yet another important view of the south is found in George P. Rawick's *From Sundown to Sunup: The Making of the Black Community*. Taking exception to the notion that slavery irreparably harmed the black family, Rawick, using slave narratives and interviews as his sources, argues that the slave community itself was an extended family, with strong bonds of affection and fellowship. Included in his bibliography are slave narratives written by women. In *Black Women Novelists: The Development of a Tradition, 1892-1976* (discussed below, in chapter two), Barbara Christian discusses the relationship of black women to the myth of the southern lady. Another investigation of black women is *Black Matriarchy: Myth or Reality?*, edited by John H. Bracey et al.; this is a collection of essays that represents both sides of the question that appears in the title. Although they present both sides, the editors clearly intend to prove it a myth.

In the sixty years that have passed since women gained the vote, there have been several accounts published of how it was won. The books discussed below reflect the best of the current scholarship on this subject. The first of these, Eleanor Flexner's *Century of Struggle: The Woman's Rights Movement in the United States*, was originally published in 1959 and reissued in a revised edition in 1975. With this book Flexner set into motion what has become the new social history of women. Although there were scholars who preceded her in this drive to retrieve women's social history, none seems to have had quite the impact that she has. This is due, in part, to the fact that her book was first published just at the cusp of the socially aware 1960s—and was reissued at the height of the current women's movement. It is also due to the fact of her thoroughness. There are few books on any subject that explore so many aspects of a question. In order to provide a comprehensive history of the women's rights movement that culminated in woman's suffrage, Flexner has investigated the social conditions of all nineteenth-century women. She includes in her study information on the middle-class white women who led the movement for suffrage and on those women not of this class who were also part of the struggle. For example, she discusses the lives and contributions of black women, immigrant women, and working-class women. She discusses the women of the northeast and those of the south and west who worked for suffrage. In short, in her history of the women's movement, Eleanor Flexner provides a detailed account of what it was like to be an American woman from the beginning of the nineteenth century to the beginning of the twentieth.

Another detailed study that does justice to the complexities and paradoxes of the fight for suffrage is Aileen S. Kraditor's *Ideas of the Woman Suffrage Movement, 1890-1920*. Of particular note is the attention Kraditor gives to the arguments forwarded by those in favor of and those opposed to woman's suffrage; because of its detailed accounts of both sides of the issue, her history is one of political process. By documenting the transformation of the suffrage movement as one from justice to expediency, Kraditor demonstrates both the political savvy of its proponents and the ideological compromises many of the leaders were willing to make in the larger effort to enfranchise women. Of interest here are the statements made by Elizabeth Cady Stanton and others that were clearly intended to work on the racial and ethnic prejudices of middle-class Americans. The suffragists were also successful in converting to their own use many of the antisuffragists' arguments; one notable success was the notion that the woman belonged in the home and not the voting booth. By emphasizing what women could do for the country, by participating in government as champions of the public weal, suffragists were able to describe their potential influence as one befitting housewives. That is, women, through the vote, would extend their domestic responsibilities to the country itself. But even in refuting the arguments of the opposition, the suffragists themselves, as Kraditor points out, were never in full agreement as to what they should claim in defense of their right to vote. Because of the paradoxes and outright contradictions in their reasoning and their obvious willingness to change their story to fit the current needs, this book is a fascinating study of political expediency and pragmatism. Kraditor also provides brief biographies of twenty-six suffragists and a bibliography of manuscript and secondary sources.

Although some feminists have taken exception to his title, William L. O'Neill's *Everyone Was Brave: The Rise and Fall of Feminism in America* is a balanced look at what O'Neill calls "the failure of feminism" (O'Neill, viii). Female equality itself has not been achieved, according to O'Neill, largely because of "the institutions of marriage and the family, as presently conceived" (O'Neill, ix; see also in this context, Carl N. Degler's *At Odds*, discussed above). It is O'Neill's contention that the early feminists—those of the 1870s—lost much of their potential support among younger women by being themselves almost obsessed with the notion of moral purity, especially in sexual matters. In his eyes, these early feminists rallied around the myths of maternity and motherhood and the concept of woman's morally superior nature—thus fatally linking and limiting themselves to the proscriptive Victorian ethos that had driven women to feminism in the first place. Suggesting that there was "fear and suspicion of sex" among most nineteenth-century feminists, O'Neill argues that the "maternal mystique" by which they sought to make their movement respectable was the very philosophy that did them in as a political force (O'Neill, 24, 36). As other historians have noted, suffragists and antisuffragists both over- and understated the inherent potential for change in the women's vote. On the one hand, suffragists argued that women, because of their moral superiority, would clean up politics and thus the country itself; on the other hand, those opposed to women's suffrage argued that the vote would change very little in the lives of American women. Of the two positions, O'Neill observes that the latter seems to be more on the mark.

In addition to those women who were active in the struggle for the vote, O'Neill examines the history of those who were active in women's organizations and clubs. In "The Structure of Social Feminism," for example, he characterizes the composition and activities of several women's organizations. Included in this brief history are the Association of Collegiate Alumnae (ACA), which was later to become the American Association of University Women (AAUW); Sorosis, precursor to the General Federation of Women's Clubs (GFWC); the National Federation of Settlements, which originated in England; and the National Consumers' League (NCL), which was, according to O'Neill, "not only a model social feminist organization but a prototypical specimen of the Progressive mentality" (O'Neill, 97). In his next chapter, "Ten Who Led the Woman Movement," O'Neill offers concise biographies of Josephine Shaw Lowell, M. Carey Thomas, Margaret Dreier Robins, Jane Addams, Anna Howard Shaw, Carrie Chapman Catt, Alice Paul, Charlotte Perkins Gilman, Florence Kelley, and Vida Scudder.

In regard to the progress made by women during the Progressive Era, O'Neill argues that it was less the result of the efforts of the suffragists than that of the overall changes of the time, such as the admission of more women to colleges and professions and the phenomenal growth, in the 1890s, of women's organizations. Of the advances made by women during and immediately after World War I, O'Neill describes them as less than expected. In fact, of the 1920s he says that for social feminists the period was one of "defeat and decay," as social reform was not compatible with the widespread fear of radicalism in the country (O'Neill, 262). The rest of O'Neill's history of the failure of feminism seeks to demonstrate the preoccupation of American society with what Betty Friedan aptly labeled the "feminine mystique."

In summary, O'Neill believes that the goals and philosophies of the social feminists—those activists and reformers who replaced the radical feminists after Reconstruction—were by definition designed to limit women's freedom because they worked from the premise that women should expand the activities of the home into the rest of the world. Another key weakness lay in the pragmatism inherent in social feminism; if women made claims for themselves on the basis of the good they would do, they could only expect to be judged on this basis. When their reforms were inadequate to the complex social problems these social feminists set out to solve, they lost much of their raison d'être. The consequence of these two weaknesses was ultimately, according to O'Neill, a moribund feminist movement—one only recently reinvigorated by the radical thinkers of the 1970s.

Taking positions similar to O'Neill and Degler, William Henry Chafe, in *The American Woman: Her Changing Social, Economic, and Political Roles, 1920-1970,* works from the premise that "sexual inequality is rooted within the social structure itself, through the allocation of different spheres of responsibility to men and women" (Chafe, viii; see also, Shulamith Firestone, *The Dialectic of Sex: The Case for Feminist Revolution,* discussed below, in chapter seven). To demonstrate his contention, Chafe examines the participation of women in politics, economics, industry, and the professions. In his introduction he reviews highlights of the Declaration of Sentiments and Resolutions passed at the 1848 Seneca Falls convention, the theories of Charlotte Perkins Gilman as expressed in *Women and Economics* (a book recently reissued for which Degler has written an introduction; discussed below, in chapter seven), the concept of the women's sphere, the struggle of the National American Woman Suffrage Association to obtain the vote, and the work of the General Federation of Women's Clubs. Chafe begins his study proper with an examination of the role of women in politics between 1920 and 1940.

Once the Nineteenth Amendment was ratified in 1920, Chafe argues, women, if they were to consolidate their power, needed to vote as a bloc; instead "women in general voted like their husbands if they voted at all, and...enthusiasm among females for reform was limited at best" (Chafe, 30). As a result, suffrage really did not measurably improve the status of women. In his next chapter, Chafe claims that the economic changes of the period have been overstated, that women were still confined to "positions traditionally set aside for females," and that a mere five percent increase in the number of women workers occurred during World War I (Chafe, 51, 52). Even in industry, the topic of Chafe's next chapter, women found little in the way of improvements, as they were discriminated against because of their sex by both management and labor unions. According to Chafe, women in the professions were also limited by the fact that the education of the time offered specialized instruction in domestic skills for women, and those women who wanted careers "were singled out for special condemnation by the proponents of homemaking" (Chafe, 106; see also, Barbara Harris, *Beyond Her Sphere,* discussed below). In his final

chapter in this section, "The Equal Rights Amendment," Chafe notes that
the proponents of the ERA were more interested in in-fighting than in
uniting "in pursuit of a common purpose" (Chafe, 131).

Part two Chafe devotes entirely to "World War II and Its Impact."
In the early years of the war employers were unwilling to hire women,
a reluctance that evaporated with the attack on Pearl Harbor in 1941.
Of the women who benefited from new hiring patterns, Chafe identifies
the black woman as benefiting the most. It was also important that women
who worked in the factories were no longer young and single, but over
thirty-five and married. If women were encouraged by the mass media and
public figures to join the labor force during the war, at its close these
same spokesmen demanded that women relinquish their jobs to returning
soldiers. Inequality also persisted in the hourly wages, as women were still
paid less than men for comparable work. Women may have held onto their
jobs but the discriminatory attitudes did not change.

In Chafe's final part, "Since the 1940s," he identifies a "deepening sense
of bewilderment among many American women over how to define their
identity" (Chafe, 199). Part of this is attributable to the almost schizophrenic
reversals in official policy during and after the war. Part is because of the
rise of what Philip Wylie calls momism. And part is the fault of such
psychological experts as Ferdinand Lundberg and Marynia Farnham who
wrote in *Modern Woman: The Lost Sex* (1947) that feminists and independent women were neurotic masochists—an attitude echoed by the women's
magazines that persisted in showing mothers as the only happy women. In
the last chapter of this section, "The Revival of Feminism," Chafe describes
three conditions that must be met for the evolution of a genuine protest
movement: "first, a point of view around which to organize; second, a
positive response by a portion of the aggrieved group; and third, a social
atmosphere which is conducive to reform" (Chafe, 227). These precondi-
tions, according to Chafe, were met in the 1960s. Although he is certainly
supportive of the causes of the contemporary feminists, he does criticize
them for not realizing that the feminine mystique permeated the nineteenth
century and was not a post-World War II invention of the mass media. In his
"Conclusion: Future Prospects," he strikes a sober note by quoting from
studies that show women's reluctance to accept the status and accomplishments of women professionals. His book is documented with copious informative footnotes.

A recent history of American women written from the perspective of
social policy—its origins and consequences—is Sheila Rothman's *Woman's
Proper Place: A History of Changing Ideals and Practices, 1870 to the
Present*. Rothman takes as her premise the fact that "every generation has
advanced its special definition of woman's proper place, and every generation has devised public and private programs to promote and enhance
that definition" (Rothman, 4-5). Her method is to define the sources and

manifestations of woman's proper place as it has evolved in the last one hundred years, then to describe and explain the public policies that have risen and fallen in response to these changing definitions of the American woman. One of the most provocative features of her book is her insistence on the unexpected negative results of social legislation intended to better all women's lives. One reason for these unanticipated consequences of so-called enlightened or progressive legislation is, according to Rothman, the largely unacknowledged differences between the middle- and lower-class white women—differences that the middle-class reformers have consistently ignored as they have worked for sweeping changes in American social policy.

Rothman's intelligent and probing book is divided into seven chapters, each of which focuses on a different aspect of the relationship between "proper womanhood" and public policy. According to Rothman, from 1870 to 1978, there have been four major policy shifts in this arena: (1) the late nineteenth century believed in a far-ranging concept of "virtuous womanhood"; (2) the Progressive Era introduced the concept of "educated motherhood"; (3) the 1920s followed with the concept of the "wife-companion"; and (4) the 1950s introduced the radically new concept of "woman as person" (Rothman, 5). Her book focuses "on each dominant model and the institutions that embodied its principles" (Rothman, 6). In her analysis she looks in depth at the influences wielded by the educational principles and practices of women's colleges, the advance of technology, and the growth of the male-dominated professions (especially the medical profession).

Among the more intriguing of Rothman's subjects is her investigation into the technological advances that resulted in apartment living and department store shopping. (On the subject of technology, see the essays that are discussed after Rothman's book.) According to Rothman, both of these urban developments permitted women to move outside the home with a never-before-experienced freedom. But rather than encouraging women to become producers of goods or technology, the department store in particular encouraged them to become consumers of the goods and technology that others (primarily men) were producing. The result of this new freedom of spirit and mobility was, ironically, not to expand but to constrict women's possibilities.

Rothman also presents a balanced look at the medical theories and practices of the last hundred years, giving special attention to so-called women's diseases. It is her conviction, as it is that of other scholars, that a grave injustice has been done women in the name of protecting them from harm. (On this, see also Barbara Ehrenreich and Deirdre English's *For Her Own Good: 150 Years of the Experts' Advice to Women* and Mary Daly's *Gyn/Ecology: The Metaethics of Radical Feminism* both discussed below, in chapters one and seven, respectively.) Rothman believes that the medical profession itself, by identifying women's normal bodily functions—such as menstruation and childbirth—as pathological, lent credence to the cultural beliefs that women were physically and mentally weak (Rothman, 24). In this context, Rothman reviews the details of Vassar's health program, a program intended to demonstrate that an educated woman need not be physically debilitated by exercising her brain. One consequence of Vassar's own rigorous insistence on the physical well-being of its female students was that, according to Rothman, it inadvertently slighted their intellectual growth by omitting the more demanding subjects that were being taken by male students at Harvard and Yale. To supplement this part of her history, Rothman includes an evaluation of the medical texts written by Silas Weir Mitchell. When Mitchell published *Fat and Blood* in 1878 (a year after Dr. Mary Putnam Jacobi published *The Question of Rest for Women During Menstruation*, in which she argued that those women who experienced menstrual pain were not somatically normal), he did so in order to promote his concept of the rest cure. But when he published *Doctor and Patient* nine years later (1887), he advocated the rest cure only in extreme cases and instead promoted the concept of "frequent physical exercise" (Rothman, 35). In sum, Rothman, rather than damning Mitchell outright—as some feminists do—suggests that here was a physician who acted in good faith and who was able to change his mind when presented with new evidence.

There are other areas of private and public policy that Rothman examines with equal care, such as her study of the women's clubs and the Protestant Nuns they gave birth to. Here, as in other instances in her book, Rothman makes a distinction between the middle and lower classes, arguing quite convincingly that "the ideal of virtuous womanhood gave a distinctly narrow and class-bound quality to social programs" (Rothman, 63; compare this to William L. O'Neill's remarks about the woman's movement in *Everyone Was Brave*, discussed above). By attributing social ills to individual moral weakness and failure, the efforts of these reformers were misguided, according to Rothman, because they "focused ameliorative efforts more on the person than on the system" (Rothman, 63). As a result, their programs were inadequate to the problems they faced. Nor were their failures limited to the lower class. One of the most poignant examples of how middle-class women tried to help others of their class lies in the history of the so-called Womans Exchanges. These institutions were set up in order to help middle-class women who, because of their husbands' deaths or other misfortunes, had become suddenly indigent. The failure of these exchanges lay in the fact that they perpetuated the fatal mythology that proper middle-class women wouldn't be caught dead trying to make a decent living. The women would bring their homemade jams and jellies and other household products to the exchange where they would be sold. But the women themselves were encouraged to come by the back stairs so no one would see them.

What should have given women a sense of self-worth—their resourcefulness in times of trouble—instead gave them a sense of shame that they were forced to work at all.

As Carl Degler does in *At Odds* (discussed above) Sheila Rothman investigates the relationship of woman to her family, especially her children and husband (as opposed to, for example, her parents or in-laws). At the heart of Rothman's discussion on "The Ideology of Educated Motherhood" is the fact that, with the rise of the experts, women lost the right to raise their own children. Very simply speaking, the experts convinced the public that child-rearing was too crucial to the future well-being of the nation to leave it in the untrained hands of mothers. Similarly, the birth and health of the child became the province of the male medical profession and eventually the state itself. Even the question of birth control has been historically a public and not a private matter. Rothman attributes this latter situation to the fact that women's responsibilities, until quite recently, have been defined in terms of their husbands and the state and not in terms of themselves. Another reason for male control of birth control Rothman attributes—most ironically—to Margaret Sanger herself. Sanger, an impassioned and thoroughly dedicated advocate of voluntary birth control, was forced by circumstances beyond her control to cede to the medical profession the right to fit and dispense pessaries—and, by extension, information about birth control itself. Rothman sees this as just another instance in which what should have been rightly the province of women became instead the province of men, and what should have been available to lower-class women became priced out of their range because they couldn't afford to go to the doctor. This example, as the others described above, is paradigmatic of the issues that Rothman raises, documents, and interprets. Hers is a book particularly valuable as a study in social history.

An essay that should be read in conjunction with Rothman's statements about the effects of technology on women is William D. and Deborah C. Andrews's "Technology and the Housewife in Nineteenth-Century America." Treating technology as both artifact and process, Andrews and Andrews argue that it significantly changed the nineteenth-century perception of housekeeping. In effect, the same technology that outside the home threatened traditional values was discovered within the home to be useful in defending them. Thus, the proponents of "domestic science," such as Catharine E. Beecher and her sister Harriet Beecher Stowe, applied the concepts of organization and efficiency—found in technological production systems—to elevating the status of women in their homes. The authors contend that Beecher herself has been misunderstood, if not misrepresented, by recent historians because of her insistence on the notion of separate spheres. According to Andrews and Andrews, Beecher and the early feminists differed only in their solution to the woman's problem, not in their definition of it. Besides offering this alternative view of Catharine

Beecher, this essay is useful as a review of the domestic science manuals that proliferated after 1830. The authors also note for the record that women, for the 1876 Centennial Exhibition in Philadelphia, chose to emphasize in their pavilion "machinery and domestic artifacts" (Andrews and Andrews, 325).

In "The Industrial Revolution Comes to the Home: Kitchen Design Reform and Middle-Class Women," Kimberley W. Carrell provides a concise summary of the innovations and inventions that helped to bring about the modern kitchen. Her point is that many of the improvements that were introduced in the twentieth century actually had their origins in Catharine Beecher's nineteenth-century domestic manuals (for a discussion of Beecher's *A Treatise on Domestic Economy*, see the introduction). Carrell identifies several major developments that contributed to the transformation of the American kitchen: 1900-1920, the development of the kitchen cabinet; the 1920s, the development of the refrigerator; 1930-1940, the development of gas and electric ranges; and in the past century the proliferation of gadgets as labor-saving devices.

Yet another view of the relationship between housework and technology is provided by Bettina Berch in "Scientific Management in the Home: The Empress's New Clothes." Scientific management, which is based on time-and-motion studies in a factory setting, originated as a way to increase the efficiency of factory workers. Between the 1890s and 1920s, however, proponents of this system had succeeded in applying its concepts to housework — an application Berch finds incongruent with the true needs of the housewife. Berch's premise is that factory work and housework are fundamentally different kinds of activities, with the former stressing the repetition of discrete tasks in a confined area and the latter a multiplicity of tasks in a more expansive area. Berch, convinced that no one has established a clear notion of what it means to save time in household tasks, contends that the slogan, Laborsaving, has been really nothing more than an advertising gimmick designed to market technology in the home. Her essay features, in its footnotes, a good review of the literature on this subject.

In " 'How to Be A Woman': Theories of Female Education in the 1950's," Marion Nowak discusses how experts in the 1950s attempted to reimmerse women in femininity and domesticity following the war years; Nowak's focus is what she describes as the "family-living courses" that were being taught at colleges and universities in the 1950s. A preliminary study on the relationship of women to technology is "A Case Study of Technological and Social Change: The Washing Machine and the Working Wife," by Ruth Schwartz Cowan, in Hartman and Banner's *Clio's Consciousness Raised* (discussed below).

Barbara J. Harris's *Beyond Her Sphere: Women and the Professions in American History* is a comprehensive study of the cultural limitations that, since the seventeenth century, have served to discourage — if not prevent—women from becoming professionals. In order to demonstrate the continuity of these social pressures that would keep women at home, Harris cites evidence from several recent studies of European and American history that demonstrate the basic misogynistic bent of the ideologies we as a nation have inherited. Referring to what she calls in chapter one "An Ideology of Inferiority," she claims that "the problem of the professional woman in the United States is one segment of the total problem of the position and role of the female in Western civilization" (Harris, 3). It is her contention, for example, that even though colonial women enjoyed more economic flexibility than their successors in the eighteenth and nineteenth centuries, they did so "within a larger context of subordination" (Harris, 20; compare this with Mary Beth Norton's *Liberty's Daughters*, discussed above). That is, not only was the seventeenth century strongly patriarchal, but most work was assigned by sex and the majority of "she-merchants" and craftswomen of the time were not married women, but widows. This latter statistic suggests to Harris "that women emerged from the domestic sphere only when necessity forced them to" (Harris, 39). Harris's point is an important one, as it tends to balance out the more favorable light that some feminist historians have shed on the economic status of colonial women.

Another valuable contribution that Harris makes to the new social history is to remind her readers that, although the cult of domesticity was not limited to middle-class women, it was originally very much a middle-class phenomenon and should be studied as such. In other words, Harris, like Sheila Rothman, perceives women's history as being most properly a study, not just of women, but of "class, region, and race" (Harris, 40).

Like many feminist historians (for example, Anne F. Scott and Eleanor Flexner, discussed above), Harris considers the Civil War to have been "a major watershed in the history of American women" (Harris, 96). Like the two world wars that would follow it, the Civil War increased the economic opportunities for American women. During this period, according to Harris, women entered new occupations, such as the civil service, and saw one of their traditional domestic responsibilities, that of nursing, become professionalized.

Harris does not neglect the backlash of the new scientism of the nineteenth century, when social conservatives invoked the authority of Darwin and others to return women to their proper place. Recounting the actual decline in the number of female medical students at this time, Harris also reports that women faced more obstacles in becoming lawyers than they did doctors. She attributes this situation to the fact that "the legal profession was institutionalized and had been granting licensing powers much earlier" (Harris, 110).

One of the explanations that Harris gives for the drop-off in professional women in the early twentieth century is the almost single-minded effort of feminists to gain the vote—a focus that left would-be professional women without political and moral support. In the 1930s, the drop-off increased because of the widely held attitude that women should not steal work from men. With the advent of World War II and the subsequent need for women to work in what had been previously male-only jobs, came what Harris refers to as a revolution in "female employment...without a corresponding shift in attitudes toward women" (Harris, 156). This discrepancy occurred, according to Harris, because the country perceived working women from an economic rather than a cultural perspective. That is, with higher inflation rates coupled with higher expectations for themselves, American families were forced, economically speaking, to sanction the concept of the working wife and mother.

Harris closes her own work with a comparison between the feminism of the twentieth century and that of the nineteenth. Among the differences she sees between the two movements is the fact that contemporary "feminists have raised the issue of marriage and the family as central to the problem of women" (Harris, 178). In their attitudes toward women working outside the home, however, the two women's movements coincide. And they do so in the face of continuing prejudice from society itself, a prejudice that Harris argues stems directly from the cult of domesticity. Perhaps most disturbing of all is the fact that women professionals themselves have internalized many of these values and continue to be controlled by them. Harris's book contains a bibliography and extremely informative footnotes.

An earlier study of the professional opportunities available to women is Elisabeth Dexter's *Career Women of America, 1776-1840*. In separate chapters Dexter outlines the kinds of jobs women held and the public reaction to their work in the fields of teaching, nursing, church work, acting, writing, shopkeeping, sewing, managing farms, and millworking. As part of her history of changing attitudes toward women's work, Dexter quotes from documents of the period that reflect both a desire for women workers and a conviction that women shouldn't work. Of the changes, she remarks that a woman who worked outside the home before 1760 "was considered simply on her own merits. After 1880 or thereabouts, such a woman was self-conscious, and her neighbors critical" (Dexter, 219). According to her research, between 1776 and 1840 women gained in the teaching profession and lost, most dramatically, in health care—findings corroborated by other scholars of professional women, with Mary Roth Walsh dissenting on the question of women doctors.

Walsh is author of the authoritative history of women in American medicine, *Doctors Wanted: No Women Need Apply: Sexual Barriers in the Medical Profession, 1835-1975*. Her thesis is that the medical establishment intentionally acted to keep women out of the profession, and that it was successful in doing so because women physicians never attained power in the male-dominated medical institutions, such as medical societies and colleges. Walsh challenges the work of those feminist historians—such as Dexter and Gerda Lerner—who claim that women lost ground in the field of medicine from the seventeenth to the nineteenth century. Observing that there is little evidence to substantiate the claim that female midwives had any real professional status, Walsh concludes that licensing was not the final blow to their decline in popularity in the nineteenth century. Furthermore, Walsh argues that women were not "sacrificed on the altar of professionalism"—a claim made by some feminist historians (Walsh, 10). Walsh's own explanation is a complex combination of economics and social theory. She finds it no coincidence, for example, that the attempts to define women by their sex organs came at the same time in the nineteenth century that women were attempting to enter male-dominated professions. Correspondingly, male physicians, Walsh observes, were subject to the same fears of sexual inadequacy and the same desire to maintain the status quo as other nineteenth-century men; they too saw the separate spheres of men and women as a source of stability in a rapidly changing world, marked by industrialization, increased immigration, and western expansion. The difference with male physicians lay in their ability to maintain the status quo by acting to prevent women easy access to medical schools, medical societies, and hospitals. Walsh also finds it significant that women demanded access to the medical profession at a time when male physicians were concerned about the "depressed state of the profession" (Walsh, 133). These men, according to Walsh, feared the wholesale entry of women into their profession because they would be an economic threat. Closely related to this fear was the fear that women would somehow feminize and thus debilitate a male profession. In short, the men feared a loss of professional status.

In addition to her perceptive and intelligent assessment of the history of women in medicine, Walsh includes copious footnotes that in themselves constitute a comprehensive bibliography of the subject. She also spends considerable time recounting the rise and fall of Samuel Gregory's Boston Female Medical College, which, when it opened on 1 November 1848, was the first women's medical college in the world. As she unfolds her argument regarding the resistance to female physicians, Walsh provides histories of several of the most notable ones, including Harriot K. Hunt, the first female doctor to practice in America; Elizabeth Blackwell, the first American woman to earn an M.D.; and Marie Zakrzewska, who with Blackwell founded the successful New England Hospital for Women and Children on 1 July 1862. This hospital became the first in America to be run entirely by and for women.

Walsh is also author of "Selling the Self-Made Woman," an essay on the nineteenth-century women who wrote stories that promoted the concept of successful professional women—authors such as Sarah Orne Jewett *(A Country Doctor)* and Elizabeth Stuart Phelps *(Dr. Zay)*.

Another look at nineteenth-century medicine and how it affected women is George James Barker-Benfield's *The Horrors of the Half-Known Life: Male Attitudes Toward Women and Sexuality in Nineteenth-Century America*. In brief, what Barker-Benfield argues is that modern gynecology developed out of male competitiveness and hostility toward women. Although some women did benefit from gynecological surgery, performed by such famous doctors as J. Marion Sims who is regarded as the father of gynecology, many were nothing more than human guinea pigs, whose bodies provided the stage on which these men sought fame and fortune. Of particular interest in this book are the biographical sketches of nineteenth-century doctors, sketches that include remarks and journal entries these men made regarding their profession. Like Walsh, Barker-Benfield places these men in a historical and social context, regarding their work as expressive of nineteenth-century sexual fears and obsessions.

Perhaps the most comprehensive study of the effects of professionalization on American women is Barbara Ehrenreich and Deirdre English's *For Her Own Good: 150 Years of the Experts' Advice to Women*. In this work the authors trace the rise of the professional experts and the concomitant decline of women's ability to control their own lives. According to them, the so-called woman question—the situation in which women are seen and treated as a problem—was a direct result of the Industrial Revolution. Ehrenreich and English contend that human behavior and thinking were radically transformed by this revolution—to the extent that society had to invent new solutions to keep women under control. In a market economy, people no longer experienced life as a unity but at the very least as a dichotomy: the male sphere identified with the marketplace, and the female sphere with the home (which had become barren of all meaningful activity except that of raising children). Because of the ethnocentricity of this market economy, according to Ehrenreich and English, women were suddenly catapulted into the role of the other, the alien. And the laws of this new market economy which encouraged this perception were themselves perceived as natural and immutable.

In order to substantiate the new view of women that emerged as a result of the Industrial Revolution, experts called upon science. Ehrenreich and English are not unaware of the ironies in using science to maintain women's subordination, since science had the potential to free both women and men from the same strictures of ignorance and superstition. But the new masculine point of view that was a correlate of the market economy insisted that woman was a problem and invoked science to prove its postulate. Rather than seeing women from a rationalist perspective, the male experts saw them from a romantic one. That is, women were defined as everything that the market was not. As is well documented by now, Darwin's theories of evolution were among the most popular of proofs marshalled by the new experts in defense of their own theory that women were inferior to—and therefore rightly subordinate to—men. In this perversion of science, as the authors assert, the experts not only betrayed women but also science itself (which, perhaps, explains some of the anti-technological attitudes expressed in recent feminist science fiction).

In contrast to Walsh's interpretation, Ehrenreich and English argue that the rise of the medical profession was accomplished largely at the expense of female midwives, whose abilities and training meant nothing in the face of the professionally educated upper-class physicians (see also, Wertz and Wertz's *Lying In* discussed below). Ehrenreich and English trace this conflict to the witch hunts of the Middle Ages (much as Mary Daly does in *Gyn/Ecology* discussed below, in chapter seven). Perhaps the most stunning insight that they offer to an understanding of professionalization is the fact that, in a market economy, doctors had to present what they could do for patients as though it were a commodity. Thus, in the late eighteenth century, heroic medicine gained popularity for its very obviousness. The extreme and often fatal treatments administered by doctors—who, of course, at the time had no concept of a germ theory of medicine—were valuable commodities because they were above all tangible evidence that the doctors were doing something to the patients. (That they might also actually be killing the patients was, of course, another matter altogether.)

With the advent of a germ theory and the rise of the laboratory scientist in the late nineteenth century came the transformation of medicine into a science itself. One sure way to keep women out of medicine was to ground it in a scientific education—a reasonable proposition—and then prevent women access to this education. Not only did the physicians gain a certain moral superiority by this move, but they consolidated their position by claiming for their own profession the aura of what had become the highly regarded scientific objectivity. Scientific medicine, of course, did have the added advantage of being able to work cures where none had been available before. But, as Ehrenreich and English observe, it was primarily the combination of their sex and their class that gave upper-class male physicians the power they needed to close their profession to all but the select brotherhood of the A.M.A.

Having established in part one of their study what they identify as "The Rise of the Experts," Ehrenreich and English in part two discuss "The Reign of the Experts." Here they discuss the sexual politics of sickness, in which the state of being female itself became, ipso facto, an illness requiring medical attention. In this section, Ehrenreich and English recount the theories of Thorstein Veblen and those of Olive Schreiner, both of whom were able to perceive the pernicious effects of what Schreiner called the female-parasitism of the leisure class, which required of a woman nothing more than that she display her husband's wealth. The response of the doctors to this newly leisured class of women was to declare that it was a woman's natural state to be an invalid. In yet another instance of class blindness, these doctors virtually declared poor, immigrant, and black women of another, less-evolved race in an effort to explain away their ability to do man's work. Ehrenreich and English do full justice to the paradoxes of this situation and the mental contortions that so-called rational (scientific) thinkers would go to in order to justify their preposterous claims about women's sickly state.

The authors include in this discussion the nineteenth-century notion that as men themselves were evolving toward a higher state, their women were slowly but surely devolving to a lower state in which they would become nothing more than vehicles for reproduction. For evidence of this, Ehrenreich and English turn to the nineteenth-century conviction that a woman could be literally identified with her ovaries and uterus. Whatever illness struck a woman could be attributed to the state of one or more of these sexual organs. One of the more extreme reactions to this belief was that expressed by several experts that an education would surely spell the end of the human race, because in exercising her brain a woman necessarily stole vital energy from her sexual organs. Eventually, if she were highly educated, she would become unable to bear children.

Ehrenreich and English conclude their disturbing and informative book with a section on "The Fall of the Experts," in which they discuss the role of American women's magazines in the revolt of mom and the rise of the single girl. In an afterword, "The End of the Romance," the authors remind us that the romantic solution succeeded because of the moral weight it carried—and that its success lay primarily in dehumanizing women. Ehrenreich and English close with the sober note that many women are confused by their recently acquired freedom of self-definition and are unable to cope with the uncertainties that they encounter at every turn. The authors also see evidence of neoromanticism in books like Marabel Morgan's *The Total Woman*. But when they look for effective antidotes to this backlash, they find only the self-help promulgated by popular psychology. The only viable answer that Barbara Ehrenreich and Deirdre English see to the rationalist-romantic dichotomy that has marked this country since the nineteenth century is a complete refurbishing of the dominant male culture. It is, as they say, a radical vision.

Additional insight to the role of the expert in the lives of American women appears in the work of John S. Haller, Jr. In "From Maidenhood to Menopause: Sex Education for Women in Victorian America," for example, Haller argues that sex manuals and the morality they reflected codified the aspirations of middle-class Americans, who "measured their greatness not by their achievements but by their principles" (Haller, 66). The bulk of his fascinating essay consists of an interpretive history of these sex-in-life manuals that the middle class utilized in raising its young women. Notable among the proscriptions, which of course included such activities as masturbation, was, remarkably, sexual congress itself; many writers envisioned the ideal marriage as one of continence and actually recommended abstinence to their readers. If sexual activity occurred in marriage it was to be solely for the purpose of procreation, and women were enjoined against having " 'any spasmodic convulsion' " because these spasms were believed to interfere with conception (Haller, 56). During pregnancy, sex was prohibited as it was believed to have a deleterious effect on the fetus. In short, by denying its own physicality, the middle class tried to distinguish itself from its lower-class counterparts.

Haller expands this essay in *The Physician and Sexuality in Victorian America*, a study he and Robin M. Haller published in 1974. This study, which includes a history of both men's and women's sexuality in the nineteenth century, is primarily noted for its in-depth account of subjects such as neurasthenia, contraception, masturbation, and venereal diseases. Also included are extensive discussions of the nineteenth-century attempt to invoke science as proof of women's inferiority as a sex and the controversy surrounding the use of corsets. Haller and Haller draw on what must be hundreds of resources, both secondary and primary; their text is replete with key phrases and quotations from sex-in-life manuals, scientific papers, and medical studies of the nineteenth century. There are also some illustrations taken from advertisements for proprietary medicines and women's undergarments. As the authors observe in their introduction, although this is a study of medical practices, it is also in part a study of feminism. Because the medical profession "held itself responsible" for the well-being of the nation, doctors "felt it necessary to bring all their professional authority to bear against" what they perceived as threats to society—including, of course, the feminist movement (Haller and Haller, xi). Although the medical profession does not emerge from this study unscathed, the authors ultimately conclude that physicians were no better able than their patients to understand or cope with the "perplexing and paradoxical problems that faced Americans in the late nineteenth century" (Haller and Haller, 303).

Lying In: A History of Childbirth in America, by Richard W. Wertz and Dorothy C. Wertz, is another book that examines the consequences to women of the professionalization of medicine. It also looks at the cultural attitudes towards a woman's sexuality, especially those that had the effect of interfering with the medical treatment a woman could receive. As part of their study, the authors trace in some detail the decline of the power and use of midwives and the increasing insinuation of male doctors into what had at one time been an exclusively female event: the act of childbirth. Not only did these male midwives (who shortly called themselves obstetricians, or, those who stand before) contribute significantly to the decline of what the authors call female solidarity, they also brought with them, out of the operating rooms and the morgues, an epidemic of puerperal fever (Wertz and Wertz, 4). The consequences to women were immediate and drastic: on the one hand, women relinquished to men the power over their own bodies, on the other, many relinquished their very lives by engaging an obstetrician. As the authors describe the nineteenth-century frame of mind: "Giving birth was the quintessential feminine act; attending birth was a fundamental expression of the controlling and performing actions suitable only for men" (Wertz and Wertz, 59). It is a transfer of power that, at least according to Mary Daly in *Gyn/Ecology*, women today still suffer from.

Other no less dire, but often preposterous, consequences were the extremes that these male doctors had to go to in order to preserve a woman's modesty while she was being examined. Because of the taboos against immodesty, women were examined for pregnancy and illness while they were fully clothed. Moreover, in many instances the doctors would either avert or close their eyes while they reached under a woman's garments to determine her physical condition. One important result of this incredible modesty was to prevent doctors from receiving sufficient clinical experience; another was to increase the paternalism between doctor and female patient. According to Richard and Dorothy Wertz, the doctors used obstetrics to gain prestige and power as a profession (Wertz and Wertz, 93). So successful were they in their efforts that they convinced women, many of whom died as a consequence of their decision, to enter hospitals to give birth. Going to the hospital for the lying-in became a status symbol, but it also increased the chances that a woman would contract childbed fever and die. Going to the hospital to give birth has become so "natural" for women, that the figures the authors cite are remarkable reminders of how "far" we have come in such a short time. In 1900, for example, fewer than 5 percent of the women gave birth in hospitals; by 1939, the figure rose to 50 percent of all women, and 75 percent of urban women (Wertz and Wertz, 133).

One of the most important conclusions that the authors draw from their history of lying-in is that women in America have, in the last two hundred years, become alienated from their own bodies. To women, as to their doctors, their own bodies have become objects. As part of their study, Wertz and Wertz offer a thorough, well-illustrated history of the development of instruments designed to facilitate difficult deliveries. They also provide selected exchanges between Dr. Oliver Wendell Holmes and his male colleagues on the publication of his monograph *Puerperal Fever As a Private Pestilence* (1855), in which he argued that the fever was contagious and carried by the doctors themselves. Although they could be expected to chafe under the suggestions that they were killing their own patients, their arrogance is astounding, one physician claiming that no "gentleman" would do such a thing (Wertz and Wertz, 122). This book is absorbing, if disturbing, reading; it is well-researched and liberally illustrated with drawings and photographs.

Female Complaints: Lydia Pinkham and the Business of Women's Medi-

cine, by Sarah Stage, is more than a history of Lydia E. Pinkham's Vegetable Compound and the sometimes less-than-scrupulously-honest family that manufactured and marketed it. Although Stage does provide a wealth of fascinating details about the origins of the compound and the family behind it, she also focuses on the medical practices and malpractices of the late nineteenth and early twentieth centuries, with an emphasis on women's disorders and their treatment. As such, *Female Complaints* is a history of the professionalization of medicine and the bitter war waged against the patent medicine industry by the physicians who perceived that these home remedies were cutting into their own business. It is also a history of the advertising industry and the intentionally misleading advertising that the patent medicine industry utilized in order to persuade an already ill-informed and gullible public of the efficacy of their herbal concoctions.

Although she gained overnight fame by becoming the company's trademark when her son, as an advertising gimmick, put her portrait on the label in 1879, Lydia Pinkham herself had little influence in the company itself. The compound, for which she is famous but which she did not invent, was first marketed in 1875. Although Lydia Pinkham herself died in 1883, the compound that carried her name prospered. One of the apparent reasons for its success was an ambitious advertising campaign that encouraged young women to write Mrs. Pinkham about their health problems; in turn they were to receive personal replies from her. The only problem with this brilliant—and effective—scheme, as Edward Bok, the muckraking editor of the *Ladies' Home Journal*, was quick to point out, was that Lydia herself was dead.

If this was a scandalous situation—and it was—the claims that the company made on behalf of the compound's power as a curative were even more outrageous. In many instances, the claims were intended, for example, to convince women that this herbal compound could act as a substitute for surgery. The history of the claims made on behalf of Lydia E. Pinkham's Vegetable Compound, therefore, is a fascinating study of the verbal contortions that the copy writers were forced into as federal regulators stiffened their requirements for honesty in advertising. At the start, the compound was purported to cure a prolapsed (fallen) uterus. By 1915, new labels claimed only that it was "recommended" for female disorders, including "Catarrhal Leucorrhea" (Stage, 189). As government pressures increased—encouraged by the lobbying efforts of the A.M.A.—labels omitted this reference and simply claimed that the compound tasted pleasant and was helpful during pregnancy and childbirth. What had once been touted, and sold, as a universal cure for all women's ailments eventually yielded to the combined efforts of the male-dominated A.M.A. and the federal government—until it was left with no real claims it could make as a legitimate medicine.

One of the ironies in its decline and fall is that Lydia Pinkham herself took a sensible approach to health and often offered excellent advice—while she was still alive—to women about the need for exercise and good food. Another of the great ironies surrounding the vegetable compound is that it contained a high percentage of alcohol and Lydia Pinkham herself was, as were many of her customers, a teetotalling abolitionist. Throughout *Female Complaints* Stage does a marvelous job of identifying these ironies that lay at the heart of the patent medicine industry itself. She consistently draws on the historical context in which decisions were made and advertising campaigns waged. Her book is valuable, therefore, as a richly informed history of the ailments that plagued women, the industries that tried to capitalize on these ailments, and the government regulations that attempted to curtail these abuses of the public trust. The book is also illustrated; the Pinkham papers are held in the Schleisinger Library of Radcliffe College.

As I have suggested and as many of the preceding works illustrate, the history of women in popular culture is primarily an interdisciplinary one, which makes it difficult to fit certain books into a single generic category. The following books, for example, straddle several fields, but primarily those of history and literature.

Kathryn Weibel's *Mirror Mirror: Images of Women Reflected in Popular Culture*, for example, is an interdisciplinary history of the images that women have assumed in American popular culture. Weibel's book is divided into five chapters, each focusing on a specific genre of popular culture: fiction, television, movies, women's magazines and magazine advertising, and fashion. Because her focus is on the images themselves, there is little theory in *Mirror Mirror*, but Weibel does provide a thorough history of her subject. Hers is a detailed, well-documented account of how women have been portrayed in these five areas of popular culture. According to her introduction, there are four dominant images that women have taken; these are the woman as "housewifely, passive, wholesome, and pretty" (Weibel, ix). As she discusses the role of women in each of the five fields of popular culture represented here, Weibel examines them through her four major images.

In chapter one, "Images of Women in Fiction," Weibel draws on the categories devised by John G. Cawelti in *Adventure, Mystery and Romance*, in which he defines the formulaic nature of popular literature. The two categories that she finds women most attracted to are those of romance and melodrama. As background for this assertion, Weibel describes *Pamela* and *Clarissa*, the two novels by Samuel Richardson that are regarded by many scholars (with the exception of Nina Baym; see her *Woman's Fiction*, discussed below, in chapter two) as the precursors of modern popular fiction. She then discusses Susanna Haswell Rowson, author of *Charlotte Temple: A Tale of Truth*, and Susan Warner, author of *The Wide, Wide World*. Weibel concludes this chapter with a discussion of Mickey Spillane's detective fiction heroines. Throughout this chapter, Weibel makes reference to the works of notable scholars in the field—a practice she maintains throughout her book, which makes it useful as a bibliographical resource.

In chapter two, she provides one of the few comprehensive essays on the role of women in American television. Recognizing, as others have, that the origins of the afternoon soap opera lie with the nineteenth-century sentimental novel, Weibel contends that their major theme is that of suffering (Weibel, 56). She also asserts that "the soap operas present the image of women as victim and encourage viewers to identify strongly with that image" (Weibel, 62). Like Horace Newcomb, she believes that the family has provided the basic metaphor of the sitcoms, from the early shows like "Ozzie and Harriet" to "All in the Family" and, less obviously perhaps, "The Mary Tyler Moore Show." In her discussion of westerns and crime shows, Weibel points out that women are seldom portrayed as strong individuals or as the protagonists and are frequently cast in the role of helpless victim—in need of a male savior. She finds in this characterization a deeply disturbing message that suggests to women that they have no power.

In her chapter on women in the movies, Weibel detects a similar disturbing trend—that in the movies of the late 1960s and 1970s women played virtually no starring roles at all. She contrasts to this the time, in the 1940s, when women dominated film and implies that some of the blame for women's absence on the screen can be attributed to the fact that directors in the 1960s were simply not interested in portraying women.

In chapter four, Weibel discusses women's magazines in conjunction with magazine advertising because she believes a study of the unchanging image of women in women's magazines is directly related to an understanding of the dynamics among "women's magazines, advertising, and the United States consumer-based economy" (Weibel, 142; for more on this, see below, in chapter three). She concludes her study with a look at the image of women in fashion and what this image has suggested about the changing role of women in society. The major question she addresses in this chapter is why women's fashions have changed so dramatically in the past two hundred years, while men's fashions, comparatively speaking, have changed very little. For part of her answer she turns to the theories of Thorstein Veblen, which are summarized in his phrase "conspicuous consumption" (described in more detail below, in chapters six and seven). This chapter, as the one on the movies, is illustrated. Weibel's footnotes contain extensive bibliographical information, with many of her sources annotated.

Another interdisciplinary study is Ernest Earnest's *The American Eve in Fact and Fiction, 1775-1914.* Earnest's thesis is that literature is not an accurate measure of women's accomplishments, interests, activities, intelligence, education, or status from the American Revolution to World War I. Although some women of this time were indeed ill-educated and content to remain homebodies, not all American women were so limited. In order to prove his thesis, Earnest uses both primary and secondary sources, documenting the portrayal of American women in literature and comparing it to how they portrayed themselves in their own letters and diaries. Of his work Earnest himself states in the epilogue, "Implicit in this whole discussion is the theory that the limited or distorted fictional picture of American women is not merely a critique of the novel, but that it has colored our whole concept of what the real women were like before World War I. They were vastly more lively, able, full blooded, and interesting human beings than we have been led to suppose" (Earnest, 270). Some of the individuals he discusses in his eleven-chapter book include: Abigail Adams, Jane Addams, Susan B. Anthony, Elizabeth Blackwell, Kate Chopin, Tennessee Claflin, Ellen Glasgow, Angelina Grimké, Sarah Grimké, Sarah Josepha Hale, Lucretia Mott, Elizabeth Cady Stanton, Harriet Beecher Stowe, M. Cary Thomas, Mercy Warren, Edith Wharton, Emma Willard, and Victoria Claflin Woodhull. Some of his topics include: birth control, sex, prostitution, and free love. Each chapter contains bibliographical footnotes of both primary and secondary sources.

To Be a Black Woman: Portraits in Fact and Fiction, edited by Mel Watkins and Jay David, is a collection of primary and secondary sources that focus on the experience of black women. Of the thirty-eight selections— written by men and women—all but six are written by blacks. The book is divided into four sections: one, "The Burden of Oppression"; two, "Black on White: The Black Woman in the White World"; three, "Black on Black: The Black Woman in the Black World"; and, four, "A Heritage Rediscovered: The New Black Woman." The purpose of this book is to provide a wide-ranging, multidisciplinary look at the status and history of American black women. The selections, according to the editors, "reflect the hardships and bitterness of the black woman's experience as well as the joy and gratification that she has achieved despite the intensity of her oppression" (Watkins and David, 11). Some of the excerpts include: an interview with Jenny Proctor, an ex-slave (quoted from *Lay My Burden Down: A Folk History of Slavery*, edited by B. A. Botkin); "The Negro Woman" by Calvin C. Hernton (from *Sex and Racism in America*); interviews from *Silent Voices: The Southern Negro Woman Today* by Josephine Carson; passages from Lorraine Hansberry's *A Raisin in the Sun*, Billie Holiday's *Lady Sings the Blues*, and Maya Angelou's *I Know Why the Caged Bird Sings*; and poetry from the work of Mari Evans and Frances W. Harper.

In their selections the editors have attempted to demonstrate that the American black woman has carried the double burden of race and sex, a burden that makes her experience unique among all Americans. It is because of her twofold oppression that Watkins and David believe that the black woman "may well be in a position to benefit more from the recent upheavals in American society than the black male"—in other words, both the Black Power Movement and the Women's Movement have the potential to improve the lives of black women (Watkins and David, 217).

Among the historical realities that the editors have illustrated here are the ways in which the black woman has been exploited by the white world and the strategies she developed in order to help her children survive in a hostile environment. Another topic the editors introduce is the "wedge driven between her and the black male"—a division the editors contend resulted in the destruction of many black families because women had to assume the roles ordinarily held by their husbands (Watkins and David, 147).

In *Black Macho and the Myth of the Superwoman*, Michele Wallace tackles the implications of two sensitive issues facing blacks today: those that result from the need for black men to assert their maleness in the face of years of discrimination, and those that arise out of the seemingly indestructible myth of the indestructible black woman. The primary victim in both instances, according to Wallace (whose feminist perspective permeates her book and provides something like a correcting factor to the male perspective of the preceding book), has been and continues to be the black woman, who suffers at the hands of black men who fight to keep her in her place in order to prove their manliness. In part one, "Black Macho," Wallace reaches into the recent history of the Civil Rights Movement and the Black Power Movement to prove that when Stokely Carmichael said the "only position of women in SNCC is prone," he spoke for most of the black male radicals of the 1960s (quoted in Wallace, 7). This attitude, in turn, Wallace attributes to an unremitting history of emasculation— physical, psychological, and economic—engraved on the souls of black men by the white power structure. Although Wallace lays the ultimate blame on whites for the black man's mistreatment of the black woman, she is not above attacking the black man for trying to emulate the white man's world, nor above criticizing the black woman for electing a subordinate role.

Wallace's study is thought-provoking and her insight merciless; she tells it as she sees it, and what she sees she most adamantly does not like. Those who fall under her critical eye include Richard Wright, Imamu Baraka, Eldridge Cleaver, and Daniel P. Moynihan. She is particularly devastating in her remarks about the infamous Moynihan Report (1965), in which he argues that the problems in the black community result directly from its "matriarchal structure...which...retards the progress of the group as a whole, and imposes a crushing burden on the Negro male" (quoted in Wallace, 109). Calling his argument "clearly ridiculous," Wallace investigates the origins and consequences of the "myth of the black superwoman"—the title of part two of her book (Wallace, 109). In this section she summarizes the lives of several admirable black women; two that attract her the most are Harriet Tubman and Sojourner Truth. She also quotes extensively from slave narratives written by black women and documents the importance of family life to slaves of both sexes. In contrast to her unstinting admiration for Tubman and Truth is Wallace's mixed feeling toward Angela Davis and Nikki Giovanni, whose work she both appreciates and condemns. What they seem to exemplify to her is the inability of black women to agree among themselves whether or not they require liberation. Wallace is less undecided. She concludes her remarkable study with a challenge to her readers: "The imperative is clear: Either we will make history or remain the victims of it" (Wallace, 177).

The Black Woman: An Anthology, edited by Toni Cade (Bambara), is a provocative assembly of black women's voices intended by the editor to represent the major issues of the 1960s. Collected here are thirty-three samples of black women's writing that range from poetry and short stories to political polemics and sociological studies. Among the issues addressed by these women are the relationships between black men and women, racism in school and society, black pride and romanticism, and what it means to be a black woman. Toni Cade herself has three entries, including "On the Issue of Roles" and "The Pill: Genocide or Liberation?" Other authors include: Nikki Giovanni, Audre Lorde, Alice Walker, Kay Lindsey, Joyce Green, Gwen Patton, and Pat Robinson. One remarkably effective polemic is Verta Mae Smart-Grosvenor's "The Kitchen Crisis," in which she talks about what she calls "kitchen consciousness" with the intention of calling to her audience's attention the fact that the decline of culinary skills represents a concomitant decline in culture itself (Cade, 119). Although she says that she does not consider herself a writer, "The Kitchen Crisis" is a brilliant piece of writing, replete with witty thrusts that cut through phony values like a well-honed kitchen blade. This example, like the others in the book, is black women's writing at its best: impassioned but controlled. These women are informed, whether it be about black history or contraception; and they are angry, whether it be about their image or their status in society. And they are working hard to change the world, to eliminate the causes of their own historical and current oppression.

In *Black Rage*, William H. Grier and Price M. Cobbs investigate the long-term effects of sexual mythology on black women; they are especially concerned with the consequences of American slavery. In chapter three, "Achieving Womanhood," the authors (both of whom are psychiatrists) describe the feelings of inadequacy found in many black women who find themselves unable to match the stereotypical image of the beautiful woman because the image is based on a white standard of beauty. Contending that a certain amount of "healthy narcissism" is necessary for women's emotional health and intellectual achievements, Grier and Cobbs argue that the "artificial standard" for beauty set by a society can indeed cause grave harm to women who do not—and cannot—fit the mold (Grier and Cobbs, 51, 40).

A more positive view of the black woman's experience is that presented by Joyce A. Ladner in *Tomorrow's Tomorrow: The Black Woman*. In this book, which takes its title from Don L. Lee's *We Walk the Way of the New World* (1970), Ladner, herself a black sociologist, depicts black womanhood as "a sociohistorical phenomenon," notable for its effectiveness and resiliency (Ladner, 270). That is, black womanhood is a successful and admirable expression of the social and historical contexts experienced by black women. Rather than seeing black women as victims of these contexts, as do Grier and Cobbs, Ladner sees them as models worthy of being emulated by white women who desire liberation. In what can only be viewed as a refreshing change from the negative picture of black women forwarded by many students of black culture, Ladner offers the fact that "Black womanhood has always been the very essence of what American womanhood is attempting to become on some levels" (Ladner, 239). She goes on to suggest that "Black women in this society are the only ethnic or racial group which has had the opportunity *to be women"* (Ladner, 280; Ladner's italics). She bases this assertion on the fact that black women have never been constrained by the false and essentially constrictive images of femininity imposed on middle-class white women. In direct contradiction to the findings of Grier and Cobbs, Ladner found in her studies of lower-class urban black adolescent females an abundance of self-love and a conviction among themselves that they were attractive and desirable. She challenges the position taken by psychologists and psychiatrists like Grier and Cobbs that black women suffer from self-hatred by claiming herself that such positions assume "that a black woman has no standards of her own and experiences self-rejection when she finds herself unable to do more than 'ape' the standards of white society" (Ladner, 75). Accusing them of condescension toward black women, Ladner identifies their self-hatred thesis as one of many myths surrounding the black experience and claims further that it is a component of the "institutional subjugation that is designed to perpetuate an oppressive class" (Ladner, 100). Although she is at all times supportive of the images of black womanhood that she finds in her studies of these black adolescents, she is not blind to the dangers inherent in the stereotype of "Sapphire," the strong black woman. Insisting that the myth of the matriarchate is unfounded in reality, Ladner attributes its existence to the fact that "within the cultural context of the dominant society, slave women were forced to assume the basic duties and responsibilities toward their families men assumed in the white world" (Ladner, 17). She concludes her study of black womanhood, therefore, with the observation that these strong black women must work toward a liberation of all black people—male and female. Ladner's book is indexed and contains a comprehensive bibliography. Throughout her text, she identifies and evaluates studies of black women and black culture, taking to task such controversial studies as Daniel P. Moynihan's *The Negro Family: The Case for National Action* (known more commonly as the Moynihan Report; see Wallace, above) and E. Franklin Frazier's *The Negro Family in the United States*— both of which blame many of the black family's problems on its supposed matriarchal structure. (For other criticism of Grier and Cobbs's work, see Pauli Murray's "The Liberation of Black Women," discussed below.)

At this time there are several outstanding documentary histories available for the study of women. Perhaps the most famous of these is Mary R. Beard's *America Through Women's Eyes*, which is a history of women's role in American life from colonial times to 1932. Beard's purpose, as she describes it, is "to illustrate, if in a fragmentary way, the share of women in the development of American society—their activity, their thought about their labor, and their thought about the history they have helped to make or have observed in the making" (Beard, 9). Beard divides her history into several different subjects and pursues what is basically a chronological order in recounting the contributions of women to American life. When contemporary primary sources are available, she uses them; when they are not, or when they are in short supply, she uses secondary materials. Beard herself introduces each chapter with a brief essay describing its contents and the historical import of the selections. Some of the most interesting material that she quotes from concerns the participation of women in business and industry, such as Helen Woodward's account of an advertising campaign she waged to introduce a new line of gingham fabrics or Mary Heaton Vorse's account of the steel industry taken from her book *Men and Steel*. One of the most absorbing first-person accounts is that provided by Anna Howard Shaw about her first months in the Michigan wilderness taken from her autobiography, *The Story of a Pioneer*. Other women are represented by letters, diaries, journals, pamphlets, and poetry—all of which contribute to the impression that women, since their arrival on these shores, have been at the heart of American cultural, literary, intellectual, and social activity.

That women are central to the American experience is also evident in the documentaries of more recent historians. One preeminent feminist historian is Gerda Lerner, whose *Black Women in White America: A Documentary History* is a meticulously edited collection of primary sources for the study of black women in American history. In her selection of material, Lerner has necessarily left much out, but she has tried, with good success, to "provide insight into the typical experience of the past by including documents relating to ordinary, anonymous women" (Lerner, xx). She has omitted material easily accessible elsewhere, such as that on the Civil Rights Movements of the 1950s and 1960s; but she has included material on and by major figures of black women's history, such as Sojourner Truth, Harriet Tubman, Mary Church Terrell, Charlotte Forten Grimké, and Shirley Chisholm. *Black Women in White America* is divided into ten major sections, many of which have additional subsections. These topics range from accounts of slavery to domestic work, from women as victims of racial and sexual oppression to black pride, from accounts of individual resistance to those of organized efforts through clubs, unions, and politics. Although the book is not indexed, its table of contents is very detailed.

Lerner has written an introduction to each section that provides background information on the documents included; in many instances, she also gives additional information on the fate of the women whose work is included here. Lerner has been careful not to overedit, however, permitting these black women to speak for themselves directly to us; for example, in order to retain the flavor of their language, Lerner has not modernized spelling or modified the texts except to shorten them occasionally. In her preface she states that black women have been "doubly invisible" because they belong to "two groups which have traditionally been treated as inferiors by American society—blacks and women" (Lerner, xvii). She also tackles the issue of black matriarchy, arguing that it is a misused term because "black women have been the most powerless group in our entire society" (Lerner, xxiii). She does make the questionable assertion, however, that "they have higher status within their own group than do white women in white society" (Lerner, xxiv).

For scholars in the field Lerner has provided one exceptionally useful section: a bibliographical essay on her sources. Remarking that many library collections do not catalogue material on black women, thus making it difficult to find material readily, if at all, Lerner informs her readers where she found material and what else is available in those collections that warrants further attention. She also comments on the kinds of problems she encountered researching this book and the strategies she employed to overcome them. She concludes her collection with a series of bibliographical notes, in which she provides annotated lists of sources in black history, women's history, slavery abolition, education, economic roles, and racism; she also provides lists of anthologies, autobiographies, and biographies.

Additional primary documents relating to the lives of American black women are available in *Black Women in American Life: Their Words, Their Thoughts, Their Feelings*, compiled by Bert James Loewenberg and Ruth Bogin. These selections range from works by such well-known black women as Harriet Tubman, Sojourner Truth, and Ida Wells-Barnett to works by the lesser-known Amanda Berry Smith, Ellen Craft, and Sarah Parker Redmond. Each section is prefaced by a brief biography of the author; the text itself contains an introductory essay by Ruth Bogin that provides a concise history of black American women in the nineteenth century. Bogin observes, for example, that, by necessity, most of the women who constitute this study "were influenced by urban conditions" and not plantation life (Loewenberg and Bogin, 5). Bogin attributes the ability of these women to survive and even flourish in less than ideal conditions to their inner reserves, which she believes were a direct product of the love they received at home. Also crucial to the survival of blacks was religion which sanctioned all the stages of womanhood and provided both a "group heritage and a creative personal impetus" (Loewenberg and Bogin, 9). Sensitive to the fact that black women have been ignored in most histories— of women, of blacks, and of the country as a whole—Bogin reminds her readers that these women have important stories to tell, that indeed they are "important carriers of black culture" (Loewenberg and Bogin, 11). This book demonstrates her assertion—and also serves to illustrate that black women are important carriers of American culture.

A companion work to Gerda Lerner's *Black Women in White America* is her more recent collection, *The Female Experience: An American Documentary*, for which she has assembled approximately one hundred documents, over half of which have never been published before. It has been her intention to include primarily those works that are otherwise not easily accessible. It has been her further intention to represent, as fully as possible, women from various ethnic groups, economic classes, and races, as well as women of different ages. The organizational framework that she uses in this collection she describes in her introduction as being derived from how women perceive themselves and organize their lives. That is, she eschews the traditional politically oriented ordering of material that is employed by male historians to explain and give shape to reality. Thus, she divides her documents into three major areas. Part one, "The Female Life Cycle," is subdivided into chapters on childhood, marriage, motherhood, and being single; housewives; aging, illness, and death. Part two, "Women in Male-Defined Society," is subdivided into chapters on education; work in and outside the home; and politics. Part three, "A New Definition of Womanhood," is subdivided into chapters on creating the new woman and women's search for independent selfhood. Among the documents included are selections from Sarah M. Grimké's previously unpublished essay "Marriage" (held by the William L. Clements Library at the University of Michigan), which can be compared profitably to Charlotte Perkins Gilman's *Women and Economics* (discussed below, in chapter seven) a portion of which Lerner also includes in this collection. Martha Coffin Wright, sister of Lucretia Mott, is represented by several entries, including letters to her daughter on the subjects of childbirth, dying, and housework. The viewpoint of the immigrant working woman is represented by several selections from Rose Schneiderman's "A Cap Maker's Story," in which she describes her own working days as a child laborer. Some of the most lively selections come from the pen of Jane Swisshelm's *Half a Century* and *Letters to Country Girls*; Swisshelm was a nineteenth-century editor (of the *St. Cloud Visiter* [sic]), noted for her acerbic wit and for having the courage to speak her mind even when she was in the minority. One of the most poignant entries is that by Frances E. Willard in which she describes how painful it was for her to give up the physical freedom of youth and become confined to the long skirts appropriate for nineteenth-century ladies (taken from *Glimpses of Fifty Years: The Autobiography of an American Woman*). Although, as these items might suggest, the bulk of Lerner's documentary is gleaned from the nineteenth century, other periods are represented. For example, the seventeenth-century trial of Anne Hutchinson for antinomian heresy is represented by excerpts from John Winthrop's account of her interrogation. Additionally, Lerner has included letters that Mary Dyer (or Dyar [?]) wrote after she was sentenced to death as a heretic in 1659. The twentieth century is represented primarily through documentation of the efforts of women to gain rights for themselves in industry, politics, and education. Also included from the twentieth century are documents pertaining to lesbianism and sexual exploitation.

Lerner's book is valuable for its primary sources and for its background information on the authors Lerner includes; this information helps place these women in a historical context. Lerner's introduction is especially useful in defining the differences between women's and men's history and in describing the development of a feminist consciousness. One point she makes here is the fact that women have been separated from one another by the threat of being labelled deviant. Women have been kept apart—and thus prevented from organizing a powerful political force—by such things as class and racial differences and, according to Lerner, by "arbitrary standards of purity and propriety" (Lerner, xxxv). It is her contention, as it is Sheila Rothman's, that the Women's Movement, to be effective, must be able to encompass women of all walks of life. Her book does much to help bring this ideal closer to reality.

Other primarily documentary studies are Nancy F. Cott's *Root of Bitterness: Documents of the Social History of American Women* and Gail Parker's *The Oven Birds: American Women on Womanhood, 1820-1920.* Cott's book, which is a collection of fifty selections, is prefaced by an introduction in which the editor briefly characterizes: the colonial period; the eighteenth century; the cult of domesticity and social change; slavery and sexuality; the nineteenth century; utopias; and gynecology. In this essay, Cott notes the peculiarly American insistence on women's sexless nature—an insistence that in the nineteenth century coexisted with the fact that women were defined solely by their sex and their reproductive capacities. She also attributes to industrialization and its resultant mass production of household goods the transformation of women from producers to consumers of commodities. Of the phenomenon of the women's clubs, she suggests that they were a natural "extension of woman's traditional role as moral and physical nurturer" (Cott, 26). The documents that Cott has included here include such selections as the "Examination of Mrs. Ann Hutchinson" for antinomianism; a "Letter from an Indentured Servant" about conditions in the colonies; Sarah Grimké's *Letters on the Equality of the Sexes;* "Narratives from Escaped Slaves"; Catharine Beecher on "Female Health in America"; Dr. Elizabeth Blackwell on "Sexual Passion in Men and Women"; and Charlotte Perkins Gilman on "Women's Evolution from Economic Dependence." Cott also provides a short bibliography of suggestions for further reading.

Gail Parker's *The Oven Birds* is arranged in a similar fashion, with the additional feature of a brief biography that prefaces each author's selection. Among the authors represented are: Lydia Huntley Sigourney, Lydia Maria Child, Angelina Grimké Weld, Catharine Beecher ("Statistics of Female Health," from *Woman Suffrage and Woman's Profession*, 1871), Harriet Beecher Stowe, Elizabeth Cady Stanton (*The Woman's Bible*, the introduction and appendix), Jane Addams, and Charlotte Perkins Gilman ("The Yellow Wallpaper" and from *The Home*, "Domestic Mythology," 1910). In her introduction, Parker characterizes all these women as being in search of heroines, of role models. She suggests, with good cause, that "the history of American feminism and literary history must be studied simultaneously if any sense is to be made of the rise and fall of the woman's movement in America" (Parker, 5). Like other women's historians, Parker finds it logical that many early feminists were Quakers because the Society of Friends permitted women to speak publicly. She accords to Elizabeth Cady Stanton the "major insight" that sentimentalism was "a fundamentally feminist reinterpretation of Calvinism" and argues further that to feminists romanticism and sentimentalism were interchangeable (Parker, 13).

As a supplement to *Ideas of the Woman Suffrage Movement*, Aileen S. Kraditor has also compiled a collection of documents on women's rights, *Up From the Pedestal: Selected Writings in the History of American Feminism*. This book, for which she has written an introduction, is divided into four major sections: one, "The Question of 'Spheres,' " which includes material from colonial writers such as Anne Bradstreet and John Winthrop and essays by Sarah Moore Grimké; two, "The Argument Becomes Specific," which includes excerpts from Catharine Beecher on women's education, Elizabeth Cady Stanton's *The Woman's Bible*, and Charlotte Perkins Gilman on economics; three, "Woman and Government," which includes the Declaration of Sentiments from the 1848 Seneca Falls Convention, and excerpts from both anti- and prosuffrage documents; and four, "Unfinished Business," which includes excerpts from the 1931 Senate hearing on the Equal Rights Amendment and the 1966 Statement of Purpose of the National Organization for Women.

One final documentary collection is worth mentioning, that by Maxine Nunes and Deanna White, called *The Lace Ghetto*. This book—which is a series of interviews, commentaries, pictures, advertisements, comics, letters, and excerpts from books on motherhood, women's rights, fashion, and sexuality—has as its emphasis Canadian popular culture, though it is by no means limited to it either in content or philosophy. As a text, it would probably be most useful as a vehicle for consciousness raising.

In the past few years, several anthologies of women's history have appeared. Many of these books are composed of papers presented at women's history conferences. Most are interdisciplinary in nature, with a focus on such areas as women in politics, education, medicine, and literature.

Clio's Consciousness Raised: New Perspectives on the History of Women,

edited by Mary S. Hartman and Lois Banner, for example, is a collection
of fourteen papers that were originally presented at the March 1973 conference, "New Perspectives on the History of Women," sponsored by the
Berkshire Conference of Women Historians (Douglass College, Rutgers
University). In her preface Mary S. Hartman points out that the book's
unity is derived from the fact that the essays focus on women who shared
a "set of common experiences"; that the essays all place women in a
social context; and that they challenge the inherited myths about women
and women's role (Hartman and Banner, vii-viii). Many of the essays included would be of particular use to a study of American popular culture because of their emphasis on women and medicine in the nineteenth
century.

In " 'The Fashionable Diseases': Women's Complaints and Their Treatment in Nineteenth-Century America," Ann Douglas Wood, for example,
contends that by the 1850s "ill health in women had become positively
fashionable and was exploited by its victims and practitioners as an advertisement of genteel sensibility and as escape from the too pressing
demands of bedroom and kitchen" (Hartman and Banner, 2). In support
of her thesis, she describes in detail what she calls the period's "fledg-
ling gynecological techniques" and does so against the cultural context
in which they were practiced (Hartman and Banner, 6). Her purpose is
not to condemn the early women's doctors for what, in retrospect, appears
to be their distinctly antifemale attitudes, but instead to understand these
attitudes as functions of their time. Nor is Wood indifferent to the social
consequences of the nineteenth-century logic that argued that "ladies get
sick *because* they are unfeminine—in other words, sexually aggressive,
intellectually ambitious, and defective in proper womanly submission and
selflessness" (Wood's italics; Hartman and Banner, 8). Because she under-
stands the cultural conditions that led to the specious reasoning of nineteenth-century physicians, Wood offers a balanced account of their contributions—both negative and positive—to the advancement of women. With
more sympathy for her male subjects than many other feminist historians,
Wood describes the rest cure invented by Silas Weir Mitchell and the gynecological treatments invented by J. Marion Sims as human responses to
women who were trapped in a society that was obsessed with female disorders.

Like Wood, Carroll Smith-Rosenberg, in "Puberty to Menopause," suggests that the "central metaphor" of the nineteenth century was one that
pictured "the female as driven by the tidal currents of her cyclical reproductive system" (Hartman and Banner, 24). The key events in this cycle
were, logically enough, menarche and menopause. Because of the century's
ambivalence to women's sexuality—denying it even as it apotheosized it—
the onset of puberty and the completion of menopause were particularly significant and stressful times for women. Puberty, according to Smith-Rosen-

berg, was a critical time in a woman's life because how she "negotiated the physiological dangers of puberty was believed to determine her health not only during her childbearing years but at menopause as well" (Hartman and Banner, 25). Similarly, menopause was perceived much as it is today, as either a time of freedom from the worries of pregnancy or a time of loss that could lead to feelings of inadequacy and depression. These attitudes, Smith-Rosenberg argues, were crucial to maintaining women's traditional role and to providing their physicians with a professional status.

In "The Lady and Her Physician," Regina Morantz demonstrates that nineteenth-century physicians were not hostile to their (female) patients. Like Wood, Morantz argues that studies of nineteenth-century physicians and their patients must be done in the proper context. But where Wood uses the cultural milieu to explain—if not exonerate—the physicians, Morantz uses the state of the profession itself. She argues, for example, that the use of "heroic" medicine—such as large doses of poisonous substances, clitoridectomies, and bleedings—were not the result of the doctors' fear of women. They were, instead, the drastic measures taken by well-meaning men who were trained in a period marked by its "scientific ignorance" (Hartman and Banner, 45). Finding evidence that these good doctors " 'tortured' men and women indiscriminately," Morantz concludes that the effort to "view the existence of Victorian women solely from the perspective of male domination has become a sterile and tedious line of inquiry" (Hartman and Banner, 47; 50-51). In taking this position, she is able to defend the efforts of Silas Weir Mitchell and to honor J. Marion Sims as "a brilliant gynecologic surgeon" (Hartman and Banner, 46).

Like the preceding essays, that by Linda Gordon, "Voluntary Motherhood: The Beginnings of Feminist Birth Control Ideas in the United States," is a marvelous compendium of little-known facts about nineteenth-century women's medicine. She reminds us, for example, that it wasn't until the 1920s that the ovarian cycle was understood and not until the 1930s that it was finally understood by American doctors. In fact, according to Gordon, doctors believed, up to the 1860s, that women, like animals, were fertile just before and after their periods. Those women who attempted to control conception by using the rhythm method were, therefore, actually increasing their chances of becoming pregnant. The very notion that women had a choice in the matter was, according to Gordon, a radical new idea for a century that had virtually identified women with pregnancy. The concept of voluntary motherhood was a limited one, however, as it did not approve of "contraceptive *devices*" or postcoital " 'washes, teas, tonics' " (Gordon's italics; Hartman and Banner, 55). The concept was supported by three types of feminists: suffragists, members of reform groups, and those of the free-love groups. Although voluntary motherhood was "accompanied by another, potentially explosive, conceptual change: the reacceptance of female sexuality," it did not encourage the rejection of traditional marriages

(Hartman and Banner, 56). Instead, according to Gordon, it became a way for women to "strengthen their positions within conventional marriages" (Hartman and Banner, 68). (Gordon is also author of *Woman's Body, Woman's Right: A Social History of Birth Control in America.*)

Although these four scholars—Wood, Smith-Rosenberg, Morantz, and Gordon—take different approaches to the question of nineteenth-century women's medicine, one point they all make is the need to view the subject in its historical, social, and intellectual context. Implicit in their work is the corollary that while current feminist perspectives are advantageous to viewing nineteenth-century women, they can also be misleading if they encourage one to gloss over the realities of a century ago. At the same time, these historians seem to agree with the position taken by Adrienne Rich (in *Of Woman Born: Motherhood as Experience and Institution,* discussed below, in chapter seven) that women will only be free when they have regained control over their own bodies, when women—and not their male doctors or their male-dominated society—define what it means to be female.

The final two essays in this collection that are pertinent to popular culture are those by Barbara Welter and Ruth Schwartz Cowan. Welter's essay, "The Feminization of American Religion, 1800-1860" (reprinted in Welter's own collection, *Dimity Convictions,* discussed below) is a study of how American Protestantism came to be feminized after the Revolutionary War. According to her theory, this change occurred because the virtues of humility and piety, among others, were not generally in demand after the war and during the expansion of the Republic. A more feminized religion, therefore, allowed for the perpetuation of these values without insisting on their centrality to American politics. The churches became, in other words, storehouses of what had been identified as the feminine virtues. "In this way," according to Welter, "the traditional religious values could be maintained in a society whose primary concerns made humility, submission, and meekness incompatible with success because they were identified with weakness" (Hartman and Banner, 138). At the same time, because of their important and visible role in church activity—if not as clergy, at least as missionaries and community volunteers—women gained a new sense of their own power to get things done and to influence the behavior of others. What had been intended as a method to exclude women and ministers from politics eventually became a route whereby women were to enter politics on their own terms. Confident from their success in church activities, many women became passionate and persuasive proponents of the suffrage movement.

Although Cowan's essay, "A Case Study of Technological and Social Change," which focuses on the effects brought by the washing machine on the working woman, is only a working paper, it does pose some crucial questions. Most importantly, Cowan questions the conventional wisdom that says that women have more time as a result of labor-saving devices in the home. What she argues is that "the diffusion of household technology among middle-class women" has precipitated a whole new set of standards by which to judge the successful homemaker (Hartman and Banner, 251). She concludes, therefore, that "there appears to be no immediate relationship" between the introduction of technology in the home and the increased number of married women in the labor force (Hartman and Banner, 251).

As these examples demonstrate, *Clio's Consciousness Raised* is a collection of thought-provoking essays that point the way for a new kind of women's history, one that is not bound by traditional methodologies and mind sets. All contain valuable information; all are thoroughly researched and footnoted. All the authors have read each other's work and often comment upon the other essays in the book.

Another anthology is *Our American Sisters: Women in American Life and Thought,* edited by Jean E. Friedman and William G. Shade. This collection, first published in 1973 and revised in 1976, contains—in the second edition—twenty-four essays that are divided into four major sections: one, "Women in Colonial America"; two, "Victorian Images"; three, "The Progressive Impulse"; and, four, "The Illusion of Equality." In making their selections for each section, the editors have attempted to represent three aspects of women's social history: "society's definition of the nature of women and their proper roles; the actual conditions of women and the social and economic functions that they performed; and women's response to their special intellectual, socioeconomic, and political problems" (Friedman and Shade, 4). In order to represent a cross section of the American woman's experience, the editors have included material on women of different ethnic, religious, and economic backgrounds.

Part one of *Our American Sisters* features such fascinating glimpses of our colonial ancestors as Edmund S. Morgan's "The Puritans and Sex," in which he argues that, contrary to rumor, the Puritans enjoyed sex and considered it a natural expression of human love—when the parties involved were married, that is. Of extramarital sex, Morgan reports, the Puritans were as "hostile" to it as they were "favorable" to it within marriage (Friedman and Shade, 13). Another look at Plymouth Colony is provided in John Demos's "Husbands and Wives," in which he describes the seventeenth-century economic, legal, and sexual relationships between men and women. Julia Cherry Spruill's "Participation in Public Affairs" documents the political activities of women who lived in the southern colonies. In "The Case of the American Jezebels: Anne Hutchinson and Female Agitation during the Years of Antinomian Turmoil, 1636-1640," Lyle Koehler argues that it was not surprising that women like Anne Hutchinson would rebel against their restrictive circumstances. Although their forms of rebellion were severely limited, Koehler argues that, in Anne Hutchinson and the antinomian movement, other dissatisfied women found a legitimate vehicle for openly expressing their resistance to "the perpetrators of the spiritual and secular status quo" (Friedman and Shade, 54). The final essay in this section, "Fruits of Passion: The Dynamics of Interracial Sex," by Winthrop D. Jordan, compares the various attitudes that the northern colonies expressed toward blacks and miscegenation with those held by the southern colonies, South Carolina in particular.

Part two, "Victorian Images," reprints Gerda Lerner's "The Lady and the Mill Girl: Changes in the Status of Women in the Age of Jackson." It also includes Ronald W. Hogeland's " 'The Female Appendage': Feminine Life-Styles in America, 1820-1860," in which Hogeland identifies four distinctive life-styles that were open to women at this time: "Ornamental," "Romanticized," "Evangelical," and "Radical" (Friedman and Shade, 134). In "A Slave Family in the Ante Bellum South," Loren Schweninger joins other historians, like Herbert Gutman and John Blassingame, who "contend that strong family loyalties developed among slaves" (Friedman and Shade, 163). Schweninger's essay is a brief history of the Thomas-Rapier family, who, through the influence of their mother, won independence for themselves and maintained feelings of "family, loyalty, unity, and love" (Friedman and Shade, 173). William L. O'Neill, in his essay, "In the Beginning," traces the origins of the first woman's rights movement in America and compares them to those of the British movement. Of both movements O'Neill observes that, after 1870, "respectability was won at the expense of intellectual adventurousness. Possibility gave way to propriety" (Friedman and Shade, 220).

Part three opens with Sondra R. Herman's "Loving Courtship or the Marriage Market? The Ideal and Its Critics, 1871-1911," in which she describes the debate about marital issues that arose in the late nineteenth century. Among the works she discusses are Charlotte Perkins Gilman's *Women and Economics* and Thorstein Veblen's *The Theory of the Leisure Class* (both of which are discussed below, in chapter seven). Other essays in this section include: Anne Firor Scott's "The 'New Woman' in the New South"; Nancy Schrom Dye's "Creating a Feminist Alliance: Sisterhood and Class Conflict in the New York Women's Trade Union League, 1903-1914"; and Jill Conway's "Women Reformers and American Culture, 1870-1930."

Part four, "The Illusion of Equality," reviews the experiences of women in the first few decades of the twentieth century. Clarke A. Chambers, for example, writes about "The Campaign for Women's Rights in the 1920's"; and James R. McGovern describes "The American Woman's Pre-World War I Freedom in Manners and Morals." Mary P. Ryan examines how these manners and morals were introduced to women in "The Projection of a New Womanhood: The Movie Moderns in the 1920s." It is Ryan's thesis that the female stars of the 1920s "served as a means of propagating new values and translating popular images into social behavior" (Friedman and Shade,

371). They were especially effective, she believes, in preparing women for the discontinuities of their lives as they tried to balance "work, home, and consumer activities" (Friedman and Shade, 383). In "The Liberation of Black Women," Pauli Murray characterizes recent examples of black history as being insensitive to black women's history — some of her examples ignore the subject altogether. Like Michele Wallace (see above), Murray does not like the fact that the desire of the black woman for liberation is regarded by many as an issue of secondary importance — second to the need of black men for liberation. What she calls for is a unified effort on the part of black women and white women "to achieve their common humanity" (Friedman and Shade, 429).

To this collection Friedman herself contributed "Contemporary Feminism: Theories and Practice," which is a comprehensive outline of the developments in feminist thinking since the 1960s. Both Friedman and Shade have also written essays to introduce each of the four parts of their book; these essays summarize the material and provide additional resources for reading. Most of the twenty-four essays they have included have extensive citations; the book itself has a brief bibliography.

Woman's Being, Woman's Place: Female Identity and Vocation in American History, edited by Mary Kelley, is a collection of twenty essays, all but two of which were presented at the Conference on the History of Women, held in October 1977 in Saint Paul, Minnesota. Part one, "Sources and Methodology," contains four essays that introduce possible approaches to women's history: Joan Hoff Wilson's "Hidden Riches: Legal Records and Women, 1750-1825"; Kim Lacy Rogers's "Relicts of the New World: Conditions of Widowhood in Seventeenth-Century New England"; Lillian Schlissel's "Diaries of Frontier Women: On Learning to Read the Obscured Patterns"; and Katharine T. Corbett's "Louisa Catherine Adams: The Anguished 'Adventures of a Nobody.' " Part two, "Identity and Vocation," constitutes the rest of the book. It contains such essays as Sumiko Higashi's "Cinderella vs. Statistics: The Silent Movie Heroine as a Jazz-Age Working Girl" (see also, her *Virgins, Vamps, and Flappers,* discussed below, in chapter four); William D. Jenkins's "Housewifery and Motherhood: The Question of Role Change in the Progressive Era"; Mary Kelley's "At War With Herself: Harriet Beecher Stowe as Woman in Conflict within the Home"; Mary H. Grant's "Domestic Experience and Feminist Theory: The Case of Julia Ward Howe"; Elisabeth Griffith's "Elizabeth Cady Stanton on Marriage and Divorce: Feminist Theory and Domestic Experience"; and Sharon O'Brien's "Tomboyism and Adolescent Conflict: Three Nineteenth-Century Case Studies" (see also, Frances Willard's "How I Learned to Ride the Bicycle," in Stephanie Twin's *Out of the Bleachers,* discussed below, in chapter six). Other essays in this collection include several on women's education and political organizations. Most of the essays focus on nineteenth-century women, and many examine the gap between what women were expected to be like and what they actually were like. All the essays are fully footnoted and are, as a consequence, valuable bibliographical sources for further study.

The Afro-American Woman: Struggles and Images, edited by Sharon Harley and Rosalyn Terborg-Penn, is a collection of nine essays on the experience of black women. In part one the editors provide an overview of the history of black women, focusing primarily on the time 1830-1930. In "Northern Black Female Workers: Jacksonian Era," for example, Harley demonstrates that the "egalitarian rhetoric of the period" was not intended to include blacks, be they male or female (Harley and Terborg-Penn, 16). As a consequence of the racial prejudice in the north, black women held virtually no factory jobs until World War I; until that time they had been employed almost exclusively as maids, housekeepers, laundresses, and seamstresses. Even as white women refused to work side by side with black women in the factory, they also—in general—declined to work with them in women's clubs and women's rights organizations. The unwillingness of whites to admit black women into their groups, when studied in conjunction with the rise of the black women's groups, raises the question in Terborg-Penn's mind as to how the two developments might be related. But, as she notes in "Discrimination Against Afro-American Women in the Women's Movement, 1830-1920," she cannot find enough information in her research to answer the question satisfactorily. Although white women were less than enthusiastic in welcoming their black sisters into reform movements, black men, according to Terborg-Penn in "Black Male Perspectives on the Nineteenth-Century Woman," were more supportive of their women than white men of theirs. In fact, most black men that she discusses saw the future of the race as dependent on the advancements of both men and women. In "The Black Woman's Struggle for Equality in the South, 1895-1925," Cynthia Neverdon-Morton details some of the social service and educational programs that black women established for poor and uneducated blacks. Although their work was often—of necessity—out of the political mainstream, what these women, such as Mary Church Terrell, president of the National Association of Colored Women, were able to accomplish was a general improvement in the lives of their people.

The final two essays in part one are somewhat out of the province of this study, but are worth mentioning. Daphne Duval Harrison recounts the contributions of "Black Women in the Blues Tradition"; Andrea Benton Rushing discusses the "Images of Black Women in Afro-American Poetry." Part two consists of three essays on individual women. Sharon Harley writes on Anna J. Cooper, author, activist, and educator. Evelyn Brooks Barnett contributes "Nannie Burroughs and the Education of Black Women." And Gerald R. Gill describes the lively vice-presidential campaign of Charlotta A. Bass, who in 1952 ran with Vincent Hallinan on the Progressive Party ticket.

In *The Majority Finds Its Past: Placing Women in History,* Gerda Lerner has collected twelve of her own essays; most have appeared elsewhere and the others were delivered as conference papers. Some of the essays are reprinted intact, with their bibliographies and footnotes updated to reflect current scholarship and with additional editorial commentary that reflects Lerner's current philosophical attitudes toward her subject. Other essays are revised and augmented versions of the originals. The collection includes four essays on the scope and underlying assumptions of women's history: "New Approaches to the Study of Women in American History" (reprinted from the *Journal for Social History* 3, Fall, 1969); "Placing Women in History: Definitions and Challenges" (revised from two conference papers and reprinted from *Feminist Studies* 3, Fall, 1975); "The Majority Finds Its Past" (reprinted from *Current History* 70, May, 1976); and "The Challenge of Women's History" (based on a lecture delivered at the Aspen Institute for Humanistic Studies, 25 August 1977). Also included are two essays on feminism: "The Feminists: A Second Look" (reprinted from the *Columbia Forum* 13, Fall, 1970) and "Women's Rights and American Feminism" (reprinted from the *American Scholar* 40, Spring, 1971). Three of the most valuable chapters are those on black American women and the special challenges they present to scholars attempting to reconstruct their history: "Black Women in the United States: A Problem in Historiography and Interpretation" (first given as a paper at the Annual Meeting of the Organization of American Historians, 1973); "Community Work of Black Club Women" (reprinted from the *Journal of Negro History* 59, April, 1974); and "Black and White Women in Interaction and Confrontation" (reprinted from *Prospects: An Annual of American Cultural Studies* 2, 1976). A related chapter is "The Political Activities of Antislavery Women" (based on a paper delivered at the Southern Historical Association Meeting, 1976). The other two chapters are Lerner's well-known essay on the negative effects of professionalization on nineteenth-century women, "The Lady and the Mill Girl: Changes in the Status of Women in the Age of Jackson" (reprinted from *American Studies* 10, Spring, 1969); and her study of the economic and social consequences of confining women to the home, "Just a Housewife" (reprinted from *Feminist Perspectives on Housework and Childcare,* edited by Amy Swerdlow, 1978). Although Lerner takes issue with some of her own earlier positions, her thinking remains provocative and challenging. Because she disagrees with herself, the collection is a study in her development as a feminist and a women's historian.

Barbara Welter's *Dimity Convictions: The American Woman in the Nineteenth Century* is a collection that brings together nine of Welter's own essays, six of which have appeared elsewhere. As such it has the strengths and flaws of any collection of this kind: it is convenient to have one source in which all of her major essays appear, but the collection, not having been edited as a book, is often repetitious and sometimes awkward in its fit. Among the essays that appear here are "Coming of Age in America: The American Girl in the Nineteenth Century" (reprinted from *Journal of Marriage and the Family,* 1969), which is a study of cultural attitudes toward menstruation, adolescence, and moral purity. Also included is Welter's famous "The Cult of True Womanhood, 1820-1860" (reprinted from the *American Quarterly* 18, Summer, 1966), in which she offers her analysis of the concept of ideal femininity. The other essays included are: "The Merchant's Daughter: A Tale from Life" (reprinted from the *New England Quarterly,* 1970); "Female Complaints" (reprinted from the *Journal of the History of Medicine,* 1970), in which she describes social attitudes toward menstruation and masturbation; "Anti-Intellectualism and the American Woman" (reprinted from *Mid-America* 48, October, 1966); "The Feminization of American Religion, 1800-1860" (also appearing in *Clio's Consciousness Raised,* edited by Mary S. Hartman and Lois Banner); "Defenders of the Faith: Women Novelists of Religious Controversy in the Nineteenth Century," in which she discusses Augusta Evans Wilson, Elizabeth Stuart Phelps, and Margaret Deland; "Murder Most Genteel: The Mystery Novels of Anna Katharine Green"; and "Mystical Feminist: Margaret Fuller, a Woman of the Nineteenth Century." In sum, Welter's book is a good source of information on the nineteenth century from various sociological and historical perspectives. It is a useful compendium.

Although Vivian Gornick's *Essays in Feminism* is not, strictly speaking, a history of women in popular culture, it does contain, among its twenty-two essays, several that are pertinent to the subject. Among those most relevant are those on Alice Paul, Agnes Smedley, and Margaret Fuller. Others are on literature, such as Gornick's essay on Henry Miller, Norman Mailer, and Saul Bellow, entitled, "Why Do These Men Hate Women?"; and the one on *The House of Mirth* and *Portrait of a Lady,* entitled "Female Narcissism as a Metaphor in Literature." Still others are on psychological studies that have been done on women, such as those by Dr. Matina Horner that Gornick discusses in "Why Radcliffe Women Are Afraid of Success" and "Why Women Fear Success." All of Gornick's essays in her collection were written between 1969 and 1978; most of them appeared originally in the *Village Voice.*

The following reference books are useful in locating material on the history of women in popular culture: *Women's Work and Women's Studies, 1973-1974,* edited by Barbara Friedman et al.; *The Women's Movement in the Seventies: An International English-Language Bibliography* and *The Women's Rights Movement in the United States, 1848-1970: A Bibliography and Sourcebook,* both by Albert Krichmar; and *Woman in America: A Guide to Information Sources,* by Virginia R. Terris.

These resources are useful in locating material on the history of black women: *The Black Family and the Black Woman: A Bibliography,* prepared by the library staff and the Afro-American Studies Department at Indiana University; "Black Women in America: An Annotated Bibliography," by Johnneta B. Cole; *The Black Woman in American Society: A Selected Annotated Bibliography*, by Lenwood G. Davis; *The Progress of Afro-American Women: A Selected Bibliography and Resource Guide*, compiled by Janet L. Sims; and *American Black Women in the Arts and Social Sciences: A Bibliographic Survey*, by Ora Williams.

Barbara Haber's *Women in America: A Guide to Books, 1963-1975* is a comprehensive annotated bibliography that includes citations on general studies of history, feminism, and black and native-American women. The annotations themselves consist of paragraph-length descriptions.

BIBLIOGRAPHY

Andrews, William D., and Deborah C. Andrews. "Technology and the Housewife in Nineteenth-Century America." *Women's Studies* 2, no. 3 (1974): 309-28.

Barker-Benfield, G[eorge] J[ames]. *The Horrors of the Half-Known Life: Male Attitudes Toward Women and Sexuality in Nineteenth-Century America*. New York: Harper & Row, 1976.

Barnett, Evelyn Brooks. "Nannie Burroughs and the Education of Black Women." In *The Afro-American Woman: Struggles and Images*, edited by Sharon Harley and Rosalyn Terborg-Penn, pp. 97-108. Port Washington, N.Y.: Kennikat Press, 1978.

Bartlett, Irving H., and C. Glenn Cambor. "The History and Psychodynamics of Southern Womanhood." *Women's Studies* 2, no. 1 (1974): 9-24.

Baym, Nina. *Woman's Fiction: A Guide to Novels by and about Women in America, 1820-1870*. Ithaca and London: Cornell University Press, 1978.

Beard, Mary R., ed. *America Through Women's Eyes*. New York: Macmillan Co., 1933.

Beauvoir, Simone de. *The Second Sex*. Translated and edited by H. M. Parshley. 1952. Reprint. New York: Alfred A. Knopf, 1968.

Berch, Bettina. "Scientific Management in the Home: The Empress's New Clothes." *Journal of American Culture* 3, no. 3 (Fall 1980): 440-45.

The Black Family and the Black Woman: A Bibliography. Bloomington, Ind.: Prepared by the library staff and the Afro-American Studies Department, Indiana University, 1972.

Bracey, John H., Jr., August Meier, and Elliott Rudwick, eds. *Black Matriarchy: Myth or Reality?* A Wadsworth Series: Explorations in the Black Experience. Belmont, Calif.: Wadsworth Publishing Company, 1971.

Cade, Toni. "On the Issue of Roles." In *The Black Woman: An Anthology*, edited by Toni Cade, pp. 101-9. New York: Signet, 1970.

———. "The Pill: Genocide or Liberation?" In *The Black Woman: An Anthology*, edited by Toni Cade, pp. 162-69. New York: Signet, 1970.

———, ed. *The Black Woman: An Anthology*. New York: Signet, 1970.

Carrell, Kimberley W. "The Industrial Revolution Comes to the Home: Kitchen Design Reform and Middle-Class Women." *Journal of American Culture* 2, no. 3 (Fall 1979): 488-99.

Chafe, William Henry. *The American Woman: Her Changing Social, Economic, and Political Roles, 1920-1970.* New York: Oxford University Press, 1972.

Chambers, Clarke A. "The Campaign for Women's Rights in the 1920's." In *Our American Sisters: Women in American Life and Thought,* edited by Jean E. Friedman and William G. Shade, pp. 323-44. 2d ed. Boston: Allyn and Bacon, 1976.

Christian, Barbara. *Black Women Novelists: The Development of a Tradition, 1892-1976.* Contributions in Afro-American and African Studies, no. 52. Westport, Conn.: Greenwood Press, 1980.

Cole, Johnneta B. "Black Women in America: An Annotated Bibliography." *Black Scholar* 3, no. 4 (December 1971): 42-53.

Conrad, Susan Phinney. *Perish the Thought: Intellectual Women in Romantic America, 1830-1860.* New York: Oxford University Press, 1976.

Conway, Jill. "Women Reformers and American Culture, 1870-1930." In *Our American Sisters: Women in American Life and Thought,* edited by Jean E. Friedman and William G. Shade, pp. 301-12. 2d ed. Boston: Allyn and Bacon, 1976.

Corbett, Katharine T. "Louisa Catherine Adams: The Anguished 'Adventures of a Nobody.'" In *Woman's Being, Woman's Place: Female Identity and Vocation in American History,* edited by Mary Kelley, pp. 67-84. Boston: G. K. Hall & Co., 1979.

Cott, Nancy F. *The Bonds of Womanhood: "Woman's Sphere" in New England, 1780-1835.* New Haven: Yale University Press, 1977.

————, ed. *Root of Bitterness: Documents of the Social History of American Women.* New York: E. P. Dutton, 1972.

Cowan, Ruth Schwartz. "A Case Study of Technological and Social Change: The Washing Machine and the Working Wife." In *Clio's Consciousness Raised: New Perspectives on the History of Women,* edited by Mary S. Hartman and Lois Banner, pp. 245-53. New York: Octagon Books, 1976.

Daly, Mary. *Gyn/Ecology: The Metaethics of Radical Feminism.* Boston: Beacon Press, 1978.

Davis, Lenwood G. *The Black Woman in American Society: A Selected Annotated Bibliography.* Boston: G. K. Hall & Co., 1975.

Degler, Carl N. *At Odds: Women and the Family in America from the Revolution to the Present.* New York: Oxford University Press, 1980.

Demos, John. "Husbands and Wives." In *Our American Sisters: Women in American Life and Thought,* edited by Jean E. Friedman and William G. Shade, pp. 24-37. 2d ed. Boston: Allyn and Bacon, 1976.

Dexter, Elisabeth. *Career Women of America, 1776-1840.* Francetown, N.H.: Marshall Jones Co., 1950.

Douglas, Ann. *The Feminization of American Culture.* New York: Alfred A. Knopf, 1977.

Dye, Nancy Schrom. "Creating a Feminist Alliance: Sisterhood and Class Conflict in the New York Women's Trade Union League, 1903-1914." In *Our American Sisters: Women in American Life and Thought,* edited by Jean E. Friedman and William G. Shade, pp. 283-300. 2d ed. Boston: Allyn and Bacon, 1976.

Earnest, Ernest. *The American Eve in Fact and Fiction, 1775-1914.* Urbana: University of Illinois Press, 1974.

Ehrenreich, Barbara, and Deirdre English. *For Her Own Good: 150 Years of the Experts' Advice to Women.* Garden City, N.Y.: Anchor Press, 1978.

Firestone, Shulamith. *The Dialectic of Sex: The Case for Feminist Revolution.* New York: William Morrow and Co., 1970.

Flexner, Eleanor. *Century of Struggle: The Woman's Rights Movement in the United States.* Rev. ed. Cambridge, Mass.: Harvard University Press, Belknap Press, 1975.

Friedan, Betty. *The Feminine Mystique.* New York: W. W. Norton & Co., 1963.

Friedman, Barbara, et al. *Women's Work and Women's Studies, 1973-1974: A Bibliography.* New York: Barnard College Women's Center, 1975. Distributed by the Feminist Press.

Friedman, Jean E. "Contemporary Feminism: Theories and Practice." In *Our American Sisters: Women in American Life and Thought,* edited by Jean E. Friedman and G. Shade, pp. 430-44. 2d ed. Boston: Allyn and Bacon, 1976.

_____, and William G. Shade, eds. *Our American Sisters: Women in American Life and Thought.* 2d ed. Boston: Allyn and Bacon, 1976.

Gherman, Dawn Lander. "Frontier and Wilderness: American Women Authors." *University of Michigan Papers in Women's Studies* 2, no. 2, pp. 7-38.

Gill, Gerald R. " 'Win or Lose—We Win': The 1952 Vice-Presidential Campaign of Charlotta A. Bass." In *The Afro-American Woman: Struggles and Images,* edited by Sharon Harley and Rosalyn Terborg-Penn, pp. 109-18. Port Washington, N.Y.: Kennikat Press, 1978.

Gilman, Charlotte Perkins. *Women and Economics: A Study of the Economic Relation Between Men and Women as a Factor in Social Evolution.* Edited with an introduction by Carl N. Degler. 1898. Reprint. New York: Harper & Row/Harper Torchbooks, 1966.

Gordon, Linda. "Voluntary Motherhood: The Beginnings of Feminist Birth Control Ideas in the United States." In *Clio's Consciousness Raised: New Perspectives on the History of Women,* edited by Mary S. Hartman and Lois Banner, pp. 54-71. New York: Octagon Books, 1976.

_____. *Woman's Body, Woman's Right: A Social History of Birth Control in America.* New York: Grossman Publishers, 1976.

Gornick, Vivian. *Essays in Feminism.* New York: Harper & Row, 1978.

_____. "Female Narcissism as a Metaphor in Literature." In her *Essays in Feminism,* pp. 218-31. New York: Harper & Row, 1978.

_____. "Why Do These Men Hate Women?" In her *Essays in Feminism,* pp. 189-99. New York: Harper & Row, 1978.

_____. "Why Radcliffe Women Are Afraid of Success." In her *Essays in Feminism,* pp. 94-107. New York: Harper & Row, 1978.

_____. "Why Women Fear Success." In her *Essays in Feminism,* pp. 84-93. New York: Harper & Row, 1978.

Grant, Mary H. "Domestic Experience and Feminist Theory: The Case of Julia Ward Howe." In *Woman's Being, Woman's Place: Female Identity and Vocation in American History,* edited by Mary Kelley, pp. 220-32. Boston: G. K. Hall & Co., 1979.

Grier, William H., and Price M. Cobbs. *Black Rage.* New York: Basic Books, 1968.

Griffith, Elisabeth. "Elizabeth Cady Stanton on Marriage and Divorce: Feminist

Theory and Domestic Experience." In *Woman's Being, Woman's Place: Female Identity and Vocation in American History*, edited by Mary Kelley, pp. 233-51. Boston: G. K. Hall & Co., 1979.

Haber, Barbara. *Women in America: A Guide to Books, 1963-1975.* Boston: G. K. Hall & Co., 1978.

Haller, John S., Jr. "From Maidenhood to Menopause: Sex Education for Women in Victorian America." *Journal of Popular Culture* 6, no. 1 (Summer 1972): 49-69.

———, [Jr.], and Robin Haller. *The Physician and Sexuality in Victorian America.* Urbana: University of Illinois Press, 1974.

Harley, Sharon. "Northern Black Female Workers: Jacksonian Era." In *The Afro-American Woman: Struggles and Images*, edited by Sharon Harley and Rosalyn Terborg-Penn, pp. 5-16. Port Washington, N.Y.: Kennikat Press, 1978.

———, and Rosalyn Terborg-Penn, eds. *The Afro-American Woman: Struggles and Images.* Port Washington, N.Y.: Kennikat Press, 1978.

Harris, Barbara J. *Beyond Her Sphere: Women and the Professions in American History.* Contributions in Women's Studies, no. 4. Westport, Conn.: Greenwood Press, 1978.

Harrison, Daphne Duval. "Black Women in the Blues Tradition." In *The Afro-American Woman: Struggles and Images*, edited by Sharon Harley and Rosalyn Terborg-Penn, pp. 58-73. Port Washington, N.Y.: Kennikat Press, 1978.

Hartman, Mary S., and Lois Banner, eds. *Clio's Consciousness Raised: New Perspectives on the History of Women.* New York: Octagon Books, 1976.

Hays, H[offman] R[eynolds]. *The Dangerous Sex: The Myth of Feminine Evil.* New York: G. P. Putnam's Sons, 1964.

Herman, Sondra R. "Loving Courtship or the Marriage Market? The Ideal and Its Critics, 1871-1911." In *Our American Sisters: Women in American Life and Thought*, edited by Jean E. Friedman and William G. Shade, pp. 233-51. 2d ed. Boston: Allyn and Bacon, 1976.

Higashi, Sumiko. "Cinderella vs. Statistics: The Silent Movie Heroine as a Jazz-Age Working Girl." In *Woman's Being, Woman's Place: Female Identity and Vocation in American History*, edited by Mary Kelley, pp. 109-26. Boston: G. K. Hall & Co., 1979.

———. *Virgins, Vamps, and Flappers: The American Silent Movie Heroine.* St. Albans, Vt.: Eden Press Women's Publications, 1978.

Hogeland, Ronald W. " 'The Female Appendage': Feminine Life-Styles in America, 1820-1860." In *Our American Sisters: Women in American Life and Thought*, edited by Jean E. Friedman and William G. Shade, pp. 133-48. 2d ed. Boston: Allyn and Bacon, 1976.

Jeffrey, Julie Roy. *Frontier Women: The Trans-Mississippi West, 1840-1880.* New York: Hill & Wang, 1979.

Jenkins, William D. "Housewifery and Motherhood: The Question of Role Change in the Progressive Era." In *Woman's Being, Woman's Place: Female Identity and Vocation in American History*, edited by Mary Kelley, pp. 142-53. Boston: G. K. Hall & Co., 1979.

Jordan, Winthrop D. "Fruits of Passion: The Dynamics of Interracial Sex." In *Our American Sisters: Women in American Life and Thought*, edited by Jean E. Friedman and William G. Shade, pp. 93-108. Boston: Allyn and Bacon, 1976.

Kelley, Mary. "At War with Herself: Harriet Beecher Stowe as Woman in Conflict within the Home." In *Woman's Being, Woman's Place: Female Identity and Vocation in American History*, edited by Mary Kelley, pp. 201-19. Boston: G. K. Hall & Co., 1979.

———, ed. *Woman's Being, Woman's Place: Female Identity and Vocation in American History*. Boston: G. K. Hall & Co., 1979.

Koehler, Lyle. "The Case of the American Jezebels: Anne Hutchinson and Female Agitation during the Years of Antinomian Turmoil, 1636-1640." In *Our American Sisters: Women in American Life and Thought*, edited by Jean E. Friedman and William G. Shade, pp. 52-75. 2d ed. Boston: Allyn and Bacon, 1976.

Kraditor, Aileen. *Ideas of the Woman's Suffrage Movement, 1890-1920*. New York: Columbia University Press, 1965.

———, ed. *Up From the Pedestal: Selected Writings in the History of American Feminism*. Chicago: Quadrangle Books, 1968.

Krichmar, Albert. *The Women's Movement in the Seventies: An International English-Language Bibliography*. Metuchen, N.J.: Scarecrow Press, 1977.

———. *The Women's Rights Movement in the United States, 1848-1970: A Bibliography and Sourcebook*. Metuchen, N.J.: Scarecrow Press, 1972.

Ladner, Joyce A. *Tomorrow's Tomorrow: The Black Woman*. Garden City, N.Y.: Doubleday & Co., 1971.

Lee, L[awrence] L[ynn], and Merrill Lewis, eds. *Women, Women Writers, and the West*. Troy, N.Y.: Whitson Publishing Co., 1979.

Lerner, Gerda. "Black and White Women in Interaction and Confrontation." In her *The Majority Finds Its Past: Placing Women in History*, pp. 94-111. New York: Oxford University Press, 1979.

———. "Black Women in the United States: A Problem in Historiography and Interpretation." In her *The Majority Finds Its Past: Placing Women in History*, pp. 63-82. New York: Oxford University Press, 1979.

———. *Black Women in White America: A Documentary History*. New York: Pantheon Books, 1972.

———. "The Challenge of Women's History." In her *The Majority Finds Its Past: Placing Women in History*, pp. 168-80. New York: Oxford University Press, 1979.

———. "Community Work of Black Club Women." In her *The Majority Finds Its Past: Placing Women in History*, pp. 83-93. New York: Oxford University Press, 1979.

———. *The Female Experience: An American Documentary*. Indianapolis and New York: Bobbs-Merrill Co., 1977.

———. "The Feminists: A Second Look." In her *The Majority Finds Its Past: Placing Women in History*, pp. 31-47. New York: Oxford University Press, 1979.

———. "Just a Housewife." In her *The Majority Finds Its Past: Placing Women in History*, pp. 129-44. New York: Oxford University Press, 1979.

———. "The Lady and the Mill Girl: Changes in the Status of Women in the Age of Jackson." In her *The Majority Finds Its Past: Placing Women in History*, pp. 15-30. New York: Oxford University Press, 1979.

———. "The Majority Finds Its Past." In her *The Majority Finds Its Past: Placing Women in History*, pp. 160-67. New York: Oxford University Press, 1979.

———. *The Majority Finds Its Past: Placing Women in History.* New York: Oxford University Press, 1979.

———. "New Approaches to the Study of Women in American History." In her *The Majority Finds Its Past: Placing Women in History*, pp. 3-14. New York: Oxford University Press, 1979.

———. "Placing Women in History: Definitions and Challenges." In her *The Majority Finds Its Past: Placing Women in History*, pp. 145-59. New York: Oxford University Press, 1979.

———. "The Political Activities of Antislavery Women." In her *The Majority Finds Its Past: Placing Women in History*, pp. 112-28. New York: Oxford University Press, 1979.

———. "Women's Rights and American Feminism." In her *The Majority Finds Its Past: Placing Women in History*, pp. 48-62. New York: Oxford University Press, 1979.

Loewenberg, Bert James, and Ruth Bogin. *Black Women in American Life: Their Words, Their Thoughts, Their Feelings.* University Park: Pennsylvania State University Press, 1976.

McGovern, James R. "The American Woman's Pre-World War I Freedom in Manners and Morals." In *Our American Sisters: Women in American Life and Thought*, edited by Jean E. Friedman and William G. Shade, pp. 345-65. 2d ed. Boston: Allyn and Bacon, 1976.

Morantz, Regina. "The Lady and Her Physician." In *Clio's Consciousness Raised: New Perspectives on the History of Women*, edited by Mary S. Hartman and Lois Banner, pp. 38-53. New York: Octagon Books, 1976.

Morgan, Edmund S. "The Puritans and Sex." In *Our American Sisters: Women in American Life and Thought*, edited by Jean E. Friedman and William G. Shade, pp. 11-23. 2d ed. Boston: Allyn and Bacon, 1976.

Murray, Pauli. "The Liberation of Black Women." In *Our American Sisters: Women in American Life and Thought*, edited by Jean E. Friedman and William G. Shade, pp. 417-29. 2d ed. Boston: Allyn and Bacon, 1976.

Neverdon-Morton, Cynthia. "The Black Woman's Struggle for Equality in the South, 1895-1925." In *The Afro-American Woman: Struggles and Images*, edited by Sharon Harley and Rosalyn Terborg-Penn, pp. 43-57. Port Washington, N.Y.: Kennikat Press, 1978.

Norton, Mary Beth. *Liberty's Daughters: The Revolutionary Experience of American Women, 1750-1800.* Boston: Little, Brown & Co., 1980.

Nowak, Marion. " 'How to Be a Woman': Theories of Female Education in the 1950s." *Journal of Popular Culture* 9, no. 1 (Summer 1975): 77-83.

Nunes, Maxine, and Deanna White. *The Lace Ghetto.* New Woman Series: 3. Toronto: New Press, 1972.

O'Brien, Sharon. "Tomboyism and Adolescent Conflict: Three Nineteenth-Century Case Studies." In *Woman's Being, Woman's Place: Female Identity and Vocation in American History*, edited by Mary Kelley, pp. 351-72. Boston: G. K. Hall & Co., 1979.

O'Neill, William L. *Everyone Was Brave: The Rise and Fall of Feminism in America.* Chicago: Quadrangle Books, 1969.

———. "In the Beginning." In *Our American Sisters: Women in American Life and Thought*, edited by Jean E. Friedman and William G. Shade, pp. 203-21. 2d ed. Boston: Allyn and Bacon, 1976.

Parker, Gail, ed. *The Oven Birds: American Women on Womanhood, 1820-1920.* Garden City, N.Y.: Doubleday Anchor Press, 1972.

Rawick, George P. *From Sundown to Sunup: The Making of the Black Community.* The American Slave: A Composite Autobiography Series. Westport, Conn.: Greenwood Press, 1972.

Rich, Adrienne. *Of Woman Born: Motherhood as Experience and Institution.* New York: W. W. Norton & Co., 1976.

Riley, Glenda. "Women in the West." *Journal of American Culture* 3, no. 2 (Summer 1980): 311-29.

Rogers, Kim Lacy. "Relicts of the New World: Conditions of Widowhood in Seventeenth-Century New England." In *Woman's Being, Woman's Place: Female Identity and Vocation in American History,* edited by Mary Kelley, pp. 26-52. Boston: G. K. Hall & Co., 1979.

Rothman, Sheila M. *Woman's Proper Place: A History of Changing Ideals and Practices, 1870 to the Present.* New York: Basic Books, 1978.

Rushing, Andrea Benton. "Images of Black Women in Afro-American Poetry." In *The Afro-American Woman: Struggles and Images,* edited by Sharon Harley and Rosalyn Terborg-Penn, pp. 74-84. Port Washington, N.Y.: Kennikat Press, 1978.

Ryan, Mary P. "The Projection of a New Womanhood: The Movie Moderns in the 1920s." In *Our American Sisters: Women in American Life and Thought,* edited by Jean E. Friedman and William G. Shade, pp. 366-84. 2d ed. Boston: Allyn and Bacon, 1976.

_____. *Womanhood in America: From Colonial Times to the Present.* New York: Franklin Watts, 1975.

Schlissel, Lillian. "Diaries of Frontier Women: On Learning to Read the Obscured Patterns." In *Woman's Being, Woman's Place: Female Identity and Vocation in American History,* edited by Mary Kelley, pp. 53-66. Boston: G. K. Hall & Co., 1979.

Schweninger, Loren. "A Slave Family in the Ante Bellum South." In *Our American Sisters: Women in American Life and Thought,* edited by Jean E. Friedman and William G. Shade, pp. 163-78. 2d ed. Boston: Allyn and Bacon, 1976.

Scott, Anne Firor. "The 'New Woman' in the New South." In *Our American Sisters: Women in American Life and Thought,* edited by Jean E. Friedman and William G. Shade, pp. 252-61. 2d ed. Boston: Allyn and Bacon, 1976.

_____. *The Southern Lady: From Pedestal to Politics 1830-1930.* Chicago: University of Chicago Press, 1970.

Sims, Janet L., comp. *The Progress of Afro-American Women: A Selected Bibliography and Resource Guide.* Westport, Conn.: Greenwood Press, 1980.

Smart-Grosvenor, Verta Mae. "The Kitchen Crisis." In *The Black Woman: An Anthology,* edited by Toni Cade, pp. 119-23. New York: Signet, 1970.

Smith, Lillian. *Killers of the Dream.* New York: W. W. Norton & Co., 1949.

Smith-Rosenberg, Carroll. "Puberty to Menopause: The Cycle of Femininity in Nineteenth-Century America." In *Clio's Consciousness Raised: New Perspectives on the History of Women,* edited by Mary S. Hartman and Lois Banner, pp. 23-37. New York: Octagon Books, 1976.

Spruill, Julia Cherry. "Participation in Public Affairs." In *Our American Sisters: Women in American Life and Thought,* edited by Jean E. Friedman and William G. Shade, pp. 38-51. 2d ed. Boston: Allyn and Bacon, 1976.

Stage, Sarah. *Female Complaints: Lydia Pinkham and the Business of Women's Medicine.* New York: W. W. Norton & Co., 1979.

Stoeltje, Beverly J. "'A Helpmate for Man Indeed': The Image of the Frontier Woman." *Journal of American Folklore* 88, no. 347 (January-March 1975): 25-41.

Terborg-Penn, Rosalyn. "Black Male Perspectives on the Nineteenth-Century Woman." In *The Afro-American Woman: Struggles and Images,* edited by Sharon Harley and Rosalyn Terborg-Penn, pp. 28-42. Port Washington, N.Y.: Kennikat Press, 1978.

———. "Discrimination Against Afro-American Women in the Women's Movement, 1830-1920." In *The Afro-American Woman: Struggles and Images,* edited by Sharon Harley and Rosalyn Terborg-Penn, pp. 17-27. Port Washington, N.Y.: Kennikat Press, 1978.

Terris, Virginia R. *Woman in America: A Guide to Information Sources.* American Studies Information Guide Series. Vol. 7. Detroit: Gale Research Co., 1980.

Veblen, Thorstein. *The Theory of the Leisure Class: An Economic Study of Institutions.* 1899. Reprint. New York: Modern Library, 1934.

Wallace, Michele. *Black Macho and the Myth of the Superwoman.* New York: Dial Press, 1979.

Walsh, Mary Roth. *Doctors Wanted: No Women Need Apply: Sexual Barriers in the Medical Profession, 1835-1975.* New Haven: Yale University Press, 1977.

———. "Selling the Self-Made Woman." *Journal of American Culture* 2, no. 1 (Spring 1979): 52-60.

Watkins, Mel, and Jay David, eds. *To Be a Black Woman: Portraits in Fact and Fiction.* New York: William Morrow and Co., 1970.

Weibel, Kathryn. *Mirror Mirror: Images of Women Reflected in Popular Culture.* Garden City, N.Y.: Doubleday Anchor Press, 1977.

Welter, Barbara. "Anti-Intellectualism and the American Woman, 1800-1860." In her *Dimity Convictions: The American Woman in the Nineteenth Century,* pp. 71-82. Athens, Ohio: Ohio University Press, 1976.

———. "Coming of Age in America: The American Girl in the Nineteenth Century." In her *Dimity Convictions: The American Woman in the Nineteenth Century,* pp. 3-20. Athens, Ohio: Ohio University Press, 1976.

———. "The Cult of True Womanhood, 1820-1860." In her *Dimity Convictions: The American Woman in the Nineteenth Century,* pp. 21-41. Athens, Ohio: Ohio University Press, 1976.

———. "Defenders of the Faith: Women Novelists of Religious Controversy in the Nineteenth Century." In her *Dimity Convictions: The American Woman in the Nineteenth Century,* pp. 103-29. Athens, Ohio: Ohio University Press, 1976.

———. *Dimity Convictions: The American Woman in the Nineteenth Century.* Athens, Ohio: Ohio University Press, 1976.

———. "Female Complaints: Medical Views of American Women." In her *Dimity Convictions: The American Woman in the Nineteenth Century,* pp. 57-70. Athens, Ohio: Ohio University Press, 1976.

———. "The Feminization of American Religion, 1800-1860." In her *Dimity Convictions: The American Woman in the Nineteenth Century,* pp. 83-102. Athens,

Ohio: Ohio University Press, 1976. [Also in *Clio's Consciousness Raised: New Perspectives on the History of Women,* edited by Mary S. Hartman and Lois Banner, pp. 137-57. New York: Octagon Books, 1976.]

_____. "The Merchant's Daughter: A Tale from Life." In her *Dimity Convictions: The American Woman in the Nineteenth Century,* pp. 42-56. Athens, Ohio: Ohio University Press, 1976.

_____. "Murder Most Genteel: The Mystery Novels of Anna Katharine Green." In her *Dimity Convictions: The American Woman in the Nineteenth Century,* pp. 130-44. Athens, Ohio: Ohio University Press, 1976.

_____. "Mystical Feminist: Margaret Fuller, a Woman of the Nineteenth Century." In her *Dimity Convictions: The American Woman in the Nineteenth Century,* pp. 145-98. Athens, Ohio: Ohio University Press, 1976.

Wertz, Richard W., and Dorothy C. Wertz. *Lying-In: A History of Childbirth in America.* New York: Free Press, 1977.

Willard, Frances E. "How I Learned to Ride the Bicycle." In *Out of the Bleachers: Writings on Women and Sport,* edited by Stephanie L. Twin, pp. 103-14. Old Westbury, N.Y.: Feminist Press, 1979.

Williams, Ora. *American Black Women in the Arts and Social Sciences: A Bibliographic Survey.* Rev. and enl. ed. Metuchen, N.J.: Scarecrow Press, 1978.

Wilson, Joan Hoff. "Hidden Riches: Legal Records and Women, 1750-1825." In *Woman's Being, Woman's Place: Female Identity and Vocation in American History,* edited by Mary Kelley, pp. 7-25. Boston: G. K. Hall & Co., 1979.

Wolfe, Margaret Ripley. "The Southern Lady: Long Suffering Counterpart of the Good Ole' Boy." *Journal of Popular Culture* 11, no. 1 (Summer 1977): 18-27.

Wood, Ann Douglas. " 'The Fashionable Diseases': Women's Complaints and Their Treatment in Nineteenth-Century America." In *Clio's Consciousness Raised: New Perspectives on the History of Women,* edited by Mary S. Hartman and Lois Banner, pp. 1-22. New York: Octagon Books, 1976.

CHAPTER 2

Women in Popular Literature

From *Charlotte Temple* (1791) to *Fear of Flying* (1973) and all the years in between, women have dominated popular American literature. The abundance of material available on the subject of women and popular literature reflects this two-hundred-year-old hegemony. It also reflects the recent resurgence of scholarly interest in women's literature, as women seek to recover what has been lost, neglected, or underestimated. Perhaps not surprisingly, although much is being written about twentieth-century women's literature, the bulk of critical attention has been focused on the nineteenth century—that remarkable period in which women assumed control over popular literature and truly made it their own. The effects of this achievement, by which women found a genuinely professional outlet for their ideas and energies, continue to mark the fiction of the late twentieth century—especially in the modern gothic romances but also in certain so-called feminist novels, such as *Memoirs of an Ex-Prom Queen*. It appears that even those writers who wish to reject their literary inheritance must give it its due, if only negatively. Thus an author like Marilyn French, in *The Women's Room*, spends considerable time in her novel of liberation in establishing the pernicious effects of the domestic mythology. If women—for bad or good—have influenced the direction of popular fiction for the past two hundred years, they have only just recently achieved distinction in that most stubbornly male field of science and fantasy fiction. With the publication in 1975 of Joanna Russ's *The Female Man*, which was followed a year later by Marge Piercy's *Woman on the Edge of Time*, however, the genre of female science fiction had truly come of age. The discussion below reflects, in some measure, the movement that women's popular literature has taken, from sentimental and domestic (or woman's) fiction to political (or feminist) and science fiction.

It also reflects the fact that critics have only just begun to explore the contributions of black women to American literature and culture. Part of the reason for the dearth of scholarship in this area is that black women's literature, even more so than white women's literature, has been quite literally lost to modern readers. The material is uncatalogued; the books are out of print and otherwise generally unavailable. Those scholars of black women's literature, in a very real sense, therefore, have had to do what amounts to basic detective work in simply locating eighteenth- and nineteenth-century black women's literature. In some instances they have had to do comparable original research in tracking down twentieth-century black women's literature. Much of this material is, of course, lost forever. Much was never written down in the first place, as very few black women learned to write until the last hundred years or so. They didn't learn because in many states it was illegal for slaves to read and write. The literature that was written down and that has survived against all odds is only just now beginning to surface. In some sense, none of this material qualifies as popular culture for the very reason that black women have not, by and large, been part of the American dream, have not represented the ideal woman whose image lies at the heart of American popular literature. In another sense, because this literature reveals a people determined to survive on their own terms, it is in every sense emblematic of the genuine American mythology and, as such, surely qualifies as literature of the popular imagination.

Lillie Deming Loshe's *The Early American Novel* is primarily useful for its bibliographical information and its plot summaries. Part one consists of a chronology of early American novels up to 1830; included are the full titles, city of publication, and first date of publication. One hundred and forty-two novels are listed, but not all are discussed in the text. The text itself contains plot summaries. Although some of Loshe's information is no longer considered by scholars to be correct (as, for example, she attributes *The Power of Sympathy; or, The Triumph of Nature* to Sarah Wentworth Morton, whereas it was actually written by William Hill Brown), on the whole her book is helpful. Part two is a general bibliography that lists reference books and the novels that Loshe refers to in her text.

Herbert Ross Brown's *The Sentimental Novel in America, 1789-1860* is perhaps the best known of the introductory works on American fiction. This book is divided into two major sections: "The Beginnings 1789-1820" provides information on the development in England and America of the genre of sentimental fiction; "The Sentimental Years 1820-1860" examines in depth the fiction of this period. Those chapters most relevant to a study of women and the sentimental novel are "Sex and Sensibility" (chapter five, part one), in which Brown discusses the female novelists and the sentimental heroine; "The Sentimental Formula" (chapter six, part one), in which he defines the typical sentimental novel's characters and plot; and "Home Sweet Home" (chapter six, part two), in which he characterizes domestic novels and their readers. For Brown, the sentimental heroine was notable for her submissiveness and willingness to suffer at the hands of her husband even the greatest abuses without complaint. The purpose of these paragons of virtue was, according to Brown, to "refine and to spiritualize man" and thus "to ennoble civilization itself" (Brown, 113). At the heart of the sentimental novel, therefore, Brown finds the conviction that humanity could be redeemed through its original instincts for good. Because in the nineteenth century it was the home that exemplified this ideal life, the most popular form of fiction was the domestic novel—a genre that, according to Brown, attracted a veritable battalion of women writers who soon "dominated the field" (Brown, 282). If domestic novels exalted the role of the woman at home, they did so in compensation for what women really experienced at home. As Brown summarizes the difference between fiction and reality, in the pages of nineteenth-century novels "are to be found the compensations in fiction for the coveted values life has failed to give them" (Brown, 322).

In *Cavalcade of the American Novel: From the Birth of the Nation to the Middle of the Twentieth Century,* Edward Wagenknecht gives a breezy and somewhat glib accounting of what he calls the "domestic sentimentalists"; yet he takes them seriously enough to observe that "it is impossible to understand nineteenth-century America without understanding them" (Wagenknecht, 82). Unable to resist the temptation, he quotes in its entirety what he calls Alexander Cowie's "recipe for the domestic novel" (taken from Cowie's *The Rise of the American Novel,* 1948, 413-15; in Wagenknecht, 83-84)—which is an amusing if simplistic parody of the sentimental plot line. Wagenknecht treats Harriet Beecher Stowe with more respect, but does identify her as one of the "domestic sentimentalists" (Wagenknecht, 91). Other American women authors who appear very briefly in this survey of the novel include: Sarah Orne Jewett, Mary Johnston, and Mary Austin. Edith Wharton, Ellen Glasgow, and Willa Cather have chapters of their own.

Additional looks at nineteenth-century literature are provided by Carl Bode, Russel B. Nye, Judith Fryer, and William Wasserstrom. In *The Anatomy of American Popular Culture,* Bode devotes two chapters to women. In "The Scribbling Women: The Domestic Novel Rules the 'Fifties,' " Bode compares the domestic novel to radio and television soap operas and offers a Jungian reading of Susan Warner's *The Wide, Wide World;* in "The Sentimental Muse" he applies Jung's ideas to the nineteenth-century poetry of Lydia Huntley Sigourney, whom he describes as "a classical example of an extremely popular bad poet" (Bode, 193). In *The Unembarrassed Muse: The Popular Arts in America,* Russel Nye provides a detailed history of the development of popular literature, finding in nineteenth-century fiction several stock characters: "the Other Woman; the Loose Woman; the Handsome Seducer; the Sick Husband; the Crude Husband; the Weak Husband; the Brave Wife; the Old Sweetheart; the Dying Child; the Martyred Wife; the Woman of Finer Feelings" (Nye, 27). Nye also identifies four basic plots and claims that the "most characteristic and predictable theme of the domestic novel was the assurance that it gave to wives and mothers that they won out in the end, no matter what the world and husbands might do to them" (Nye, 27). Judith Fryer, in *The Faces of Eve: Women in the Nineteenth-Century American Novel,* examines the more serious fiction of the period — namely, that by James, Hawthorne, Melville, and Howells — in an effort to characterize the role of Eve in the myth of the new world. Fryer finds basically four images of Eve in this fiction, each of which provides a chapter title: The Temptress, The American Princess, The Great Mother, and The New Woman. Both Nye's and Fryer's books contain useful bibliographies of American fiction. William Wasserstrom's *Heiress of All the Ages: Sex and Sentiment in the Genteel Tradition* argues that the writers in the genteel tradition transformed the British novels of sentimentality and sensibility into forms expressive of the American experience. At the heart of this fiction was the conviction that American women exemplified the American culture. Of these heroines Wasserstrom observes that they were neither wholly good nor wholly bad but somehow managed to be both (Wasserstrom, 37). Although his is a survey of the entire period, Wasserstrom reserves the bulk of his comments for Henry James, whom he regards as the one genius of the genteel tradition. Edith Wharton he describes as an imitator of James and "only a slightly better amateur" than Henry B. Fuller and Robert Herrick (Wasserstrom, 55).

As evident from some of the above studies, many critics have been less than impressed with the popular fiction written by women in the nineteenth century. Two notable exceptions to this attitude are taken by Helen Waite Papashvily and Nina Baym, both of whom take the genre as seriously as it was presumably intended to be taken. Papashvily's thesis in *All the Happy Endings: A Study of the Domestic Novel in America, the Women Who Wrote It, the Women Who Read It, in the Nineteenth Century* is that nineteenth-century women rebelled against their domestic imprisonment by reading and writing domestic novels. Of the authors she discusses, Papashvily found that most were upper-middle-class women who began to write when they were quite young and did so out of economic necessity; most were disappointed by a man who somehow betrayed their trust, a pattern that Papashvily describes as a "chronic grievance" (Papashvily, xvi). Observing that a mere 10 percent of American women were interested in the 1848 Seneca Falls Convention for women's rights, she points out that readers of domestic novels constituted a more popular but less obvious rebellion against the status quo. Regarding domestic novels as "handbooks" of feminine revolt, Papashvily, in the fourteen chapters of her own book, demonstrates their seditious intentions (Papashvily, xvii). In chapter one, "All Women — All Enchained — All Enchanted," she sets the stage for her argument by describing the formulaic plot of Susan Warner's *The Wide, Wide World* (1850), the heroine of which is a pious, tearful young orphan. In "The Revolt — Active and Passive," Papashvily describes the social effects

of the Industrial Revolution that transferred women's work from the home
to the factory and created the concept of the ornamental life. In "The Rise
of the Fallen," Papashvily traces the eighteenth-century literary background
that led to the phenomenal success of the nineteenth-century domestic
novel. Here she quotes Sydney Smith, who asked in 1820, " 'In the four
quarters of the globe who reads an American book?' " (Papashvily, 25).
(This would be a question answered with a vengeance a mere decade later.)
In this chapter Papashvily describes such popular novels as Susanna Haswell Rowson's *Charlotte Temple;* Hannah Webster Foster's *The Coquette;*
Tabitha Tenney's satirical *Female Quixotism;* and Mrs. P. D. Manvill's
Lucinda, the Mountain Mourner, which Papashvily identifies as the last
of its kind to use a fallen woman as its heroine. Noting that American
heroines had to be duped or otherwise coerced into illegal sexual liaisons,
Papashvily observes that this phenomenon can be attributed to the economics of the time: women were far too much in demand to squander know-
ingly their chances for happiness and security.

Chapter four, "The New Reader," opens with an account of the changes
in American life from 1830 to 1850 that led to the rise of the domestic
novel. Events to which Papashvily attributes this rise include the establishment of public schools after the inauguration of Andrew Jackson; the
introduction of cast plates in 1813 that made printing easier; the increase
in subscription libraries; and the perfection of the kitchen stove and the
sewing machine, developments that gave women more time in which to
read. This was a period in which annuals, such as *The Friendship's Wreath*
and *The Garland*, became popular and ladies' magazines proliferated—
both events increasing the publishing opportunities for women writers.
Three authors that Papashvily discusses as cases in point are Sarah Josepha
Hale, Catharine Maria Sedgwick, and Hannah F. S. Lee.

Chapter five—ironically taking its title from Hawthorne's bitter complaint, "The Scribbling Women"—briefly describes the successful careers
of Hale and Mrs. E. D. E. N. Southworth and more fully elucidates those
of the two men who dominated the field in the 1840s, J. H. Ingraham and
T. S. Arthur. Chapter six, "The Death of the Master," is devoted to the
writing career of Harriet Beecher Stowe. Papashvily's unusual thesis regarding *Uncle Tom's Cabin* is that it helped foster the woman's rebellion "by
sounding the death knell of the master" (Papashvily, 74). This theme continues in chapter seven, "The Mutilation of the Male," in which Papashvily
discusses the career of Caroline Lee Hentz. In this context Papashvily argues that female authors invented the concept of the absent or diminished
husband in order to free their heroines to act independently without fear
of social retribution. And she adds, somewhat acerbically, "Those women
who were not fortunate enough to get a bad husband had to make one"
(Papashvily, 94).

In the next chapter, "Keepers of the Keys to the Kingdom," she reintroduces the subject of the remarkably competent and pious orphan girl with which she opens her study. According to Papashvily, female superiority needed to be "established and maintained" and was so largely by the vehicle of the child wonders like Fleda Ringgan in Susan Warner's *Queechy*, whose competence changes the farming methods of her entire neighborhood; or Gerty in Maria Cummins's *The Lamplighter*, who at the tender age of eight keeps house for the man who takes her in (Papashvily, 95). Both of these children, as well as Ida Ross in Marion Harland's *Alone*, are spiritually superior beings whose behavior becomes a model for their elders. According to Papashvily's interpretation, these young spiritual leaders exemplified the new authority that nineteenth-century women, as religious paragons, could enjoy in real life.

Chapter nine, "A New Heroine—and Hero," more fully elucidates the life of Mrs. E. D. E. N. (Emma Dorothy Eliza Nevitte) Southworth. With the publication of *The Deserted Wife*, Southworth found a way to remove the husbands from her fiction altogether and thus free her heroines for more responsibility. With *Capitola; or, The Hidden Hand*, she introduced a heroine who was, according to Papashvily, "radiant, vigorous and active...daring and confident, perpetually young and always beautiful" (Papashvily, 128). In contrast to the strength and willfulness of Southworth's heroines was the hero of *Ishmael; or, In the Depths*, whom Papashvily describes as "obliging, docile and agreeable" (Papashvily, 133).

In "Joy of Battle," Papashvily theorizes that women enjoyed the battle between the sexes, evidence for which she finds in Mary Jane Holmes, whose work she describes as containing "irony and humor" (Papashvily, 149). In "Choice of Weapons," Papashvily describes the life and work of Augusta Jane Evans, author of the enormously popular *St. Elmo*. It is in this chapter that Papashvily identifies what she calls the "militant frigidity" of women, the origins of which she attributes to their desire for revenge (Papashvily, 168). The final two chapters, "The Time of Victory" and "Common Sense in the Household," trace the decline of the domestic novel. In her epilogue Papashvily remarks that the "emasculation process continues" in the popular fiction of the 1950s (Papashvily, 211). Her book contains a bibliographical addendum.

In *Woman's Fiction: A Guide to Novels by and about Women in America, 1820-1870*, Nina Baym takes exception to the term "domestic sentimentalism" as used in reference to nineteenth-century fiction written by women, preferring instead the more accurate and less value-laden term "woman's fiction." Baym is particularly critical of the former term because, in her words, it emphasizes not the plot but a "presumed ambience in the fiction" (Baym, 24). The term she suggests in its stead she applies to fiction written by women for women that was characterized by a "particular story" (Baym, 22). This story is basically one of a young woman who, deprived of support, learns to take care of herself; although details vary from story to story, "all involve the heroine's accepting herself as female while rejecting the equation of female with permanent child" (Baym, 17). For this and other reasons, Baym argues that nineteenth-century woman's fiction was not in direct lineage with Samuel Richardson's novels of sensibility. Instead she finds the antecedents in the novel of manners, such as those by Fanny Burney and Maria Edgeworth. In contrast to Papashvily's reading of these novels, Baym finds in them an obvious if limited feminism that was intended to educate readers to accept responsibility for their actions. Regarding these novels more highly than most critics, Baym describes them as being about how "the heroine perceives herself" (Baym, 19). Their message, according to Baym, is a psychological one that says, in short, women see themselves falsely as helpless creatures with no egos — a perception that "accounts for woman's degraded and dependent position in society" (Baym, 19).

Domesticity, in these novels, although limiting women to an extent, "was intended not to keep woman back but to advance her" (Baym, 180). Like other scholars of the period, Baym interprets the cult of domesticity as a response to the negative social changes brought by industrialization. Those authors who advocated domesticity were thus forwarding the notion that women in the home could wield genuine influence; in short, women in these novels had the ability — the moral obligation — to transform themselves and, by extension, reform their societies. That they were described as being able to do so in a domestic milieu that emphasized almost exclusively personal relations suggests a significant difference between the nineteenth and twentieth centuries. These authors, as Baym astutely remarks, did not think in terms of "classes, castes, or other institutional structures" but in terms of "personal relations" (Baym, 18). The epitome of personal relations was the home itself, which had the potential for effecting the greatest social change. In their conviction that humans were social products the authors of these novels, according to Baym, reflected the Victorian concept of self. In sum, to Victorians the home was not so much a place or "a space but a system of human relations" (Baym, 49).

In her study Baym traces the heyday of the woman's novel and its subsequent decline in the late nineteenth century. One possible cause of the decline and eventual disappearance of the woman's novel Baym attributes to the fact that "after the Civil War, the idea of expanding woman and her world began to oppose the domestic ideology rather than cooperate with it" (Baym, 50). Before it disappeared completely, however, the woman's novel was transmuted into the Elsie Dinsmore series and works like Louisa May Alcott's *Little Women*—that is, didactic books for little girls. Its only contemporary manifestation at the adult level is the Gothic romance (Baym, 296).

Although there are no footnotes in Baym's book, she does write of the woman novelists and their works in great detail, providing as a consequence a thorough historical and literary account of the woman's novel.

She begins her work with Catharine M. Sedgwick and concludes with Augusta Evans. Of Mrs. E. D. E. N. Southworth's work, Baym observes that it "constitutes a flamboyant rejection of the expected literary behavior of women writers" (Baym, 114). In comparing the work of Southworth and Caroline Lee Hentz, Baym suggests that the difference lies in part in the fact that, although both authors created strong women, Hentz's are "more ladylike and 'ethereal' " than Southworth's (Baym, 126). Whereas Southworth seems to relish all "strong emotions," Hentz does not (Baym, 129). Although Hentz shared Southworth's criticism of the patriarchy, she seemed less inclined to condemn it altogether and thus consistently married off her heroines to decent men.

In almost an aside Baym makes one of her most important observations about the literature that she is discussing, and that is that the heroines frequently run away when faced with a particularly distressing situation. Unlike some of their male counterparts in literature, however, these women improve their lot by running—they do so, according to Baym, because "they know where they are going and because running away is not a final gesture but a beginning" (Baym, 135).

Other authors included in this marvelous study are Susan Warner and her sister Anna Warner; Mary Jane Holmes; and Marion Harland (pseudonym of Mary Virginia Hawes Terhune). Of the difference between the Warners and the others, Baym observes that the latter turned to writing, not from economic necessity, but "for autonomy and for satisfaction" (Baym, 177). In doing so, of course, they risked disapprobation because they were violating the social code that middle-class women only worked when they had to. The fact that these women could build successful careers on their writing—without being impoverished or pretending to be—suggests to Baym that "authorship appears to be the first profession in America that accepted women without special gender-imposed entrance requirements" (Baym, 178). At the same time, of course, women were supposed to write only for other women.

Other novelists that Baym includes are the obscure Caroline Chesebro'; Harriet Beecher Stowe, whom Baym refuses to identify as an author of woman's fiction because of her focus on other issues; and Augusta Evans, for whom she reserves the highest praise. Calling Evans's heroines "the strongest, most brilliant, and most accomplished" of the lot, Baym remarks that they are not forced by circumstance to go it alone but that they elect to be independent (Baym, 278). As such, they walk a tightrope—as did their author—between what was acceptable behavior for women and what was not. This tension Baym believes accounts in part for some of Evans's success. Baym's own success derives from the fact that her account is enthusiastic yet balanced, her observations original and fresh without being farfetched. One could almost hope, in reading *Woman's Fiction,* that the genre had endured.

Baym includes a brief but helpful bibliographical essay and a chronology of novels.

The following essays are of interest because they discuss not only early American literature but also early American women writers and how they flourished in what were, generally speaking, restrictive circumstances. In "Profile: Susanna Rowson, Early American Novelist," Wendy Martin contrasts the idealized heroine of the domestic novels that Rowson made so popular with Rowson's own life of "adventure, risk-taking, and self-assertion" (Martin, 7). Martin explains this ironic disjuncture by the fact that "the mystique of passive femininity" and women's concomitant social and economic dependency were so pervasive that Rowson "apparently overlooked the implications" of her own life in establishing what was to become an exceedingly durable stereotype of American women (Martin, 7). Elmer F. Suderman, in "Elizabeth Stuart Phelps and the Gates Ajar Novels," observes what he only half-jokingly calls the centennial celebration of Phelps's novels about the afterlife. Remarking on the exceedingly domestic view of heaven that Phelps portrays in her Gates Ajar novels, Suderman faults her and others of this school for being unable—or unwilling— to grapple with the "august theme" that they had "stumbled on" (Suderman, 103). He also faults their loyal readers with being content with so impoverished a vision of heaven. Ann Douglas Wood, in "Mrs. Sigourney and the Sensibility of the Inner Space," gives almost an Eriksonian reading of Lydia Huntley Sigourney's vapid poetry, arguing that Sigourney "used her poetry to advertise herself as a docile and willing prisoner of the womb" (Wood, 170). In point of fact, as Wood points out, Sigourney herself was no prisoner at all but an aggressive woman who, by force of will, transformed herself into a very bad but exceptionally successful poet. What Wood finds most remarkable in this woman was her "unconscious and uncanny ability to adapt herself to the patterns laid out for the women of her day, and to exploit them" (Wood, 181). A genuine entrepreneur, Sigourney "used poetry to gain social mobility" and "as a means for a kind of militant sublimation" (Wood, 181). (Further discussion of Sigourney can be found in Wood's *The Feminization of American Culture* discussed above, in chapter one.) Wood forwards a similar interpretation of "Fanny Fern" (pen-name of Sara Willis, who married three times; her husbands were Charles Eldredge, Samuel Farrington, and James Parton). In "The 'Scribbling Women' and Fanny Fern: Why Women Wrote," Wood argues that Fanny Fern "waged a curious and confused battle" against the restrictions of the "feminine subculture"—and did so through the forms of the subculture itself (Wood, 17). In her fiction, such as *Ruth Hall*—a novel that even Hawthorne admired—Fern uses her heroine, who is an author herself, to communicate her conviction that writing can be used by women to escape the limitations and domestic confinements that men would have them accept as natural consequences of being female. Fern wrote, in other words, to protest woman's condition and to offer an escape from it.

An essay that compares the incredible success of the nineteenth-century woman's novelists to their immediate successors is Ann Douglas Wood's "The Literature of Impoverishment: The Woman Local Colorists in America 1865-1914." In the first part of her essay, Wood describes what she calls the "aggressive and feminist" sensibility of the sentimental women writers who dominated the field of fiction from 1800 to 1860 (Wood, 5). According to Wood, these writers used the façade of the sentimental heroine as a device to assert "the richness of womanhood and the plenitude of their resources" (Wood, 10). These women turned to writing as a profession in the first place because it was, except for teaching, the only one available to them; moreover, it was one that they could disguise as thoroughly feminine even as they were using it for the very "unfeminine" end of making money. In contrast to these enormously popular and successful writers were those women Local Colorists whose work appeared after the Civil War. As a watershed in the history of women, the Civil War is important because it opened new professions for them. Wood uses this fact to explain, in part, why "fewer rebellious feminine spirits were turning to the literary life as the logical outlet for their ambitions" (Wood, 13). Unlike their predecessors who carved out new territory for themselves in literature and who were themselves quite mobile in their own lives, the Local Colorists set a "pattern of retreat" (Wood, 14). The women of their fiction, instead of being powerful and influential denizens of the household, are "superfluous as individuals" and "superannuated as a sex" (Wood, 17). Wood sees the home in the Local Colorists' fiction as being not a flexible symbol of woman's strength, but a concrete fixed symbol of death and decay (Wood, 21). Similarly, the heroine herself has been transformed from the young woman or girl of sentimental fiction into an old woman. In Wood's view, the Local Colorists were in some sense simply describing life as they saw it in a world damaged by war. In another, they were exaggerating the conditions in order to protest against them. But, finally, in Wood's words, "they were corpse watchers. They were half in love with what it was their fineness to know were rotting timbers and bare and beautifully bleached bones: impoverishment was the legacy they left" (Wood, 32). This essay is thoroughly documented with over sixty informative footnotes; it also features a chart that compares the family backgrounds of the sentimental novelists and the Local Colorists that Wood includes in her discussion.

Taking as her premise the fact that popular literature reflects the private concerns of its audience, Carolyn Forrey, in "The New Woman Revisited," examines the heroines of eight novels written by women in the late nineteenth century. What she finds in this fiction is that although the New Woman was often portrayed sympathetically, she had no real place in what remained a traditionally patriarchal society. The New Woman, a term popularized by journalists in the 1890s, was characteristically self-reliant, well educated, and eager to experience life on her own terms. The problem she faced was that there was no equally liberated male counterpart with whom she could share her life; thus many New Woman heroines remained unmarried. Others who married and later repented of this decision found the only outlet for their passions to be suicide, since society most certainly did not countenance free love for women. Among the novels that Forrey discusses are Louisa May Alcott's *Jo's Boys* (1886); Sarah Orne Jewett's *A Country Doctor* (1884); Ellen Glasgow's *The Descendant* (1897); Amelia Barr's *Between Two Loves* (1889); and Kate Chopin's *The Awakening* (1899). The institutions that Forrey identifies as thwarting "feminine aspirations" were those of "marriage and morality" (Forrey, 53). It is in the popular fiction of the late nineteenth century that Forrey believes we can best discover those "basic personal and social dilemmas" that troubled women but which the suffragists played down in an effort to win the vote (Forrey, 54).

Until the recent publication of *Women, Women Writers, and the West* (see below), one of the very few studies of the role of women in the West was John G. Cawelti's *The Six-Gun Mystique*, in which he contends that women are the "primary symbols of civilization in the western" (Cawelti, 47). As such, they clash with the masculine code of the West. In some instances, women are transformed into the male's companion, as for example, Georgianna Stockwell in Zane Grey's *The Code of the West*. In the more contemporary westerns, Cawelti finds the nineteenth-century duality of the good (blonde) and bad (brunette) women symbolized respectively in the schoolteacher and the dance hall girl, "or between the hero's Mexican or Indian mistress and the WASP girl he may ultimately marry" (Cawelti, 48). Just as the hero is often torn between these two types of women, the town itself, in Cawelti's view, reflects the ambiguity of civilization itself (Cawelti, 49). An essay that builds on Cawelti's work is Anne Falke's "The Art of Convention: Images of Women in the Modern Western Novels of Henry Wilson Allen." Falke's point is that Allen, who writes under the names Clay Fisher and Will Henry, manages to utilize female stereotypes without being a slave to them. His women characters are, therefore, more real than most heroines of conventional western fiction.

Women, Women Writers, and the West, edited by Lawrence L. Lee and Merrill Lewis, is a collection of eighteen essays, ten of which were presented originally as papers at the October 1976 meeting of the Western Literature Association at Western Washington University; the other eight were solicited by the editors for their collection between then and 1977. Many of the essays directly address the question of the effects of the male myth on frontier women. In "Women's Literature and the American Frontier: A New Perspective on the Frontier Myth," for example, Susan H. Armitage illustrates how the traditionally male myth of the frontier West "seriously misrepresented the frontier reality"—primarily because it omits or otherwise devalues the experience of the women (Lee and Lewis, 6). Jeannie McKnight, in "American Dream, Nightmare Underside: Diaries, Letters, and Fiction of Women on the American Frontier," also works to correct the frontier myth by describing the lives of women as they saw themselves; primarily what she focuses on are the travails of women and their need for the friendship and community of other women. There are several essays that discuss the image and role of women in literature, such as those on Hamlin Garland, Gertrude Atherton, O. E. Rølvaag, and Conrad Richter. Others focus on "The Woman as Writer," such as Bernice Slote's "Willa Cather and the Sense of History" and Sylvia B. Lee's "The Mormon Novel: Virginia Sorensen's *The Evening and the Morning.*" Most of the essays are well documented with informative footnotes.

The next few works also focus on myth and literature. In "The American Galatea," for example, Judith H. Montgomery contends that all aspects of early American culture encouraged what she calls "the development of the Pygmalion myth"—a myth she finds central to the work of Henry James and Nathaniel Hawthorne (Montgomery, 890). According to Montgomery, by the end of the nineteenth century, the American Galatea had degenerated into such complete dependence on her male creator and possessor that she had become "generically unfit for survival" (Montgomery, 898). Her successor was the American bitch. Dolores Barracano Schmidt, in "The Great American Bitch," argues that this negative image of the American woman resulted directly from the social changes that, by 1920, had given women the vote. Crediting Hemingway, Lewis, Fitzgerald, and Anderson with the invention of this stereotype, Schmidt suggests that it was out of the "fears and wishes" of these male authors that the bitch evolved (Schmidt, 905). She sees it as no coincidence that the rise of the bitch was an integral part of the literature of insecurity that dominated the 1920s. Rather than seeing the bitch, who is usually a wife and sometimes also a mother, as a victim of a sexist society that would keep her subordinate and out of the halls of power and influence, these male writers portrayed her as the cause of "marital unhappiness, infidelity, divorce, and alienation" (Schmidt, 904). Both Montgomery's and Schmidt's essays were originally presented as part of the MLA Workshop on Feminist Literature and Feminine Consciousness (27 December 1970). Both appeared with other essays (see, for example, Lillian S. Robinson's "Dwelling in Decencies," discussed below, in chapter seven).

Picking up on the idea of myth, Wendy Martin, in an essay not directly related to popular literature but of interest to women's popular culture, argues that the American novel since its inception has been an instrument of Puritan morality and bourgeois ethics. In "Seduced and Abandoned in the New World: The Image of Woman in American Fiction," Martin recounts the fate of several heroines, from Charlotte Temple to Hester Prynne and Isabel Archer, concluding that American novels reward the passive woman while punishing the woman who has the courage to act on her own volition. After tracing the decline and fall of these and other heroines, Martin concludes that what this culture needs is a new mythology of women that overturns the Christian myth of the fallen woman.

A response to Martin's call can be found in Grace Stewart's *A New Mythos: The Novel of the Artist as Heroine 1877-1977.* This book is especially useful to a study of women in popular literature because Stewart identifies the aesthetic and psychological problems faced by women writers who are forced to create heroines against a patriarchal background. According to Stewart, this patriarchal literary tradition handicaps the woman writer in two specific ways: by limiting what she can become as a woman and what she can do and say as a writer. These conflicts—between what the patriarchal mythos requires and what the woman artist desires—Stewart finds at the heart of those *Künstlerromanen* that have heroines instead of heroes. Taking her cue from Phyllis Chesler (see, for example, *Women and Madness*) and other feminists, Stewart traces in these novels variations on the myth of Demeter and Persephone—a myth she regards as suggestive of the problems faced by the artist as heroine. The myth is particularly appropriate in this application because of its emphasis on the relationship between mothers and daughters—a conflict that Stewart sees as central to most of the *Künstlerromanen* she discusses. The two central characters in this myth help to explain the difficulties faced by women who would become artists. Demeter represents both the Good and the Terrible Mother: the Mother that nurtures and the Mother that destroys. As such she represents the biological destiny of women and the fate that would-be female artists must overcome. Persephone, representing the innocent maiden, is eternally trapped between the male and the female worlds that do battle for her soul. The myth, therefore, is one of sorrow and loss from the perspective of both Demeter and Persephone. It is also a myth of rebellion, as Demeter "challenges the patriarchal order on behalf of her daughter" (Stewart, 46).

In chapter four, "The Artist as Heroine: Her Journey to the Interior," Stewart traces the quest for identity that female artists engage in, a quest that parallels that taken by male artists. If the purpose and the preliminary adventures are comparable in the journeys of the two sexes, the consequences—the moment of revelation or recognition—are not. Stewart's summary of this difference is both cogent and distressing when she remarks that "Whereas the typical mythic hero destroys the minotaur, marries the heroine, and assumes the throne, the heroine must accept the demon, reject the hero, and live in misery if she is to retain her identity as an artist" (Stewart, 178). In other words, where the hero is exalted by his society, the heroine remains alienated from hers and is all too often identified with the monster itself. In the new mythos—which is written from an awareness of society's indifference or outright hostility to the woman artist—the victory arises when the woman artist, against all teachings to the contrary, accepts herself for what she is, be it "a freak, a monster, a dybbuk, or a Medusa" (Stewart, 178).

The novels that Stewart includes in her study are American, English, and Canadian. They include such well-known works as Sylvia Plath's *The Bell Jar,* Doris Lessing's *The Golden Notebook,* Virginia Woolf's *Orlando,* Erica Jong's *Fear of Flying,* and Margaret Atwood's *Surfacing;* they also include less familiar works like May Sinclair's *Mary Olivier: A Life,* Esther M. Broner's *Her Mothers,* and Elizabeth Stuart Phelps's *The Story of Avis.* Although perhaps only Jong's and Phelps's novels strictly qualify as popular fiction, Stewart's approach lends itself well to a study of the role of the woman artist in the popular imagination. Furthermore, by identifying a new mythos, Stewart provides a new standard by which to evaluate the popular image of the woman artist; by this she also provides what is perhaps the original mythological context for that staple of popular literature—the Terrible Mother.

In *Reaching Out: Sensitivity and Order in Recent American Fiction by Women,* Anne Z. Mickelson discusses selected novels and stories of twelve contemporary authors in order to determine whether or not there is what she calls a "new woman" emerging in our literary imaginations. Her answer is, apparently, yes and no. In order to answer her question, Mickelson focuses on the portraits of women in the work of several best-selling authors, allotting a chapter each to Joyce Carol Oates ("Sexual Love in the Fiction of Joyce Carol Oates"), Erica Jong ("Flying or Grounded?"), Lois Gould ("The Musical Chairs of Power"), Gail Godwin ("Order and Accommodation"), and Joan Didion ("The Hurting Woman"). In another chapter, "Winging Upward: Black Women," she discusses Sarah E. Wright, Toni Morrison, and Alice Walker. In her final chapter, "Piecemeal Liberation," she looks at the work of Marge Piercy, Sara Davidson, Marilyn French, and Grace Paley. She finds, overall, in the work of these women a common concern with identity and egalitarianism (whether between the sexes or the races) and a desire to create new forms for expressing their ideas—features she identifies as being characteristic of all American fiction.

Although she spends considerable time examining the relationships between men and women and those among women, perhaps her most rewarding approaches are those that center on the study of the relationships that these fictional women have with their own bodies. She contrasts, for example, the uneasy relationship that the women of Oates's fiction have with their bodies to the "celebration of the female body" found at the end of Erica Jong's *Fear of Flying* and *How To Save Your Own Life* (Mickelson, 35). The problems that Joan Didion's Maria Wyeth *(Play It As It Lays)* experiences with her own body, Mickelson attributes to the "prefabricated male language" in which she operates (Mickelson, 95). Similarly, Mickelson argues that authors like Toni Morrison and Grace Paley, who are "dislodging...woman from old assumptions about her body and the world outside it," are, in a fundamentally important way, modifying our very language (Mickelson, 236). For example, the physical violence that Toni Morrison's Sula *(Sula)* is capable of wreaking on herself and others is significant because violence, as Mickelson suggests, has been historically a male prerogative—in fiction and in real life. As if to corroborate this observation and illustrate its bitter consequences, Mickelson has included in her study Lois Gould's *A Sea-Change,* in which the heroine, Jessie Waterman, is literally raped with a gun. In response to this violation of her self, Jessie eventually transforms herself into a man—a rather unsatisfactory, if efficacious, solution to save herself from further violation. Another solution to the physical and psychological abuse that women suffer at the hands of men is to live without them, as exemplified by the communal living, the lesbian relationships, and the woman's hard-won ability to live alone that are found in novels like Marge Piercy's *Small Changes* and Marilyn French's *The Women's Room.* As an introduction to the philosophical and social concerns of some of our most provocative writers, *Reaching Out* is most satisfactory; implicit in the text are questions that Mickelson herself would be quick to point out beg for more attention. Her book is scholarly and provides a useful historical context for these twelve contemporary women authors.

Taking a less sympathetic view of contemporary women's fiction, Jane Larkin Crain, in "Feminist Fiction," investigates the phenomenon of popular feminist novels that seem less to honor the strengths of women than parade their psychotic weaknesses. The novels she discusses—all written after the advent of women's liberation—consistently have as their protagonists women who are, in Crain's terms, pathologically passive; all "suffer intensely but for no apparent reason" (Crain, 61). As a consequence of their one-dimensional shapes, these women, and the other characters in the novels—specifically the men—become little more than allegorical. The novels themselves, therefore, do little more than demonstrate their author's polemical conviction that women are condemned to fulfill roles that men determine for them. If nothing else Crain's point of view is provocative. The novels she includes are: Sue Kaufman's *Diary of a Mad Housewife* and *Falling Bodies;* Lois Gould's *Such Good Friends* and *Final Analysis;* and Erica Jong's *Fear of Flying.*

In "Somebody's Trying to Kill Me and I Think It's My Husband: The Modern Gothic," Joanna Russ explicates several typical modern Gothic novels, concluding that they are "a direct expression of the traditional feminine situation" that somehow validates the feminine mystique (Russ, 671). Of the heroines in these novels, Russ remarks that they are comparable to housewives on vacation. They have almost obsessive interests in and abilities to describe—even at the most tense moments—the details of costume and furnishings. And, as appropriate for a vacation, the settings are always in exotic locations. Quoting extensively from several novels, Russ notes that those passages in which dress and house are described sound like women's magazine articles—a not surprising similarity as readers of Gothic novels are also readers of ladies' magazines. What strikes Russ the most about these novels—besides their ability to avoid, glamorize, and vindicate housewives, all at the same time—is the contrast between the dangerous activity surrounding the heroine and her own utter passivity (Russ, 675, 678). Regarding this passivity, she remarks (much as she does in "What Can a Heroine Do? Or Why Women Can't Write" discussed below) that "the Heroine's suffering is the principle [sic] action of the story *because it is the only action she can perform*" (Russ, 686; Russ's italics). In short, given the limitations of our patriarchal culture and the ancillary limitations on our literature, this is the only kind of adventure open to the "conventionally feminine heroine" (Russ, 686). Kay J. Mussell's "Beautiful and Damned: The Sexual Woman in Gothic Fiction" canvasses a wider range of novels and concludes that they consistently portray two kinds of woman: the conventional, virtuous heroine; and the nonconforming, passionate "other" woman. Although the "other" woman's beauty and sexuality exceed that of the heroine's, it is the plainer, domestic heroine who gets the man in the end—and does so precisely because she represents traditional sexual standards.

Women's bodies—as objects and as icons—have always been crucial to American popular culture. Sometimes women's bodies are important for their presence, as in advertising and other visual media, and sometimes for their absence, as in the films of the 1960s. Because women have been identified for so long with their bodies, many radical feminist thinkers have tried to deny a woman's physicality in an effort to free women from the Freudian notion that anatomy is destiny. Others, like Adrienne Rich, are now calling for a rehabilitation of the body, for a fuller knowledge of what it means to experience the world through (or in) a female body. One literary critic who examines some of the issues surrounding this subject is Nancy Regan. In "A Home of One's Own: Women's Bodies in Recent Women's Fiction," Regan investigates several popular novels that focus on what happens when a woman learns to inhabit her own body. Appropriately Regan opens her essay with a discussion of Gothic novels, in which houses symbolize women's bodies. Both Victoria Holt and Phyllis A. Whitney, for example, "transmute the concept of what it's like to be inside a female body into what it's like to live in a mysterious house. And the point is, in all Gothics: it's dangerous!" (Regan, 776). Other fiction that deals with the question without relying on symbols or other forms of displacement are novels like *Fear of Flying* and *Looking for Mr. Goodbar*, both of which, according to Regan, narrate the " 'adventures' of a woman who decides to inhabit her bodilyself [sic] fully, though not necessarily without guilt" (Regan, 777). Regan finds value in what she regards as Jong's otherwise disappointing novel because it makes the point that the first step to accepting and enjoying one's sexuality is narcissism. That is, a woman, if she is to inhabit her body successfully, must love and accept it. Regan is fully aware of the implicit irony of Jong's position that equates a positive self image with narcissism, since popular culture itself preaches the gospel of narcissism as the secret to happiness. In contrast to Isadora Wing, who enjoys her body and its sexuality, is Theresa Dunn, heroine of *Looking for Mr. Goodbar*. Terry, whose body is literally scarred and crippled, is, according to Regan, trapped and victimized by her body. The failure in Regan's opinion is one that can be attributed to an absence of narcissism; in short, Terry does not like her body because she imagines that others are hypercritical of its flaws. What Regan hopes to find, in future feminist fiction, are heroines who successfully complete the quest for their bodies, who learn that their place is at home in their own female bodies.

There are several essays useful to a study of women and popular literature in Susan Koppelman Cornillon's anthology, *Images of Women in Fiction: Feminist Perspectives*. Joanna Russ's "What Can a Heroine Do? Or Why Women Can't Write," for example, provides a concise summary of the myths that dominate our literature—myths that are, in all cases, male oriented. Russ's point is that these myths simply do not work for women and that, if women want to write about women, they will have to find other forms of expression for their ideas. One suggestion she makes is that women writers should begin to utilize the lyric mode, which she defines as "*the organization of discrete elements* (images, events, scenes, passages, words, what-have-you) *around an unspoken thematic or emotional center*" (Russ's italics; Cornillon, 12). Another suggestion is for women to write detective, supernatural, or science fiction—all genres that already employ "myths which have nothing to do with our accepted gender roles" (Cornillon, 17). Discussion of "The Image of Women in Science Fiction," Russ's second essay in this collection, can be found below.

Kathleen Conway McGrath, in "Popular Literature as Social Reinforcement: The Case of *Charlotte Temple*," suggests that this novel enjoyed incredible popularity in the eighteenth century because it reinforced "prevailing social norms" (Cornillon, 24). Cornillon herself, in her own essay, "The Fiction of Fiction," argues that women experience themselves not directly, but indirectly through male culture—a situation she sees reflected in popular literature like Joyce Carol Oates's *them*. Of Oates and others, Cornillon says that they, as individualists, fail to see themselves as part of an oppressed group—a blindness that affects their fiction because they identify themselves with male values.

On the other hand, Ellen Morgan, in "Humanbecoming: Form and Focus in the Neo-Feminist Novel," identifies what she considers to be the three major ideas of neofeminism: that women are conditioned to be female; that the relationship between men and women is a power struggle; and that women are human. Morgan finds these three ideas illustrated in Alix Kates Shulman's *Memoirs of an Ex-Prom Queen*, a book that she regards as a neofeminist novel—that is, one written during and influenced by the current woman's movement. She feels that three basic forms reflect the struggle that is at the heart of this movement; these are the *Bildungsroman*, the historical novel, and the propaganda novel. *Memoirs*, in her opinion, is a cross between a *Bildungsroman* and a historical novel.

Other essays of note in this collection include Carole Zonis Yee's "Why Aren't We Writing About Ourselves"; Nina Baym's "The Women of Cooper's *Leatherstocking Tales*"; Linda Ray Pratt's "The Abuse of Eve by the New World Adam"; Nan Bauer Maglin's "Fictional Feminists in *The Bostonians* and *The Odd Women*"; and John Cornillon's "A Case for Violet Strange." Lillian S. Robinson and Lise Vogel's "Modernism and History" and Fraya Katz-Stoker's "The Other Criticism: Feminism vs. Formalism" are discussed below, in chapter seven.

Cornillon's book concludes with a bibliography that was later revised and expanded by the Sense and Sensibility Collective and published under the title *Women and Literature: An Annotated Bibliography of Women Writers*. Both versions of the bibliography include annotated entries on works of fiction and criticism; the emphasis in both is on the twentieth century.

In *What Manner of Woman: Essays on English and American Life and Literature*, Marlene Springer has collected a number of very fine original essays that have application to women and popular literature. The first half of her book concentrates on British literary history; the six chapters that compose the second half focus on the American experience as it is reflected in popular and mainstream literature. All the essays are well documented with bibliographical footnotes; and the text itself is thoroughly indexed, a real boon in an anthology of this nature. The essays under consideration below are arranged in chronological order, as they appear in the collection.

In "Images of Women in Early American Literature," Ann Stanford provides a concise summary of the roles women played in literature and society from 1620 to 1800. She notes that because the writings of the seventeenth century were mostly pragmatic and reportorial in nature, "the images of women in the literature are often accounts of real women, usually brief and fragmented" (Springer, 184, 187). The women she focuses on in her essay, therefore, are: Anne Hutchinson, who appeared in print as a result of her antinomian teachings and trial; Anne Bradstreet, whose poetry reflects the "educated, intellectually vigorous immigrant"; Mrs. Mary Rowlandson, who was author of the most popular of the century's Indian captivity tales; and Sarah Kemble Knight, who during this period made a five-month journey on horseback from Boston to New York (Springer, 190). With the advent of the eighteenth century came native periodical publications and with them a new kind of writer and literature. In 1722, according to Stanford, "the *Courant* began to publish fictitious letters concerned with particular problems of women" (Springer, 201). Calling these "the earliest fictional characters in American literature," Stanford claims that these stereotypes did reflect the real problems faced by women who were still under the domination of their fathers and husbands (Springer, 201). She then goes on to discuss the sentimental novel of seduction as represented by William Hill Brown's *The Power of Sympathy* (1789) and Susanna Rowson's *Charlotte Temple* (1791). Charles Brockden Brown she characterizes as making a "serious effort to understand and improve the conditions of women" in *Alcuin* (1798), *Wieland* (1798), and *Ormond* (1799). She concludes her essay with the observation that the women in seventeenth-century literature "are large, heroic figures," while those in the eighteenth have lost much of this stature (Springer, 207). Stanford's contribution to this collection is documented with many suggestions for further reading in both the primary sources and the background history of the period.

Nina Baym, in her essay "Portrayal of Women in American Literature, 1790-1870," takes up where Stanford leaves off, with a little overlap, as she begins her study with a review of Charles Brockden Brown. Before discussing the literature directly, however, Baym presents a historical and social overview of the period in American literature that she covers, suggesting that "the fact of sex in a highly discriminatory society ensured some common features in the lives of women all over the nation" (Springer, 211). The ideology of the period as it affected women she identifies as being domestic and paternalistic. Women were expected to stay at home and had virtually no rights under the law. "By the 1850s," according to Baym, "middle-class ideology had elevated one image of woman—the home-loving woman, pleasing, conservative, and virtuous, a comfort and delight to her husband, an ideal to her children—into a national model" (Springer, 213). Coincidental with this national repression of a woman's individuality were reform movements in which women began to assert themselves and their rights. Strong, positive portraits of women, however, did not find their way into much of the literature of this time, as they had in the fiction of Charles Brockden Brown. Of Brown, Baym says he "condemns the entire moral, political, legal, and domestic structures of American life" in his "four-part feminist dialogue called *Alcuin*" (Springer, 215). After Brown, the imaginative picture of women became dramatically less prominent. The examples Baym draws from, to demonstrate the attenuation of women's stature, include the works of Washington Irving, Ralph Waldo Emerson, Henry David Thoreau, Walt Whitman, Herman Melville, and Edgar Allan Poe; in other words, most of the major literary figures of the nineteenth century. Two male exceptions to this rule were James Fenimore Cooper, whose women in the *Leatherstocking Tales* although "not central...are present and important in each"; and Nathaniel Hawthorne who "made women in themselves a central focus in his writing" (Springer, 216, 224). The other exceptions were Margaret Fuller who is remembered for *Woman in the Nineteenth Century* (1845), "a transcendental manifesto for women's rights," and Emily Dickinson whose poetic persona is "a significant woman character" who writes about what it is like to be female at this time (Springer, 218, 227). Baym closes her discussion of the nineteenth century with a quick look at the popular writers, such as Susan Warner, Augusta Jane Evans, and Louisa May Alcott, whom she characterizes as having used "a trio of female types: diabolic, angelic, and human women" (Springer, 228). In establishing these types, Baym makes it a point to distinguish between the angel-woman and the genuine heroine. "This heroine," she says, "has psychological strength, moral stamina, and intellectual ability—she is not at all like the weak, clinging, nonrational, and inferior creature of the era's ideology" (Springer, 230). Baym's footnotes constitute a very helpful annotated bibliography of primary and secondary sources on this period of American literature and history.

The final four essays in Springer's *What Manner of Woman* are not as central to the study of women in popular literature as the ones already cited, but they do offer pertinent historical and literary background information that would be useful to such a study. Martha Banta, in "They Shall Have Faces, Minds, and (One Day) Flesh: Women in Late Nineteenth-Century and Early Twentieth-Century American Literature," examines the central issues and the character types in major American literature of this period. For her the central issues are those of "property, value, force, and unity"; the character types are "(1) the Bitch-Virgin; (2) the Mother; (3) the Spinster; (4) the Victim; (5) the Heroine—(a) the Heroine as Idol; (b) the Heroine of Ideas" (Springer, 237, 250). The authors Banta discusses include Henry James, Henry Adams, William Dean Howells, Mark Twain, Frank Norris, Theodore Dreiser, and Emily Dickinson. In his essay, " 'Combat in the Erogenous Zone': Women in the American Novel between the Two World Wars," James W. Tuttleton looks at the fiction of Fitzgerald, Hemingway, and Faulkner from the premise that "few of the political and social reforms in behalf of women in the twenties and thirties had much real effect on their situation" (Springer, 274). Martha Masinton and Charles G. Masinton take a similar approach to the fiction of Mailer, Updike, and Bellow in their essay, "Second-class Citizenship: The Status of Women in Contemporary American Fiction." Although they concentrate on novels written by men, the Masintons also discuss in passing some contemporary feminist fiction, such as that by Sue Kaufman, Alix Kates Shulman, Marge Piercy, Joyce Carol Oates, and Joan Didion. The position that these two scholars take is that the roles of women in "contemporary novels derive primarily from myth and stereotype" (Springer, 297). The fiction by males works within these stereotypes, that by females (feminists) against them. In the final essay, " 'Free in Fact and at Last': The Image of the Black

Woman in Black American Fiction," Elizabeth Schultz surveys the fiction of several black authors and concludes that, contrary to popular opinion, black women are most definitely not invisible in these works. Not only does Schultz's essay counter the notion that black women are absent from literature, but it also provides a concise history of the fiction written by both black men and black women. As such, it fills in the blanks left by much American literary history.

Although the subject of Mary Allen's *The Necessary Blankness: Women in Major American Fiction of the Sixties* is, by definition, not that of popular literature, her book warrants brief mention here because she characterizes the women in this fiction in terms relevant to popular culture. That is, she finds that the women in the work of John Barth, Thomas Pynchon, James Purdy, Ken Kesey, Philip Roth, John Updike, Joyce Carol Oates, and Sylvia Plath are notable for their negative capabilities. They are, in other words, blank or empty creatures, without a sense of humor, inclined to madness, neurotic, materialistic, and often failed, manipulative mothers. Although the authors she studies are major, the women they portray coincide with popular images found in less serious literature and in other popular culture genres. Allen includes a bibliography and an index to her work. A companion work to this would be Katherine Rogers's *The Troublesome Helpmate: A History of Misogyny in Literature*, which is a highly selective study of works in English that exhibit misogynistic attitudes. Of relevance to the study of American literature is chapter seven, "The Fear of Mom: The Twentieth Century," which includes descriptions of H. L. Mencken, Sinclair Lewis, Ernest Hemingway, and Philip Wylie. In *The Resisting Reader: A Feminist Approach to American Fiction*, Judith Fetterley, working from the premises that literature is political and American literature male, looks at the fiction of major American male authors.

In 1972, Carolyn G. Heilbrun published a short article in *Saturday Review* called "The Masculine Wilderness of the American Novel." In this essay, she compares what she calls the "male-fantasy novel of America"—such as James Dickey's *Deliverance* or those of Hemingway and Fitzgerald of a generation earlier—with those of Charles Dickens, concluding that they all share "profoundly anti-androgynous" qualities (Heilbrun, 41). She was to elaborate on her concept of androgyny a year later in a full-length study, *Toward a Recognition of Androgyny*, in which she identifies the concept as an ideal toward which both men and women should strive in life and literature. Although androgyny excited considerable critical interest, its vogue was short-lived with radical feminist thinkers. Mary Daly, for example, attacked it in 1978 by calling it a "semantic abomination" (Daly, *Gyn/Ecology: The Metaethics of Radical Feminism*, xi).

As I have suggested, although much has been written about the image of white women in American popular literature, very little work has been done on the image and role of women of color. One study that helps to correct this lacuna is Barbara Christian's *Black Women Novelists: The Development of a Tradition, 1892-1976.* Christian's work is important because it provides a historical, interpretive introduction to the subject of black women as authors and subjects of fiction. Although the bulk of her study focuses on three contemporary novelists—Paule Marshall, Toni Morrison, and Alice Walker—who would not be regarded as writers of popular literature, Christian's introductory essay contains information vital to an understanding of black women in American popular fiction. This essay is of particular interest because it examines the role of the black woman against the context of the cult of domesticity and the rise of the lady of leisure. According to Christian, black women until quite recently have been relegated to four roles in literature—roles that had their origins in the cultural mythology that white women were frail and pure. The most common image of the black woman in nineteenth-century literature was that of the mammy, what Christian calls the "necessary correlate to the lady" (Christian, 12). In a very real sense, if the white woman was to exemplify the myth of the lady at all, she had to rely on the strength and capabilities of black women slaves. Although the mammy remained mostly in the background of antebellum literature, her physical appearance—a black earth mother in a kerchief—is one that we all recognize immediately, suggesting that it has become part of our collective imagination. The second and equally enduring image of the black woman that we have inherited from the nineteenth century is that of the loose black woman. This image developed, Christian suggests, because of the dominant myth of the white woman's asexuality and the accompanying myth of the black race's superior sexuality.

The other two images are the tragic mulatta and the conjure woman. The mulatta was the black woman who, by an unfortunate circumstance of birth, had just enough black blood in her to be regarded legally as a black, but who also looked like a white woman. The tragedy in her situation is clear, as she belonged to neither world—but from all appearance belonged with the white world. The conjure woman Christian contrasts with the religious white woman; the conjure woman enjoyed real power, whereas the white woman only had the semblance of power in her piety. Of the four images of black women, Christian finds the conjure woman to have had the greatest power in reality; all four she considers were necessary for the perpetuation of the myth of the southern lady.

Noting the emphasis on appearance in this mythology, Christian comments on the identification of a woman's being with her body and suggests that it was impossible for a black woman to become a heroine because, by her looks alone, she was disqualified. Even abolitionist novels perpetuated the stereotypes—primarily that of the tragic mulatta—as their intention was to gain the sympathetic attention of the white audience. Christian describes the goal of these novelists as that of protesting against the dehumanizing conditions of slavery. The problem they faced, therefore, was not to establish the black woman as a heroine but as a human.

In contrast to the images of black women in fiction—as described above—were those of the oral tradition, the slave narratives and songs. Because the oral tradition was expressive of black values, it was not subject to the limitations of the white mythology. The women of these narratives and songs could be—and were—women of all shades of brown and black.

Although the Harlem Renaissance (1917-1929) opened new frontiers for the black artist, those who did write lacked models, working as they did in what Christian calls the "vacuum of unarticulated tradition" (Christian, 40). The two greatest black women novelists to come out of this period, Jessie Redmon Fauset and Nella Larsen, retained as their heroines, for example, the traditional light-skinned heroine of the nineteenth century who was too refined to fit into the black world. Although the heroine of Zora Neale Hurston's *Their Eyes Were Watching God* (1937) is also a light-toned mulatta, Janie Crawford, unlike the fictional heroines who preceded her, is a black woman who finds her identity when she is most closely in tune with her own black culture. It wasn't until 1937, therefore, that black women authors were truly freed from the stereotypic images of mammy, whore, tragic mulatta, and conjure woman. But if black women writers are no longer confined to these four roles for their heroines, the images themselves linger on with a perverse life of their own. (See, for example, Jean Carey Bond's "Reader's Forum: The Media Image of Black Women" discussed below, in chapter five.)

Although many black scholars raise the issue of stereotyping in order to condemn it, Mary Helen Washington, in "Black Women Image Makers," asserts that it is time to lay these stereotypes to rest and get on with "the business of reading, absorbing and giving critical attention to those writers whose understanding of the black woman can take us forward" (Washington, 11). Her own essay covers the work of Maya Angelou, Alice Walker, Paule Marshall, Gwendolyn Brooks, and Toni Cade Bambara.

Washington has also edited a collection of short fiction, *Black-Eyed Susans: Classic Stories by and about Black Women*, which, as her title suggests, focuses on the black woman's experience. In her introduction, Washington surveys the various expressions of this experience, emphasizing at all times the viewpoint of the black women authors themselves. In conformance with the major themes that she finds in the work of recent black artists, Washington divides her introduction and her book into six categories: "Growing Up Black and Female"; "The Black Woman and the Myth of the White Woman"; "The Black Mother-Daughter Conflict"; "The Black Woman and the Disappointment of Romantic Love"; and "Reconciliation." What Washington illustrates in these ten stories is that many black women authors "have broken through the old myths and fantasies about black women"—those fantasies that portray the black woman as an unyielding figure of strength, a powerful and uncomplicated monolithic figure (Washington, xxxi). Thus, in Jean Wheeler Smith's "Frankie Mae," we follow the inevitable destruction of a young girl who is forced, by white society, to grow up before she is ready. Although Frankie is noble in her survival, she is doomed. By the time she is nineteen she has had four children; she dies giving birth to her fifth. Selections from Toni Morrison's *The Bluest Eye* and Gwendolyn Brooks's *Maud Martha* bear witness to the self-hatred attendant upon black women who are trapped by the white standards of beauty. Washington's book ends on a note of reconciliation, however, in Alice Walker's "A Sudden Trip Home in the Spring," in which Sarah Davis confirms her love of her family and her desire to become a sculptor, by vowing at the end to "make my grandpa up in stone" (Washington, 154). A brief biography is provided for each author; a selected bibliography is also included.

Another valuable sourcebook is *Sturdy Black Bridges: Visions of Black Women in Literature*, edited by Roseann P. Bell, Bettye J. Parker, and Beverly Guy-Sheftall. This volume is divided into three parts: one, "The Analytical Vision," a series of fifteen critical essays; two, "The Conversational Vision," a series of nine interviews and conversations with black authors and critics; and, three, "The Creative Vision," a series of poems, stories, and plays that focus on the black woman. Of particular interest in part one of this collection are the following: a summary article on black women poets from Phillis Wheatley to Margaret Walker by Gloria T. Hull, one of a similar nature on autobiographies of black women by Mary Burgher, two essays on Alice Walker—one by Mary Helen Washington and the other by Chester J. Fontenot—and an essay on the role of voodoo practices in Zora Neale Hurston's fiction. Part two contains interviews with men and women, including Ann Petry, Toni Cade Bambara, Toni Morrison, George E. Kent, and Addison Gayle. This last interview, conducted by Roseann P. Bell, is provocative in that Gayle takes to task for their portraits of black men many of the most popular of the contemporary black women writers, including Gayl Jones and Alice Walker. Part three contains work by the famous and the obscure, including Paule Marshall, Mari Evans, Nikki Giovanni, and Audre Lorde. In addition to the extensive coverage of Afro-American authors, *Sturdy Black Bridges* also contains considerable material on African and Caribbean women writers. There is also an extensive bibliography on black women writers that is divided into six categories: (1) General: Historical, Sociological, Literary; (2) Bibliographies; (3) Anthologies; (4) Interviews; (5) Discussion of Black Female Characters in Works by Male Authors; and (6) Individual Authors. This latter list features Maya Angelou, Toni Cade Bambara, Gwendolyn Brooks, Nikki Giovanni, Lorraine Hansberry, Zora Neale Hurston, June Jordan, Nella Larsen, Audre Lorde, Paule Marshall, Toni Morrison, Alice Walker, Phillis Wheatley, and others. The book is illustrated with photographs and drawings of black women. Although much of what appears here is not technically popular culture, this book, because there is so very little written on the role of black women in literature, is a must for someone studying the subject of African-American women in literature and culture. (See also, Mel Watkins and Jay David's *To Be a Black Woman: Portraits in Fact and Fiction*, discussed above, in chapter one.)

Bibliographical sources on the subject of black women and literature include the following: *The Black Family and the Black Woman: A Bibliography*, prepared by the library staff and the Afro-American Studies Department at Indiana University; Russell C. Brignano's *Black Americans in Autobiography*; Lenwood G. Davis's *The Black Woman in American Society: A Selected Annotated Bibliography*; Janet L. Sims's *The Progress of Afro-American Women: A Selected Bibliography and Resource Guide*; and Ora Williams's *American Black Women in the Arts and Social Sciences: A Bibliographic Survey*.

In 1975 the *Journal of Communication* published a three-part symposium, "Women in Detective Fiction," that was based on papers originally presented at the Fourth Annual Meeting of the Popular Culture Association in May 1974. Although the focus is primarily on British detective fiction, the comments made about the reasons women murder and the role of the spinster detective provide a background useful to a study of this genre as it pertains to women. The essays are: Agate Nesaule Krouse and Margot Peters's "Why Women Kill"; Mary Jane Jones's "The Spinster Detective"; and Earl F. Bargainnier's "I Disagree."

Bobbie Ann Mason's *The Girl Sleuth: A Feminist Guide* is a good introduction to detective fiction written for young girls. Mason includes a brief publishing history of the Stratemeyer Syndicate, which, since 1910, has originated over one hundred series, including the popular Bobbsey Twins, Hardy Boys, and Nancy Drew books. James P. Jones, in "Nancy Drew, WASP Super Girl of the 1930s," characterizes Nancy as representative of the middle-class values of the 1930s; in the books that were written between 1930 and 1941, Jones notes that blacks and immigrant peoples were negatively stereotyped, as were policemen. When the series was partially rewritten in the 1960s and 1970s, its authors removed the most egregious examples of stereotyping. In an essay that is given a rather misleading title, "Nancy Drew, Ballbuster," Lee Zacharias suggests that the Nancy Drew series has been popular because it fulfills all the fantasies of its preteen female readers, who long for the confidence, mobility, and superiority that they see in Nancy. For Zacharias, Nancy is neither feminine nor a feminist—she is outside roles that would restrict her freedom. The power she holds over the men in the series is her superior ability to solve crimes. For a discussion of adult detective fiction, see Arnold R. Hoffman's "Social History and the Crime Fiction of Mary Roberts Rinehart," an essay that also includes a complete bibliography of her major works.

Most of the critical material on women in science fiction appears in journals or general collections, although there are a few books on individual authors. One of the most widely quoted essays is Joanna Russ's "The Image of Women in Science Fiction," which appears in Susan Koppelman Cornillon's *Images of Women in Fiction* (see above). According to Russ, "There are plenty of images of women in science fiction. There are hardly any women" (Cornillon, 91). She bases this observation on the fact, which has been echoed by others, that most writers of science fiction, themselves male, simply extrapolate the social mores of their own time into their stories of the future. Pamela Sargent makes similar observations in "Women in Science Fiction," an essay that appeared as part of a special issue on women in *Futures* (October 1975). Sargent, who is author of the introduction to *Women of Wonder*, an anthology of women's science fiction, argues that current science fiction simply "reflects |the| attitudes" of the twentieth century (Sargent, 433). Finding in earlier authors the tendency to model their "future worlds on past societies which had subordinated women," she suggests that it is hardly surprising to discover that these authors were not interested in speculating about alternative life styles for women (Sargent, 433-34). Like other feminist critics, Sargent is less than enthusiastic about the domesticated women in Robert Heinlein's fiction, although—virtually alone among her peers—she does give him credit for trying to portray worlds in which women have the opportunity to become professionals and technicians. Sargent concludes her article with brief discussions of Ursula K. Le Guin's *The Dispossessed* and Joanna Russ's *The Female Man*. She also provides a bibliography, which includes novels, collections, short stories, and essays.

Mary Kenny Badami, in her 1976 essay, "A Feminist Critique of Science Fiction," speaks for many readers when she argues persuasively that feminist criticism is sorely needed in science fiction if for no other reason than to compensate for the lack of a woman's point of view in the genre. Badami summarizes women's participation in science fiction as being that of non-characters, nonfans, and nonwriters. As a feminist critic, she is particularly interested in correcting this situation because books that were written twenty or forty years ago continue to be read, and their implicit (and explicit) condemnations of women continue, in her opinion, to help shape society even now. Convinced that authors consciously and unconsciously reveal their values in their fiction, Badami thinks it is time to point out the lingering prejudices found in the science fiction written by men and to move beyond them to a more socially enlightened view of the future. Accompanying her article is "A Checklist of SF Novels with Female Protagonists," compiled by George Fergus. Originally assembled in 1975, this annotated checklist reinforces Badami's thesis that women do not appear as major characters in science fiction. Fergus's list, which was culled from literally thousands of science fiction novels, contains exactly sixty-four entries.

In "New Worlds, New Words: Androgyny in Feminist Science Fiction,"
Pamela Annas takes a slightly different approach from that taken by Badami. Annas questions why women themselves have not written much science fiction—that is, until quite recently. Her explanation is that a writer
needs to feel part of a community or a tradition in order to posit an
alternate one. Because women have not been able to imagine radical
changes in their lives, according to Annas, the form of science fiction has not
appealed to them. In addition she suggests that the form of writing attractive
to the oppressed or newly emancipated is autobiographical because it per-
mits these individuals to unite themselves with their society's past history.
Androgyny Annas proposes as a solution or a "political response" because
it can be used as a "utopian possibility that transcends sexual dualism"
(Annas, 155). Among the works that Annas discusses are Ursula K. Le Guin's
The Left Hand of Darkness and *The Dispossessed*, Theodore Sturgeon's
Venus Plus X, Joanna Russ's *The Female Man*, and Marge Piercy's *Woman
on the Edge of Time*.

Beverly Friend discusses many of these same novels in her contribution
to Thomas D. Clareson's collection, *Many Futures, Many Worlds: Theme
and Form in Science Fiction* (1977). For her study, "Virgin Territory: The
Bonds and Boundaries of Women in Science Fiction," Friend isolates the
kinds of roles women have played in science fiction. One of her categories
is "Women as Gadgets (or Gadgets as Women)," such as the cyborg Helva
in Anne McCaffrey's *The Ship Who Sang* and the well-known everyman's
dream woman, the robot Helen O'Loy in the story by that name written
by Lester del Rey. Although Helva is an exception to the generalization
made by Friend that "woman-as-gadget" is all too often "woman-as-idiot,"
Friend's comparison fits the women of much male science fiction (Clareson,
143). Another author who also concludes ruefully that the negative stereotypes of women are "remarkably persistent" is Susan Wood, in her well-
documented essay, "Women and Science Fiction," that appears in *Algol*
(Wood, 10). Wood's article, which includes both informative footnotes and
a brief bibliography, sums up much of the previous work done in the field.
Like other feminist critics, Wood calls for more real people in science
fiction, not just their images (see Russ, above) and for serious attempts
on the part of the authors of the genre to envision truly different cultures,
not just extrapolations of their own. Sounding a lot like Elizabeth Janeway
(in *Man's World, Woman's Place: A Study in Social Mythology*, discussed
below, in chapter seven), Wood observes that "Many of the images of
women in science fiction...seem to be distortions of archetypes we have
barely begun to understand, much less reject" (Wood, 12).

Two women who write science fiction and also write about it are Anne
McCaffrey and Marion Zimmer Bradley. McCaffrey, in "Hitch Your Dragon to a Star: Romance and Glamour in Science Fiction" (which appears
in Reginald Bretnor's *Science Fiction Today and Tomorrow*), makes her

classic observation that "Science fiction, then and to a great extent now, is more cerebral than gonadal" (Bretnor, 279). But then she goes on to demonstrate that both "romance" and "glamour," if taken in their original meanings, have always been characteristic of both fantasy and science fiction. She further points out that women's most important contribution to science fiction has been their interest in developing believable characters. Marion Zimmer Bradley, in her introduction to *The Keeper's Price*, a collection of Darkover stories written by Bradley and her fans, attributes to "Star Trek" the sudden and recent interest that women have had in writing science fiction and fantasy. She sees "Star Trek" as having opened up a whole new world of imaginative possibilities for women who otherwise have not been "encouraged, in our society, to create their own fantasy worlds" (Bradley, 9). Bradley encourages women to write science fiction and scorns the notion that male editors won't publish women, attributing to Donald Wolheim (of DAW Books, publishers of the Darkover series) the remark that "two out of three of the best new writers turn out to be female" (Bradley, 8).

Of all the women who now write science fiction—and the number is growing—the one who continues to receive the most critical attention is Ursula K. Le Guin. Joe De Bolt, for example, has edited a collection of essays on her work entitled *Ursula K. Le Guin: Voyager to Inner Lands and Outer Space*. Barry N. Malzberg's introduction to this volume focuses on Le Guin's concern with the relationship between individuals and their culture. De Bolt himself has provided a short, but interesting, biography of Le Guin, in which we learn that she came by her interest in anthropology quite naturally, as it was her parents' occupation. She was born on 21 October 1928—St. Ursula's Day. James W. Bittner's contribution is a bibliographical essay, "A Survey of Le Guin Criticism"; this is a substantial essay that runs eighteen pages. In addition the book contains essays on her fantasy, *The Earthsea Trilogy*; the sociological content in her work; her debt to Taoism; and her science. Another collection of essays is *Ursula K. Le Guin*, edited by Joseph D. Olander and Martin Harry Greenberg. Among the most interesting of the essays, which range from psychological and archetypal studies of her journey motif to her evolutionary and social theories, is "Androgyny, Ambivalence, and Assimilation in *The Left Hand of Darkness*," by N. B. Hayles. Hayles uses the dialectics of what she calls the "double valence" of Le Guin's androgyny to demonstrate the book's structural unity (Olander and Greenberg, 97). This collection of essays also features a bibliography compiled by Marshall B. Tymn.

In the essay mentioned above by Hayles, she acknowledges her debt to Martin Bickman's "Le Guin's *The Left Hand of Darkness*: Form and Content," in which he observes that "the complex patterning of the book is not so much a way to tell the story as it is the story itself" (Bickman, 42). Arguing that the book's form and content "make a seamless whole," he goes on to suggest that "Genly Ai is the structuring consciousness of the book, that his 'story' is not only those sections he tells in his own person, but the selection and ordering of everything that appears" (Bickman, 42).

Susan Wood also approaches Le Guin's work through a paradigm that suggests order. In "Discovering Worlds: The Fiction of Ursula K. Le Guin," which appears in volume two of Thomas Clareson's *Voices for the Future*, Wood claims that "the ethical concept underlying her work [is] a celebration of life itself, through a joyful acceptance of its patterns" (Clareson, 154). Variously identifying Le Guin's structures as maps and webs of meaning, Wood goes on to say that the central figures in her fiction "embody aspects of the artist seeking truth and expressing its patterns" (Clareson, 156). Wood's essay encompasses all the major works of Le Guin and shows their relationship to one another.

Le Guin herself talks about her writing in a lecture she delivered at a science fiction festival at the Institute of Contemporary Arts in London. In "Science Fiction and Mrs. Brown," which is collected in *Science Fiction at Large*, edited by Peter Nicholls, Le Guin raises the question, "Can a science fiction writer write a novel?" (Nicholls, 7). That is, can science fiction be about human beings, can it have at its center characters and not gimmicks. To answer this in the affirmative, Le Guin uses her own novels as examples. Of her work she says: "A book does not come to me as an idea, or a plot, or an event, or a society, or a message; it comes to me as a person. A person seen, seen at a certain distance, usually in a landscape" (Nicholls, 24). To her the process of writing, therefore, is one of discovery, in which she tries to get to know the person she has pictured. This is how she came to write both *The Left Hand of Darkness* and *The Dispossessed*, stories that required her to invent entire worlds in order to understand the characters she had imagined. Le Guin also talks about her writing in the introduction of the 1976 edition of *The Left Hand of Darkness* and in the introductions to the individual stories in *The Wind's Twelve Quarters*. In the latter book she makes a significant editorial change in "Winter's King," a story that led to *The Left Hand of Darkness*. In the revised version of this story Le Guin retains the male forms of official titles (such as "king") but, in response to feminist criticism, uses feminine pronouns to refer to these officials. Thus, the "king" is "she."

Science-Fiction Studies: Selected Articles on Science Fiction, 1973-1975, edited by R. D. Mullen and Darko Suvin, is an anthology of several articles that appeared in volumes one and two (issues 1-7) of *Science-Fiction Studies*. Among the essays of interest are Joanna Russ's "Towards an Aesthetic of Science Fiction" and Ursula K. Le Guin's "Surveying the Battlefield." Also included is the special issue on Le Guin that appeared in November 1975 (*SFS* 2: 203-274). This issue contains a select bibliography, an essay by Le Guin herself called "American SF and the Other," an essay on the structure of her science fiction, three on her utopian narratives, one on her politics, and one by Darko Suvin called "Parables of De-Alienation: Le Guin's Widdershins Dance."

If the scholars have been moved to extraordinary effort on behalf of Ursula K. Le Guin, the fans have been inspired on behalf of Marion Zimmer Bradley. Not only have several of them published under her editorship their own collection of Darkover stories, *The Keeper's Price* (mentioned above), but they have set up a society called "Friends of Darkover" which publishes the *Darkover Newsletter* and *Starstone 1* (this last edited by Marion Zimmer Bradley and Walter Breen). Walter Breen has also compiled the *Darkover Concordance* which contains a foreword by Bradley, the chronological sequence of the Darkover novels, a guide to pronunciation of Darkover words, the concordance itself, and several appendixes that feature ballads, oaths, songs, proverbs, and the publishing histories and story summaries of all the novels.

Samuel R. Delany has written an introduction for Joanna Russ's *Alyx*, a book that collects several of Russ's works, including "I Thought She Was Afeared Till She Stroked My Beard" (first published as "I Gave Her Sack and Sherry"), "The Barbarian," *Picnic on Paradise*, and "The Second Inquisition." Delany's focus is on Russ's language, more specifically on her ability to blend the narrative forms of sword-and-sorcery and science fiction and in so doing expand the mind of her readers. (Delany couches much of his discussion of Russ's technique in an analogy based on the transformation of a society from a barter to a money system. His essay is, therefore, useful also in understanding his own work, *Tales of Nevèrÿon*.)

In 1980, Roger C. Schlobin published *Andre Norton: A Primary and Secondary Bibliography* in the Masters of Science Fiction and Fantasy series edited by L. W. Currey. According to the compiler, this bibliography is complete to date. It is divided into four major sections: fiction, miscellaneous media, nonfiction, and a fully annotated criticism section (including biography and selected reviews). The book is indexed by titles and authors; it also contains two appendixes, one categorizing Norton's work by genre, the other identifying series and sequels. For the book, Schlobin has written a critical introduction that reminds us just how prolific and diverse Andre Norton's writing has been over the years. One point worth mentioning is that "Andre Norton" is the legal name Alice Mary Norton used once she began publishing novels; it is not, therefore, technically speaking, a pseudonym. Her pseudonym is "Andrew North." The genres successfully tackled by this remarkable woman include science fiction and fantasy, historical novels, westerns, and adventure tales. Between 1934 and 1979, Andre Norton published eighty-seven novels (Schlobin, xv).

There are a few general reference books in science fiction that provide information on women. For example, Thomas D. Clareson's *Science Fiction Criticism: An Annotated Checklist* indexes work on Le Guin, Andre Norton, and C. L. Moore. Marshall B. Tymn and Roger C. Schlobin's *The*

Year's Scholarship in Science Fiction and Fantasy, 1972-1975 is a continuation of Clareson's work and is the first of a projected series that is
slated to appear at four-year intervals. It contains information on books,
monographs, articles, reprints, and dissertations; the current volume includes studies on Le Guin, McCaffrey, and Norton. Tymn and Schlobin
also have collaborated with L. W. Currey to compile and edit *A Research
Guide to Science Fiction Studies*. This is a selective checklist of annotated
primary and secondary sources for both fantasy and science fiction. Special
features include a list of periodicals in the field and their addresses and
a list of sources for acquisition purposes. In *Speaking of Science Fiction:
The Paul Walker Interviews*, Walker includes interviews (which were done
by letter) with Le Guin, Russ, McCaffrey, Norton, Zenna Henderson,
and Leigh Brackett. According to the figures quoted by Walker, the best-
selling science fiction author after Robert Heinlein is Andre Norton. Robert
Reginald's *Science Fiction and Fantasy Literature: A Checklist, 1700-1974*,
volume one, includes authors, titles, series, awards, and indexes; volume
two is composed of biographical sketches of contemporary science fiction
authors.

Scattered throughout *Science Fiction: History, Science, Vision* by Robert
Scholes and Eric S. Rabkin are various observations pertinent to a study of
women in science fiction. They also discuss in some detail Russ's *The Female Man* and Le Guin's *The Dispossessed* and *The Left Hand of Darkness*.
Although Sam J. Lundwall, in *Science Fiction: What It's All About*, discusses women, he reveals his antifemale bias in his chapter heading, "Wom-
en, Robots, and Other Peculiarities."

Several other reference works are useful to a general study of women
and popular literature. Frank Luther Mott's *Golden Multitudes: The Story
of Best Sellers in the United States*, for example, describes popular fiction
from colonial times to 1945. It also contains three helpful appendixes:
"Overall Best-Sellers in the United States"; "Better Sellers"; and "Annual
Best-Sellers in the Book Stores." Of the twenty-one books that, as of 1945,
had sold over two million copies, five were by women: Harriet Beecher
Stowe's *Uncle Tom's Cabin*, Mrs. E. D. E. N. Southworth's *Ishmael*, Louisa
May Alcott's *Little Women*, Margaret Mitchell's *Gone With the Wind*,
and Betty Smith's *A Tree Grows in Brooklyn*. James D. Hart provides an
interpretive history of women's fiction in *The Popular Book: A History of
America's Literary Taste*. This book is well indexed with several categories
that pertain to women's fiction and history; it also contains a bibliographical
checklist.

Suzanne Ellery Greene's *Books for Pleasure: Popular Fiction 1914-1945*
analyzes the contents of best-selling books according to the time in which
they were popular. The books that were popular from 1914 to 1916, for
example, she describes as emphasizing the family, especially the relationship between parent and child. The period 1918 to 1927 she identifies as

one of "Exoticism, Rebellion, and Search"; in the books popular in this time she finds a search for meaning against the new sense of freedom that accompanied World War I. As a result of the depression the popular fiction of the 1930s focused on more traditional values, characterized by "a tendency to return to differentiating between the sexes in the realms of thought and action" (Greene, 89). Only in Viña Delmar's *Bad Girl* (1928) does a woman play a more important role than the man; women in the fiction of the late 1920s and throughout the 1930s tended to be more like the heroine of Hervey Allen's *Anthony Adverse* (1933), who was content with a role in life secondary to her husband's. By the Second World War, women once more became central figures in the best-sellers. In summary, from 1914 to 1945 Greene sees in popular fiction a general movement toward complexity and maturity in both the plots and the characters themselves.

Lyle H. Wright, in "A Statistical Survey of American Fiction, 1774-1850," identifies the country's earliest best-selling books based on the number of editions they went through. Another strictly bibliographical work is Alice Payne Hackett and James Henry Burke's *80 Years of Best-Sellers, 1895-1975* (this updates two previous editions entitled respectively, *60 Years...* and *70 Years...*).

In 1979 Carol Fairbanks published *More Women in Literature: Criticism of the Seventies* in which she updated her earlier bibliography, *Women in Literature: Criticism of the Seventies* (published under the name Carol Fairbanks Myers). Both versions of this bibliography contain thousands of citations; the revised edition features criticism on over one thousand authors. These bibliographies are international in scope and confined to work that was actually published during the 1970s. The subjects of these essays and critical works, however, range from Sappho to the 1970s.

Other bibliographies appear in appendix three.

BIBLIOGRAPHY

Allen, Mary. *The Necessary Blankness: Women in Major American Fiction of the Sixties.* Urbana: University of Illinois Press, 1976.
Annas, Pamela J. "New Worlds, New Words: Androgyny in Feminist Science Fiction." *Science-Fiction Studies* 5, no. 2 (July 1978): 143-56.
Armitage, Susan H. "Women's Literature and the American Frontier: A New Perspective on the Frontier Myth." In *Women, Women Writers, and the West,* edited by L[awrence] L. Lee and Merrill Lewis, pp. 5-11. Troy, N.Y.: Whitson Publishing Co., 1979.
Badami, Mary Kenny. "A Feminist Critique of Science Fiction." *Extrapolation* 18, no. 1 (December 1976): 6-19.
Banta, Martha. "They Shall Have Faces, Minds, and (One Day) Flesh: Women in Late Nineteenth-Century and Early Twentieth-Century American Literature." In *What Manner of Woman: Essays on English and American Life and Literature,* edited by Marlene Springer, pp. 235-70. New York: New York University Press, 1977.

Bargainnier, Earl F. "I Disagree." *Journal of Communication* 25, no. 2 (Spring 1975): 113-19.

Baym, Nina. "Portrayal of Women in American Literature, 1790-1870." In *What Manner of Woman: Essays on English and American Life and Literature,* edited by Marlene Springer, pp. 211-34. New York: New York University Press, 1977.

———. *Woman's Fiction: A Guide to Novels by and about Women in America, 1820-1870.* Ithaca and London: Cornell University Press, 1978.

———. "The Women of Cooper's *Leatherstocking Tales.*" In *Images of Women in Fiction: Feminist Perspectives,* edited by Susan Koppelman Cornillon, pp. 135-54. Bowling Green, Ohio: Bowling Green University Popular Press, 1972.

Bell, Roseann P., Bettye J. Parker, and Beverly Guy-Sheftall. *Sturdy Black Bridges: Visions of Black Women in Literature.* Garden City, N.Y.: Doubleday Anchor Press, 1979.

Bickman, Martin. "Le Guin's *The Left Hand of Darkness:* Form and Content." *Science-Fiction Studies* 4, no. 1 (March 1977): 42-47.

Bittner, James W. "A Survey of Le Guin Criticism." In *Ursula K. Le Guin: Voyager to Inner Lands and Outer Space,* edited by Joe De Bolt, pp. 31-49. Port Washington, N.Y.: Kennikat Press, 1978.

The Black Family and the Black Woman: A Bibliography. Bloomington, Ind.: Prepared by the library staff and the Afro-American Studies Department, Indiana University, 1972.

Bode, Carl. "The Scribbling Women: The Domestic Novel Rules the 'Fifties." In his *The Anatomy of American Popular Culture, 1840-1861,* pp. 169-87. Berkeley, Calif.: University of California Press, 1959.

———. "The Sentimental Muse." In his *The Anatomy of American Popular Culture, 1840-1861,* pp. 188-200. Berkeley, Calif.: University of California Press, 1959.

Bond, Jean Carey. "Reader's Forum: The Media Image of Black Women." *Freedomways* 15, no. 1 (Winter 1975): 34-37.

Bradley, Marion Zimmer. "Introduction: A Word from the Creator of Darkover." In *The Keeper's Price,* edited by Marion Zimmer Bradley, pp. 7-15. New York: Daw Books, 1980.

Breen, Walter. *Darkover Concordance: A Reader's Guide.* Foreword by Marion Zimmer Bradley. Illustrations by Melisa Michaels. Berkeley, Calif.: Pennyfarthing Press, 1979.

Bretnor, Reginald, ed. *Science Fiction, Today and Tomorrow: A Discursive Symposium.* New York: Harper & Row, 1974.

Brignano, Russell C. *Black Americans in Autobiography: An Annotated Bibliography of Autobiographies and Autobiographical Books, Written since the Civil War.* Durham: Duke University Press, 1974.

Brown, Herbert Ross. *The Sentimental Novel in America, 1789-1860.* Durham: Duke University Press, 1940.

Cawelti, John G. *The Six-Gun Mystique.* Bowling Green, Ohio: Bowling Green University Popular Press, 1970.

Chesler, Phyllis. *Women and Madness.* Garden City, N.Y.: Doubleday & Co., 1972.

Christian, Barbara. *Black Women Novelists: The Development of a Tradition, 1892-1976.* Contributions in Afro-American and African Studies, no. 52. Westport, Conn.: Greenwood Press, 1980.

Clareson, Thomas D., ed. *Many Futures, Many Worlds: Theme and Form in Science Fiction.* Kent, Ohio: Kent State University Press, 1977.
_____. *Science Fiction Criticism: An Annotated Checklist.* Kent, Ohio: Kent State University Press, 1972.
_____, ed. *Voices for the Future: Essays on Major Science Fiction Writers.* 2 vols. Bowling Green, Ohio: Bowling Green University Popular Press, 1976, 1979.
College English. Special issue on women, 32, no. 8 (May 1971).
Cornillon, John. "A Case for Violet Strange." In *Images of Women in Fiction: Feminist Perspectives,* edited by Susan Koppelman Cornillon, pp. 206-15. Bowling Green, Ohio: Bowling Green University Popular Press, 1972.
Cornillon, Susan Koppelman. "The Fiction of Fiction." In *Images of Women in Fiction: Feminist Perspectives,* edited by Susan Koppelman Cornillon, pp. 113-30. Bowling Green, Ohio: Bowling Green University Popular Press, 1972.
_____, ed. *Images of Women in Fiction: Feminist Perspectives.* Bowling Green, Ohio: Bowling Green University Popular Press, 1972.
Crain, Jane L. "Feminist Fiction." *Commentary* 58, no. 6 (December 1974): 58-62.
Daly, Mary. *Gyn/Ecology: The Metaethics of Radical Feminism.* Boston: Beacon Press, 1978.
Darkover Newsletter, no. 9-10. Berkeley, Calif.: Friends of Darkover, 1978.
Davis, Lenwood G. *The Black Woman in American Society: A Selected Annotated Bibliography.* Boston: G. K. Hall & Co., 1975.
De Bolt, Joe. "A Le Guin Biography." In *Ursula K. Le Guin: Voyager to Inner Lands and Outer Space,* edited by Joe De Bolt, pp. 13-28. Port Washington, N.Y.: Kennikat Press, 1978.
_____, ed. *Ursula K. Le Guin: Voyager to Inner Lands and Outer Space.* Port Washington, N.Y.: Kennikat Press, 1978.
Delany, Samuel R. Introduction to *Alyx* by Joanna Russ, pp. v-xxiv. Boston: G. K. Hall & Co./Gregg Press, 1976.
Douglas, Ann. *The Feminization of American Culture.* New York: Alfred A. Knopf, 1977.
Fairbanks, Carol. *More Women in Literature: Criticism of the Seventies.* Metuchen, N.J. and London: Scarecrow Press, 1979.
Falke, Anne. "The Art of Convention: Images of Women in the Modern Western Novels of Henry Wilson Allen." *North Dakota Quarterly* 42, no. 2 (Spring 1974): 17-27.
Fergus, George. "A Checklist of SF Novels with Female Protagonists." *Extrapolation* 18, no. 1 (December 1976): 20-27.
Fetterley, Judith. *The Resisting Reader: A Feminist Approach to American Fiction.* Bloomington, Ind. and London: Indiana University Press, 1978.
Fiedler, Leslie. *Love and Death in the American Novel.* New York: Criterion Books, 1960.
Forrey, Carolyn. "The New Woman Revisited." *Women's Studies* 2, no. 1 (1974): 37-56.
Friend, Beverly. "Virgin Territory: The Bonds and Boundaries of Women in Science Fiction." In *Many Futures, Many Worlds: Theme and Form in Science Fiction,* edited by Thomas D. Clareson, pp. 140-63. Kent, Ohio: Kent State University Press, 1977.

Fryer, Judith. *The Faces of Eve: Women in the Nineteenth-Century American Novel.* New York: Oxford University Press, 1976.

Gornick, Vivian, and Barbara K. Moran, eds. *Woman in Sexist Society.* New York: Basic Books, 1971.

Greene, Suzanne Ellery. *Books for Pleasure: Popular Fiction, 1914-1945.* Bowling Green, Ohio: Bowling Green University Popular Press, 1974.

Hackett, Alice Payne, and James Henry Burke. *80 Years of Best-Sellers, 1895-1975.* New York: R. R. Bowker Co., 1977.

Hart, James D. *The Popular Book: A History of America's Literary Taste.* New York: Oxford University Press, 1950.

Hayles, N. B. "Androgyny, Ambivalence, and Assimilation in *The Left Hand of Darkness*." In *Ursula K. Le Guin,* edited by Joseph D. Olander and Martin Harry Greenberg, pp. 97-115. New York: Taplinger Publishing Co., 1979.

Heilburn, Carolyn. "The Masculine Wilderness of the American Novel." *Saturday Review* 55 (29 January 1972): 41-44.

———. *Toward a Recognition of Androgyny.* 1973. Reprint. New York: Harper & Row/Colophon Books, 1974.

Hoekstra, Ellen. "The Pedestal Myth Reinforced: Women's Magazine Fiction, 1900-1920." In *New Dimensions in Popular Culture,* edited by Russel B. Nye, pp. 45-48. Bowling Green, Ohio: Bowling Green University Popular Press, 1972.

Hoffman, Arnold R. "Social History and the Crime Fiction of Mary Roberts Rinehart." In *New Dimensions in Popular Culture,* edited by Russel B. Nye, pp. 153-71. Bowling Green, Ohio: Bowling Green University Popular Press, 1972.

Honey, Maureen. "The 'Celebrity' Magazines." In *New Dimensions in Popular Culture,* edited by Russel B. Nye, pp. 59-77. Bowling Green, Ohio: Bowling Green University Popular Press, 1972.

Janeway, Elizabeth. *Man's World, Woman's Place: A Study in Social Mythology.* New York: William Morrow and Co., 1971.

Jones, James P. "Nancy Drew, WASP Super Girl of the 1930s." *Journal of Popular Culture* 6, no. 4 (Spring 1973): 707-17.

Jones, Mary Jane. "The Spinster Detective." *Journal of Communication* 25, no. 2 (Spring 1975): 106-12.

Katz-Stoker, Fraya. "The Other Criticism: Feminism vs. Formalism." In *Images of Women in Fiction: Feminist Perspectives,* edited by Susan Koppelman Cornillon, pp. 315-27. Bowling Green, Ohio: Bowling Green University Popular Press, 1972.

Krouse, Agate Nesaule, and Margot Peters. "Why Women Kill." *Journal of Communication* 25, no. 2 (Spring 1975): 98-105.

Lee, L[awrence] L[ynn], and Merrill Lewis, eds. *Women, Women Writers, and the West.* Troy, N.Y.: Whitson Publishing Co., 1979.

Lee, Sylvia B. "The Mormon Novel: Virginia Sorensen's *The Evening and the Morning*." In *Women, Women Writers, and the West,* edited by L[awrence] L. Lee and Merrill Lewis, pp. 209-18. Troy, N.Y.: Whitson Publishing Co. 1979.

Le Guin, Ursula K. "American SF and the Other." In *Science-Fiction Studies: Selected Articles on Science Fiction, 1973-1975,* edited by R[ichard] D. Mullen and Darko Suvin, pp. 238-40. Boston: G. K. Hall & Co./Gregg Press, 1976.

———. Introduction to *The Left Hand of Darkness.* 1969. Reprint. New York: Ace Books, 1976.

_____. "Science Fiction and Mrs. Brown." In *Science Fiction at Large: A Collection of Essays, by Various Hands, about the Interface between Science Fiction and Reality,* edited by Peter Nicholls, pp. 13-33. New York: Harper & Row, 1976.

_____. "Surveying the Battlefield." In *Science-Fiction Studies: Selected Articles on Science Fiction, 1973-1975,* edited by R|ichard| D. Mullen and Darko Suvin, pp. 52-54. Boston: G. K. Hall & Co./Gregg Press, 1976.

_____. *The Wind's Twelve Quarters.* New York: Bantam Books, 1976.

Loshe, Lillie Deming. *The Early American Novel.* New York: Columbia University Press, 1907.

Lundwall, Sam J. *Science Fiction: What It's All About.* New York: Ace Books, 1971.

McCaffrey, Anne. "Hitch Your Dragon to a Star: Romance and Glamour in Science Fiction." In *Science Fiction, Today and Tomorrow: A Discursive Symposium,* edited by Reginald Bretnor, pp. 278-92. New York: Harper & Row, 1974.

McGrath, Kathleen Conway. "Popular Literature as Social Reinforcement: The Case of *Charlotte Temple.*" In *Images of Women in Fiction: Feminist Perspectives,* edited by Susan Koppelman Cornillon, pp. 21-27. Bowling Green, Ohio: Bowling Green University Popular Press, 1972.

McKnight, Jeannie. "American Dream, Nightmare Underside: Diaries, Letters, and Fiction of Women on the American Frontier." In *Women, Women Writers, and the West,* edited by L|awrence| L. Lee and Merrill Lewis, pp. 25-44. Troy, N.Y.: Whitson Publishing Co., 1979.

Maglin, Nan Bauer. "Fictional Feminists in *The Bostonians* and *The Odd Women.*" In *Images of Women in Fiction: Feminist Perspectives,* edited by Susan Koppelman Cornillon, pp. 216-36. Bowling Green, Ohio: Bowling Green University Popular Press, 1972.

Malzberg, Barry N. "Circumstance as Policy: The Decade of Ursula K. Le, Guin." Introduction to *Ursula K. Le Guin: Voyager to Inner Lands and Outer Space,* edited by Joe De Bolt, pp. 5-9. Port Washington, N.Y.: Kennikat Press, 1978.

Martin, Wendy. "Profile: Susanna Rowson, Early American Novelist." *Women's Studies* 2, no. 1 (1974): 1-8.

_____. "Seduced and Abandoned in the New World: The Image of Woman in American Fiction." In *Woman in Sexist Society: Studies in Power and Powerlessness,* edited by Vivian Gornick and Barbara K. Moran, pp. 226-39. New York: Basic Books, 1971.

Masinton, Martha, and Charles G. Masinton. "Second-class Citizenship: The Status of Women in Contemporary American Fiction." In *What Manner of Woman: Essays on English and American Life and Literature,* edited by Marlene Springer, pp. 297-315. New York: New York University Press, 1977.

Mason, Bobbie Ann. *The Girl Sleuth: A Feminist Guide.* Old Westbury, N.Y.: Feminist Press, 1975.

Mickelson, Anne Z. *Reaching Out: Sensitivity and Order in Recent American Fiction by Women.* Metuchen, N.J.: Scarecrow Press, 1979.

Montgomery, Judith H. "The American Galatea." *College English* 32, no. 8 (May 1971): 890-99.

Morgan, Ellen. "Humanbecoming: Form and Focus in the Neo-Feminist Novel." In *Images of Women in Fiction: Feminist Perspectives,* edited by Susan Koppelman Cornillon, pp. 183-205. Bowling Green, Ohio: Bowling Green University Popular Press, 1972.

Mott, Frank Luther. *Golden Multitudes: The Story of Best Sellers in the United States.* 1947. Reprint. New York: R. R. Bowker Co., 1960.

Mullen, R[ichard] D., and Darko Suvin, eds. *Science-Fiction Studies: Selected Articles on Science-Fiction, 1973-1975.* Boston: G. K. Hall & Co./Gregg Press, 1976.

Mussell, Kay J. "Beautiful and Damned: The Sexual Woman in Gothic Fiction." *Journal of Popular Culture* 9, no. 1 (Summer 1975): 84-89.

Myers, Carol Fairbanks. *Women in Literature: Criticism of the Seventies.* Metuchen, N.J.: Scarecrow Press, 1976.

Nicholls, Peter, ed. *Science Fiction At Large: A Collection of Essays, by Various Hands, about the Interface between Science Fiction and Reality.* New York: Harper & Row, 1976.

Nye, Russel B. *The Unembarrassed Muse: The Popular Arts in America.* New York: Dial Press, 1970.

_____, ed. *New Dimensions in Popular Culture.* Bowling Green, Ohio: Bowling Green University Popular Press, 1972.

Olander, Joseph D., and Martin Harry Greenberg, eds. *Ursula K. Le Guin.* Writers of the Twenty-first Century Series. New York: Taplinger Publishing Co., 1979.

Papashvily, Helen Waite. *All the Happy Endings: A Study of the Domestic Novel in America, the Women Who Wrote It, the Women Who Read It, in the Nineteenth Century.* New York: Harper & Brothers, 1956.

Pratt, Annis. "The New Feminist Criticism." *College English* 32, no. 8 (May 1971): 872-78.

Pratt, Linda Ray. "The Abuse of Eve by the New World Adam." In *Images of Women in Fiction: Feminist Perspectives,* edited by Susan Koppelman Cornillon, pp. 155-74. Bowling Green, Ohio: Bowling Green University Popular Press, 1972.

Regan, Nancy. "A Home of One's Own: Women's Bodies in Recent Women's Fiction." *Journal of Popular Culture* 11, no. 4 (Spring 1978): 772-88.

Reginald, R[obert]. *Science Fiction and Fantasy Literature: A Checklist, 1700-1974.* 2 vols. Vol. 2, *Contemporary Science Fiction Authors.* Detroit: Gale Research Co., 1979.

Robinson, Lillian S. "Dwelling in Decencies: Radical Criticism and the Feminist Perspective." In her *Sex, Class, and Culture,* pp. 3-21. Bloomington, Ind. and London: Indiana University Press, 1978.

_____, and Lisa Vogel. "Modernism and History." In *Sex, Class, and Culture,* edited by Lillian S. Robinson, pp. 22-46. Bloomington, Ind. and London: Indiana University Press, 1978.

Rogers, Katherine. *The Troublesome Helpmate: A History of Misogyny in Literature.* Seattle: University of Washington Press, 1966.

Russ, Joanna. *Alyx.* Boston: G. K. Hall & Co./Gregg Press, 1976.

_____. "The Image of Women in Science Fiction." In *Images of Women in Fiction: Feminist Perspectives,* edited by Susan Koppelman Cornillon, pp. 79-94. Bowling Green, Ohio: Bowling Green University Popular Press, 1972.

_____. "Somebody's Trying to Kill Me and I Think It's My Husband: The Modern Gothic." *Journal of Popular Culture* 6, no. 4 (Spring 1973): 666-91.

_____. "Towards an Aesthetic of Science Fiction." In *Science-Fiction Studies: Selected Articles on Science Fiction, 1973-1975,* edited by R[ichard] D. Mullen and Darko Suvin, pp. 8-15. Boston: G. K. Hall & Co./Gregg Press, 1976.

_____. "What Can a Heroine Do? Or Why Women Can't Write." In *Images of Women in Fiction: Feminist Perspectives,* edited by Susan Koppelman Cornillon, pp. 3-20. Bowling Green, Ohio: Bowling Green University Popular Press, 1972.

Sargent, Pamela. "Women in Science Fiction." *Futures* 7, no. 5 (October 1975): 433-41.

Schlobin, Roger C. *Andre Norton: A Primary and Secondary Bibliography.* Masters of Science Fiction and Fantasy, edited by L. W. Currey. Boston: G. K. Hall Reference Books, 1980.

Schmidt, Dolores B. "The Great American Bitch." *College English* 32, no. 8 (May 1971): 900-905.

Scholes, Robert, and Eric S. Rabkin. *Science Fiction: History, Science, Vision.* New York: Oxford University Press, 1977.

Schultz, Elizabeth. "'Free in Fact and at Last': The Image of the Black Woman in Black American Fiction." In *What Manner of Woman: Essays on English and American Life and Literature,* edited by Marlene Springer, pp. 316-44. New York: New York University Press, 1977.

Sense and Sensibility Collective. *Women and Literature: An Annotated Bibliography of Women Writers.* 2d ed. rev. and enl. Cambridge, Mass.: Sense and Sensibility Collective, 1973.

Sims, Janet L., comp. *The Progress of Afro-American Women: A Selected Bibliography and Resource Guide.* Foreword, Bettye Thomas. Westport, Conn.: Greenwood Press, 1980.

Slote, Bernice. "Willa Cather and the Sense of History." In *Women, Women Writers, and the West,* edited by L[awrence] L. Lee and Merrill Lewis, pp. 161-71. Troy, N.Y.: Whitson Publishing Co., 1979.

Springer, Marlene, ed. *What Manner of Woman: Essays on English and American Life and Literature.* New York: New York University Press, 1977.

Stanford, Ann. "Images of Women in Early American Literature." In *What Manner of Woman: Essays on English and American Life and Literature,* edited by Marlene Springer, pp. 184-210. New York: New York University Press, 1977.

Starstone 1. Edited by Marion Zimmer Bradley and Walter Breen. Berkeley, Calif.: Published by the Friends of Darkover, 1978.

Stewart, Grace. *A New Mythos: The Novel of the Artist as Heroine, 1877-1977.* St. Albans, Vt.: Eden Press Women's Publications, 1979.

Suderman, Elmer F. "Elizabeth Stuart Phelps and the Gates Ajar Novels." *Journal of Popular Culture* 3, no. 1 (Summer 1969): 91-106.

Suvin, Darko. "Parables of De-Alienation: Le Guin's Widdershins Dance." In *Science Fiction Studies: Selected Articles on Science Fiction, 1973-1975,* edited by R[ichard] D. Mullen and Darko Suvin, pp. 295-304. Boston: G. K. Hall & Co./Gregg Press, 1976.

Tuttleton, James W. "'Combat in the Erogenous Zone': Women in the American Novel between the Two World Wars." In *What Manner of Woman: Essays on English and American Life and Literature,* edited by Marlene Springer, pp. 271-96. New York: New York University Press, 1977.

Tymn, Marshall B., and Roger C. Schlobin. *The Year's Scholarship in Science Fiction and Fantasy, 1972-1975.* Kent, Ohio: Kent State University Press, 1979.

————, and L. W. Currey, comps. and eds. *A Research Guide to Science Fiction Studies: An Annotated Checklist of Primary and Secondary Sources for Fantasy and Science Fiction.* New York: Garland Publishing, 1977.

Wagenknecht, Edward. *Cavalcade of the American Novel: From the Birth of the Nation to the Middle of the Twentieth Century.* New York: Henry Holt and Co., 1952.

Walker, Paul. *Speaking of Science Fiction: The Paul Walker Interviews.* Oradell, N.J.: LUNA Publications, 1978.

Washington, Mary Helen. "Black Women Image Makers." *Black World* 23, no. 10 (August 1974): 10-18.

————, ed. *Black-Eyed Susans: Classic Stories by and about Black Women.* Garden City, N.Y.: Doubleday Anchor Press, 1975.

Wasserstrom, William. *Heiress of All the Ages: Sex and Sentiment in the Genteel Tradition.* Minneapolis: University of Minnesota Press, 1959.

Watkins, Mel, and Jay David, eds. *To Be a Black Woman: Portraits in Fact and Fiction.* New York: William Morrow and Co., 1971.

Williams, Ora. *American Black Women in the Arts and Social Sciences: A Bibliographic Survey.* Rev. and enl. ed. Metuchen, N.J.: Scarecrow Press, 1978.

"Women in Detective Fiction: Symposium." *Journal of Communication* 25, no. 2 (Spring 1975): 98-119.

[Wood,] Ann Douglas. *The Feminization of American Culture.* [See Douglas, Ann.]

Wood, Ann Douglas. "The Literature of Impoverishment: The Women Local Colorists in America, 1865-1914." *Women's Studies* 1, no. 1 (1972): 3-45.

————. "Mrs. Sigourney and the Sensibility of the Inner Space." *New England Quarterly* 45, no 2 (June 1972): 163-81.

————. "The 'Scribbling Women' and Fanny Fern: Why Women Wrote." *American Quarterly* 23, no. 1 (Spring 1971): 3-24.

Wood, Susan. "Discovering Worlds: The Fiction of Ursula K. Le Guin." In *Voices for the Future: Essays on Major Science Fiction Writers,* edited by Thomas D. Clareson, vol. 2, pp. 154-79. Bowling Green, Ohio: Bowling Green University Popular Press, 1979.

————. "Women and Science Fiction." *Algol: The Magazine About Science Fiction* 16, no. 1 [whole no. 33] (Winter 1978-1979): 9-18.

Wright, Lyle H. "A Statistical Survey of American Fiction, 1774-1850." *Huntington Library Quarterly* 2 (1938-1939): 309-18.

Yee, Carole Zonis. "Why Aren't We Writing About Ourselves?" In *Images of Women in Fiction: Feminist Perspectives,* edited by Susan Koppelman Cornillon, pp. 131-34. Bowling Green, Ohio: Bowling Green University Popular Press, 1972.

Zacharias, Lee. "Nancy Drew, Ballbuster." *Journal of Popular Culture* 9, no. 4 (Spring 1976): 1027-38.

CHAPTER 3

Women in Magazines and Magazine Fiction

In many respects, the history of women's magazines parallels the history of women's literature and the history of American advertising. Since their inception in the early nineteenth century, women's periodicals have featured as staple fare both fiction and poetry calculated to appeal to women readers. Complementing this entertainment component have been advertisements directed toward women and the magazines' editorial content, which also has been addressed specifically to women. Research into the history of women's magazines, therefore, crosses several different, but interrelated, fields as the works cited below demonstrate.

Cynthia L. White's *Women's Magazines, 1693-1968* is a comprehensive history of British and American periodicals published primarily for women. The portion of her book most relevant to a study of American popular culture is chapter eight, in which White provides a brief sketch of what she calls "The Women's Press in America." As part of her history she characterizes several individual magazines and quotes from personal interviews she held with publishers' representatives. Several of her appendixes are also helpful. For example, appendix one lists "Periodicals Intended Primarily for the Woman Reader, 1693-1968." Appendixes four and five provide the circulation figures of several prominent weekly and monthly women's magazines. Appendix nine is a "Classified List of American Women's Periodicals, 1968"; this list is annotated with information that includes name of publisher, date of origin, type of magazine, and circulation. Helen Woodward's *The Lady Persuaders* is another study that focuses only on women's magazines. Although Woodward's book contains a wealth of information about magazines like *Godey's Lady's Book*, *McCall's*, *Ladies' Home Journal*, and *Cosmopolitan*, it is virtually undocumented and its facts are not always to be trusted. Much of Woodward's information is firsthand, however, as she worked for years at *Woman's Home Companion*. But Woodward is not without her prejudices: near the end of the book she admits that she dislikes women's magazines. In describing the differences between men's and women's magazines, she observes that the latter "tell their readers what to do; they teach them, they command them, they threaten and promise them" (Woodward, 6). Calling women's magazines "trade papers for women," Woodward also claims that they contain propaganda that is intended to "make the man more feminine and the woman more masculine" (Woodward 8; 12). Remarking on the terminology used in the magazine trade, Woodward observes that the word *lady* appeared in magazines and magazine titles of the early 1800s because the term *woman* was considered an insult to refined females (Woodward, 15). In the transition period when *woman* replaced *lady*, which was accomplished by World War I, editors often hedged and used instead the term *girl* (Woodward, 103). Thus in 1908 when Woodward herself worked for the *Woman's Home Companion*, the "girls" on the staff didn't "work"—they "went to business." They didn't "have jobs"—they "accepted positions" (Woodward, 108).

Woodward attributes the decline of women's magazines in the 1930s to the fact that they reduced the amount of practical information that they were dispensing through their self-help departments. By 1958, when the *Woman's Home Companion* itself was defunct, the magazines had lost the focus that had been provided by domineering editors—such as Edward Bok—and, in effect, were floundering among an onslaught of other mass media, such as television, radio, and newspapers.

A more scholarly study of women's periodicals appears as part of Frank Luther Mott's *A History of American Magazines, 1741-1930.* This important work is especially valuable in that it is thoroughly indexed. Each of the first four volumes has its own index, and the final (fifth) volume includes a cumulative index for the entire work. In all five of the indexes there are extensive entries on women and women's subjects. Volumes one through four contain essays on various topics in magazine history, which are followed by a section entitled "Sketches of Important Magazines." Volume five is composed entirely of sketches and the index. Because women's magazines have played a crucial role in the development of the American periodical, Mott gives them careful consideration in his *History.* His essays cover such subjects as "female education" and the "woman question." He also quotes liberally from the prospectus of each magazine that he highlights, as well as providing a concise publishing history of the magazine. All five volumes are illustrated. (For a brief discussion of Mott's ideas about magazine advertising, see below, in chapter six.)

Another, less extensive, general history is James Playsted Wood's *Magazines in the United States.* Although his focus is not women's magazines per se, Wood does provide considerable information about the genre. He begins his discussion of women's magazines by describing several family magazines that sought, through special features, to attract female readers. Among the magazines he discusses in this context are the *American Magazine*, the *Saturday Evening Post*, and Graham's *Lady's and Gentleman's*

Magazine. In the first issue of the *American Magazine* in 1787, for example, Noah Webster promised that " 'his *fair readers* may be assured that no inconsiderable pains will be taken to furnish them entertainment' " (quoted in Wood, 23; Webster's italics). In 1821 the *Saturday Evening Post* featured a department called "The Ladies' Friend." George Graham's magazine in the 1840s tried to appeal to women by publishing sentimental literature by Mrs. Frances Osgood, Mrs. Ann Stephens, and Mrs. Lydia Huntley Sigourney.

Perhaps the most famous of the early women's magazines was *Godey's Lady's Book*, which was founded by Louis Antoine Godey and edited by Sarah Josepha Hale (for discussion of Hale, see below). Of *Godey's* Wood observes that it "affected the manners, morals, tastes, fashions in clothes, homes, and diet of generations of American readers" (Wood, 51). Wood also gives an extensive history of the *Ladies' Home Journal*, another influential woman's magazine that was run by a powerful, socially responsible editor. *Ladies' Home Journal* had been established in 1883 by Cyrus H. K. Curtis, who in 1889 hired Edward Bok as his editor. Under Bok's leadership, the *Ladies' Home Journal* initiated several reform movements, in which Bok himself campaigned against such social evils as venereal disease and patent medicines. (For a more thorough history of Bok's attacks against the patent medicine industry, see Sarah Stage's *Female Complaints: Lydia Pinkham and the Business of Women's Medicine*, discussed above, in chapter one.) Other women's magazines that Wood includes in his study are *McCall's*, *Harper's Bazaar*, and *Vogue*. Although this single-volume history does not index the topic of women, it does index journal titles and the major figures in the field. It also contains a brief bibliography.

Theodore Peterson's *Magazines in the Twentieth Century* is a study of contemporary periodicals (not all of which have made it into the 1980s). The chapters that are most relevant to a study of women include "Advertising: Its Growth and Effects" (for a brief outline of his ideas, see below, in chapter six) and "The Old Leaders That Survived" (sketches of *McCall's*, *Ladies' Home Journal*, and others).

Of all the women involved in magazine publishing, Sarah Josepha Hale continues to attract the most critical attention. Two early works on this remarkable woman are Ruth Finley's *The Lady of Godey's: Sarah Josepha Hale* and Isabelle Webb Entrikin's *Sarah Josepha Hale and Godey's Lady's Book*. Both are well-documented biographies and both reflect the esteem in which Hale is held by these scholars—an admiration that occasionally interferes with their ability to evaluate her work. Finley's book contains nine color reproductions from *Godey's* and other illustrations, but focuses primarily on Hale herself. Entrikin's book emphasizes the magazine itself and includes a thorough history of Hale's own very considerable contributions, which often consisted of as much as 50 percent of an issue's entire contents; this book also contains a bibliography. More recent evaluations of Hale's accomplishments (such as that found in Ann Douglas's *The*

Feminization of American Culture, which is discussed above, in chapter one) regard her in a less favorable light, finding her apolitical stance reactionary and unmitigated by her support for women's education. None of the scholars, however, tries to underestimate her power and her influence on American magazines and mores. For example, Dominic Ricciotti, in "Popular Art in *Godey's Lady's Book:* An Image of the American Woman," suggests that the magazine "not only anticipated but also helped to formulate the feminine taste in art so prevalent in America following the Civil War" (Ricciotti, 10). Hale accomplished this by selecting art work that complemented her editorial policies. In keeping with the sentimental literature that she published and her emphasis on the moral persuasiveness of American women, Hale selected, according to Ricciotti, illustrations of two basic kinds: one, romantic images of escape that complemented the magazine's fiction; and, two, pictures that "espoused the moral, nationalistic, and cultural aims of the art populizers, emphasizing the association of women with those aims" (Ricciotti, 8).

Whether or not they approve of the editorial content of women's magazines, most scholars accept the fact that these publications have been instrumental in socializing American women and in creating an image of the idealized American woman. One feminist writer who roundly criticizes these magazines for inventing and perpetuating a feminine mythology is Betty Friedan. The basic argument of her book, *The Feminine Mystique*, is that women, largely through the efforts of "writers and editors in the media," have been brainwashed into thinking that their "highest value" lies in fulfilling their femininity (Friedan, 155; 37). Although, as William Henry Chafe points out in *The American Woman* (discussed above, in chapter one), Friedan exaggerates her case against the magazines when she claims that they invented the feminine mystique, she does have a valid complaint. That is, the women's magazines may not have originated the myth of the American woman, but they certainly do continue to worship the happy homemaker and sacrifice on her altar the independent career woman. (For more discussion on Friedan's work, see below, in chapter seven.)

There are several recent studies that corroborate the fact that women's magazines have been instrumental in perpetuating the feminine mystique. In "The Passive Female: Her Comparative Image by Class and Culture in Women's Magazine Fiction," for example, Cornelia Butler Flora reports that women's magazine fiction, as a rule, reinforces the concept of passive females. Similarly, Ellen Hoekstra's study, "The Pedestal Myth Reinforced: Women's Magazine Fiction, 1900-1920," demonstrates that the fiction of four early twentieth-century magazines—*Ladies' Home Journal, Good Housekeeping, Woman's Home Companion*, and the *Delineator*—describes women as wanting to remain on their so-called pedestals. Hoekstra's essay appears in *New Dimensions in Popular Culture*, edited by Russel B. Nye, which also contains Maureen Honey's "The 'Celebrity' Magazines." In this essay Honey notes that publications like *Photoplay* and *Modern Screen* make it clear to women that "the ultimate happiness comes in being a housewife" (Nye, 64). Another study that reinforces Friedan's position is Helen H. Franzwa's "Working Women in Fact and Fiction," in which Franzwa compares the government statistics on women who work outside the home to those that appear in a sample of stories taken from *Ladies' Home Journal, McCall's,* and *Good Housekeeping* during the years 1940 and 1970. In her sample Franzwa discovered that the one constant in all the stories was that of defining women in terms of men; that is, the women were portrayed in one of the following four roles: "single and looking for a husband; housewife-mother; spinster; widowed or divorced—soon to remarry" (Franzwa, 106). Notably not one married woman had a job outside the home. As Franzwa remarks, all these images of women in magazine fiction contradict reality, as in 1967, for example, 37 percent of married women held paying jobs (Franzwa, 104).

Looking at women's magazines from a slightly different angle, Phyllis Tortora, in "Fashion Magazines Mirror Changing Role of Women," concludes that magazines such as *Godey's, Peterson's,* the *Delineator, Harper's Bazaar,* and *Vogue,* have found it in their best interests to provide editorial commentary on contemporary women's issues. Although these magazines have not always taken a liberal or progressive stance, they have offered their opinions on education for women, universal suffrage, and minimum wages. As an exception to this pattern, Tortora notes, however, that fashion magazines did not acknowledge the rapid changes in women's roles that characterized the period from 1930 to 1960. Tortora explains this fact by pointing out that the questions raised by working mothers are irrelevant to the needs of the fashion industry, observing that these specialty magazines present only the "image" of the liberated woman, not her "substance" (Tortora, 23).

Kathryn Weibel takes a similar approach to women's magazines in *Mirror Mirror: Images of Women Reflected in Popular Culture* (also discussed above, in chapter one). According to Weibel in chapter four, "Images of Women in Women's Magazines and Magazine Advertising," women have been at the heart of the publishing and advertising industries because of three assumptions made about women (Weibel, 142). That is, publishers and advertisers since the nineteenth century have generally assumed, one, that women read more magazines than men; two, that women buy most of the commodities for the home; and, three, that women can be induced to buy more by a careful manipulation of their self-image (Weibel, 142). To demonstrate her thesis, Weibel recounts the history of women's magazines from *Godey's Lady's Book,* when it was edited by Sarah Josepha Hale, to *Cosmopolitan,* when it was transformed by Helen Gurley Brown. Characterizing the image of women in the majority of American magazines as ["housewifely, passive, wholesome, and pretty,"] Weibel suggests that this is a composite portrait consciously designed by publishers and advertisers to [help them sell more products to women] (Weibel, 142). In this chapter Weibel also discusses *Ms.* magazine and *Essence* in the context of the political activism of the 1960s and 1970s, suggesting that there is considerable room in the publishing industry for more magazines that directly address the serious issues of today's world.

A book that is composed almost entirely of illustrations is Jane Trahey's *Harper's Bazaar: 100 Years of the American Female;* although the book is fun to browse through, it contains no interpretive text. Instead it contains several literary selections that are intended to reveal *Harper's* unique contributions to American culture. A rather flip but informative article is Robin Reisig's "The Feminine Plastique," which is a behind-the-scenes look at *Cosmopolitan* magazine. Reisig describes *Cosmo,* as it is run by Helen Gurley Brown, as being "one of the most heavily edited magazines in any field" and as providing its readers with ["its own style of soft-core pornography"] (Reisig, 28; 27). On a more serious note, Bertha-Monica Stearns, in "Before *Godey's,*" describes most of the forgotten ladies' magazines that paved the way for *Godey's*—and by extension *Cosmopolitan.* According to Stearns, between 1784 and 1860 "at least one hundred periodicals designed for women appeared in America" (Stearns, 248). That *Godey's* lasted as long as it did and that *Cosmopolitan* continues to breeze along seem remarkable accomplishments in light of the death rate of this particular type of publication.

Although they surely have dominated our culture, the images of women found in women's magazines are not the only ones familiar to us. Those icons of women that appear in men's magazines, such as *Playboy* and *Penthouse,* are equally, if more recently, pervasive and persuasive. In fact, it is the "availability" of the Playmate of the Month that Richard A. Kallan and Robert D. Brooks believe lies at the heart of *Playboy's* success. In "The Playmate of the Month: Naked But Nice," Kallan and Brooks argue that it is the combination of availability and clean sex that "for two decades... [has] functioned to legitimize the nude centerfold" (Kallan and Brooks, 329). Lee D. Rossi seems to agree with their premise when he compares the women pictured in *Playboy* with those of two of its competitors. In "The Whore vs. The Girl-Next-Door: Stereotypes of Woman in *Playboy, Penthouse,* and *Oui,*" Rossi observes that *Penthouse* and *Oui* create "fictions" about nameless females that invite the audience to fill in their own (perverse) details. *Playboy,* on the other hand, portrays "real" women who have names, families, and personalities. All three magazines Rossi finds, not surprisingly, to be "hostile" to the women's movement (Rossi, 92).

Two books that focus on women and the mass media are Matilda Butler and William Paisley's *Women and the Mass Media: Sourcebook for Research and Action* and Gaye Tuchman, Arlene Kaplan Daniels, and James

Benet's *Hearth and Home: Images of Women in the Mass Media*. Butler and Paisley's book is a gold mine of information on sexism in television, magazines, newspapers, and advertising. In making their case that sexism is rampant in the media, the authors review all the major studies and summarize their findings. In an effort to help those who want to protest the sexism, Butler and Paisley describe how editorial decisions are made and suggest effective ways of challenging these decisions. They conclude their book with an appendix, "Additional Resources for Research and Action," that provides the names and addresses of organizations that fight sexism in media and of several prominent advertising agencies and their accounts.

Hearth and Home is an anthology of essays on women in magazines and television. (For a discussion of those essays on television, see below, in chapter five). In her introductory essay, "The Symbolic Annihilation of Women by the Mass Media," Gaye Tuchman argues that mass media both reflect and transmit the major values of our society. Summarizing the assumptions of women's magazines, she remarks that they "continue to assume that every woman will marry, bear children and 'make a home'" (Tuchman et al., 24; for further discussion of her essay as it pertains to television per se, see below, in chapter five). Three essays follow that specifically address the image of women in magazines. Marjorie Ferguson, in "Imagery and Ideology: The Cover Photographs of Traditional Women's Magazines," reports on her in-depth study of the three largest British women's magazines. E. Barbara Phillips compares the portrayal of women in "Magazine Heroines: Is *Ms.* Just Another Member of the *Family Circle*?" Her conclusion is that it is not, that there are significant differences between the magazines in terms of what women they focus on. In her study Phillips herself focuses on the occupation of the women featured in these magazines. Not surprisingly she discovers that *Family Circle* features women who are housewives and *Ms.* those who aren't; in other words, *Family Circle* caters to traditional domestic values and *Ms.* to the more recently expressed feminist values. She observes further, however, that the *Ms.* heroine, whom she describes as "the New Woman for the New Order," may be more liberal than her *Family Circle* counterpart but she is not liberated (Tuchman et al., 128). Phillips asserts this on the basis that *Ms.* seems to lock women into the reactionary bind that somehow there is such a thing as a sex-specific "feminine consciousness" (Tuchman et al., 128). Carol Lopate's "Jackie!" outlines how various kinds of magazines portray Jackie Kennedy Onassis and what these differences suggest about the women who read these magazines. For example, mainstream magazines like *Ladies' Home Journal* focused on Jackie's wealth; *Family Circle*, which Lopate identifies as working class, focused on Jackie as wife and mother; the gossip magazines focused on sex and sin, even if it meant misleading their readers and manipulating the facts. The political effect of all this differentiation is, according to

Lopate, to affirm the status quo. Jackie is all things to all readers; thus a magazine's readers can identify with her as she is and—more importantly—without changing themselves.

In 1980, the *Journal of American Culture* ran an issue on magazines, edited by Dorey Schmidt. Among the essays included are three of particular interest to women and popular culture. Maureen Honey's "Recruiting Women for War Work: OWI and the Magazine Industry During World War II" describes the efforts of the Magazine Bureau of the Office of War Information to provide appropriate government propaganda for magazine readers. Founded in June, 1942, the bureau "coordinated government publicity needs with information disseminated by magazines and proposed themes for articles, fiction and editorials which were designed to create favorable attitudes toward government programs" (Honey, 49). Among the most important of its activities were those involved with increasing the number of women in the work force, activities that, according to Honey, took up most of the bureau's time between 1943 and 1944. Once women were no longer needed in the factories, the bureau's publication, the *Magazine War Guide*, asked publishers to concentrate on the problems in the homes—problems that women, by implication, would have to quit their jobs in order to solve. In short, Honey demonstrates that the OWI formally approved the use of popular culture as government propaganda. In a lighter vein, Donna Rose Casella Kern outlines nineteenth-century formula magazine fiction in "Sentimental Short Fiction by Women Writers in *Leslie's Popular Monthly.*" Dividing her discussion into two time periods, 1876-1885 and 1885-1900, Kern finds the first period dominated by formulaic sentimental fiction and the second increasingly concerned with adventure fiction. In the first category, women are portrayed as dependent creatures who belong at home; they are usually strongly attached to their fathers and their mothers are usually dead. In the second category, which came on the scene as women were taking jobs outside the home, the heroine is more independent and strong-willed and not always obsessed—as her earlier counterpart had been—with romantic love. In short, as the audience changed, so did the fiction. The third essay is Lynne Masel-Walters's "To Hustle with the Rowdies: The Organization and Functions of the American Woman Suffrage Press." In this study of the suffrage press, which spans the late nineteenth and early twentieth century, Masel-Walters is less concerned with the journals' contents than with their mode of operation. The major difference that she perceives between the journals of the first and the second wave of suffrage organizations is that the first were run by amateurs who were always short of operating funds and the second by more experienced professional journalists who frequently were also women of means. Masel-Walters details the fates of such journals as Elizabeth Cady Stanton and Susan B. Anthony's *The Revolution*, which was briefly underwritten by the eccentric George Francis Train; the more durable *Woman's Journal* which in 1917 was renamed the *Woman Citizen*, when it was bought by the National American Woman Suffrage Association; and the *New Northwest*, which was run by Abigail Scott Duniway. Observing that these suffrage publications focused exclusively on women's interests—white, middle-class women's interests—she remarks that it is not surprising that among the subscribers were very few men, minorities, or working-class women. Nor, given their topical interest and the ultimate success of their mission, is it surprising that most of these suffrage journals died for lack of interest after 1920.

Reference books in the area of women's magazines include the following resources. The *Standard Periodical Directory* indexes women's periodicals under the headings "Women's Liberation" and "Women's Fashions." *Ulrich's International Periodicals Directory* indexes a "Women's Interests" section, which in the 1979-1980 edition runs for nearly ten pages. Especially helpful in an uncertain field where publications come and go at an alarming rate is *Ulrich's* section on cessations, as it gives the publishing history of defunct periodicals. The Library of Congress's *New Serial Titles* is useful for tracking down libraries that have holdings of some of the more obscure—and short-lived—journals in women's studies. Virginia R. Terris's mammoth bibliography, *Woman in America: A Guide to Information Sources*, contains an appendix that gives the names and addresses of women's periodicals. (Also, see below, appendix one for a similar list.) Susan Cardinale's *Special Issues of Serials About Women, 1965-1975* is an annotated listing, arranged alphabetically by serial title, of special issues of periodicals that are not published primarily for women. (Also, see below, appendix two for another list of special issues.) Lenwood G. Davis, in *The Black Woman in American Society: A Selected Annotated Bibliography*, includes a directory of "Selected Current Black Periodicals." Janet L. Sims's *The Progress of Afro-American Women: A Selected Bibliography and Resource Guide* includes citations for magazines and special periodical issues that relate to black women.

BIBLIOGRAPHY

Butler, Matilda, and William Paisley, eds. *Women and the Mass Media: Sourcebook for Research and Action.* New York: Human Sciences Press, 1979.

Cardinale, Susan. *Special Issues of Serials About Women, 1965-1975.* Monticello, Ill.: Council of Planning Librarians, 1976.

Chafe, William Henry. *The American Woman: Her Changing Social, Economic, and Political Roles, 1920-1970.* New York: Oxford University Press, 1972.

Davis, Lenwood G. *The Black Woman in American Society: A Selected Annotated Bibliography.* Boston: G. K. Hall & Co., 1975.

Douglas, Ann. *The Feminization of American Culture.* New York: Alfred A. Knopf, 1977.

Entrikin, Isabelle Webb. *Sarah Josepha Hale and Godey's Lady's Book.* Lancaster, Pa.: Lancaster Press, 1946.

Ferguson, Marjorie. "Imagery and Ideology: The Cover Photographs of Traditional Women's Magazines." In *Hearth and Home: Images of Women in the Mass Media,* edited by Gaye Tuchman, Arlene Kaplan Daniels, and James Benet, pp. 97-115. New York: Oxford University Press, 1978.

Finley, Ruth E. *The Lady of Godey's: Sarah Josepha Hale.* Philadelphia: J. B. Lippincott Co., 1931.

Flora, Cornelia Butler. "The Passive Female: Her Comparative Image by Class and Culture in Women's Magazine Fiction." *Journal of Marriage and the Family* 33, no. 3 (August 1971): 435-44.

Franzwa, Helen H. "Working Women in Fact and Fiction." *Journal of Communication* 24, no. 2 (Spring 1974): 104-9.

Friedan, Betty. *The Feminine Mystique.* New York: W. W. Norton & Co., 1963.

Hoekstra, Ellen. "The Pedestal Myth Reinforced: Women's Magazine Fiction, 1900-1920." In *New Dimensions in Popular Culture,* edited by Russel B. Nye, pp. 45-58. Bowling Green, Ohio: Bowling Green University Popular Press, 1972.

Honey, Maureen. "The 'Celebrity' Magazines." In *New Dimensions in Popular Culture,* edited by Russel B. Nye, pp. 59-77. Bowling Green, Ohio: Bowling Green University Popular Press, 1972.

———. "Recruiting Women for War Work: OWI and the Magazine Industry During World War II." *Journal of American Culture* 3, no. 1 (Spring 1980): 47-52.

Kallan, Richard A., and Robert D. Brooks. "The Playmate of the Month: Naked But Nice." *Journal of Popular Culture* 8, no. 2 (Fall 1974): 328-36.

Kern, Donna Rose Casella. "Sentimental Short Fiction by Women Writers in *Leslie's Popular Monthly*." *Journal of American Culture* 3, no. 1 (Spring 1980): 113-27.

Library of Congress. *New Serial Titles, 1976-1979.* 2 vols. Washington, D.C.: Library of Congress, 1980.

Lopate, Carol. "Jackie!" In *Hearth and Home: Images of Women in the Mass Media,* edited by Gaye Tuchman, Arlene Kaplan Daniels, and James Benet, pp. 130-40. New York: Oxford University Press, 1978.

Masel-Walters, Lynne. "To Hustle With the Rowdies: The Organization and Functions of the American Woman Suffrage Press." *Journal of American Culture* 3, no. 1 (Spring 1980): 167-83.

Mott, Frank Luther. *A History of American Magazines, 1741-1930.* 5 vols. 1938-1939. Reprint. Cambridge, Mass.: Harvard University Press, Belknap Press, 1966.

Nye, Russel B., ed. *New Dimensions in Popular Culture.* Bowling Green, Ohio: Bowling Green University Popular Press, 1972.

Peterson, Theodore. *Magazines in the Twentieth Century.* 2d ed. Urbana: University of Illinois Press, 1964.

Phillips, E. Barbara. "Magazine Heroines: Is *Ms.* Just Another Member of the *Family Circle?*" In *Hearth and Home: Images of Women in the Mass Media,* edited by Gaye Tuchman, Arlene Kaplan Daniels, and James Benet, pp. 116-29. New York: Oxford University Press, 1978.

Reisig, Robin. "The Feminine Plastique." *Ramparts,* March 1973, pp. 25-29, 53-55.

Ricciotti, Dominic. "Popular Art in *Godey's Lady's Book:* An Image of the American Woman, 1830-1860." *History of New Hampshire* 27, no. 1 (1972): 3-26.

Rossi, Lee D. "The Whore vs. The Girl-Next-Door: Stereotypes of Woman in *Playboy, Penthouse,* and *Oui*." *Journal of Popular Culture* 9, no. 1 (Summer 1975): 90-94.

Sims, Janet L., comp. *The Progress of Afro-American Women: A Selected Bibliography and Resource Guide.* Westport, Conn.: Greenwood Press, 1980.

Stage, Sarah. *Female Complaints: Lydia Pinkham and the Business of Women's Medicine.* New York: W. W. Norton & Co., 1979.

Standard Periodical Directory. 5th ed. New York: Oxbridge Communications, 1977.

Stearns, Bertha-Monica. "Before *Godey's.*" *American Literature* 2 (1930): 248-55.

Terris, Virginia R. *Woman in America: A Guide to Information Sources.* American Studies Information Guide Series, vol. 7. Detroit: Gale Research Co., 1980.

Tortora, Phyllis. "Fashion Magazines Mirror Changing Role of Women." *Journal of Home Economics* 65, no. 3 (March 1973): 19-23.

Trahey, Jane, ed. *Harper's Bazaar: 100 Years of the American Female.* New York: Random House, 1967.

Tuchman, Gaye. "Introduction: The Symbolic Annihilation of Women by the Mass Media." In *Hearth and Home: Images of Women in the Mass Media*, edited by Gaye Tuchman, Arlene Kaplan Daniels, and James Benet, pp. 3-38. New York: Oxford University Press, 1978.

_____, Arlene Kaplan Daniels, and James Benet, eds. *Hearth and Home: Images of Women in the Mass Media.* New York: Oxford University Press, 1978.

Ulrich's International Periodicals Directory, 1979-1980. 18th ed. New York: R. R. Bowker Co., 1979.

Weibel, Kathryn. *Mirror Mirror: Images of Women Reflected in Popular Culture.* Garden City, N.Y.: Doubleday Anchor Press, 1977.

White, Cynthia L. *Women's Magazines, 1693-1968.* London: Michael Joseph, 1970.

Wood, James Playsted. *Magazines in the United States.* 3d. ed. New York: Ronald Press Co., 1971.

Woodward, Helen. *The Lady Persuaders.* New York: Ivan Obolensky, 1960.

CHAPTER *4*

Women in Film

Because women in film have a visual impact on their audiences, it is not surprising that most of the early criticism that has been done on the subject has focused on the image of women in film. Other approaches have been to discuss the roles of women in film as sociopolitical events that project the culture's paternalistic or misogynistic attitudes. Still other approaches are to treat movies as part of our social mythology and women in film as iconographic statements about this mythology. The works discussed below represent all of these approaches in one way or another. Although women in film is no longer the neglected subject it once was, there is still much to be written about and much to be discovered. One area of serious neglect remains the subject of black women in film. To date, there are only two comprehensive studies of women in film; there are no comprehensive studies of black women in film.

The two most comprehensive studies of women and film are those by Marjorie Rosen and Molly Haskell. Although both scholars cover much of the same material in their historical analyses, their approaches are considerably different. Rosen's approach in *Popcorn Venus: Women, Movies and the American Dream* is a sociopolitical one that interprets film in the context of social and political changes. Haskell's approach in *From Reverence to Rape: The Treatment of Women in the Movies* is to analyze individual films and trends in the context of the history of the film industry itself. The difference is significant. Rosen attempts to show how the movies reflect — or deflect — historical reality. Haskell, on the other hand, is less concerned about the relationship of art to life and more concerned about the art itself.

In *Popcorn Venus*, Rosen works from the premise that, from the beginning, there has been a paradoxical cause-and-effect relationship between film and society. On the one hand, she believes that the movies have hastened women's liberation by changing the way women see the world. On the other, she finds at the heart of the film industry an unspoken but very real male conspiracy to use movies to keep women in their place.

Working from this double-edged premise, Rosen tries to show how specific films "fit" the time period in which they were made. Her text, therefore, is largely a social history in and of itself, as she describes the social and political developments that have affected women in the past half century. Although Rosen places individual films in their historical context, she does not have an unbiased view of American history. Her point of view is clearly feminist, and as a feminist she is clearly critical of much of what the film industry has produced. Because of this situation, there is throughout her text the possibility—at least—that what she is saying about films is more a reflection of her own philosophy than that of the filmmakers themselves. It is a difficult issue to resolve satisfactorily and one that certainly is paralleled, for example, in the conflicting interpretations that feminist historians bring to the subject of nineteenth-century medicine. But whatever its interpretive weaknesses, *Popcorn Venus* is a detailed and fascinating account of the changing roles of women in society and their changing images in film.

An example of the way she interprets the history of film occurs in her treatment of Mary Pickford. Pickford, from Rosen's perspective, is the perfect example of the Victorian woman; that is to say, she exemplifies the nineteenth-century attitude that the ideal woman is pure, innocent, and childlike. But if Pickford pleased—and reassured—her Victorian audience, as she most certainly did, she neither pleases nor reassures Rosen. Rosen, from the distance of half a century, calls her a "freak who denied—in fact, made repugnant—all that was inevitable about womanhood" (Rosen, 42).

Molly Haskell's *From Reverence to Rape: The Treatment of Women in the Movies* examines the paradoxes inherent in the fact that the film industry has been dominated by women but controlled by men. That is, the majority of the big stars—at least until the last decade or so—have been women, but the directors and producers have been, with few exceptions, men. In describing the central place of women in film, Haskell argues that the "conception of woman as idol, art object, and visual entity is, after all, the first principle of the aesthetic of film as a visual medium" (Haskell, 7). In other words, the cinematic image of woman is comparable to that of an icon, representing values not her own but those of her male directors and producers. Or, as Haskell puts it, "women, by the logistics of film production and the laws of Western society, generally emerge as the projections of male values" (Haskell, 39).

In her introductory chapter, "The Big Lie," Haskell describes some of the problems that emanate from the fact that our culture has accepted the myth of woman's inferiority. Like Rosen, Haskell believes that the film industry has been instrumental in "reinforcing the lie" (Haskell, 2). The irony is that while women have been portrayed as being inferior and rightly subordinate to men, the female stars themselves have enjoyed extraordinary success, power, and influence. Even though women have been central to the film industry since its inception, they have received little serious critical attention. Haskell warns those critics who hope to correct this situation that, even though women have much to protest in their cinematic portrayals, they should be wary of "grafting a modern sensibility onto the past" (Haskell, 30). In making this statement, Haskell almost seems to be addressing Marjorie Rosen who, as I have suggested already, does impose her feminist perspective on the history of American film. Because Haskell for the most part heeds her own warning, her book is less of an attack on earlier films and filmmakers and more of an interpretive history of the genre.

Of the tendency of the films of the 1920s to utilize types, for example, Haskell reminds us that both the vamp and the virgin, while certainly recognizable as types, were portrayed differently within each type. Every actress who played the vamp brought her own special signature to the type; just as did everyone who played the virgin. And if films seemed to typify women more than men, Haskell remarks, it is because women were "more central to the myths of the period" (Haskell, 49). What Haskell implies by this observation is that we can be critical of the Victorian period itself for stereotyping women, but we shouldn't pick out a single form of mass culture and blame it for its contributions to the myth. D. W. Griffith's child heroines Haskell discusses in the context of the Victorian ideal, adding that the "urge to return to childhood, to recover an innocence both historical and personal," is entrenched in the American psyche (Haskell, 61). She sees these young women, moreover, as being relatively complex; of all Griffith's heroines, Haskell describes Lillian Gish as being the "most emotionally resourceful and intense" (Haskell, 56).

In her account of the films of the 1930s Haskell spends considerable time describing how the enactment of the Production Code affected the portrayal of women on screen. On the one hand, she considers the Production Code to have been particularly detrimental to women's sexuality. That is, before the code women were permitted sexual desires as natural expressions of their humanity. After the code, which was above all things anti-sex in its intentions, those women who were sexual were portrayed as somehow unnatural or monstrous. On the other hand, the Production Code facilitated the development of new women's roles on screen. If women couldn't be sex goddesses anymore, they had to be something; the solution, according to Haskell, was to make them working women. Thus the Production Code, which denied women expression of their sexuality, did in the long run help to liberate them.

In trying to characterize pre- and post-Production Code films, Haskell compares the personae of stars like Marlene Dietrich, Jean Harlow, and Mae West with that of Shirley Temple. Of the three sex goddesses Haskell remarks that they are hedonists who are committed to the idea of sensuality (Haskell, 109). Harlow she describes as lascivious, Dietrich and West as androgynous. Her description of West is particularly astute as she suggests that West was "a hypothetical, sexually aggressive woman; and woman as sex object turned subject" (Haskell, 115). Although sex to Mae West was more verbal than actual or physical, she is still regarded by many as being a major reason for the implementation of the Production Code, an event that spelled her ruin as a star. She and the other sex goddesses of the early 1930s were replaced by what Haskell calls "deviates in disguise" (Haskell, 123). The prime example of the "virgin worship" is, according to Haskell, none other than Shirley Temple (Haskell, 123).

Haskell devotes an entire chapter to the woman's film and remarks as she does so that it is a "damning comment" on American society that there even is such a genre as *woman's* film (Haskell, 153). Between the woman's films of the 1930s and 1940s Haskell sees a considerable difference. The heroines of the 1930s woman's films Haskell describes as "spunkier and more stoical" than those of the 1940s (Haskell, 172). The heroines of the 1940s fluctuated between those who were self-denying and passive and those who were brittle and aggressive (Haskell, 172).

With the advent of the 1940s Haskell sees the signs that indicated that women were about to be replaced by men on screen. The perfect equilibrium that Haskell sees in the films of the 1930s by the 1940s begins to waver. She attributes this new imbalance to the social changes brought by the war, not the least of which was the entry of women into the work force. In her opinion, in the films of the 1940s there was a certain " 'disease' and even impotence that lurked beneath the surface of male characters" that cannot be "entirely accounted for by plot" (Haskell, 194). In the context of these films of the 1940s, Haskell discusses two types of extraordinary women that emerged with sudden clarity at this time. One she calls the superfemale, the woman who is exceedingly feminine but unhappy with her situation; unwilling to give up her advantages as a woman, she turns her excess energies on the people around her—with dire consequences for them and often herself. The other she calls the superwoman, the woman who arrogates unto herself male qualities. Those who fit these two categories Haskell identifies as Vivien Leigh as Scarlett O'Hara for the first and Joan Crawford for the second. Those who underwent a transformation from superfemale to superwoman Haskell identifies as Bette Davis and Rosalind Russell.

Of the 1950s films, Haskell observes that they were, by and large, disguises for the rebellion that was fermenting within society itself (on this subject, see also Brandon French's *On the Verge of Revolt,* discussed below). It is at this time in the history of film that Haskell sees the metaphor of woman as actress solidified. What had been a healthy concept of role playing became in this period so feminized that it carried primarily negative implications. Perhaps the quintessential example of this role-playing woman was Marilyn Monroe, a woman whom Haskell claims it is almost impossible to judge because of the fact of her suicide. Marilyn Monroe was so important to the 1950s that Haskell suggests that "if she hadn't existed we would have had to invent her, and we did, in a way" (Haskell, 255). She exemplifies to Haskell the 1950s' insistence that women existed only for the gratification of male needs.

But even if Marilyn Monroe was a distortion of womanhood, she at least appeared on the screen, a presence that Haskell finds sorely lacking in the films of the 1960s and early 1970s. In this decade Haskell sees a steady deterioration of the role of women on screen, until eventually, in some films, women disappear altogether. Haskell concludes her book with a lament for the women of the past who, even if they weren't perfect, did relate to one another and to men and who, as of 1973, seem to her to have been replaced entirely by men. (See also, Kathryn Weibel's *Mirror Mirror: Images of Women Reflected in Popular Culture*, discussed above, in chapter one.)

Two other books that were published the same year as Rosen's and Haskell's are Joan Mellen's *Women and Their Sexuality in the New Film* and Marsha McCreadie's *The American Movie Goddess*. Mellen's book is a collection of essays on American and Continental films. Half of her chapters are devoted to filmmakers. As a historian of film, Mellen is at her best when she discusses trends and looks for sociological or psychological explanations, as she does in her chapters on the bourgeois woman, female sexuality, and lesbianism in film. Of contemporary cinema, she remarks that "one searches in vain...for a new perception of women which assumes their capacities and value" (Mellen, 15). In contrast, she writes that the films of the 1940s "produced films about autonomous women" (Mellen, 17). In these women's films, actresses like Katharine Hepburn, Joan Crawford, and Bette Davis "portrayed career women in open struggle to assert the right to such aspirations and they showed boundless energy in achieving them" (Mellen, 17). Mellen also includes a chapter entitled "The Mae West Nobody Knows," in which she offers, albeit somewhat uneasily, a feminist interpretation of West's life and films. Marsha McCreadie's *The American Movie Goddess* is an anthology of essays and brief quotations that is intended to be used as a sourcebook for an introductory college writing course.

A more scholarly work is Karyn Kay and Gerald Peary's *Women and the Cinema: A Critical Anthology*. These essays, some of which are reprints and some originals, fall under no critical umbrella. They range from feminist perspectives and theory to interviews with women in film production. The book is divided into seven sections, each with its own bibliography. Part one, "Feminist Perspectives," features an interpretive essay on the life and work of Dorothy Arzner. In "Dorothy Arzner's *Dance, Girl, Dance*," Karyn Kay and Gerald Peary describe Arzner as a director who "documented the lives of women at all phases of consciousness, wrestling for

love, career, independence, integrity" (Kay and Peary, 10). Another essay in this section is Diane Giddis's "The Divided Woman: Bree Daniels
in *Klute,*" in which Giddis describes Fonda-as-Bree as managing to express "one of the greatest of contemporary female concerns: the conflict
between the claims of love and the claims of autonomy" (Kay and Peary,
27). Arguing that Bree's conflict goes deeper than the one between her
good and bad self, Giddis builds a convincing case by demonstrating that
the more she becomes emotionally involved with Klute, the more vulner-
able and less self-sufficient she becomes. Janet Maslin, in "Hollywood
Heroines under the Influence: Alice Still Lives Here," investigates the subtext of *Alice Doesn't Live Here Anymore* and *A Woman under the Influence.* Although she is impressed by both movies, she regards neither
as making feminist statements. The films fail to provide a truly feminist
perspective, in her opinion, because "neither Alice nor Mabel is quite
responsible for her own behavior" (Kay and Peary, 44). Jeanine Basinger, in
search of what she calls "positive portraits" of women, turns to movies
of the 1940s for "Ten That Got Away" (Kay and Peary, 61). What she is
looking for are examples of women who take control of their own lives,
women who make it in the "man's" world, and women who have positive
relationships with other women. Among the films she describes as featur-
ing these kinds of women are the mid-to-late-1940s films: *National Velvet,* starring Elizabeth Taylor; *The Shocking Miss Pilgrim,* starring Betty
Grable; *Beyond the Forest,* starring Bette Davis; and *Roughly Speaking,*
starring Rosalind Russell.

Part two of Kay and Peary's anthology contains autobiographical statements from Louise Brooks and Greta Garbo, a brief portrait of Mae West by
Stark Young, and one of Marlene Dietrich by Alexander Walker. It also
contains an essay by Janice Welsch, entitled "Actress Archetypes in the
1950s: Doris Day, Marilyn Monroe, Elizabeth Taylor, Audrey Hepburn,"
in which she identifies Day as the archetypal sister, Monroe as the archetypal mistress, Taylor as the archetypal mother, and Hepburn as the archetypal daughter. What application these archetypes have to a study of
film is not entirely clear; nor is the emphasis on the 1950s in Welsch's
title clear, as she does not limit her discussion to films made in this decade. Part two concludes with a selection from Simone de Beauvoir's book
on Brigitte Bardot and an essay by Molly Haskell on Liv Ullmann.

Part three, "Women in American Production," and part four, "Experi-
mentalists and Independents," focus on Alice Guy Blache, Lois Weber,
Dorothy Arzner, Ida Lupino, Stephanie Rothman, Germaine Dulac, Joyce
Wieland, among others. Part five, "Women and Political Films," features a
study of women in films that were produced at Warners in the 1930s, an
interview with Jane Fonda and one with Lina Wertmuller. Part six is a collection of "Polemics" that covers, among other topics, the work of Howard
Hawks and Lina Wertmuller.

Part seven, "Feminist Film Theory," contains an excerpt from Claire Johnston's "Women's Cinema as Countercinema," in which she examines the question of female stereotyping in the context of mythological theories. In this essay, which here is entitled "Myths of Women in the Cinema," Johnston contends that myth, "as a form of speech or discourse, represents the major means in which women have been used in the cinema: myth transmits and transforms the ideology of sexism and makes it invisible…and therefore natural" (Kay and Peary, 409). The implication of this premise is that iconography can be turned against itself; that is, the mythic content of stereotypes "can be used as a shorthand for referring to an ideological tradition in order to provide a critique of it" (Kay and Peary, 409). Taking issue with other feminist critics, Johnston does not believe that Mae West subverted sexual mythology, arguing instead that her persona is "entirely consistent with sexist ideology" (Kay and Peary, 411). Laura Mulvey approaches the notion of iconography from a different perspective in "Visual Pleasure and Narrative Cinema." In this fascinating essay, Mulvey examines film from a psychoanalytical point of view, using Freud's theories of sexuality as her reference. In order to explain the pleasure that the audience experiences when watching traditional narrative cinema, she uses two contradictory notions: the pleasures of voyeurism, or scopophilia, and the pleasures of narcissism, or identification with the object being viewed. What she argues is that the men in the audience identify with the hero who regards the heroine as a sexual object; the male viewers, therefore, enjoy both a narcissistic experience in seeing "themselves" projected on screen and a scopophiliac experience in seeing women on screen. Women in the audience, on the other hand, are caught between the awkward prospect of trying to identify with the male hero and the self-destructive prospect of identifying with the female sex object. Mulvey makes additional observations in this highly recommended essay, but suffice it to say that she concludes that women, who have played the passive role to men's active role on and off screen, "cannot view the decline of the traditional film form with anything much more than sentimental regret" (Kay and Peary, 428).

In addition to its many excellent essays, *Women and the Cinema* contains a list of selected filmographies of the women directors cited in the text and a general bibliography.

Two books that focus on films from particular eras are those by Sumiko Higashi and Brandon French. In *Virgins, Vamps, and Flappers: The American Silent Movie Heroine,* Higashi describes, in considerable detail, the characterization of women in early American films. Because she was able to view nearly all of the films she discusses (a filmography follows the text), her book is a valuable record of this period. Like Marjorie Rosen, Higashi also discusses the images of women in the context of the social values of the time, taking as her premise "that a society's feminine ideal is related in complex ways to its moral climate and values" (Higashi, iii).

Her book, which is liberally illustrated with scenes from the movies she discusses, includes separate chapters on Lillian Gish and Mary Pickford— whom she characterizes, along with Theda Bara, as the "silent screen actresses who best represented the Victorian tradition" (Higashi, 169). Other chapters focus on the vampire, the sentimental heroine and the fallen woman, the working girl, the "new woman," sex and marriage in film, and what she calls the "uncharacteristic heroine"—those who don't fit the pattern of Jazz Age films. Higashi provides a comprehensive bibliography that includes books, articles, and collections; in writing this book, she interviewed several women in the field, including Lillian Gish and Lois Wilson. (For another look at this period in film, see Mary P. Ryan's "The Projection of a New Womanhood: The Movie Moderns in the 1920s" in *Our American Sisters: Women in American Life and Thought,* discussed above, in chapter one.)

Brandon French's *On the Verge of Revolt: Women in American Films of the Fifties* analyzes the "double text" of thirteen films that illustrate what French calls the "culture's schizoid 'double-think' " of the 1950s (French, xxi). That is, French claims that these films, while appearing to promote the concept of "women's domesticity and inequality," also illustrate the "malaise of domesticity and the untenably narrow boundaries of the female role" (French, xxi). French's approach to these films, which include *Shane* (1953), *Picnic* (1956), and *Some Like It Hot* (1959), is similar to the approaches taken by Helen Papashvily (*All the Happy Endings*) and Nina Baym (*Woman's Fiction*) to the fiction of the 1850s (for discussion of Papashvily's and Baym's books, see above, in chapter two). In other words, French regards these films as expressive of the cultural mythology of the 1950s and, in many instances, expressive of women's dissatisfaction with this mythology. In her attacks on the source of the "domestic female image" of the 1940s and 1950s, French sounds like Betty Friedan in *The Feminine Mystique* (French, xvii; for a discussion of Friedan's book, see chapters three and seven). For example, French attributes the resurgence of this image to the efforts of "certain sociologists, psychologists, anthropologists, educators, authors, and physicians, as well as the organs of mass media, which preached the dangers of women's lost femininity and the bounties which awaited women within the boundaries of the traditional female role" (French, xvii–xviii). Lurking beneath the dominant images of domestic tranquility, according to French, lay the ever-present possibility of open rebellion on the part of disenchanted women. It is this tension between illusion and reality that French believes the movies of the 1950s capture "with a surprising degree of fidelity" (French, xxi). To discuss the differences among the films, she divides them into three categories: those between 1950 and 1952 showed women who were in transition between accepting their domesticity and asserting their equality; those between 1953 and 1956 portrayed women who were unhappy because they were starved for sex; and those between 1957 and 1959 camouflaged their radical message of antidomesticity in a nun's habit (French, xxii). French's book includes a selected bibliography, a directory of distributors and other film rental information; it is also illustrated.

In *Sex in the Movies: The Celluloid Sacrifice,* Alexander Walker compares the on-screen images of movie stars with their off-screen experiences. In doing this, Walker provides brief biographies of most of the major American sex goddesses from Theda Bara to Elizabeth Taylor. He has made his selection from those stars "whose careers and lives off screen formed their characters in a way that assisted the peculiar kind of sex appeal associated with them on the screen" (Walker, 12-13). Of Theda Bara, who was transformed from Theodosia Goodman into a sex goddess by William Fox, Walker claims that she was the "first star to have a screen personality specially fabricated for her" (Walker, 23). To Mae West, however, he gives full credit for being entirely "self-made and self-sustaining" (Walker, 79). The downfall of Harlow and Monroe he suggests was caused by their desire to become legitimate actors in a "system that is geared to [their] glorification" (Walker, 121). Among the other women that Walker discusses are Clara Bow, Mary Pickford, Marlene Dietrich, and Greta Garbo. Of particular interest is his essay on the rise and fall of censorship in American films, an essay in which he explores the relationship between the Production Code and the Catholic Legion of Decency—and their collaborative efforts to destroy the professional career of Mae West. One weakness in this book is that Walker, who must have read Philip Wylie's *Generation of Vipers* (see the introduction, above), is convinced that the United States is a matriarchy inherently destructive of its men. To prove that the American male has been castrated by Doris Day of all people, Walker quotes from various comedies of the 1960s in an essay entitled "The Last American Massacre." Although this certainly sounds like unabashed misogyny, the rest of the book is more rational.

In *Sex Psyche Etcetera in the Film,* Parker Tyler offers a rather glib assessment of the careers of famous actresses in his essay "The Awful Fate of the Sex Goddess." Although he strives for ironic disapproval of their treatment, his own approach seems to be antiwoman and is, ultimately, superficial. In eight pages, for example, he covers the history of no fewer than fifteen women in film, observing that they were "lovely hoaxes foisted upon a naive, gullible and dated public of both sexes: the gaga identifiers (female) and the gasping adorers (male)" (Tyler, 22). An anthology of more thoughtful essays on the subject is *Sexuality in the Movies,* edited by Thomas R. Atkins. Part one, "Social and Cultural Perspective," offers essays on cinematic sexuality, American film censorship, the current rating system, and morality and the movies. Part two, "Categories and Genres," contains essays on monster movies and sex, homosexuality, and the genre sex film. Part three, "Contemporary Landmarks," features interpretations of six different films: *I Am Curious Yellow, Midnight Cowboy, Carnal Knowledge, Deep Throat, Last Tango in Paris,* and *Cries and Whispers.* The book is liberally illustrated.

Martha Wolfenstein and Nathan Leites's well-known essay, "The Good-Bad Girl," appears in their *Movies: A Psychological Study.* The phenomenon of the good-bad girl in American film, the authors believe, results from the tension of having to choose between the polar opposites of the sexy bad woman and the affectionate good woman. Instead of choosing, many filmmakers try to incorporate both stereotypes into the good-bad girl. The examples Wolfenstein and Leites base their discussion on include *Gilda, Till the End of Time, The Big Sleep,* and *The Strange Love of Martha Jones.* (This essay is reprinted in Bernard Rosenberg and David Manning White's *Mass Culture: The Popular Arts in America.*) Another critic who identifies sexual stereotyping in film is Howard Haymes. In "Movies in the 1950s: Sexism from A to Zapata," Haymes finds cinematic examples of female stereotyping that correspond to those literary stereotypes identified by Simone de Beauvoir in *The Second Sex.* Although Haymes does nothing with this list, his idea has possibilities.

Lewis Jacobs's *The Rise of the American Film: A Critical History,* although it contains no specific topics on women in film, is useful as a general guide to the history of film. The most relevant chapter to a study of women is perhaps his discussion of the "Growing Sophistication of Film Content: The Vamp, Satire, Romance." Jacobs does tend to slight women directors; his reference to Dorothy Arzner, for example, is to say that she was a cutter "who worked on *The Covered Wagon*" (Jacobs, 330). He gives more credit to Anita Loos and June Mathis. Of Loos he claims she "did much to broaden the range of screen subjects and refine the tone of movies" in her capacity as screenwriter (Jacobs, 219). He calls June Mathis "one of the most important scenarists in motion pictures" during the 1920s and "the most esteemed scenarist in Hollywood" (Jacobs, 328; 349). Jacobs's book is illustrated and contains a bibliography of books, articles, documents, periodicals, and film catalogues.

To date, almost nothing has been written about the role of nonwhite women in films. Although recent histories of blacks in films and filmmaking have included some discussion of black women, most focus on the contributions of black men in the field. Lindsay Patterson's *Black Films and Film-makers: A Comprehensive Anthology from Stereotype to Superhero* does include an essay by Edward Mapp entitled "Black Women in Films: A Mixed Bag of Tricks," in which Mapp discusses the degrading roles that black women have played in film since the inception of the medium. The stereotypes that Mapp identifies are the same as those identified by Barbara Christian in her historical introduction to *Black Women Novelists* (discussed above, in chapter two); that is, in fifty years of film, Mapp finds that black women have been limited to only a handful of parts, characterized primarily by the mammy, the tragic mulatta, and the maid. Another study of stereotypes is Donald Bogle's *Toms, Coons, Mulattoes, Mammies, and Bucks: An Interpretive History of Blacks in American Film.* Bogle identifies Nina Mae McKinney as having played the "movies' first black whore" in *Hallelujah* (1929) (Bogle, 31). Contending that the 1930s were notable for the presence of black servants on screen, Bogle offers the examples of Louise Beavers in *She Done Him Wrong* (1933) and Bill "Bojangles" Robinson in *The Littlest Rebel* (1935). Other famous black artists that Bogle discusses include Hattie McDaniel, who won an academy award for her role of mammy in *Gone With the Wind,* Hazel Scott, Lena Horne, Ethel Waters, Dorothy Dandridge, Diahann Carroll, Beah Richards, Diana Ross, and Cicely Tyson.

In April 1973, the Afro-American Studies and American Studies departments of Boston University sponsored a symposium on *Black Images in Films, Stereotyping, and Self-Perception as Viewed by Black Actresses* (appearing in print as Occasional Paper number two). The most valuable part of the text of this symposium, as far as a study of black women in film is concerned, is the panel discussion, "Focus on the Actress as a Person and a Profession," in which Susan Batson, Cynthia Belgrave, Ruby Dee, Beah Richards, and Cicely Tyson participated. Following their discussion of the problems faced by black actresses is a question and answer section in which Batson, Belgrave, and Richards offer their solutions for combating racism in film.

Peter Noble's *The Negro in Films* is a general history of blacks in film, with brief biographies of major black actresses, such as Lena Horne, Ethel Waters, Louise Beavers, and Hattie McDaniel. Nobel's book is illustrated and contains an appendix that lists the films from 1902 through 1948 that feature blacks or focus on racial themes. James P. Murray's *To Find an Image: Black Films from Uncle Tom to Super Fly* provides another concise history of blacks in film; Murray also discusses the more contemporary black actresses such as Diahann Carroll, Dionne Warwick, Diana Ross, and Judy Pace. Murray includes an appendix that lists black films by year from 1970 to 1973, and by the decade from 1910 to the 1960s, and as a group for the very earliest films. A final feature of his book is a list of all the black stars who have been nominated for academy awards. In the generously illustrated *Black Film Stars,* Eileen Landay includes several biographies of black actresses as well as brief descriptions of their major films. Some of the stars she includes are Louise Beavers, Hattie McDaniel, Butterfly McQueen, Lena Horne, Ruby Dee, and Diana Sands.

Other book-length studies of blacks in film that mention—if only in passing—the role of black women are the following: Thomas Cripps, *Black Film as Genre;* Daniel J. Leab, *From Sambo to Superspade: The Black Experience in Motion Pictures;* Edward Mapp, *Blacks in American Films: Today and Yesterday;* Gary Null, *Black Hollywood: The Negro in Motion Pic-*

tures; and Jim Pines, *Blacks in Films: A Survey of Racial Themes and Images in the American Film.*

Phyllis Rauch Klotman's *Frame by Frame—A Black Filmography* contains over three thousand entries that relate to blacks in films. These entries are divided into three major areas: an alphabetical listing of films, an appendix containing names and addresses of production companies and distributors, and a bibliography of blacks in film. The book contains five name indexes that are categorized by profession: black performers, black authors, black screenwriters, black producers, and black directors. The book's scope is international and covers the period from 1900 to 1977. The term *black* is used to refer to Afro-Americans, black Americans, black Latin Americans, black Africans, and Afro-Caribbeans. According to Klotman, those films listed include those with "black themes or subject matter—even before blacks acted in them; films that have substantial participation by blacks as writers, actors, producers, directors, musicians, animators, or consultants; and films in which blacks appeared in ancillary or walk-on roles" (Klotman, xiii). Each filmography contains as much of the following information as it was possible for Klotman to obtain: film title, series title, narrator, cast, writer, producer, director, studio, company, technical information, date and country of origin, type, distributor, archive, and a brief annotation. Another bibliography is Anne Powers's *Blacks in American Movies: A Selected Bibliography,* which contains listings from books, periodical articles, and other sources that contain general information about blacks in American films.

In the late 1960s and early 1970s, several film journals—in response to the women's movement, no doubt—ran special series and special issues on women in film. In 1966, for example, *Films and Filming* ran a four-part series, "The Heroine," by Kevin Gough-Yates. Although these articles are marred by the author's masculine bias, they do provide a concise history of the roles permitted women in American and Continental films until the mid-1960s. In part one, Gough-Yates focuses on heroines who play what he regards as masculine roles, noting that this form of behavior is permissible only in certain circumstances—namely in times of war and in essentially matriarchal situations. The dated quality of Gough-Yates's remarks can be seen in the following observation he makes: "The importance of not being dominated sexually by the male is a recurrent motif in films where the girl [sic] is essentially violating traditional standards" (Gough-Yates, part one, 25). Although Gough-Yates's essays are, for the most part, free of judgmental statements, at times he does seem to have accepted the sexual code that he describes (an acceptance that is no doubt partially explained by the fact that the articles were written in 1966). Of *Queen Christina* and *Now Voyager,* for example, he concludes that their heroines, having initially been misguided, go "through a therapeutic experience which involves a moral and spiritual awakening": in other words, they learn to conform to society's expectations for women (Gough-Yates, part one, 26). He also remarks, without comment, that self-sacrifice is the quality most valued in heroines. In part two, he emphasizes those heroines who "falsely identify their functions in society with sexual achievement," such as the heroine of *The Roman Spring of Mrs. Stone* (Gough-Yates, part two, 31). In part three, he looks at the bitch, whom he characterizes as one who "initiates all her relationships and then controls them towards her own ends, playing an essentially masculine or active part. Her motives are always disingenuous, springing from a desire for money, social advancement, or even neurotic impulse" (Gough-Yates, part three, 42). For this independent spirit and selfish behavior, the bitch, as Gough-Yates observes, must ultimately be punished because she has violated the code of behavior for women. In part four, he distinguishes between the fallen angel and the good-bad girl, taking his definition of the latter from the work done by Martha Wolfenstein and Nathan Leites (discussed above). The good-bad girl Gough-Yates regards as the reverse of the bitch; the fallen angel as the supplement to the vamp. He summarizes the redemption of these heroines as occurring as a result of male attention or male dominance. Whereas much of what Gough-Yates observes about the sexual conventions as portrayed in film is valid and to the point, much is by now simply outdated and some is even offensive.

The next year, 1967, *Films and Filming* ran another multi-issue series on women, "Where Have All the Stylists Gone?" by Eric Braun. This five-part series focuses on "leading ladies who were mainly great stylists, though not by any means always great actresses" (Braun, part 1, 51). By style, he means "a combination of personality, individuality and authority," exemplified by such actresses as Greta Garbo, Lauren Bacall, Sophia Loren, and Mae West. Those women who, to his taste, have no style are Elizabeth Taylor, Debbie Reynolds, and Kim Novak. Braun attributes to the war years what he perceives as the "general decline of style" in American films from the 1940s on, when the studios' intention was to promote pin-ups (Braun, part 3, 14). Braun's purpose is a bit silly, but he does provide an interesting history of women movie stars.

Film Library Quarterly devoted its Winter 1971-1972 issue to "Women in Film." In this issue, Janet Sternburg, in "Revealing Herself," discusses four novels and one film that she believes express what it is like to be a woman; observing that women are only recently revealing the truths about their lives, she concludes that film and fiction are effective vehicles in this effort. The film she discusses is *Growing Up Female: As Six Become One*; the novels, *Up the Sandbox, Walking Papers, The Bluest Eye,* and *An American Girl*. If the work of women is inspirational to other women, that of some male directors continues to demean women, according to Lillian Gerard in "Belles, Sirens, Sisters." Gerard examines three films, *McCabe and Mrs. Miller, Carnal Knowledge*, and *Sunday, Bloody Sunday*, that she contends portray women as subservient creatures, unable to think for themselves or succeed on their own. Some real women who have succeeded on their own are Maya Deren, Germaine Dulac, and Madeline Anderson. The careers of the first two are recounted by Regina Cornwell in "Maya Deren and Germaine Dulac: Activists of the Avant-Garde"; the third is interviewed by the staff of *Film Library Quarterly* in "An Interview with Madeline Anderson on the Making of *I Am Somebody.*" The issue concludes with reviews of "Films by and about Women."

Take One, which is published in Montreal, ran a special issue "Women and Film," in January, 1972. This issue includes an interview with Shirley Clarke, reviews of women's films, and filmographies of Canadian women directors. In addition it features "Women on Women in Films," which consists of responses by women filmmakers to a questionnaire about how the fact of their sex has affected their work; and "Thoughts about the Objectification of Women" by Barbara Martineau. In the fall of 1972 *The Velvet Light Trap* also ran a special issue, "Sexual Politics and Film." (Back issues of this are no longer available, and I have been unable to procure a copy.)

Two essays that review the 1972 First International Festival of Women's Films are Marjorie Rosen's "Women, Their Films, and Their Festival" and Catherine Calvert's "Five Women Filmmakers: How They Started, Where They're Going." Rosen's essay discusses the festival in detail, including several of the films that were shown. Calvert uses the festival as a springboard to discuss the careers of Rosalind Schneider, Amalie Rothschild, Madeline Anderson, Claudia Weil, and Julia Reichert. As an adjunct to this essay, Eleanor Perry addresses the question "Is There a Female Film Aesthetic?"

The following resources are helpful in finding material on women in film. Rosemary Ribich Kowalski's *Women and Film: A Bibliography* contains over two thousand briefly annotated entries on women in film in the United States and abroad. The citations are divided into four main categories: women as performers, women as filmmakers, images of women, and women columnists and critics. Kaye Sullivan's *Films for, by and about Women* is an annotated list of films related to women. Sullivan includes a directory of film sources and filmmakers with their addresses and an index of women filmmakers and their films. Sharon Smith's *Women Who Make Movies* is an illustrated directory of bibliographical information on American and foreign filmmakers since 1896. It contains a current listing of American women filmmakers, lists of organizations and distributors, and a bibliography. Jeanne Betancourt's *Women in Focus* is an alphabetical compendium of more than seventy-five films about women (some have been written and directed by women, others by men, but all have a feminist perspective). Each film is thoroughly annotated. *Women in Focus* also contains a bibliography of film periodicals and secondary sources about women. The Women's Film Co-Op publishes a catalogue describing short and feature films by and about women; it can be ordered from the Co-Op at 200 Main

Street, Northampton, MA 01060. The Women's History Research Center sells *Films by and/or about Women* that lists hundreds of films, filmmakers, and distributors. This catalogue is annotated and provides complete rental information. It can be ordered from the Research Center at 2325 Oak Street, Berkeley, CA 94708.

Linda Batty's *Retrospective Index to Film Periodicals, 1930-1971* lists the entire contents of fourteen film journals from their inception through December 1971 and the film reviews and articles from the *Village Voice*. This index is divided into three sections: individual films (titles), subjects, and book review citations. Subjects relevant to women that Batty lists are: "Actors and Actresses," "Stars," "Women," and "Women and the Cinema." Another bibliography, Richard Dyer MacCann and Edward S. Perry's *The New Film Index: A Bibliography of Magazine Articles in English, 1930-1970*, lists magazine articles but not film reviews. It contains a handful of subject listings pertinent to women and film, such as that on "Women Producers, Directors, and Technicians" and several on "Film Content as a Reflection of Society." The *Motion Picture Almanac* is a gold mine of information about individual stars and films; the entire text of the original Production Code of Ethics appears in the 1936-1937 edition (pages 903-4). Ian and Elizabeth Cameron's rather fatuous little book, *Dames*, contains seventy-four mini-descriptions of those women in films that the Camerons consider to be female heavies, tarts, or singers. They include only those actresses who were still alive as of 1939. The biographies average only about twenty-five words each, but they are accompanied by individual filmographies.

BIBLIOGRAPHY

Atkins, Thomas R., ed. *Sexuality in the Movies.* Bloomington, Ind.: Indiana University Press, 1975.

Basinger, Jeanine. "Ten That Got Away." In *Women and the Cinema: A Critical Anthology,* edited by Karyn Kay and Gerald Peary, pp. 61-72. New York: E. P. Dutton, 1977.

Batty, Linda. *Retrospective Index to Film Periodicals, 1930-1971.* New York and London: R. R. Bowker Co., 1975.

Baym, Nina. *Woman's Fiction: A Guide to Novels by and about Women in America, 1820-1870.* Ithaca and London: Cornell University Press, 1978.

Betancourt, Jeanne. *Women in Focus.* Dayton, Ohio: Pflaum Publishing, 1974.

Black Images in Films, Stereotyping, and Self-Perception as Viewed by Black Actresses. Proceedings of a symposium sponsored by Afro-American Studies and American Studies, Boston University, 13-14 April 1973. Occasional Paper no. 2. Boston: Afro-American Studies Program, Boston University, 1974.

Bogle, Donald. *Toms, Coons, Mulattoes, Mammies, and Bucks: An Interpretive History of Blacks in American Films.* New York: Viking Press, 1973.

Braun, Eric. "Where Have All the Stylists Gone?" *Films and Filming* 13, no. 8 (May 1967): 50-55; no. 9 (June 1967): 38-43; no. 10 (July 1967): 12-16; no. 11 (August 1967): 10-14; no. 12 (September 1967): 12-16.

Calvert, Catherine. "Five Women Filmmakers: How They Started, Where They're Going." *Mademoiselle* 76, no. 1 (November 1972): 144-45, 195-97.

Cameron, Ian, and Elizabeth Cameron. *Dames.* New York: Frederick A. Praeger, 1969.

Christian, Barbara. *Black Women Novelists: The Development of a Tradition, 1892-1976.* Contributions in Afro-American and African Studies, no. 52. Westport, Conn.: Greenwood Press, 1980.

Cornwell, Regina. "Maya Deren and Germaine Dulac: Activists of the Avant-Garde." *Film Library Quarterly* 5, no. 1 (Winter 1971-1972): 29-38.

Cripps, Thomas. *Black Film as Genre.* Bloomington, Ind. and London: Indiana University Press, 1978.

"Films by and about Women." Rev. essay. *Film Library Quarterly* 5, no. 1 (Winter 1971-1972): 46-59.

French, Brandon. *On the Verge of Revolt: Women in American Films of the Fifties.* New York: Frederick Ungar Publishing Co., 1978.

Friedan, Betty. *The Feminine Mystique.* New York: W. W. Norton & Co., 1963.

Gerard, Lillian. "Belles, Sirens, Sisters." *Film Library Quarterly* 5, no. 1 (Winter 1971-1972): 14-21.

Giddis, Diane. "The Divided Woman: Bree Daniels in *Klute.*" In *Women and the Cinema: A Critical Anthology,* edited by Karyn Kay and Gerald Peary, pp. 26-36. New York: E. P. Dutton, 1977.

Gough-Yates, Kevin. "The Heroine." *Films and Filming* 12, no. 8 (May 1966): 23-27; no. 9 (June 1966): 27-32; no. 10 (July 1966): 38-43; no. 11 (August 1966): 45-50.

Haskell, Molly. *From Reverence to Rape: The Treatment of Women in the Movies.* New York: Holt, Rinehart and Winston, 1973.

Haymes, Howard. "Movies in the 1950s: Sexism from A to Zapata." *Journal of the University Film Association* 26, no. 1-2 (1974): 12, 22.

Higashi, Sumiko. *Virgins, Vamps, and Flappers: The American Silent Movie Heroine.* St. Albans, Vt.: Eden Press Women's Publications, 1978.

"An Interview with Madeline Anderson on the Making of *I Am Somebody.*" By the FLQ staff. *Film Library Quarterly* 5, no. 1 (Winter 1971-1972): 39-41.

Jacobs, Lewis. *The Rise of the American Film: A Critical History.* Rev. ed. New York: Columbia Teachers College Press, 1967.

Johnston, Claire. "Myths of Women in the Cinema." In *Women and the Cinema: A Critical Anthology,* edited by Karyn Kay and Gerald Peary, pp. 407-11. New York: E. P. Dutton, 1977.

Kay, Karyn, and Gerald Peary. "Dorothy Arzner's *Dance, Girl, Dance.*" In *Women and the Cinema: A Critical Anthology,* edited by Karyn Kay and Gerald Peary, pp. 9-25. New York: E. P. Dutton, 1977.

_____, eds. *Women and the Cinema: A Critical Anthology.* New York: E. P. Dutton, 1977.

Klotman, Phyllis Rauch. *Frame by Frame—A Black Filmography.* Bloomington, Ind. and London: Indiana University Press, 1979.

Kowalski, Rosemary Ribich. *Women and Film: A Bibliography.* Metuchen, N.J.: Scarecrow Press, 1976.

Landay, Eileen. *Black Film Stars.* New York: Drake Publishers, 1973.

Leab, Daniel J. *From Sambo to Superspade: The Black Experience in Motion Pictures.* Boston: Houghton Mifflin Co., 1975.

MacCann, Richard Dyer, and Edward S. Perry. *The New Film Index: A Bibliography of Magazine Articles in English, 1930-1970.* New York: E. P. Dutton, 1975.

McCreadie, Marsha, ed. *The American Movie Goddess.* New York: John Wiley & Sons, 1973.

Mapp, Edward. "Black Women in Films: A Mixed Bag of Tricks." In *Black Films and Film-makers: A Comprehensive Anthology from Stereotype to Superhero,* edited by Lindsay Patterson, pp. 196-205. New York: Dodd, Mead & Co., 1975.

———. *Blacks in American Films: Today and Yesterday.* Metuchen, N.J.: Scarecrow Press, 1972.

Martineau, Barbara. "Thoughts about the Objectification of Women." *Take One* 3, no. 2 (November-December 1970): 15-18.

Maslin, Janet. "Hollywood Heroines under the Influence: Alice Still Lives Here." In *Women and the Cinema: A Critical Anthology,* edited by Karyn Kay and Gerald Peary, pp. 44-49. New York: E. P. Dutton, 1977.

Mellen, Joan. *Women and Their Sexuality in the New Film.* New York: Horizon Press, 1973.

Motion Picture Almanac. Edited by Richard Gertner. New York: Quigley Publishing Co., 1980.

Mulvey, Laura. "Visual Pleasure and Narrative Cinema." In *Women and the Cinema: A Critical Anthology,* edited by Karyn Kay and Gerald Peary, pp. 412-28. New York: E. P. Dutton, 1977.

Murray, James P. *To Find an Image: Black Films from Uncle Tom to Super Fly.* Indianapolis and New York: Bobbs-Merrill Co., 1973.

Noble, Peter. *The Negro in Films.* Literature of Cinema Series. New York: Arno Press and New York Times, 1970.

Null, Gary. *Black Hollywood: The Negro in Motion Pictures.* Secaucus, N.J.: Citadel Press, 1975.

Papashvily, Helen Waite. *All the Happy Endings: A Study of the Domestic Novel in America, the Women Who Wrote It, the Women Who Read It, in the Nineteenth Century.* New York: Harper & Brothers, 1956.

Patterson, Lindsay, ed. *Black Films and Film-makers: A Comprehensive Anthology from Stereotype to Superhero.* New York: Dodd, Mead & Co., 1975.

Perry, Eleanor. "Is There a Female Film Aesthetic?" *Mademoiselle* 76, no. 1 (November 1972): 145.

Pines, Jim. *Blacks in Films: A Survey of Racial Themes and Images in the American Film.* London: Studio Vista/Cassell & Collier Macmillan Publishers, 1975.

Powers, Anne. *Blacks in American Movies: A Selected Bibliography.* Metuchen, N.J.: Scarecrow Press, 1974.

Ramsaye, Terry, ed. *1936-1937 International Motion Picture Almanac.* New York: Quigley Publishing Co., 1936.

Rosen, Marjorie. *Popcorn Venus: Women, Movies and the American Dream.* New York: Coward, McCann & Geoghegan, 1973.

———. "Women, Their Films, and Their Festival." *Saturday Review* 55 (12 August 1972): 31-36.

Rosenberg, Bernard, and David Manning White, eds. *Mass Culture: The Popular Arts in America.* Glencoe, Ill.: Free Press, 1963.

Ryan, Mary P. "The Projection of a New Womanhood: The Movie Moderns in the

1920s." In *Our American Sisters: Women in American Life and Thought,* edited by Jean E. Friedman and William G. Shade, pp. 366-84. 2d ed. Boston: Allyn and Bacon, 1976.

"Sexual Politics and Film." Special issue of *The Velvet Light Trap,* no. 6 (Fall 1972).

Smith, Sharon. *Women Who Make Movies.* New York: Hopkinson and Blake, 1975.

Sternburg, Janet. "Revealing Herself." *Film Library Quarterly* 5, no. 1 (Winter 1971-1972): 7-12, 60-64.

Sullivan, Kaye. *Films for, by and about Women.* Metuchen, N.J.: Scarecrow Press, 1980.

Tyler, Parker. *Sex Psyche Etcetera in the Film.* New York: Horizon Press, 1969.

Walker, Alexander. "Marlene Dietrich: At Heart a Gentleman." In *Women and the Cinema: A Critical Anthology,* edited by Karyn Kay and Gerald Peary, pp. 93-98. New York: E. P. Dutton, 1977.

_____. *Sex in the Movies: The Celluloid Sacrifice.* Baltimore: Penguin Books, 1968. (Original title, *The Celluloid Sacrifice.* London: Michael Joseph, 1966.)

Weibel, Kathryn. *Mirror Mirror: Images of Women Reflected in Popular Culture.* Garden City, N.Y.: Doubleday Anchor Press, 1977.

Welsch, Janice. "Actress Archetypes in the 1950s: Doris Day, Marilyn Monroe, Elizabeth Taylor, Audrey Hepburn." In *Women and the Cinema: A Critical Anthology,* edited by Karyn Kay and Gerald Peary, pp. 99-111. New York: E. P. Dutton, 1977.

Wolfenstein, Martha, and Nathan Leites. "The Good-Bad Girl." In their *Movies: A Psychological Study,* pp. 25-47. Glencoe, Ill.: Free Press, 1950.

"Women and Film." Special issue of *Take One* 3, no. 2 (January 1972).

"Women in Film." Special issue of *Film Library Quarterly* 5, no. 1 (Winter 1971-1972).

"Women on Women in Films." *Take One* 3, no. 2 (November-December 1970): 10-14.

Women's Film Co-Op. *1972 Catalogue.* Northampton, Mass.: Women's Film Co-Op, 1972.

Women's History Research Center. *Films by and/or about Women: Directory of Filmmakers, Films, and Distributors Internationally, Past and Present.* Berkeley, Calif.: Women's History Research Center, 1972.

Wylie, Philip. *Generation of Vipers.* New York: Rinehart and Co., 1942.

Young, Stark. "What Maisie Knows: Mae West." In *Women and the Cinema: A Critical Anthology,* edited by Karyn Kay and Gerald Peary, pp. 90-92. New York: E. P. Dutton, 1977.

CHAPTER 5

Women in Television

Most of the studies that have been done on the subject of women and television have a methodology that is decidedly based in the social sciences or in communications. Those scholars who have a primary interest in literature are not yet flocking to television to investigate the image and role of women in telefiction or situation comedies. As a consequence, very few truly interpretive essays are included in the discussion below. Most of the information, quite simply, remains statistical. Various television genres—such as commercials, comedies, and news reporting—are represented, but much work remains to be done on them. Much work also needs to be done in defining the field of women and television itself. Because television is so obviously a visual medium, it would seem that there are infinite possibilities for approaching the question of women on television from the perspectives of perceptual theory. One promising approach in this direction is taken in *Hearth and Home*.

As mentioned above (in chapter three), *Hearth and Home: Images of Women in the Mass Media*, edited by Gaye Tuchman et al., is a scholarly inquiry into several forms of mass media, including that of television. In her introduction, "The Symbolic Annihilation of Women by the Mass Media," Tuchman identifies the two ideas central to this collection of essays: the reflection hypothesis and symbolic annihilation. The reflection hypothesis, very simply stated, assumes that the media "reflect dominant societal values" (Tuchman et al., 7). Symbolic annihilation means that a group—in this case, women—is either at times absent altogether or otherwise trivialized to the extent that it might as well not exist at all. According to Tuchman, all of television, including drama, children's programs, and commercials, "proclaims that women don't count for much" (Tuchman, 10). George Gerbner raises a provocative issue in "The Dynamics of Cultural Resistance," where he claims that the image of women on television is deteriorating instead of improving. Asserting that television is the "new religion," Gerbner claims that it plays the same role in our lives as the monolithic Catholic church did before the Reformation (Tuchman et al., 47). It is, in short, "a cosmic force or a symbolic environment" into which one is born and about which one has little choice (Tuchman et al., 47). Given the conservative nature of this contemporary institution, it is not really surprising, therefore, to discover that, according to Gerbner at least, "the media appear to be cultivating resistance and preparing for a last-ditch defense" against the liberating forces of feminism (Tuchman et al., 50). Judith Lemon, in "Dominant or Dominated? Women on Prime-Time Television," confirms much of what Gerbner asserts when she reports that "television maintains societal stereotypes in its portrayal of power" (Tuchman et al., 52). She also reports, however, that social class plays a larger role in this dominance than does sex, although the impact of sex is not negligible. Lemon notes a difference between the treatment of black and white women in terms of dominance. Because television tends to depict stereotypical family situations, black women are often portrayed as dominant at home, a portrayal that perpetuates the myth of the black matriarch. Thus, black women, when in all-black situations on television, enjoy more dominance than white women do in comparable all-white situations. Other essays in this section include Stephen Schuetz and Joyce N. Sprafkin's "Spot Messages Appearing within Saturday Morning Television Programs" and Muriel S. Cantor's "Where Are the Women in Public Broadcasting?" Following the essays, at the end of the book, is Helen Franzwa's "The Image of Women in Television: An Annotated Bibliography." This bibliography includes research studies, public-interest reports, and popular articles. It is divided into several sections, including adult entertainment, public affairs, commercials, and children's programs. It also includes information on organizations that are "concerned about the portrayal of women in the media," including their addresses (Tuchman et al., 296). An alphabetical list of references follows the bibliography.

An interpretive study of most of the genres of television, from situation and domestic comedies to the news, is Horace Newcomb's *TV: The Most Popular Art*. An annotated listing of all television programs is available in Vincent Terrace's *The Complete Encyclopedia of Television Programs, 1947-1979*. This two-volume work includes the names of the main characters and the actors and actresses who played them, the number of episodes filmed, the dates of the programs, and a brief synopsis of the premise.

Two books that discuss the relationship between soap operas and their fans are Robert La Guardia's *The Wonderful World of TV Soap Operas* and Manuela Soares's *The Soap Opera Book*. La Guardia claims for the soaps that they were "important ego-builders for women long before anyone ever heard of Women's Liberation" (La Guardia, 7). He goes on to assert that these daytime serials have helped to counter "the trend of putting down women in movies and especially on nighttime television" (La Guardia, 7). The rest of part one is taken up with a history of the soaps on radio and television; part two consists of the complete plot summaries of seventeen soaps. Manuela Soares's book, which is extensively illustrated, contends that the soaps' appeal is related to the fantasies of their audience. In chapter six she outlines what she considers to be the major archetypes among soap opera characters. For the women characters they are: the young-and-vulnerable romantic heroine; the rival; the suffering antagonist; the meddlesome and villainous mother/grandmother; the benevolent mother/grandmother; and the career woman (Soares, 57-71).

Another look at the soaps is provided by Madeleine Edmondson and David Rounds (the latter a veteran actor in the serials) in *From Mary Noble to Mary Hartman: The Complete Soap Opera Book*, which updates their earlier study, *The Soaps: Daytime Serials of Radio and TV*. Although Edmondson and Rounds provide considerable information about the genre, their format is a bit cute, as they present much of their material in dialogue. They also fail to footnote their material and are often vague about its source. Clearly, Edmondson and Rounds are well versed in their field, but their book does suffer from their attempts to de-emphasize their research. As a result, they fail to make their secondary sources generally accessible to their readers and, in the end, come dangerously close to insulting the very audience they sought to charm.

In 1974, the *Journal of Communication* ran a special issue on women and television; most of the essays are primarily statistical and offer only very brief interpretations of the data. One of the most widely quoted of these essays is Mildred Downing's "Heroine of the Daytime Serial," which characterizes the women on soap operas as "strong, warm, and fallible" (Downing, 130). From her observations of literally hundreds of episodes in 1973, Downing concludes that the image of the daytime heroine is "far from unacceptable"; in fact, this heroine "may be the most worthy of emulation" of any characters on television in that she feels responsible for others and is able to function as herself and not just as an adjunct to males (Downing, 137). Although women in daytime serials are generally portrayed realistically in terms of human qualities, Downing does observe that women are shown actually working only in emergency situations and that, in general, the older they get the less likely they are to work outside the home. Also, in aggregate, they are younger than the men in the series. In "Women in TV Commercials," Alice E. Courtney and Thomas W. Whipple analyze the findings of four studies of television commercials that were conducted from April 1971 to February 1973. Their conclusion is that these studies demonstrate that "women are not portrayed as autonomous, independent human beings, but are primarily sex-typed" (Courtney and Whipple, 117). Other essays in this issue include that by Helen White Streicher discussed below; Ann Beuf's "Doctor, Lawyer, Household Drudge"; Kay Mills's "Fighting Sexism on the Airwaves"; Nancy S. Tedesco's "Patterns in Prime Time"; and Joseph Turow's "Advising and Ordering: Daytime, Prime Time."

In "Daytime Television: You'll Never Want to Leave Home," Carol Lopate analyzes the content and implicit messages of game shows and soap opera, concluding that these programs "make the family palatable" (Lopate, 81). That is, each kind of show demonstrates the primary role of the family in determining a meaningful existence for women. Remarking on the general powerlessness of the game show contestants, who are at the mercy of the avuncular MCs and fate itself (in the form of good or bad luck), Lopate observes that in this world "it does not matter that most things are beyond one's control, because it is a world of bountifulness" (Lopate, 72). In the world of the soaps, the family is so important that "people cannot be involved with each other unless they are somehow related" (Lopate, 77). In short, daytime television by glamorizing and romanticizing the family implicitly repeats the message that the family itself—and only the family—can fulfill one's deepest needs and most exotic fantasies. In effect, daytime television, according to Carol Lopate, denies women the time and the inclination to become themselves; it does this by convincing women that it is only in a communal setting, and not in isolation, that one achieves a meaningful identity.

A brief but cogent assessment of the image and role of black women on television is that by Jean Carey Bond, "Reader's Forum: The Media Image of Black Women." In this essay, Bond discusses four television shows that feature black women: the made-for-television movie, "The Autobiography of Miss Jane Pittman" (based on the novel by Ernest Gaines); the short-lived detective series "Get Christy Love"; and the sitcoms "That's My Mama?" and "Good Times." Behind the apparent progress that blacks have made simply by appearing more frequently on television, Bond finds a pernicious tendency to use the blacks to forward the values of white culture. Thus, she notes, in the "Autobiography" all of the black men that are close to Miss Jane Pittman are destroyed, a pattern that convinces Bond that the movie was intended as a message to blacks to stay in their place. The series "Get Christy Love" Bond challenges because its heroine too closely resembles the stereotypical black whore image of southern literature; "Good Times" and "That's My Mama?," on the other hand, perpetuate the myth of the black superwoman, the matriarch. In short, Bond finds little to praise in the versions of black women she sees on television. For another interpretation of how television contributes to the debilitating myths that control women, see Lillian S. Robinson's "What's My Line?" (discussed below, in chapter seven).

Carol Traynor Williams, in "It's Not So Much, 'You've Come a Long Way, Baby'—as 'You're Gonna Make It After All,'" emphasizes the group cooperation, behind the camera and in front of it, that makes the "Mary Tyler Moore Show" unique among situation comedies. Williams, in fact, finds the sitcom label generally inappropriate for this show because of its ability to humanize its characters. That is, rather than relying strictly on humor, this show has made it a point to develop the relationships among the characters to the extent that it is often capable of dealing with real problems in a believable or realistic context. Arthur Asa Berger, on the other hand, attacks one of the "Mary Tyler Moore" spinoffs in "Rhoda's Marriage: Plain Janes Have Less Pains" in his *The TV-Guided American*. Berger faults "Rhoda," not only because it is "sentimental and meretricious," but because it "takes itself more seriously" than other situation comedies and "claims to raise our consciousness"—something Berger claims it fails to do because it is too trivial (Berger, 75).

Two studies made of television cartoons that run on Saturday and/or Sunday morning demonstrate that males outnumber women and that women are, by and large, relegated to secondary positions of importance in the story lines. In "The Girls in the Cartoons," Helen White Streicher found that, generally speaking, "females were less numerous than males, made fewer appearances, had fewer lines, played fewer 'lead roles,' were less active, occupied many fewer positions of responsibility, were less noisy, and were more preponderantly juvenile than males" (Streicher, 127). In "From Olive Oyl to Sweet Polly Purebread: Sex Role Stereotypes and Televised Cartoons," Richard M. Levinson finds the same pattern of discrimination and concludes that "television's portrayal of the sexes in cartoons does not accurately mirror real world events but it does reflect real world *values* concerning traditional sex-role assumptions" (Levinson, 568; Levinson's italics).

Newscasting and reporting are two other areas of television in which the status of women is less than ideal. In *Women in Television News*, Judith S. Gelman reports on the personal experiences of several women whom she interviewed in the early 1970s. Although the conclusions she draws are somewhat obvious, the interviews she held do provide an interesting composite picture of the typical woman in television news. Not surprisingly, appearance is the key to success; although the women are expected to be basically competent, "hiring practices continue to reflect an emphasis on youth and attractiveness, so that the visual image becomes the basic asset for a newswoman" (Gelman, 166). Gelman's book contains a career chronology of the women she interviewed and a bibliography of secondary sources.

For a brief history of women in television, see also Kathryn Weibel's *Mirror Mirror: Images of Women Reflected in Popular Culture* (discussed above, in chapter one).

BIBLIOGRAPHY

Berger, Arthur Asa. *The TV-Guided American*. New York: Walker and Co., 1976.
Beuf, Ann. "Doctor, Lawyer, Household Drudge." *Journal of Communication* 24, no. 2 (Spring 1974): 142-45.
Bond, Jean Carey. "Reader's Forum: The Media Image of Black Women." *Freedomways* 15, no. 1 (Winter 1975): 34-37.

Cantor, Muriel S. "Where Are the Women in Public Broadcasting?" In *Hearth and Home: Images of Women in the Mass Media,* edited by Gaye Tuchman, Arlene Kaplan Daniels, and James Benet, pp. 78-89. New York: Oxford University Press, 1978.

Courtney, Alice E., and Thomas W. Whipple. "Women in TV Commercials." *Journal of Communication* 24, no. 2 (Spring 1974): 110-18.

Downing, Mildred. "Heroine of the Daytime Serial." *Journal of Communication* 24, no. 2 (Spring 1974): 130-37.

Edmondson, Madeleine, and David Rounds. *From Mary Noble to Mary Hartman: The Complete Soap Opera Book.* New York: Stein and Day, 1976.

_____. *The Soaps: Daytime Serials of Radio and TV.* New York: Stein and Day, 1972.

Franzwa, Helen. "The Image of Women in Television: An Annotated Bibliography." In *Hearth and Home: Images of Women in the Mass Media,* edited by Gaye Tuchman, Arlene Kaplan Daniels, and James Benet, pp. 273-99. New York: Oxford University Press, 1978.

Gelman, Judith S. *Women in Television News.* New York: Columbia University Press, 1976.

Gerbner, George. "The Dynamics of Cultural Resistance." In *Hearth and Home: Images of Women in the Mass Media,* edited by Gaye Tuchman, Arlene Kaplan Daniels, and James Benet, pp. 46-50. New York: Oxford University Press, 1978.

La Guardia, Robert. *The Wonderful World of TV Soap Operas.* Rev. ed. New York: Ballantine Books, 1977.

Lemon, Judith. "Dominant or Dominated? Women on Prime-Time Television." In *Hearth and Home: Images of Women in the Mass Media,* edited by Gaye Tuchman, Arlene Kaplan Daniels, and James Benet, pp. 51-68. New York: Oxford University Press, 1978.

Levinson, Richard M. "From Olive Oyl to Sweet Polly Purebread: Sex Role Stereotypes and Televised Cartoons." *Journal of Popular Culture* 9, no. 3 (Winter 1975): 561-72.

Lopate, Carol. "Daytime Television: You'll Never Want to Leave Home." *Feminist Studies* 3, nos. 3-4 (Spring-Summer 1976): 69-82.

Mills, Kay. "Fighting Sexism on the Airwaves." *Journal of Communication* 24, no. 2 (Spring 1974): 150-55.

Newcomb, Horace. *TV: The Most Popular Art.* Garden City, N.Y.: Anchor Press, 1974.

Robinson, Lillian S. "What's My Line?" In her *Sex, Class, and Culture,* pp. 310-42. Bloomington, Ind., and London: Indiana University Press, 1978.

Schuetz, Stephen, and Joyce N. Sprafkin. "Spot Messages Appearing within Saturday Morning Television Programs." In *Hearth and Home: Images of Women in the Mass Media,* edited by Gaye Tuchman, Arlene Kaplan Daniels, and James Benet, pp. 69-77. New York: Oxford University Press, 1978.

Soares, Manuela. *The Soap Opera Book.* New York: Harmony Books, 1978.

Streicher, Helen White. "The Girls in the Cartoons." *Journal of Communication* 24, no. 2 (Spring 1974): 125-29.

Tedesco, Nancy S. "Patterns in Prime Time." *Journal of Communication* 24, no. 2 (Spring 1974): 119-24.

Terrace, Vincent. *The Complete Encyclopedia of Television Programs, 1947-1979.* 2 vols. South Brunswick, N.J.: A. S. Barnes, 1979.

Tuchman, Gaye. "Introduction: The Symbolic Annihilation of Women by the Mass Media." In *Hearth and Home: Images of Women in the Mass Media,* edited by Gaye Tuchman, Arlene Kaplan Daniels, and James Benet, pp. 3-38. New York: Oxford University Press, 1978.

————, Arlene Kaplan Daniels, and James Benet, eds. *Hearth and Home: Images of Women in the Mass Media.* New York: Oxford University Press, 1978.

Turow, Joseph. "Advising and Ordering: Daytime, Prime Time." *Journal of Communication* 24, no. 2 (Spring 1974): 138-41.

Weibel, Kathryn. *Mirror Mirror: Images of Women Reflected in Popular Culture.* Garden City, N.Y.: Doubleday Anchor Press, 1977.

Williams, Carol Traynor. "It's Not So Much, 'You've Come a Long Way, Baby'—As 'You're Gonna Make It After All.'" *Journal of Popular Culture* 7, no. 4 (Spring 1974): 981-89.

See p. 128

CHAPTER 6

Women in Advertising, Fashion, Sports, and Comics

The focus in this chapter is on woman as a body. Although women were granted the vote in 1920, it has only been in the past few years that women have reclaimed the rightful ownership of their bodies. Until the nineteenth century, men, in a very real way, literally owned the bodies of their wives. Under the law, a woman who married became a *femme couverte* or "dead in the law"; that is to say, she had no legal existence except through her husband. It wasn't until New York State granted married women property rights just before the Civil War that the economic stranglehold of men over women was loosened. Black women, of course, were legally regarded as their master's chattel—a status reconfirmed by the 1857 Dred Scott decision and only officially overturned in 1863 with the Emancipation Proclamation and in 1865 with the adoption of the Thirteenth Amendment. Regardless of their legal status, however, women, both white and black, continued to be treated by men as though they were property to be displayed. Thus, from its inception, advertising was directed at the woman who, wishing only to catch and keep her man, was willing to reshape and clothe her body to please him. (That in reality it was men who caught and kept their women was a fact left ignored.) Preying on women's fears, advertising capitalized on the notion that a woman's body was plastic, an object capable of infinite transformations. And women, trapped by the cult of the lady, were afraid not to be in fashion. Even the most ardent feminists gave up the notion of dress reform because they could not stand up under the public ridicule and humiliation they were subject to when they wore such practical clothes as shorter skirts and bloomers. Thus women, to be fashionable and to survive economically, pinched, squeezed, and otherwise mutilated their bodies.

Reform in dress coincided with increased mobility brought about by industrialization and with the increased opportunities for women to work outside the home. It was also helped along by the invention of the bicycle in the late nineteenth century. As women enjoyed more freedom in sports and other physical exercise, their clothes kept pace with their activity. One of the major differences between the current feminist movement and the earlier one is that today's women have claimed the right to their own bodies. Although there were some efforts made by earlier feminists to understand and control their bodies, it has only been within the past twenty years or so that women have been successful in this venture. In 1965 the Supreme Court overturned the last state law that barred contraception and in 1973 declared abortion legal. During this time, several self-help health groups—such as the Boston Women's Health Book Collective—have been organized to counsel women about their bodies. That women have made great strides in reinhabiting their bodies is also evident in women's underground comics which first cropped up in the early 1970s. These comics have as one of their major topics what it is like to menstruate. Other topics include sex—with men and with other women—birth control, and the effects of trying to become well-groomed and beautiful by wearing the right clothes and makeup. All the stories in these underground comics are illustrated quite graphically and many assert the right of women to be exactly what they want to be—even if they are not what is commonly regarded as attractive. One group that has been particularly affected by popular standards of beauty consists of those black women, who, by virtue of their color, cannot fulfill the idealized image of the beautiful woman— because this image is a white one. The slogan Black Is Beautiful, which gained popularity in the 1960s as a consequence of and a rallying point for the Black Power Movement, indicates a serious attempt on the part of blacks to refuse to allow the white majority society to determine its values.

For purposes of clarity, I have divided this chapter into four subsections: advertising, fashion, sport, and comics. The bibliography that follows this chapter reflects these divisions.

WOMEN IN ADVERTISING

Some of the more useful resources for a study of women in advertising are the advertising manuals themselves, as they reveal both the conscious and the unconscious attitudes that advertisers have taken toward women. The two major ways to break down the subject of women in advertising are: women as the object of advertising and women as the subject of advertising. The first is a study of the premise that it is possible to sell things specifically to women. The second is the study of how women appear in advertising; how they are used to sell goods—be it to men or women, or men and women.

Carl A. Naether's well-known text, *Advertising to Women*, for example, takes as its premise that women are a "distinct class of buyers" (Naether, v). According to the introduction—written by a woman—women are the "shoppers of the world" (Naether, xiii). Naether's book, published in 1928, is a guide, therefore, as to how one might most effectively attract the attention of this particular group who, at the time the book was written, were said to "buy from 80 to 90 percent of the things in general use in our daily life" (Naether, 4). Although Naether offers what was undoubtedly sound advice for the 1920s, his subtext accounts for the historical value of his book. He maintains, for example, that advertising copy should be written by men, then checked over by women "for the purpose of feminizing it" (Naether, 19). Clearly addressing a male audience, he also urges his readers to maintain, in conversation with women, "an attitude of patience, refinement, and respect" (Naether, 25). The key word in this list, of course, is "patience," as though women would try the patience of any male who tries to converse with them on a meaningful level (Naether, 25). Obviously regarding women as natural narcissists, he says that a woman would "find it hard" to perceive any thing or any body as "not relating in some more or less definite way *to her*" (Naether, 32-33; Naether's italics). Contributing his own bit of influence to the transformation of women from producers to consumers of goods, he states baldly that "shopping is as much a woman's *business* as making money is a man's" (Naether, 52; emphasis added). He apparently tries to justify his strange—and strained—use of the word *business* by claiming that it is a "broad, almost *professional*, purchasing power which the modern woman wields" (Naether, 53; emphasis added). As respectful as he is of women's purchasing power, he is disrespectful of their intelligence and individuality. It is the emotional pitch that he favors, arguing that the more emotional the appeal the more effective it will be. He attributes to all women the abiding desire to look young and sexually appealing. Thus, he says, the "wish of well-nigh every woman is to possess eyes that, softly shaded by long beautiful lashes, radiate brilliantly; a complexion that is smooth and velvety, showing rosy health through cheeks and lips; hands that are well shaped and white and soft; and whatever else she considers needful to make her physical self pleasing to the point of magnetic springs largely from the desire to fascinate the other sex" (Naether, 133). The passage does not end here, but this quotation is sufficient to reveal some of the most basic of Naether's beliefs about women. It also demonstrates, convincingly, that the feminine mystique was being constructed long before the 1950s. Moreover, it reveals through the single phrase, "white and soft," that black women were not the focus of Naether's selling strategies—nor were they emblems of the ideal American beauty. Finally, by emphasizing women's emotional nature and the dominance of her feelings, Naether was perpetuating a stereotype whose legacy continues to haunt us.

As an advertising textbook, *Advertising to Women* is, one hopes, outdated. But as a source of social attitudes and the vehicles for expressing them, it is invaluable. It is copiously illustrated with examples of real advertisements and sample sales letters. More than its author ever dreamed, it is indeed a thorough study of advertising to women. Another outdated, yet often cited, text is Janet L. Wolff's *What Makes Women Buy: A Guide to Understanding and Influencing the New Woman of Today*.

General histories of advertising are Frank S. Presbrey's monumental 1929 work, *The History and Development of Advertising*, and Robert Atwan, Donald McQuade, and John W. Wright's *Edsels, Luckies, and Frigidaires*. Of women's advertising, Atwan et al. claim that it is still, as it was in the nineteenth century, "an idealization of women's domestic roles in an industrialized society" (Atwan et al., 6). In contrast to the woman as housewife are those advertisements directed toward men, in which women are portrayed as sex objects. As part of their history, Atwan et al. include a section on the history of sex in American advertising, in which they state that sex in advertising is no more prevalent than a hundred years ago—just more explicit (Atwan et al., 326). Their text is illustrated with 250 advertisements from family magazines over the last century; these magazines include *Time, Life, Newsweek, Ladies' Home Journal, Mademoiselle, Vogue, The New Yorker, Penthouse,* and *Playboy*.

Both Frank Luther Mott and Theodore Peterson, in their respective studies of American magazines, devote considerable space to the rise of magazine advertising from the late nineteenth to the early twentieth century. Both regard the development of advertising as intimately related to the history and success of American magazines. Both also attribute the increased emphasis on advertising to the effects of the Industrial Revolution and the increased use of brand names at the turn of the century. Mott, in *A History of American Magazines, 1885-1905*, volume four, remarks that the one factor responsible for the 1905 peak in advertising "was the increasing use of trade-marked goods" (Mott, 33). Among the earliest brand names that appeared in American magazines were Pears' Soap in 1883 and Eastman Kodak and Quaker Oats in the 1890s; in the late 1880s bicycles were extensively advertised, with no fewer than thirty-eight different companies represented in the March 1896 issue of *Cosmopolitan* (Mott, 24). With the influx of advertisements, the magazine industry itself was transformed, according to Theodore Peterson; in *Magazines in the Twentieth Century*, he characterizes the change as one that led publishers away from exclusively editorial concerns to consumer concerns. He notes that although magazine advertising appeared as early as 10 May 1741 (the date he assigns as the one on which the first magazine advertisement appeared in the United States, in the *General Magazine and Historical Chronicle*; Peterson, 20), it wasn't until after the Civil War that advertisements appeared in any volume. Like Mott, he too quotes Edward Bok's autobiography in which this former editor of the *Ladies' Home Journal* claims that he was, in 1896, the first editor to integrate the magazine's fiction content into its advertising pages. Peterson concludes that advertising, which had once been scorned by many publishers, now wields considerable—if implicit—influence in the management of some publications; it has also been known, although only infrequently, to affect the editorial content of certain magazines. The implications of this for women are many and have been explored to some extent by some of the following scholars.

One of the most widely quoted authorities on the subject of women and advertising is the anthropologist Erving Goffman, author of *Gender Advertisements*. For the publication in 1979 of this monograph, Vivian Gornick has written an explanatory introduction. In this introduction, Gornick suggests that Goffman's most important idea in *Gender Advertisements* is the "connection he makes between our image of women and the behavior of children" (Goffman, viii). Like Trevor Millum and George Gerbner (discussed below and in chapter five, respectively), Gornick argues that the "social purpose" of advertising is to convince us to behave as the men and women depicted are behaving (Goffman, vii). She finds Goffman's own remarks about the reality of advertising particularly crucial, especially when he points out that advertisements *"as pictures...*are not perceived as peculiar and unnatural" (Goffman, ix; Goffman's italics). Goffman opens his discussion of the content of advertisements with a discussion of ceremony and display, noting that displays—as in a photograph, for example—"provide evidence of the actor's *alignment* in a gathering" (Goffman, 1; Goffman's italics). He finds it particularly significant, therefore, that women are, as a general rule, always positioned in attitudes of subordination to men in advertisements. In this, women are analogous to children with reference to adult males.

Working from the psychology of perception, Goffman takes as his premise that perception of pictures and of reality is a learned activity and that "this learning draws deeply and fallibly on past experience" (Goffman, 12). In other words, in our society "we learn to decode small flat tracings [pictures] for large, three dimensional scenes in a manner somewhat corresponding to the way we have learned to interpret our visual images of real objects" (Goffman, 12). Thus, we perceive and regard pictures and the reality to which they refer as roughly equivalent. Remarkably, in part because advertisements are "intentionally choreographed to be unambiguous," the reality they portray is often "fuller and richer" than our perception of the real thing (Goffman, 23). In other words, advertisers create a fiction that is, in some respects, more real than reality. By drawing on our own past experience with ritualized situations, the advertisers can speak effectively and unambiguously to us. Conversely, if we study the presentation of gender, the ceremonial displays that they portray, we can perhaps "begin to see what we ourselves might be engaging in doing" (Goffman, 27).

Thus, as Gornick suggests in her introduction, it is of the essence that Goffman, through his analysis of the magazine advertisements in his book, informs us that women are pictured in the following subordinate fashion to men: women are shorter than men; women's hands do not grasp objects firmly; men instruct women; women appear to be drifting in reverie while men's eyes are focused purposefully; women appear helpless (Goffman, viii). That these pictures are not, as Goffman and Gornick remind us, perceived as unnatural—by most people—suggests some serious problems with how we perceive women. In support of his ideas Goffman reprints and analyzes over five hundred magazine photographs. His introductory essay contains valuable reference materials, especially on the theories of perception.

Although Trevor Millum's *Images of Women: Advertising in Women's Magazines* focuses exclusively on British magazines, it does suggest some possible approaches to the subject of women in advertising. Millum's approach is basically an interdisciplinary one based on theories of reality and visual perception, in which he draws on the work of such thinkers as Peter Berger and Thomas Luckmann and the philosopher Susanne K. Langer (who, somewhat inexplicably, appears as a "he" in Millum's book). Another of his sources is Erving Goffman. Working from the premise that advertising functions as retransmission, Millum says that advertising reinforces and reveals "some of the major preoccupations and cultural values of a society" (Millum, 45). In its need to communicate efficiently and its desire to communicate effectively, advertising works in stereotypical— that is, easily recognizable—images. Thus, "what is in general terms middle class becomes the norm, the standard against which we measure ourselves, that which we must desire if we wish to be normal" (Millum, 52). In summary, that which is merely a "particular reality is presented as if it were the only reality" (Millum, 52). After establishing his methodological framework, Millum recounts the process by which advertisements are created and then analyzes several that have appeared in British publications.

Lucy Komisar provides a feminist perspective on advertising in "The Image of Woman in Advertising," in which she asseverates that advertising is "an insidious propaganda machine for a male supremacist society" (Gornick and Moran, 207). After outlining the demeaning roles that women play in advertising, Komisar concludes, in somewhat rueful hopefulness, that women ironically—and quite unintentionally—may be forced by these wretched images into a new awareness of themselves. In this hope she appears to echo Goffman's claim that studying advertising can help us to see ourselves—or help us to see how we see ourselves. (For another look at the sex-typing in advertising, see Alice E. Courtney and Thomas W. Whipple's "Women in TV Commercials," discussed above, in chapter five.)

Early in the 1970s, concerned with the articulate criticism being leveled at advertising by feminist leaders, the National Advertising Review Board established a panel, chaired by Dr. Aurelia Toyer Miller of the University of Massachusetts, Amherst, to investigate the charges that advertising was rampantly sexist. In 1975, *Advertising Age* published the full text of this special report, "Advertising Portraying or Directed to Women." This report acknowledges the truth of the accusations and notes that the problem "is real and will not go away by itself" ("Advertising," 75). Women, they found, were indeed portrayed too often as housewives and too infrequently as professionals; women were also featured as sex objects to the exclusion of their individuality. The problem that the panel found with the image of woman as a housewife lay not so much in its content as in its "endless procession" ("Advertising," 75). In addition, according to the panel, women were portrayed too often as stupid and as needing to rely on men to solve their problems. The panel summed up its discoveries by observing that "the image of the housewife in advertising appears frequently to be not only a circumscribed one, but also a person with a warped sense of values" ("Advertising," 75). In order to combat these damaging portraits of women in advertising, the panel assembled a checklist of questions that an advertising agency should ask itself about the contents of its advertisements; the checklist is divided into questions intended to elicit positive and negative responses. In short, the panel urges the advertiser to ask " 'How would I like to be depicted in this way?' " ("Advertising," 76).

In 1976, the *Journal of Communication* ran a special section, "Equality in Advertising," consisting of five studies that focus on the image of women and minorities in advertising. "Selling Women, Selling Blacks," by James D. Culley and Rex Bennett, updates several studies of television and print commercials that were done in the early 1970s; in their study of 1974 advertisements, Culley and Bennett discovered that women were still being portrayed primarily as housewives. They also confirmed the fact that blacks appear in almost no general circulation magazines and that when they do they are part of crowd scenes. On a related topic, Michael K. Chapko surveyed the portrayal of blacks in all the issues of *Ebony* magazine for 1970, 1972, and 1974. He found that, whereas blacks pictured had darker skin in the more recent magazine ads, women, on the average, were lighter than the men. A study of inverse progress in advertising is Alison Poe's "Active Women in Ads." For this study Poe examined for their sports content over seven thousand advertisements appearing in the *Saturday Evening Post, Cosmopolitan,* and the *Ladies' Home Journal* during 1928, 1956, and 1972. She found that, contrary to her expectations, the "representation of women in sports did not increase but in fact lessened"; in short, there were more advertisements that pictured women engaged in physical activity or sports in 1928 than there were in either 1956 or 1972. The final two studies in this special issue are: Charlotte G. O'Kelly and Linda Edwards Bloomquist, "Women and Blacks on TV," and Suzanne Pingree et al., "A Scale for Sexism." All the essays are based on statistical methodology with only minimal interpretation of the data. However, all do contain substantial information about previous studies.

Information about particular advertising agencies is available in the *Standard Directory of Advertising Agencies.* According to the June 1980 *Directory,* for example, Advertising to Women, Incorporated, was founded in 1975, with the purpose of specializing in advertising to women. Although the chairman of the board is a man, the president and creative director is a woman—Lois Geraci Ernst. Among the accounts this agency holds are the Charles of the Ritz Group, the Personal Care Division of Gillette Company, and *Good Housekeeping.* Another agency run by a woman is Shirley Polykoff Advertising, Incorporated, which was founded by Polykoff herself in 1971 after her successes with Foote, Cone and Belding, for whom she created the phenomenally successful Clairol hair-coloring series, "Does she...or doesn't she?" and "The closer he gets the better you look." Polykoff describes her rise to success, which culminated in 1967 when she was voted the National Advertising Woman of the Year, in her autobiography, *Does She...or Doesn't She? And How She Did It.* According to the *Directory,* her agency holds accounts for Bristol-Myers Company (Body on Tap Shampoo), Clairol (Miss Clairol Haircoloring), and Vick's Toiletry Products—to name but a few.

WOMEN IN FASHION

Among the texts available on the general history of fashion is R. Turner Wilcox's *Five Centuries of American Costume,* which details the origins and modifications of American fashion; this book is illustrated with drawings and contains a bibliography. Alice Morse Earle's *Two Centuries of Costume in America, 1620-1820* is another general outline of fashion history. J. Anderson Black and Madge Garland's *A History of Fashion* is useful for its glossary of terms, its selected bibliography, and its list of costume collections found in museums. This text is liberally illustrated with colored photographs and drawings. Karlyne Anspach's *The Why of Fashion* is a college-level textbook on the subject; as such it is useful as an introduction to the various ways one can approach the field. Anspach includes references to several other works, such as Edmund Bergler's *Fashion and the Unconscious* (1953) and Gregory Stone's "Appearance and the Self." Like others whose work preceded or coincided with the resurgence of feminism in the mid-1960s, Anspach falls into numerous perceptual traps in her view of women. She says, for example, that "Each girl strives for the feminine ideal—to be fascinating...young and glamorous...beautiful...attractive to men" (Anspach, 31; Anspach's ellipses). For an investigation into the subject of fashion as it appears in art, see Anne Hollander's *Seeing through Clothes,* in which she "explores the idea that in civilized western life the clothed figure looks more persuasive and comprehensible in art than it does in reality" (Hollander, xi). A book that treats clothes as "the mirror of history" is Estelle Ansley Worrell's *American Costume, 1840-1920,* which is illustrated by the author.

Two books that trace the production side of fashion and how the development of mass production changed both clothes and the people who wear them are Claudia B. Kidwell and Margaret C. Christman's *Suiting Everyone: The Democratization of Clothing in America* and Sandra Ley's *Fashion for Everyone: The Story of Ready-to-Wear. Suiting Everyone* was written to accompany the exhibition of that name that was held at the Smithsonian

Institution; it contains lavish photographs of textile mills, sewing machines, cutting machines, advertisements from magazines and catalogs, and the exhibits themselves.

A brief but useful summary of different fashions that American women have worn since the early nineteenth century is in Kathryn Weibel's *Mirror Mirror: Images of Women Reflected in Popular Culture,* chapter five, "Images of the Fashionable Woman." Weibel seems to have drawn her major ideas from those of Thorstein Veblen and Simone de Beauvoir when she explains that "one function of the wives of wealthy men has always been to display their wealth" (Weibel, 177). In her account of changing fashions, Weibel discusses the contributions of the great couturiers such as Christian Dior and Coco Chanel. Her essay is illustrated with line drawings that make clear the various images of the fashionable woman. (Weibel's book is also discussed above, in chapters one and three.)

A more thorough introduction to the entire field of fashion is the collection of essays, *Dress, Adornment, and the Social Order,* edited by Mary Ellen Roach and Joanne Bubolz Eicher. This anthology covers several different approaches to fashion, including the origins of dress and ornamentation; rituals and morality in dress; social organization and dress; the relationships of dress to self-concepts and maturation; stability and change in patterns of dress. Although there are few essays that focus exclusively on women and fashion, there are several that are useful to a study of the subject. In "Themes in Cosmetics and Grooming," for example, Murray Wax (a market researcher) offers several generalizations about why women try to make themselves more attractive through cosmetics and dress. Wax suggests that women dress themselves "in anticipation of a *social situation,*" that sociability is more important than sexuality in determining what a woman will wear (Roach and Eicher, 44, 45; Wax's italics). Wax, as most of the other contributors, takes it as a given that in modifying her body a woman improves its appearance. "The woman," he remarks, "who has the patience, the skill, and, most important, the eager and self-disciplined attitude toward her body can—even with limited natural resources—make of her appearance something aesthetically interesting and sexually exciting" (Roach and Eicher, 44). Perhaps most incredible in this context is the report written by Theo K. Miller, Lewis G. Carpenter, and Robert B. Buckley. In their "Therapy of Fashion" (written in 1960), they describe an experiment conducted in a mental hospital among female patients; this experiment was "designed to recreate *healthy feminine characteristics* in a selected group of women patients" (Roach and Eicher, 269; emphasis added). The experiment began with a fashion show, which was followed by individual consultation in which experts advised patients on what suited them best, and concluded with a fashion show in which the test group modeled the clothes they had designed and made themselves. If we are to believe this account, this project was responsible for the redemption or at least the improved conditions of several patients. One patient is quoted as saying that, after one of the classes, " 'all at once the clouds rolled back, the sun was shining, and I felt *like myself* again' " (Roach and Eicher, 270; emphasis added). Although I have no major reservations about the premise that serious neglect of one's appearance can be a sign of or a corollary to mental illness—and a reversal of this neglect a sign of or corollary to recovery or improvement—I find disturbing the authors' assumptions (and one presumes the experimenter's assumptions) about what constitute "healthy feminine characteristics." Implicit in this entire report is the notion that a healthy woman is one who conforms to society's dictates regarding her appearance. (Phyllis Chesler's *Women and Madness* should be read as an antidote to this article, as should Simone de Beauvoir's *The Second Sex;* discussed below, in chapter seven.)

On a related issue is Lawrence Langner's "Clothes and Government," which is a discussion of the political uses to which clothes are put. In Langner's view, "one of mankind's most ingenious uses of clothing is to employ it to demonstrate the authority of individuals or groups and to transform this authority into the power of government" (Roach and Eicher, 124). Langner goes on to say that "one of man's first innovations was to use clothes to assist him in dominating others" (Roach and Eicher, 124). Although Langner is using the male pronoun generically, we might, with some gain, use it in its sex-specific meaning and apply his observations to how men have used clothing to dominate women; Langner himself, however, seems unaware of this possible application of his ideas as he focuses exclusively on class and caste as social and economic stratifications. One might profitably compare what he is saying here (in 1959) to what feminists were arguing about women's clothes in the late nineteenth century. One also might look at the uniform of the businessman and the recent spate of advice books addressed to women who want careers in business, in which they are adjured to dress, in effect, like the men. (See also Una Stannard's essay discussed below.)

Yet another provocative essay is Ernest Crawley's history of the origins of certain fashions. In "The Sexual Background of Dress," he informs us that the Elizabethan farthingale, which later became transmuted into the hoops and the crinoline, was "like most other feminine fashions in dress ...invented by courtesans" (Roach and Eicher, 73). In other words, those innovations that most exaggerated the woman's breasts and hips were introduced by women who made a living with their bodies. In piquant contrast to this is the passage from the New Jersey sumptuary laws quoted by Elizabeth B. Hurlock in "Sumptuary Law." When New Jersey was still a British colony, it passed a law that read, in part, that any woman who might " 'impose upon, seduce, or betray into matrimony any of his Majesty's subjects, by virtue of scents, cosmetics, washes, paints, artificial teeth, false hair, or high-heeled shoes, shall incur the penalty of the law now in force against witchcraft and like misdemeanors' " (Roach and Eicher, 299). From this passage it appears that the men of New Jersey understood the true meaning of the word *glamour*—that is, to cast a spell.

Perhaps the best feature of Roach and Eicher's book is its incredibly long and fully annotated bibliography, which runs for sixty pages. The essays themselves remain tied to their time and, as such, make far too many unsettling assumptions about women. To give them credit, however, they constitute a substantial resource and a helpful introduction to a complex subject.

Perhaps the most interesting period in the study of American fashion is the reform movement of the nineteenth century. During this time several notable feminists, including Elizabeth Cady Stanton and Sarah M. Grimké, worked valiantly for reform in woman's dress in the belief that the long heavy skirts and cinched waists were inimical to woman's health and general well-being. Two essays that provide insights to this movement are Robert E. Riegel's "Women's Clothes and Women's Rights" and Jeanette C. Lauer and Robert H. Lauer's "The Battle of the Sexes: Fashion in Nineteenth-Century America." Riegel's essay covers the period of reform, roughly between 1851 and 1920. Summarizing the feminist objections to women's dress in the mid-nineteenth century, Riegel suggests that they were based on the question of women's health and the conviction that "current feminine clothes incited immorality" (Riegel, 390). In the latter view, according to Riegel, the feminists were supported by the conservative element who were themselves critical of what they considered to be the "immodest and immoral" nature of women's dress (Riegel, 391). At the beginning of the reform movement, the feminists argued that women's dress was the workings of a male conspiracy designed to keep women economically and physically helpless—and thus slaves to marriage. By the end of the movement, the reformers were blaming "greedy manufacturers intent upon large profits" (Riegel, 400). Various mid-century proponents of dress reform included Lydia Sayer, who fought for it in her publication *The Sibyl* even after she had been deserted by the feminists who felt dress reform was deflecting from more important issues. Although few went so far as recommending nudity as a solution, Riegel does cite evidence that Charlotte Perkins Gilman proposed it as a solution to the immorality incited by provocative dress. Another, less radical but still quite unusual solution was that of Dr. Mary E. Walker, who simply wore men's clothes—and was occasionally arrested for doing so. By the late nineteenth century, the reform movement had attenuated considerably, in part because women did not like to suffer public abuse by wearing more comfortable but less proper dress and because fashion itself was changing without the efforts of the agitators. By the twentieth century, women were already enjoying more education and more opportunities in the professions, so the early arguments of the feminists, who had claimed that heavy cumbersome clothes would keep them out of useful work, were no longer valid. In short, as Riegel observes, dress reform had followed, not precipitated, the emancipation of American women (Riegel, 401). Riegel's essay is lavishly documented with both primary and secondary sources.

In "The Battle of the Sexes: Fashion in Nineteenth-Century America," Jeanette C. Lauer and Robert H. Lauer discuss what they consider to be the four major beliefs that constituted the struggle for reform in women's dress in the second half of the nineteenth century. That is, because, in general, the nineteenth century held that certain clothes were appropriate for each sex, women who violated fashion taboos were perceived as going against the natural (God-given) order of things. Second, the fashion of the day, with its emphasis on corsets and long, heavy skirts, was regarded as instrumental in keeping women subordinate to men and ensconced in the home; certainly it limited their mobility and prevented them from engaging in most physical activities. Third, which constituted a sort of double bind, women were scorned—primarily by men—for permitting themselves to be dictated to by fashion, although men mocked those women who attempted to counter the fashion by wearing such innovative garments as bloomers. Finally, in direct relationship to the previous belief, men were convinced that they had a right to dictate what women wore. From this list, it is clear that Lauer and Lauer perceive the conflict over women's dress to be intimately involved with the larger issue of women's rights. Their essay is illustrated and their argument bolstered with quotations from both sides of the reform question, including a derisive song entitled "The Bloomer Costume" which was popular in 1851.

Some of the sources that Riegel and Lauer and Lauer draw on are available in Aileen Kraditor's *Up from the Pedestal: Selected Writings in the History of American Feminism,* which includes a short section on "The Relation of Women's Fashions to Woman's Status" in the nineteenth century. For example, Kraditor quotes from Sarah M. Grimké's 1838 article, "Dress of Women," in which Grimké remarks that men are "ever ready to encourage" vanity of dress in women as a way to keep women from achieving equality (Kraditor, 123). In an undated manuscript Elizabeth Smith Miller describes how and why she designed what came to be known as the Bloomer costume, which Amelia Bloomer popularized in her publication *The Lily.* In a series of letters Gerrit Smith and Elizabeth Cady Stanton debate the relationship between fashion and equality. Smith argues that those "doctrines and sentiments" that keep women subordinate would die out if women only were to "give up the irrational modes" of dress that so clearly express their bondage to men (Kraditor, 126). Smith goes on to argue that if women do not throw off their "clothes-prison," all the strivings of the woman's movement will be for naught (Kraditor, 128). Stanton replies that where Smith claims to be radical, what she would like to see is a revolution of institutions, not of dress, that she has "no reason to hope that pantaloons would do more for us than they have done for man himself" (Kraditor, 130). In an impassioned 1871 essay, *Constitutional Equality a Right of Woman,* Tennessee Claflin condemns the current fashion for its hypocrisy, its interference with free movement, and for contributing to "the class of complaints known as Female Weakness" (Kraditor, 134). Of women's expensive ornamental dress, Thorstein Veblen, in *Theory of the Leisure Class* (1899), remarks that the "reason for all this conspicuous leisure and attire on the part of women lies in the fact that they are servants to whom, in the differentiation of economic functions, has been delegated the office of putting in evidence their master's ability to pay" (Kraditor, 136; on Veblen, see also below).

Although the issue of dress reform was overshadowed by the Civil War, it did not completely die out among its proponents. One indication of its status is evident in the speech delivered by Marie M. Jones to the 1864 World's Health Convention in New York City. In this speech, *Woman's Dress: Its Moral and Physical Relations,* which is available on microfiche as part of the Pamphlets in American History, Jones makes the pragmatic suggestion that women should treat fashion as "it really is, a matter of health and convenience, not of principle" (Jones, 29). This conclusion is somewhat surprising as she expends considerable energy attacking dress as "the idol at which woman" has worshipped; she has also recommended replacing the constricting fashion of the nineteenth century with the Reform Dress—for which she includes patterns (Jones, 5). Like other proponents of reform, Jones argues that fashionable dress has literally and figuratively "dwarfed" and "crippled" woman's "mind, heart, soul, and body" (Jones, 5-6). Corsets she identifies as "death-dealing instruments" (Jones, 16). Her ideal solution is the short skirted Reform Dress that hangs more loosely on the woman's body; but because she suffered public humiliation and abuse while wearing such a dress, her compromise is to "make the long dress hygienic" (Jones, 24). She compromises primarily because she believes that dress should not impair a person's well-being, and she argues, with considerable merit, that there is little advantage to wearing a more comfortable dress if doing so brings public scorn upon one. Martyrdom, in other words, is not for everyone.

Exactly thirty years later, in 1894, Thorstein Veblen, in "The Economic Theory of Women's Dress," added a new element to the controversy over women's clothing—that of the economics of "conspicuous consumption" (Veblen, 205). Arguing that fashion has become "an index of the wealth of its wearer—or, to be more precise, of its owner, for the wearer and the owner are not necessarily the same person," Veblen asserts that "almost the sole function of women" is to demonstrate "her economic unit's ability to pay" (Veblen, "Economic," 199, 200). Citing the three "cardinal principles of the theory of woman's dress" as expensiveness, novelty, and ineptitude, Veblen explains women's dress as clothing that is intended to—or at least appear to—"hamper, incommode, and injure the wearer, for in so doing it proclaims the wearer's pecuniary ability to endure idleness and physical incapacity" (Veblen, "Economic," 204, 203). Thus the skirt endures as a major feature of clothing precisely because, in Veblen's view, "it is cumbrous" (Veblen, "Economic," 203). Veblen elaborates on this theory of fashion in *The Theory of the Leisure Class* (1899). In chapter seven, "Dress as an Expression of the Pecuniary Culture," he reiterates much of what he said in his earlier essay and adds some pertinent remarks about the function of the corset, which he terms "a mutilation, undergone for the purpose of lowering the subject's vitality and rendering her permanently and obviously unfit for work" (Veblen, *Theory*, 172). On the subject of corsets, Veblen goes on to say in his book that the truly wealthy, who are beyond the possible aspersion that they must work manually, have taken to not wearing corsets. Those who do wear them are lower-class women who, on special occasions, desire to emulate the leisured class and those of the higher social classes who "have recently and rapidly risen into opulence" (Veblen, *Theory*, 185). That is, the corset is popular during the period of transition from lower to higher "levels of pecuniary culture" (Veblen, *Theory*, 185).

Although Veblen seems quite certain of his interpretation of the role of the corset in women's fashion, scholars more recently have identified it as something of a controversial issue. In "The Exquisite Slave: The Role of Clothes in the Making of the Victorian Woman," for example, Helene Roberts posits several interpretations of woman's dress. Roberts's basic thesis is that women's clothes "clearly projected the message of a willingness to conform to the submissive-masochistic pattern" of femininity and also "helped mold female behavior to the role of the 'exquisite slave' " (Roberts, 557). The paradigmatic example that Roberts focuses on is the corset and the practice of tight-lacing, which she claims became almost a cult among some women. In direct opposition to Roberts's remarks about the corset and tight-lacing is David Kunzle's essay (printed in the same issue of *Signs*), "Dress Reform as Antifeminism: A Response to Helene E. Roberts's 'The Exquisite Slave: The Role of Clothes in the Making of the Victorian Woman.' " Kunzle claims that there is not sufficient evidence to support a theory of pandemic tight-lacing; he also claims, contrary to what Roberts says, that those who did practice it were of the lower and not the middle classes.

If corsets were de rigueur for the best-dressed ladies of the nineteenth century, so were they included in the designs of these ladies' bathing costumes, according to Claudia B. Kidwell in *Women's Bathing and Swimming Costume in the United States*. In the early nineteenth century, as Kidwell describes it, it was fashionable for men and women to immerse themselves in the water at spas, at the beach, or at bathing houses—not for physical exercise, but as a therapeutic, medicinal treatment that required almost no exertion at all. Thus the costumes worn for bathing were not designed for movement in the water, but as camouflage to disguise the features of the human body—especially in the case of women, who are often pictured as being fully dressed while standing waist-deep in water. As the century progressed, however, so did the attitudes toward proper bathing costumes. In the 1850s, for example, women wore drawers with long-skirted dresses; by the 1870s women were becoming more fashion-conscious and by the 1890s were wearing what was called the princess-style bathing costume, which was constructed of blouse and trousers in one piece with a skirt that buttoned at the waist and which could be removed for bathing.

Concurrent with these changes were the attitudes toward physical exercise—including swimming. Although Benjamin Franklin had recommended swimming to his friends, it didn't catch on in America until the nineteenth century. In 1846 James Arlington Bennet published *The Art of Swimming,* in which he urged both men and women to learn how to swim. It wasn't until much later in the century, however, that women actually began swimming in any great numbers, one reason being, of course, that it would have been impossible—if not fatal—to swim in the cumbersome bathing costumes of the period. Although the 1890s witnessed an increased interest in women's sports, swimming as a competitive sport didn't gain favor until the twentieth century. In 1909 Adeline Trapp became the first woman to swim the East River in New York City and she did so in a fairly practical one-piece swimming suit—for which she was chastised by some reporters for being immodest. (She compromised in subsequent swims by wrapping herself in cloaks or other protective garments as she emerged from the water.) In 1912 the Stockholm Olympics included a 100-meter race for women swimmers, which suggests that swimming, as a sport, had been officially sanctioned.

Even though there were at this time advertisements for swimming suits in various catalogues and ladies' magazines, the editorial content of the magazines continued to stress the bathing costume. But in 1921, when Jantzen ran a national advertising campaign to publicize its new knit swimming suit line, the gap was breached. Rapidly what had once been a practical response to the requirements of swimming became almost overnight a fashion sensation, with women being urged to purchase at least one new suit each season. By the 1930s, suits no longer had trunks that covered their legs, and the skirt itself was barely identifiable as a skirt. By the 1940s, the two-piece suit with its bare midriff was popular, and women who once had been too weighted down to move in the water had become enthusiastic and accomplished swimmers. In some respects, therefore, it is accurate to say that the increased freedom of mobility that women have won for themselves in the past century and a half is directly reflected in their swim wear.

If the role of technology is implicit in much of what Kidwell suggests, it is more directly addressed in the following two essays. In "Feminine Hygiene, Fashion, and the Emancipation of American Women," for example, Fred E. H. Schroeder posits a complex series of interrelationships among women's liberation, fashion, and the development of sanitary napkins and tampons. It is Schroeder's belief that the advances in technology—from the 1890s when mail-order catalogues carried menstrual products to 1921 when Kotex was introduced—have had a direct bearing on women's fashions. Women's skirts remained long and bulky throughout the nineteenth century and into the twentieth, according to Schroeder, in part as protective camouflage for the menstruating woman who didn't wish to be humiliated by having her condition made public. With the invention of celluloid fabrics, which was stimulated by the war shortages, women were given the opportunity to purchase inexpensive, disposable sanitary products that offered more reliable protection than the menstrual cloths they had been accustomed to wearing under their heavy skirts and many petticoats. Thus, Schroeder argues that mass marketing of sanitary napkins—and eventually tampons —directly contributed to woman's increasing freedom in the realm of fashion by allowing her, without peril, to shorten her skirts and wear sporty clothes.

The role of technology in democratizing fashion is discussed in "Everywoman's Jewelry: Early Plastics and Equality in Fashion," by Eleanor Gordon and Jean Nerenberg. After establishing a brief history of the changes in women's fashion that were made possible by the advent of new production processes in the early twentieth century, the authors focus on the changes in fashion wrought by the development of synthetic materials that we today loosely refer to as plastics. What the authors find important about the emergence of plastic costume jewelry is the fact that it was accepted, not as a substitute or imitation of expensive jewelry, but as a mode of decoration in its own right. Furthermore, plastic or costume jewelry was cheap enough that virtually everyone could afford to buy it, an option enjoyed by both the very rich and the relatively poor women of America. It also contributed to the concept that fashion could be youthful and even amusing; as the authors put it, it "provided fashion for everyone to laugh at, to enjoy, to wear" (Gordon and Nerenberg, 643). As such, it helped destroy the same class barriers that fashion had heretofore worked to uphold.

An essay that treats fashion as an expression of sexual class and not just economic class is "The Mask of Beauty" by Una Stannard. Basing her thinking on the work of several well-known theorists, Stannard investigates the myth that women are the beautiful sex, concluding that the "cult of beauty in women...is, in fact, an insanity, for it is posited on a false view of reality" (Gornick and Moran, 130). Offering a panoramic view of the self-mutilation that women have undertaken in the hope of making themselves beautiful, she remarks laconically that "the pursuit of beauty" must be "a great anesthetic" (Gornick and Moran, 120; on the subject of women's self-mutilation, see also Mary Daly, *Gyn/Ecology: The Metaethics of Radical Feminism*, discussed below, in chapter seven). It is Stannard's conviction that the publicly acclaimed beauties, such as those in beauty contests, are intended as models of the role all women are expected to play; that is, women are "articles of conspicuous consumption in the male market" (Gornick and Moran, 123). In this statement, Stannard borrows some of the ideas of Thorstein Veblen (see above); she also reflects some of the ideas forwarded by Charlotte Perkins Gilman in *Women and Economics*, in which Gilman states that women, by economic necessity, are forced into exaggerating their female characteristics in order to attract a man (see chapter seven). Stannard, when she discusses narcissism and its social purpose, seems to draw on the thinking of Simone de Beauvoir (see *The Second Sex*, discussed below, in chapter seven). Observing that women are taught to regard themselves as sex objects, Stannard argues that the consequence of this brainwashing is to instill in women a permanent infantile narcissism. As sexual objects, women function as foils to men, buttressing their insecure masculinity by their own exaggerated femaleness. In short, according to Stannard, it is the function of fashion—be it cosmetics or dress—to strengthen the superiority of men by insuring the subordination of "the false peacock of the species" (Gornick and Moran, 122).

Another theoretical approach to women's fashion, "Icons of Popular Fashion," appears in Ray B. Browne and Marshall Fishwick's collection of essays, *Icons of America*. In this particular essay, Valerie Carnes argues that "fashion (in the sense of style or 'manners') forms a visible, popular iconology, revealing much about our values, attitudes, and assumptions about 'the good life'" (Browne and Fishwick, 228). Beginning with the politically charged 1960s, Carnes sees a new significance to fashion in the United States and a new source of its models. As she puts it, "fashion became more than itself. More than ever before, it was a code, a secret system of signals, a highly complex and subtle iconology that both shaped and reflected the volatile social values and ideologies of the decade" (Browne and Fishwick, 231). Rather than looking to Hollywood and its stars for their models as they had in the 1940s and 50s, women of the 1960s looked to the purveyors of fashion itself. There they found such paradigms of fashion as "Realgirls, Swingers, Gamines, Ingenues, Kooks...Hippie Girls, Beautiful Creatures, Free Souls"—all recognizable by their extreme youth, their boyish, skinny figures, and their sense of adventure (Browne and Fishwick, 231). According to Carnes, several institutions contributed to the growth and popularity of this new fashion icon; among those she identifies are the fashion industry itself, the magazine and advertising industries, and what she calls the "entertainment media" (Browne and Fishwick, 231). In Carnes's opinion, these institutions were so successful in promulgating a new ideal of dress—and, by implication, a new ideal of womanhood itself—because they filled the moral vacuum that was at the heart of the Me generation. In a time when the past was suspect and solutions to complex problems were supposed to be instantaneous, this "new iconology of surfaces" met the superficial needs of what were essentially superficial people (Browne and Fishwick, 231). With individual expression deemed the highest good, "the ultimate iconographical gesture" in a consumer-oriented society is that of buying and wearing clothes (Browne and Fishwick, 236-37). Fashion became a shorthand route to and expression of identity. In effect, clothing expressed the politics and values of its wearers. No longer was it necessary to spend years coming to a political or philosophical position. Instead, according to Carnes, by making a simple purchase of clothing one could obtain the right "uniform" and—hey, presto!—automatically become a card-carrying member of whatever group one desired. In McLuhan's terms, the medium (fashion) was the massage (message).

As this summary suggests, Carnes, in "Icons of Popular Fashion," moves from the peculiarly female role in fashion to a more universal one. In the first part of her essay, she focuses primarily on the changing appearances of women in the 1960s and explains these changes in sociological terms based on the institutionalization of fashion icons. In the second part of her essay, she turns to the general effects on the society itself that a surface iconology can have. Using Walter Weisskopf's concept of a value-empty society, she argues that the surface icons of popular fashion are particularly appealing to persons who are forced to look inward for all value and meaning. Because of its ability to establish an ever-changing "personal style," clothing becomes the most valued commodity (Browne and Fishwick, 236). Fashion, in other words, is indistinguishable from the human being. Carnes's essay is illustrated with photographs of fashions representative of the 1960s.

Although her focus is British, Annette Drew-Bear, in "Cosmetics and Attitudes Towards Women in the Seventeenth Century," does provide a fascinating account of what cosmetics were in use at that time. By quoting widely from drama and poetry, she also demonstrates the seventeenth-century notion that the use of cosmetics was related to sexual promiscuity and deceptiveness.

WOMEN IN SPORTS

Janice Kaplan's *Women and Sports* is less a history than an investigation into the relationship between women and athletics—and that between women and their bodies. This is a comprehensive, well-balanced look at the status of women in American sports which has been written for the amateur sports enthusiast. As such, it offers suggestions for how women can become more involved in sport and what the benefits of an active life can be. The book is footnoted and contains comments from other female athletes, both professionals and amateurs. It is divided into nine chapters, each presenting a different approach to the question of women and sports.

"The New Image" asks what athletics can do for women and discusses how women athletes are perceived. In this section Kaplan examines the role of big business in women's sports, such as that taken by Colgate-Palmolive and Virginia Slims who have sponsored professional competition in golf and tennis, respectively. "Physiology" looks at how women have felt alienated from their bodies; one cause of this alienation Kaplan suggests comes from the social attitudes that women are expected to have toward their own bodies. Addressing the question of skill, Kaplan suggests that girls, for example, don't throw a ball as well as boys simply because "they haven't practiced" as much (Kaplan, 34). In this chapter Kaplan also provides data on the percentage of fat in women's bodies, their skeletal structure, and the effects of training on menstruation and pregnancy. In other words, she is providing accurate, scientific information that she hopes will combat the mythology that would keep women off the playing fields for their own good. In "Femininity and Feminism," she goes one step farther in document-ing the problems that some women have had in reconciling their athletic capabilities to the notion of femininity. To do this she looks at the careers of several ice-skating champions, such as Tenley Albright, Peggy Fleming, Janet Lynn, Dorothy Hamill, and Linda Fratianne—all of whom are remem-bered for their beauty as much as their skating. In this light, Kaplan also looks at the recent phenomenon of anorexia nervosa, as a consequence of which girls literally starve themselves to death.

As a counterpoint to this chapter, Kaplan argues in "Sex and Sports" that, contrary to myth, participation in athletics actually increases a woman's sexuality and her sexual responsiveness. To reinforce this assertion, Kaplan points out, in "Everyone Can Do It," that exercise is beneficial in reducing stress and anxiety. Up to this point in her study, she has demonstrated the advantages of engaging in sports—not just as a student, but as an adult. To do this she has taken pains to debunk the negative stereotypes and myths that have plagued women's athletics, and she has done this successfully by referring to current research on women's physiology and by interviewing numerous women athletes—all of whom are well content with the relationship they have with their own bodies.

The final four chapters complete the self-help portion of her book. In "Choosing a Sport," she offers candid, useful advice about how to select physical exercise that is suitable for the individual woman and therefore likely to be maintained. In "Nutrition, Diets, and Secret Potions," she discusses the need for a proper diet. In "Competition and Attitude" she argues reasonably enough that women should be allowed not just to play sports but to compete in them—even if it means against men. In "Moving On" Kaplan repeats her basic contentions that women have made progress in sport and that sports themselves can keep women in touch with their bodies. This is a very upbeat book, designed primarily to encourage women to incorporate physical activity into their daily lives. As a record of recent medical and psychological studies that validate the advantages of sports to women, it is also quite informative.

Some of the most intellectually stimulating approaches to the subject of women and sport are those contained in Carole A. Oglesby's collection of essays, *Women and Sport: From Myth to Reality*. For her book, Oglesby has assembled work from twelve different experts in the field, and most of the essays are original pieces, not reprints. Her book is divided into two major parts: one, "Women's Sport: Society and Ourselves," with three subsections; and two, "Women's Sport: Myth, Reality, and Social Change," with no subsections. In an introductory essay, "Prologue: The Myth," Betty Spears provides a quick overview of the history of women in sports; beginning with accounts of Greek attitudes toward women's athletics, she moves to summaries of the changing attitudes held by Americans. She notes that in the Puritan colonies, for example, "little if any recreation was permitted," so not surprisingly women were not active in sports (Oglesby, 7). By the nineteenth century, however, American women had their own national championships in golf (1885) and tennis (1887). What Spears does, in other words, is resurrect forgotten information and in so doing present a balanced picture of women's participation in and exclusion from sports.

Section one of part one, "Society and the Female Body," is composed of two chapters. Jackie Hudson's study, "Physical Parameters Used for Female Exclusion from Law Enforcement and Athletics," reviews the extensive research and literature on women's and men's physical capabilities and characteristics. Her paper is very detailed (she cites over one hundred sources) and intended to demonstrate that the theories and data that men draw on when they attempt to keep women out of law enforcement and sports are both misleading and incorrect. Although Sharon Mathes's study is more inconclusive than Hudson's, she does pose some intriguing questions. What she wants to know, as she says in "Body Image and Sex Stereotyping," is whether a person's willingness to participate in sports can be correlated positively with how she feels about or sees her own body. That is, Mathes wants to establish what the relationship is between self-perception and the kinds and levels of physical activity a person engages in. In Mathes's opinion, most of the research done in this area has not been conducted in enough depth to provide reliable answers. Her purpose, therefore, seems to be to stimulate interest in further studies on these issues.

Section two, "Society, Sport, and Sexuality," contains three essays. In Carole Oglesby's "The Masculinity/Femininity Game: Called on Account of..." (her ellipsis), she posits that "traditional sport has been a social mode (a socialization process) for the particular stylization of sexuality which is normative in our society" (Oglesby, 76). But if sport has helped to define our traditional images of masculinity and femininity, it can also be used, according to Oglesby, to redefine them. Arguing that current constructions of masculinity and femininity harm both males and females by alienating persons from themselves, Oglesby proposes a redefinition of the terms *masculine* and *feminine*. Identifying sexuality as "a quality of human interaction," she would like to see "masculinity" defined in terms of a man's ability to interact successfully with females; and "femininity" defined in terms of a woman's ability to interact successfully with men (Oglesby, 84-85). She is, in other words, trying to treat sexuality not as a genetic given, but as a form of self-perception. Rather than using sports to train men to be more masculine — in the traditional sense of the concept — she wants to use sports to train both men and women to become more androgynous. Oglesby's ideas are complemented by those of Mary E. Duquin in "The Androgynous Advantage." Distinguishing between a male's "instrumental" activities and a woman's "expressive" behavior, Duquin discusses the consequences of treating sports solely as agents of masculine orientation. Like Oglesby, she too would like to see sports perceived as androgynous activities, intended to bring out both instrumental and expressive behavior in both sexes. Patricia Del Rey, cognizant of the sexual polarities in contemporary society, focuses on the problems active women have in coping in a situation that is far from the androgynous ideal envisioned by Oglesby and Duquin. Her contribution to this collection, "The Apologetic and Women in Sport," which is reprinted from D. M. Landers and R. W. Christina's *Psychology of Motor Behavior and Sport*, summarizes the often contradictory attitudes that female athletes have about themselves as women and what strategies they invoke to retain their femininity in male-dominated and male-oriented professions. What is particularly intriguing about all three of the essays in this section is the fact that the relationship between the body and self-perception is the paramount issue; what this suggests is a new field of inquiry that integrates perceptual and sports theory and does so in a social and historical context. Sport, as these scholars imply, is not only a physical activity but also mental and psychological constructs. As such, its literature is at the heart of the new feminist criticism.

Section three, "Society, Sport Involvement, and Sport Achievement," also contains three theoretical, highly researched essays that look into the relationship between women and sport. Susan L. Greendorfer, in "Socialization into Sport," reviews the literature in this field and concludes that there are several "unexplored topics which merit attention" (Oglesby, 130). She calls for more precise definitions of the term *sport*, for more comparative studies between women who participate in athletics and those who don't, and more between male and female participants. She concludes that the woman who engages in sports activity begins to do so early in life and that "peers, family and teachers-coaches represent three social systems influencing female socialization into sport" (Oglesby, 131). She cites over 170 studies. Susan Birrell, in "Achievement-Related Motives and the Woman Athlete," examines the myths surrounding the female athlete. Of particular interest are her discussions of what she calls "Achievement-Related Motives," which she breaks down into questions about "the *need to achieve* (or hope of success), the *fear of failure*, and the *fear of success*" (Birrell's italics; Oglesby, 145). After reviewing more than one hundred sources, Birrell concludes that studies of women's fear of success may be seriously flawed and that women can be taught to develop their motivation to achieve. (For a discussion of Matina Horner's studies of women's fear of success, see Vivian Gornick's *Essays in Feminism*, discussed above, in chapter one.) In the final chapter in this section, "Beliefs About Success and Failure: Attribution and the Female Athlete," Maureen C. McHugh, Mary E. Duquin, and Irene Hanson Frieze apply to women athletes a form of "attribution theory" that deals with causal explanations of success or failure. Suggesting that this theory has "important implications for coaches and female athletes" alike, McHugh et al. argue that its application "may increase both the performance levels and the self-esteem and confidence of female athletes" (Oglesby, 188).

Part two, "Women's Sport: Myth, Reality, and Social Change," is composed of four chapters. Wilma Scott Heide's "Feminism for a Sporting Future" is a call for more widespread participation of women in sports and for absolute equality in terms of facilities and equipment. Heide also argues that women need to teach sport to other women because of the positive role-modeling possible in these circumstances. In "Federal Civil Rights Legislation and Sport," Elizabeth R. East reviews the provisions, enforcement, and applications of four federal laws: the Equal Pay Act of 1963 as Amended by the Education Amendments of 1972; Title VII of the Civil Rights Act of 1964 as Amended by the Equal Employment Opportunity Act of 1972; Executive Order 11246 as Amended by Executive Order 11375 (combatting sex discrimination in education); and Title IX of the Education Amendments of 1972. In "The ERA and Women's Sport: An Hypothetical Trial Case," Carol L. Rose presents her version of the "opposing arguments that can be expected to be brought before the first court to hear a case involving sex discrimination in interscholastic athletics" once the Equal Rights Amendment has been ratified (Oglesby, 222). In "Women and the Sport Governance System," Carole A. Oglesby presents for analysis the "structure of the international sport governance system" (Oglesby, 247).

Another publication that investigates the issues surrounding Title IX is "What Constitutes Equality for Women in Sport? Federal Law Puts Women in the Running." This pamphlet was prepared by the Project on the Status and Education of Women of the Association of American Colleges and was written by Margaret Dunkel; it is an ERIC document. This essay is primarily useful in identifying the issues that surround the exceedingly complex question in its title; the essay is not intended to answer the question but to demonstrate its complexity and the implications of possible solutions. It is followed by helpful citations and a bibliography of resources, published and unpublished, relating to the question of women in sport.

Like Carol Oglesby's *Women and Sport*, Stephanie L. Twin's *Out of the Bleachers: Writings on Women and Sport* is a welcome addition to a field still largely ignored by feminist scholars. Although Twin's book is not as scientifically oriented as Oglesby's, it does provide a serious look at the subject of women and sport. *Out of the Bleachers* is divided into three parts: (1) "Physiology and Social Attitudes: Separating Fact from Fiction"; (2) "Sportswomen: Reflections on Their Lives"; and (3) "The Structure of Women's Sports: Looking to the Future." The first few essays of part one contain facts about women and sports that have been gleaned from recent scientific studies on the effects of physical activity on women's bodies. The essays that constitute the second half of part one reflect the social mythologies that have prevented women from taking themselves seriously as athletes. These essays are notable for their historical interest, as, for example, Arabella Kenealy's 1899 "Woman as Athlete," in which she argues that women do not have enough energy to engage in sports and still remain feminine or ladylike. Her argument is based on the premise that individuals have a limited amount of "force" or energy to expend in a lifetime, and that force spent in physical activity can only be stolen from that required for other activities. Women who insist on exercising strenuously, according to this belief, are automatically less feminine because they do not have sufficient energy to put into their womanly qualities. Also included in this section is a 1912 essay by Dudley A. Sargent, M.D., entitled, "Are Athletics Making Girls Masculine? A Practical Answer to a Question Every Girl Asks." Dudley's answer is that women need exercise fully as much as men do; but, in order to prevent women from developing masculine physical traits, sports should be adapted especially for women. A second view of women as "truncated males" is that posited by Paul Weiss in "Women Athletes," reprinted from his 1969 *Sport: A Philosophical Inquiry*.

Part two of *Out of the Bleachers* contains essays by and about female athletes. Included in this section is a biographical essay on Willye B. White and an autobiographical essay by Althea Gibson. Of particular historical note is Frances E. Willard's 1895 essay, "How I Learned to Ride the Bicycle"—a feat she accomplished when she was fifty-three years old. Part three contains an essay on Title IX and essays by two of the most provocative thinkers in the field, Jack Scott ("A Radical Ethic for Sports") and Harry Edwards ("Desegregating Sexist Sport"). It also contains a brief but comprehensive history of women and sports, written by Twin herself. This is a well-researched essay that provides a perspective on the subject not found elsewhere. *Out of the Bleachers*, as few books have done, manages to be both nonsexist and nonracist. As a result, it provides a valuable perspective on women's popular culture. It is also profusely illustrated with photographs of women athletes.

Although Donna Mae Miller's *Coaching the Female Athlete* is primarily directed toward those individuals in the profession of coaching women, it does contain some information of use to those studying the role of women in sports. Of special note are the bibliographies that follow each of her eleven chapters and the first two chapters themselves. Chapter one, "Dimensions of Athletic Programs for Girls and Women," summarizes the history of women in athletics, the current situation (early 1970s), and the potential problems inherent in women's athletics. Chapter two, "Dimensions of the Athlete," focuses on psychosociologic and physiologic considerations. The rest of the chapters are devoted to practical advice on how to help female athletes develop motor skills, how to increase their motivation, how to train and condition their bodies, how to measure and evaluate their performance, and how to teach them. Miller sees in Catharine Beecher's calisthenic program that she introduced at her Hartford Female Seminary in 1828 and in Delphine Hanna's Women's Gymnasium and Field Association that she inaugurated at Oberlin College in 1904 the precursors of organized women's athletics in America. In describing the social pressures that discouraged women from becoming athletes before the twentieth century, Miller states that "a feminine picture of women was conjured up, which seemed to militate against females doing anything more physical than stamping their feet and screaming" (Miller, 5). It is an apt image that Miller supports by reference to several recent studies on the female athlete's perception of herself as a woman. Miller's book is indexed and contains an appendix of illustrated weight-training exercises.

Complementing the scholarly research on women and sport are the articles that have appeared recently in popular magazines. In 1973, *Sports Illustrated*, for example, ran a three-part series, "Women in Sport," by Bil Gilbert and Nancy Williamson, in which they reported on the status of women's athletics and amateur sports. These three articles—"Women Are Getting a Raw Deal"; "Are You Being Two-Faced?"; "Programmed to Be Losers"— are primarily valuable for their anecdotal content. Although the authors seem certain that the attitudes towards women's sports are changing, their articles present conclusive evidence that old ideas die hard. Perhaps the paradigmatic example is that of Ellen Cornish. Cornish was a high school senior in 1972; she was at the time one of the best distance runners in the country but was unable to compete at the high school level because her school did not have a woman's track program. In an effort to give her practice competing, her coach arranged for her to run noncompetitively against the males in a dual meet with a local school. According to Gilbert and Williamson's report, as the race neared its end, "with Cornish fighting for the lead, she was pulled off the track" (Gilbert and Williamson, "Programmed," 62). The two coaches had made a prerace agreement to do this in order to "protect the male runners from the mor- ale-shattering possibility of being beaten by a girl, a possibility that was probable" (Gilbert and Williamson, 62). Such incidents speak volumes; unfortunately for women athletes such incidents are all too common, as these three articles illustrate.

For its cover story on 3 June 1974, *Newsweek* magazine ran "Sports-womanlike Conduct." This story, heavily illustrated, mostly describes the careers of famous women athletes like golf pro Carol Mann, tennis star Billie Jean King, and world-class sprinter Wyomia Tyus. It also includes lesser known figures like jockeys Robyn Smith and Mary Bacon, marathoner Nina Kuscsik, cyclist and speed skater Sheila Young, and golfer Cathy Duggan. In September 1974, *WomenSports* ran a special issue, "Revolution in Women's Sports," in which it offered stories on how federal legislation pertains to women's athletics and others on how to finance women's sports. Four years later, on 26 June 1978, *Time* magazine ran a cover story, "Comes the Revolution." This story, written by B. J. Phillips—a woman who is one of *Time*'s regular sportswriters—begins, rather cutely, with a series of entertaining anecdotes but then does move on to discuss Title IX. Ellie McGrath, in an accompanying essay, "The Weaker Sex? Hah!," reports on women's physiology, including the relationship of sports to menstruation and pregnancy and the effects of exercise on a woman's muscles. On 18 May, 1980, the *New York Times Magazine* section carried a cover story, "Sex Differences in Sports," in which P. S. Wood surveys the anatomical differences between men and women and their respective physical advantages in terms of athletics.

In their book, *Beyond Sugar and Spice: How Women Grow, Learn, and Thrive,* Caryl Rivers, Rosalind Barnett, and Grace Baruch include a chapter on "The Sporting Life: The Second Baseperson Is Here to Stay." In this chapter they report on the prejudicial attitudes regarding women in sport that they discovered as part of a survey. For example, they discovered that many sexually integrated classes don't make the girls play under the same rules as the boys. More positively, the authors themselves provide strategies that parents can employ to avoid sexual stereotyping as they raise their children.

One well-known writer in sports who has not escaped sexual bigotry is James A. Michener. Although he is a self-professed feminist, his history, *Sports in America,* contains only one chapter on women in sport. In this chapter, "Women in Sports," rather than providing much needed information on the history of women's sports, he focuses his attention on how an athletic budget might be divided so women get their fair share under the provisions of Title IX. Using the criteria of fun, health, and public entertainment, he would divide his model budget of nearly 4 million dollars so fun receives 30 percent, health 30 percent, and public entertainment 40 percent; of these fractions, men would receive $2,989,000 or 77 percent of the total and women $911,000 or 23 percent of the total (Michener, 139). On another subject, Michener recommends against allowing boys and girls to compete with one another after the age of thirteen or fourteen. He takes this position because he is afraid of the effects on a boy of losing to a girl; it would be a defeat, according to Michener, that could be "interpreted as a failure in manliness" (Michener, 126).

Remarkably, given his obvious prejudice against women in sport, Michener's television series, "James Michener's America," actually does a credible job in its "Women in Sports." This film, which is directed and produced by Bud Greenspan, is a sixty-minute PBS production that offers a history of women in sport and a report on their current status. Michener narrates the film and interviews several women athletes—amateur and professional. Included are interviews with Kathy V. Switzer (who was the first woman to run in the Boston Marathon), Wyomia Tyus (the only black in the film), Chris Evert Lloyd, Janet Guthrie, Nancy Lopez, Miki King Hogue, and Donna deVarona. Melissa Ludke Lincoln, the writer for *Sports Illustrated* who demanded and received access to the men's locker room, appears, as does Le Anne Schreiber, who in 1978 was named head of the sports department at the *New York Times.* In order to refute the myth that sports harm women physically, the film also includes an interview with Dr. Roy Collins, an orthopedic surgeon who speaks knowledgeably about the physiology of women athletes.

WOMEN IN COMICS

Although the following works do not feature women artists, they do provide historical background on comics as an art form. Maurice Horn's *The World Encyclopedia of Comics* contains a short history of comics, an analytical summary of comics, and an extensive alphabetical listing of entries relevant to comics. It also contains the full text of the 1954 Code of the Comics Magazine Association of America. This code states in part that "all wild, unsavory, gruesome illustrations shall be eliminated" and that no "profanity, obscenity, smut, vulgarity, or words or symbols which have acquired undesirable meanings" shall be permitted (Horn, 751). In the years since the inception of this code, underground comics that violate its proscriptions have proliferated. Two illustrated histories of this intransigent genre are Mark James Estren's *A History of Underground Comics,* which includes excerpts of correspondence between Estren and Trina Robbins; and Don Donahue and Susan Goodrick's *The Apex Treasury of Underground Comics.*

For those interested in the heroines of Marvel comics, Stan Lee has published a collection of reprints, *The Superhero Women,* that features these characters. Each reprint is preceded by a rather flippant two-page essay on the origin of the character. Among those appearing in this book are Medusa, Red Sonja, Sue Storm, Lyra the Femizon, and Shanna the She-Devil. Typical of the remarks that Lee makes are those regarding Red Sonja, who he says "perhaps best typifies the new equality between male and female. Granted, she's lovely, luscious, and every inch a woman. Yet, combat is her calling and adventure is her life" (Lee, 35). This woman warrior is barely clothed in a bikini.

A more legitimate woman warrior is Wonder Woman, and in 1972 *Ms.*

magazine published a special retrospective on the original *Wonder Woman* comics that William Moulton Marston created in 1941. This book, which is in full color, contains both the comics and an introduction by Gloria Steinem and an interpretive essay by Phyllis Chesler. Of Wonder Woman, Steinem observes that she, while not perfect, still "symbolizes many of the values of the women's culture that feminists are now trying to introduce into the mainstream" (n.p.). Chesler places Wonder Woman in the mythological context of Amazons in "The Amazon Legacy." Of the 1940s strips—Marston died in 1947, after which the strip became less feminist— Chesler remarks that "women are seen as natural leaders who could rule the world" (n.p.). Even though the strip is "futuristic" in such assumptions, it is also realistic, to Chesler's mind, as "it clearly portrays the fact that women have to be better and stronger than men to be given a chance in a man's world" (n.p.).

Maurice Horn's *Women in the Comics* is a pictorial history of female characters in comic strips. His book, which is something of an encyclopedia, is arranged chronologically with each section prefaced by a brief history of the period. It is lavishly illustrated and contains a helpful bibliography. The commentary itself is a bit too superficial to be helpful except inasmuch as it provides publishing information.

It is Philippe Perebinossoff's premise, in "What Does a Kiss Mean? The Love Comic Formula and the Creation of the Ideal Teen-Age Girl," that love comics reflect and reinforce the qualities that popular culture expects its young women to have. Basically, these consist of wanting to be popular and, ultimately, to be married and to be a good wife. Some of the themes in these comics are standard to popular culture; that is, women (or girls) cannot trust other women; clothes can transform even the plainest female into a beauty; it is possible to fall in love at first sight; and a woman's place is in the home. In short, according to Perebinossoff, these comics "support the status quo" (Perebinossoff, 833).

Comics that most certainly do not reinforce the status quo are those underground comics written by women, such as Trina Robbins, Lyn Chevli, and Joyce Sutton. In "Women Libeled: Women's Cartoons of Women," Delores Mitchel takes a look at the work of these women and others. The focus of Mitchel's essay is the humor in women's underground comics, as it appeared in a random sample of twenty "comix" published by women artists in California between 1970 and 1976. Of these comics Mitchel reports that females make up 75 to 100 percent of the cast of characters in any one comic (Mitchel, 598). She also concludes that they are "overtly autobiographical," a situation that leads to certain ambiguities in the comics themselves (Mitchel, 598). As Mitchel observes, the women themselves have "experienced social conditioning which encourages aspirations for beauty and poise; yet the comic artist's forte lies in debunking the ideal and the heroic" (Mitchel, 598). Possibly because of this uncomfortable fit, the comic artists satirize these ideals and often themselves for getting caught up in them; they also include a lot of humor that is "based on clothing, cosmetic and hair styles, and household furnishings" (Mitchel, 602). Nor are they above satirizing advertising and women's magazines, which they obviously perceive as trying to manipulate women. In short, according to Mitchel's study, most of the humor she finds in these women's underground comics "is based on the contrast between ideal, socially conditioned expectations and the disillusioning reality characters encounter" (Mitchel, 604). Mitchel's footnotes contain some valuable bibliographical information.

In 1979 the *Journal of Popular Culture* ran an in-depth issue on "Comics as Culture," edited by M. Thomas Inge. Of particular interest in this issue are two essays: Jack Shadoian's "Yuh Got Pecos! Doggone, Belle, Yuh're As Good As Two Men" and Ronald Levitt Lanyi's interview, "Trina, Queen of the Underground Cartoonists." Shadoian's essay focuses on the little-known phenomenon of the genuinely heroic women of the western comics in the late 1940s and early 1950s. Although these stunningly beautiful heroines were no doubt created for—and enjoyed by—a male audience, they are notable for their aggressive, courageous behavior. Among the heroines that Shadoian discusses are Buffalo Belle, Rhoda Trail, Buckskin Belle, and Prairie Kate. Lanyi's interview is with Trina Robbins, a feminist underground cartoonist who edited in 1970 *It Ain't Me, Babe,* the first feminist comic, and in 1977 *Wet Satin,* a collection of women's erotic fantasies. The interview, while providing firsthand information about Robbins herself, is also interesting because she and Lanyi have different views of her work. Lanyi insists on finding phallic symbolism in many of her drawings, and she claims it just isn't there. Another interview with Trina Robbins appears in *Comix Book,* no. 5; this one, conducted by Ed Ward, covers Robbins's early years as a cartoonist and describes how she got started in underground comics.

Investigations into social cartoons have been conducted by Cheris Kramer, who studied the folk linguistics of captions in such popular magazines as the *New Yorker, Playboy, Cosmopolitan,* and *Ladies' Home Journal.* In "Folk Linguistics: Wishy-Washy Mommy Talk: Study of Sex Language Differences through Analysis of *New Yorker* Cartoons," she reports that in these cartoons women speak less often than men, in fewer places than men (women speak primarily in domestic situations, in the home), and less forcefully than men. In "Stereotypes of Women's Speech: The Word from Cartoons," she reports that according to the cartoons she studied, women speak ineffectively and with more restraints on their subjects. In both essays Kramer describes a test she administered to her students, in which they were asked to identify the probable speaker when given only the captions of several cartoons. Although her students did not always agree with the stereotyping behind or inherent in the cartoon captions, they were able, to a statistically significant extent, to identify the sex of the speaker. This would seem to validate her thesis that social cartoons are barometers of folklore because their "humor depends on the exaggeration of popular stereotypes of human behavior" (Kramer, "Folk Linguistics...," 83).

For studies of television cartoons, see Helen White Streicher's "The Girls in the Cartoons" and Richard M. Levinson's "From Olive Oyl to Sweet Polly Purebread: Sex Role Stereotypes and Televised Cartoons", both discussed above, in chapter five).

BIBLIOGRAPHY

ADVERTISING

"Advertising Portraying or Directed to Women." *Advertising Age* 46, no. 16 (21 April 1975): 72, 75-76.

Atwan, Robert, Donald McQuade, and John W. Wright. *Edsels, Luckies, and Frigidaires: Advertising the American Way.* A Delta Special. New York: Dell Publishing Co., 1979.

Chapko, Michael K. "Black Ads Are Getting Blacker." *Journal of Communication* 26, no. 4 (Autumn 1976): 175-78.

Courtney, Alice E., and Thomas W. Whipple. "Women in TV Commercials." *Journal of Communication* 24, no. 2 (Spring 1974): 110-18.

Culley, James D., and Rex Bennett. "Selling Women, Selling Blacks." *Journal of Communication* 26, no. 4 (Autumn 1976): 160-74.

"Equality in Advertising." Special section in *Journal of Communication* 26, no. 4 (Autumn 1976): 160-200.

Gerbner, George. "The Dynamics of Cultural Resistance." In *Hearth and Home: Images of Women in the Mass Media,* edited by Gaye Tuchman, Arlene Kaplan Daniels, and James Benet, pp. 46-50. New York: Oxford University Press, 1978.

Goffman, Erving. *Gender Advertisements.* Introduction by Vivian Gornick. 1976. Reprint. Cambridge, Mass.: Harvard University Press, 1979.

Gornick, Vivian. Introduction to *Gender Advertisements,* by Erving Goffman, pp. vii-ix. 1976. Reprint. Cambridge, Mass.: Harvard University Press, 1979.

———, and Barbara K. Moran, eds. *Woman in Sexist Society: Studies in Power and Powerlessness.* New York: Basic Books, 1971.

Komisar, Lucy. "The Image of Woman in Advertising." In *Woman in Sexist Society: Studies in Power and Powerlessness,* edited by Vivian Gornick and Barbara K. Moran, pp. 207-17. New York: Basic Books, 1971.

Millum, Trevor. *Images of Women: Advertising in Women's Magazines.* Totowa, N.J.: Rowman and Littlefield, 1975.

Mott, Frank Luther. *A History of American Magazines, 1885-1905.* Vol. 4. Cambridge, Mass.: Harvard University Press, Belknap Press, 1957.

Naether, Carl A. *Advertising to Women.* New York: Prentice-Hall, 1928.

O'Kelly, Charlotte G., and Linda Edwards Bloomquist. "Women and Blacks on TV." *Journal of Communication* 26, no. 4 (Autumn 1976): 179-84.

Peterson, Theodore. "Advertising: Its Growth and Effects." In his *Magazines in the Twentieth Century,* pp. 18-43. 2d ed. Urbana: University of Illinois Press, 1964.

Pingree, Suzanne, Robert Parker Hawkins, Matilda Butler, and William Paisley. "A Scale for Sexism." *Journal of Communication* 26, no. 4 (Autumn 1976): 193-200.
Poe, Alison. "Active Women in Ads." *Journal of Communication* 26, no. 4 (Autumn 1976): 185-92.
Polykoff, Shirley. *Does She... or Doesn't She? And How She Did It.* Garden City, N.Y.: Doubleday & Co., 1975.
Presbrey, Frank S. *The History and Development of Advertising.* Garden City, N.Y.: Doubleday, Doran & Co., 1929.
Standard Directory of Advertising Agencies. In *The Agency Red Book,* no. 190. Skokie, Ill.: National Register Publishing Co., June 1980.
Wolff, Janet L. *What Makes Women Buy: A Guide to Understanding and Influencing the New Woman of Today.* New York: McGraw-Hill, 1958.

FASHION

Anspach, Karlyne. *The Why of Fashion.* Ames: Iowa State University Press, 1967.
Beauvoir, Simone de. *The Second Sex.* Translated and edited by H. M. Parshley. 1952. Reprint. New York: Alfred A. Knopf, 1968.
Black, J. Anderson, and Madge Garland. *A History of Fashion.* New York: William Morrow and Co., 1975.
Browne, Ray B., and Marshall Fishwick, eds. *Icons of America.* Bowling Green, Ohio: Bowling Green University Popular Press, 1978.
Carnes, Valerie. "Icons of Popular Fashion." In *Icons of America,* edited by Ray Browne and Marshall Fishwick, pp. 228-40. Bowling Green, Ohio: Bowling Green University Popular Press, 1978.
Chesler, Phyllis. *Women and Madness.* Garden City, N.Y.: Doubleday & Co., 1972.
Claflin, Tennessee [or Tennie C.]. From *Constitutional Equality a Right of Woman.* 1871. Reprint. In *Up From the Pedestal: Selected Writings in the History of American Feminism,* edited by Aileen S. Kraditor, pp. 131-34. Chicago: Quadrangle Books, 1968.
Crawley, Ernest. "The Sexual Background of Dress." In *Dress, Adornment, and the Social Order,* edited by Mary Ellen Roach and Joanne Bubolz Eicher, pp. 72-76. New York: John Wiley & Sons, 1965.
Daly, Mary. *Gyn/Ecology: The Metaethics of Radical Feminism.* Boston: Beacon Press, 1978.
Drew-Bear, Annette. "Cosmetics and Attitudes Towards Women in the Seventeenth Century." *Journal of Popular Culture* 9, no. 1 (Summer 1975): 31-37.
Earle, Alice Morse. *Two Centuries of Costume in America, 1620-1820.* Vol. 1. 1903. Reprint. New York: Benjamin Blom, 1968.
Gilman, Charlotte Perkins. *Women and Economics: A Study of the Economic Relation between Men and Women as a Factor in Social Evolution.* Edited with an introduction by Carl N. Degler. 1898. Reprint. New York: Harper & Row/ Harper Torchbooks, 1966.
Gordon, Eleanor, and Jean Nerenberg. "Everywoman's Jewelry: Early Plastics and Equality in Fashion." *Journal of Popular Culture* 13, no. 4 (Spring 1980): 629-44.
Gornick, Vivian, and Barbara K. Moran, eds. *Woman in Sexist Society: Studies in Power and Powerlessness.* New York: Basic Books, 1971.

Grimké, Sarah Moore. From "Dress of Women." In *Up from the Pedestal: Selected Writings in the History of American Feminism*, edited by Aileen S. Kraditor, pp. 122-23. Chicago: Quadrangle Books, 1968.

Hollander, Anne. *Seeing through Clothes.* New York: Viking Press, 1978.

Hurlock, Elizabeth B. "Sumptuary Law." In *Dress, Adornment, and the Social Order*, edited by Mary Ellen Roach and Joanne Bubolz Eicher, pp. 295-301. New York: John Wiley & Sons, 1965.

Jones, Marie M. *Woman's Dress: Its Moral and Physical Relations, Being an Essay Delivered before the World's Health Convention, New York City, November, 1864.* New York: Miller, Wood & Co., 1865.

Kidwell, Claudia B. *Women's Bathing and Swimming Costume in the United States.* U.S. National Museum Bulletin 250. Contributions from the Museum of History and Technology Paper 64. Washington, D.C.: Smithsonian Institution Press, 1968.

———, and Margaret C. Christman. *Suiting Everyone: The Democratization of Clothing in America.* Washington, D.C.: Smithsonian Institution Press, 1974.

Kraditor, Aileen S., ed. *Up from the Pedestal: Selected Writings in the History of American Feminism.* Chicago: Quadrangle Books, 1968.

Kunzle, David. "Dress Reform as Antifeminism: A Response to Helen E. Roberts's 'The Exquisite Slave: The Role of Clothes in the Making of the Victorian Woman.'" *Signs: Journal of Women in Culture and Society* 2, no. 3 (Spring 1977): 570-79.

Langner, Lawrence. "Clothes and Government." In *Dress, Adornment, and the Social Order*, edited by Mary Ellen Roach and Joanne Bubolz Eicher, pp. 124-27. New York: John Wiley & Sons, 1965.

Lauer, Jeanette C., and Robert H. Lauer. "The Battle of the Sexes: Fashion in Nineteenth-Century America." *Journal of Popular Culture* 13, no. 4 (Spring 1980): 581-89.

Ley, Sandra. *Fashion for Everyone: The Story of Ready-to-Wear, 1870-1970.* New York: Charles Scribner's Sons, 1975.

Miller, Elizabeth Smith. "On the Bloomer Costume." In *Up from the Pedestal: Selected Writings in the History of American Feminism*, edited by Aileen S. Kraditor, pp. 123-24. Chicago: Quadrangle Books, 1968.

Miller, Theo K., Lewis G. Carpenter, and Robert B. Buckey. "Therapy of Fashion." In *Dress, Adornment, and the Social Order*, edited by Mary Ellen Roach and Joanne Bubolz Eicher, pp. 269-70. New York: John Wiley & Sons, 1965.

Riegel, Robert E. "Women's Clothes and Women's Rights." *American Quarterly* 15, no. 3 (Fall 1963): 390-401.

Roach, Mary Ellen, and Joanne Bubolz Eicher, eds. *Dress, Adornment, and the Social Order.* New York: John Wiley & Sons, 1965.

Roberts, Helene. "The Exquisite Slave: The Role of Clothes in the Making of the Victorian Woman." *Signs · Journal of Women in Culture and Society* 2, no. 3 (Spring 1977): 554-69.

Schroeder, Fred E. H. "Feminine Hygiene, Fashion, and the Emancipation of American Women." *American Studies* 17, no. 2 (Fall 1976): 101-10.

Smith, Gerrit. "Correspondence Between Gerrit Smith and Elizabeth Cady Stanton." In *Up from the Pedestal: Selected Writings in the History of Amer-*

ican Feminism, edited by Aileen S. Kraditor, pp. 124-31. Chicago: Quadrangle Books, 1968.

Stannard, Una. "The Mask of Beauty." In *Woman in Sexist Society: Studies in Power and Powerlessness,* edited by Vivian Gornick and Barbara K. Moran, pp. 118-30. New York: Basic Books, 1971.

Stanton, Elizabeth Cady. "Correspondence Between Gerritt Smith and Elizabeth Cady Stanton." In *Up from the Pedestal: Selected Writings in the History of American Feminism,* edited by Aileen S. Kraditor, pp. 124-31. Chicago: Quadrangle Books, 1968.

Veblen, Thorstein. "The Economic Theory of Women's Dress." *Popular Science Monthly* 46 (November 1894): 198-205.

_____. From *The Theory of the Leisure Class.* 1899. Reprint. In *Up from the Pedestal: Selected Writings in the History of American Feminism,* edited by Aileen S. Kraditor, pp. 135-36. Chicago: Quadrangle Books, 1968.

_____. *The Theory of the Leisure Class: An Economic Study of Institutions.* 1899. Reprint. New York: Modern Library, 1934.

Wax, Murray. "Themes in Cosmetics and Grooming." In *Dress, Adornment, and the Social Order,* edited by Mary Ellen Roach and Joanne Bubolz Eicher, pp. 36-45. New York: John Wiley & Sons, 1965.

Weibel, Kathryn. *Mirror Mirror: Images of Women Reflected in Popular Culture.* Garden City, N.Y.: Doubleday Anchor Press, 1977.

Wilcox, R. Turner. *Five Centuries of American Costume.* New York: Charles Scribner's Sons, 1963.

Worrell, Estelle Ansley. *American Costume, 1840-1920.* Harrisburg, Pa.: Stackpole Books, 1979.

SPORTS

Birrell, Susan. "Achievement-Related Motives and the Woman Athlete." In *Women and Sport: From Myth to Reality,* edited by Carole A. Oglesby, pp. 143-71. Philadelphia: Lea & Febiger, 1978.

"Comes the Revolution." Cover story, *Time,* 26 June 1978, pp. 54-59.

Del Rey, Patricia. "The Apologetic and Women in Sport." In *Women and Sport: From Myth to Reality,* edited by Carole A. Oglesby, pp. 107-11. Philadelphia: Lea & Febiger, 1978.

Dunkel, Margaret. "What Constitutes Equality for Women in Sport? Federal Law Puts Women in the Running." Washington, D.C.: Project on the Status and Education of Women of the Association of American Colleges, April 1974. [Available on ERIC.]

Duquin, Mary E. "The Androgynous Advantage." In *Women and Sport: From Myth to Reality,* edited by Carole A. Oglesby, pp. 89-106. Philadelphia: Lea & Febiger, 1978.

East, Elizabeth R. "Federal Civil Rights Legislation and Sport." In *Women and Sport: From Myth to Reality,* edited by Carole A. Oglesby, pp. 205-19. Philadelphia: Lea & Febiger, 1978.

Edwards, Harry. "Desegregating Sexist Sport." In *Out of the Bleachers: Writings on Women and Sport,* edited by Stephanie L. Twin, pp. 188-91, 196-97. Old

Westbury, N.Y.: Feminist Press, 1979.

Gilbert, Bil, and Nancy Williamson. "Are You Being Two-Faced?" *Sports Illustrated,* 4 June 1973, pp. 44-48, 51-54.

_____. "Programmed to be Losers." *Sports Illustrated,* 11 June 1973, pp. 60-67 et passim.

_____. "Sport Is Unfair to Women." *Sports Illustrated,* 28 May 1973, pp. 88-98.

_____. "Women Are Getting a Raw Deal." *Sports Illustrated,* 28 May 1973, pp. 88-98; 4 June 1973, pp. 44-54; 11 June 1973, pp. 60-67 et passim.

Gornick, Vivian. *Essays in Feminism.* New York: Harper & Row, 1978.

Greendorfer, Susan L. "Socialization into Sport." In *Women and Sport: From Myth to Reality,* edited by Carole A. Oglesby, pp. 115-40. Philadelphia: Lea & Febiger, 1978.

Heide, Wilma Scott. "Feminism for a Sporting Future." In *Women and Sport: From Myth to Reality,* edited by Carole A. Oglesby, pp. 195-202. Philadelphia: Lea & Febiger, 1978.

Hudson, Jackie. "Physical Parameters Used for Female Exclusion from Law Enforcement and Athletics." In *Women and Sport: From Myth to Reality,* edited by Carole A. Oglesby, pp. 19-57. Philadelphia: Lea & Febiger, 1978.

Kaplan, Janice. *Women and Sports.* New York: Viking Press, 1979.

Kenealy, Arabella. "Woman as Athlete." In *Out of the Bleachers: Writings on Women and Sport,* edited by Stephanie L. Twin, pp. 35-37, 42-52. Old Westbury, N.Y.: Feminist Press, 1979.

McGrath, Ellie. "The Weaker Sex? Hah!" *Time,* 26 June 1978, p. 60.

McHugh, Maureen C., Mary E. Duquin, and Irene Hanson Frieze. "Beliefs About Success and Failure: Attribution and the Female Athlete." In *Women and Sport: From Myth to Reality,* edited by Carole A. Oglesby, pp. 173-91. Philadelphia: Lea & Febiger, 1978.

Mathes, Sharon. "Body Image and Sex Stereotyping." In *Women and Sport: From Myth to Reality,* edited by Carole A. Oglesby, pp. 59-72. Philadelphia: Lea & Febiger, 1978.

Michener, James A. "James Michener's America: Women in Sports." PBS program. Directed and produced by Bud Greenspan, 1980.

_____. *Sports in America.* New York: Random House, 1976.

Miller, Donna Mae. *Coaching the Female Athlete.* Philadelphia: Lea & Febiger, 1974.

Oglesby, Carole A. "The Masculinity/Femininity Game: Called on Account of ..." In *Women and Sport: From Myth to Reality,* edited by Carole A. Oglesby, pp. 75-88. Philadelphia: Lea & Febiger, 1978.

_____. "Women and the Sport Governance System." In *Women and Sport: From Myth to Reality,* edited by Carole A. Oglesby, pp. 247-54. Philadelphia: Lea & Febiger, 1978.

_____, ed. *Women and Sport: From Myth to Reality.* Philadelphia: Lea & Febiger, 1978.

Phillips, B. J. "Comes the Revolution." *Time,* 26 June 1978, pp. 54-59.

"Revolution in Women's Sports." Special issue of *WomenSports,* September 1974.

Rivers, Caryl, Rosalind Barnett, and Grace Baruch. *Beyond Sugar and Spice: How Women Grow, Learn, and Thrive.* New York: G. P. Putnam's Sons, 1979.

Rose, Carol L. "The ERA and Women's Sport: An Hypothetical Trial Case." In

Women and Sport: From Myth to Reality, edited by Carole A. Oglesby, pp. 221-46. Philadelphia: Lea & Febiger, 1978.

Sargent, Dudley A. "Are Athletics Making Girls Masculine? A Practical Answer to a Question Every Girl Asks." In *Out of the Bleachers: Writings on Women and Sport,* edited by Stephanie L. Twin, pp. 52-62. Old Westbury, N.Y.: Feminist Press, 1979.

Scott, Jack. "A Radical Ethic for Sports." In *Out of the Bleachers: Writings on Women and Sport,* edited by Stephanie L. Twin, pp. 182-87. Old Westbury, N.Y.: Feminist Press, 1979.

Spears, Betty. "Prologue: The Myth." In *Women and Sport: From Myth to Reality,* edited by Carole A. Oglesby, pp. 1-15. Philadelphia: Lea & Febiger, 1978.

"Sportswomanlike Conduct." *Newsweek,* 3 June 1974, pp. 50-55.

Twin, Stephanie L., ed. *Out of the Bleachers: Writings on Women and Sports.* Series: Women's Lives Women's Work. Old Westbury, N.Y.: Feminist Press, 1979.

Weiss, Paul. "Women Athletes." In *Out of the Bleachers: Writings on Women and Sport,* edited by Stephanie L. Twin, pp. 62-75. Old Westbury, N.Y.: Feminist Press, 1979.

Willard, Frances E. "How I Learned to Ride the Bicycle." In *Out of the Bleachers: Writings on Women and Sport,* edited by Stephanie L. Twin, pp. 103-14. Old Westbury, N.Y.: Feminist Press, 1979.

Wood, P. S. "Sex Differences in Sports." *New York Times Magazine* (section 6), 18 May 1980, pp. 30-33, 38, 96, 98, 100, 102, 104.

COMICS

Chesler, Phyllis. "The Amazon Legacy." In *Wonder Woman.* A *Ms.* Book. New York: Holt, Rinehart and Winston and Warner Books, 1972. (n.p.)

Donahue, Don, and Susan Goodrick, eds. *The Apex Treasury of Underground Comics.* Illustrated. New York: Links Books, 1976.

Estren, Mark James. *A History of Underground Comics.* San Francisco: Straight Arrow Books, 1974.

Horn, Maurice. *Women in the Comics.* New York: Chelsea House, 1977.

———, ed. *The World Encyclopedia of Comics.* Illustrated. New York: Chelsea House, 1976.

Kramer, Cheris. "Folk Linguistics: Wishy-Washy Mommy Talk: Study of Sex Language Differences through Analysis of *New Yorker* Cartoons." *Psychology Today* 8, no. 1 (June 1974): 82-85.

———. "Stereotypes of Women's Speech: The Word from Cartoons." *Journal of Popular Culture* 8, no. 3 (Winter 1974): 624-30.

Lanyi, Ronald Levitt. "Trina, Queen of the Underground Cartoonists." An interview. *Journal of Popular Culture* 12, no. 4 (Spring 1979): 737-54.

Lee, Stan. *The Superhero Women.* New York: Simon and Schuster, 1977.

Levinson, Richard M. "From Olive Oyl to Sweet Polly Purebread: Sex Role Stereotypes and Televised Cartoons." *Journal of Popular Culture* 9, no. 3 (Winter 1975): 561-72.

Mitchel, Delores. "Women Libeled: Women's Cartoons of Women." *Journal of*

Popular Culture 14, no. 4 (Spring 1981): 597-610.

Perebinossoff, Philippe. "What Does a Kiss Mean? The Love Comic Formula and the Creation of the Ideal Teen-Age Girl." *Journal of Popular Culture* 8, no. 4 (Spring 1975): 825-35.

Shadoian, Jack. "Yuh Got Pecos! Doggone, Belle, Yuh're As Good As Two Men." *Journal of Popular Culture* 12, no. 4 (Spring 1979): 721-36.

Steinem, Gloria. Introduction to *Wonder Woman.* A *Ms.* Book. New York: Holt, Rinehart and Winston and Warner Books, 1972. (n.p.)

Streicher, Helen White. "The Girls in the Cartoons." *Journal of Communication* 24, no. 2 (Spring 1974): 125-29.

Ward, Ed. "Trina." An interview with Trina Robbins. *Comix Book,* no. 5. Edited by Denis Kitchen, pp. 47-48. Princeton, Wis.: Kitchen Sink Enterprises, a Division of Krupp Comic Works, 1976.

Wonder Woman. Introduction by Gloria Steinem. Interpretative Essay by Phyllis Chesler. A *Ms.* Book. New York: Holt, Rinehart and Winston and Warner Books, 1972.

CHAPTER 7

Theories of Women in
Popular Culture

Although there is not a lot of theoretical material that is specifically addressed to the question of women in popular culture, there are several scholars whose works are applicable to the subject. Some of these scholars and their ideas have been discussed in the preceding chapters; for the most part they do not appear again in the discussion below. Not all genres are equally represented by theoreticians, but a brief survey might include the following: in history, Gerda Lerner, Ann Douglas (Wood), and Sheila Rothman; in literature, Nina Baym, Barbara Christian, and Joanna Russ; in magazines, Betty Friedan; in film, Marjorie Rosen, Molly Haskell, and Sumiko Higashi; in television, George Gerbner; in advertising, Erving Goffman; in fashion, Thorstein Veblen and Valerie Carnes; and in sport, Mary E. Duquin, Sharon Mathes, and Carole A. Oglesby.

The following discussion of theoretical studies is divided into two major time frames; those works that preceded the 1960s and those that followed. There are five major works which I have included that came out before 1960. These works appear to be the seminal texts on which current scholarship is based and from which it derives much of its own radicalism. Although all these texts do not relate specifically to American women and culture, their ideas are certainly pertinent to the subject and therefore should be mentioned at least in passing.

The first of these works is Mary Wollstonecraft's *A Vindication of the Rights of Woman* which was first published in London in 1792 and in which she argues for the equality of the sexes. As long as women are economically and socially dependent upon men, Wollstonecraft remarks, so will they be "cunning, mean, and selfish" (Wollstonecraft, 143). Wollstonecraft further attributes to the economic and social inequities between the sexes the fact that "women at present are by ignorance rendered foolish or vicious" (Wollstonecraft, 192). It would be to the greater good of society, therefore, for a revolution to take place that would put women on an equal footing with men; in short, having freed women from their slavish chains, men would find them "more observant daughters, more affectionate sisters,

more faithful wives, more reasonable mothers—in a word, better citizens"
(Wollstonecraft, 150). The negative attributes that Wollstonecraft assigns
to women she finds not their natural condition but the consequences of
their oppression.

The second of these seminal texts is also British in origin—John Stuart
Mill's *The Subjection of Women.* In this 1869 essay Mill observes that
women's subjection, if it were only a question of logic, could be disputed
and overturned relatively easily. But he finds that women's subjection is
more an emotional than a rational issue and, as such, nearly impossible to
eradicate. Describing women as being in a state of bondage, Mill remarks
that "each individual of the subject-class is in a chronic state of bribery
and intimidation combined" (Mill, 11). This is to say that women are beholden for their very lives to their masters—to men. But men, according to
Mill, require of women more than simple obedience; men, he says, "want
their sentiments" (Mill, 14). And in order to obtain these favors men have
"put everything in practice to enslave their minds" (Mill, 15). They have,
that is, "turned the whole force of education to effect their purpose" (Mill,
15). What his compatriots regard as the natural state of women is, therefore, in Mill's words "an eminently artificial thing—the result of forced
repression in some directions, unnatural stimulation in others" (Mill, 21).
Although in these observations Mill sounds remarkably modern, contemporary feminists do take issue with one of his central ideas. And this is his
notion that it is not, generally speaking, "a desirable custom, that the wife
should contribute by her labor to the income of the family" (Mill, 47).
Rather, the wife should run the home and be responsible for the "domestic
expenditure" (Mill, 47).

Like Wollstonecraft, Mill attributes to the legal and social inequities between the sexes "all the selfish propensities, the self-worship, the unjust
self-preference, which exist among mankind" (Mill, 80). He also contends
that men do not truly know women, remarking in what may be his most
widely quoted summary of the situation that "we may safely assert that
the knowledge which men can acquire of women, even as they have been
and are, without reference to what they might be, is wretchedly imperfect
and superficial, and always will be so, until women themselves have told
all that they have to tell" (Mill, 25).

Another nineteenth-century study of the role of women in society is
Charlotte Perkins Gilman's *Women and Economics: A Study of the Economic Relation between Men and Women as a Factor in Social Evolution.*
In this book Gilman forwards the theory that women of the nineteenth
century are "modified to sex to an excessive degree" because they are born
and bred to consider males their "economic environment" (Gilman, 39).
Working out of three of the major intellectual schools of the late nineteenth century—Darwinism, socialism, and progressivism—Gilman, in what
was a best-seller in its time, blames society—much as do Wollstonecraft

and Mill—for restricting the development of women. In what is the most famous passage of this tract, Gilman sums up the experience of women thus: "Wealth, power, social distinction, fame—not only these, but home and happiness, reputation, ease and pleasure, her bread and butter—all, must come to her through a small gold ring. This is a heavy pressure. It has accumulated behind her through heredity, and continued about her through environment" (Gilman, 71). As the solution to such a debilitating situation and truncated existence, Gilman proposes a radical restructuring of society, which includes such measures as institutionalized child care and public dining facilities—both intended to free women from the strictures of domestic living. Arguing for a more egalitarian form of marriage, Gilman intended thereby to provide the opportunity for both men and women to work outside the home, convinced as she was that all human beings have a fundamental need to work and to be rewarded for their labors.

For this 1966 reprint of the 1898 edition of Gilman's *Women and Economics,* Carl N. Degler has written a biographical essay in which he describes the personal experiences that led Gilman to her radical point of view regarding marriage. (One of her experiences, that of undergoing Silas Weir Mitchell's rest cure, almost literally drove her insane and provided the inspiration for her famous short story, "The Yellow Wallpaper." See introduction above.) Degler also points out that the information that Gilman utilizes in this polemic is not based on original research and is often, in fact, incorrect. But in applying this information to women and women's condition, however, Gilman is both original and brilliantly effective, as evidenced by the fact that much contemporary feminist thinking seems to derive directly from her ideas.

Before discussing these modern feminists, however, two other seminal texts—Thorstein Veblen's *The Theory of the Leisure Class: An Economic Study of Institutions* and Simone de Beauvoir's *The Second Sex*—need to be mentioned. Veblen's 1899 study is based, in part, on his 1894 essay, "The Economic Theory of Women's Dress," in which he introduced his concept of woman's dress as an example of "conspicuous consumption" (both of Veblen's works are discussed above, in chapter six). Simone de Beauvoir draws on this theory in her own work, which is based also on theories of existential philosophy. Although de Beauvoir is writing about French women in particular, she ranges throughout history and several different cultures in order to demonstrate her premise that women have been relegated to the subordinate role of the "other" by men who regard themselves as "subject." As a consequence of their subordination women have been locked into a state of being that is antithetical to the existential concept of becoming. That is to say, men have the opportunity to grow, to become something new, but women are expected to remain the same throughout their lives. In this context, some of de Beauvoir's most interesting essays are those in which she focuses on the role of the woman's body in

modern civilization. In chapter nine, "Dreams, Fears, Idols," for exa
she observes—just as Veblen does—that one of the primary functio
woman in "bourgeois society" has been "*to make a good showing*," that is to
show off her husband's wealth through her own appearance (de Beauvoir, 175;
de Beauvoir's italics). In chapter eighteen, "Social Life," de Beauvoir returns
to this notion and explores its consequences, finding that the tendency in
Western cultures has been for a woman to identify her very being with her
body. And in chapter twenty-two, "The Narcissist," she describes this ultimate form of self-worship, in which women all too often indulge themselves
for lack of more creative activities. Some of *The Second Sex* is by now outdated in its information, some is certainly controversial, but in its entirety
it remains valuable for its ability to inspire and for its amazing compendium
of historical and biological facts pertinent to the female experience.

One of the most provocative books to come out of the recent feminist
movement, and one that is clearly dependent in part on the preceding
seminal studies just discussed, is Shulamith Firestone's *The Dialectic of
Sex: The Case for Feminist Revolution.* In this book, Firestone challenges
the two assumptions dearest to the heart of the paternalistic Western world:
love and the family. Working out of the Marxism and existentialism implicit
in de Beauvoir, Firestone takes the concept of dialectical materialism and
applies it to the sexual class division in Western society. Although her
method is in the Marxist tradition, she is not content with Marx's analysis
because of his antifemale biases. Another of her influences is Freud, who,
she argues, was absolutely correct in perceiving sex as the central issue
of our time. Where Freud errs, she says, is in accepting the status quo;
those of the neo-Freudian school she characterizes by their emphasis on
adjustment, their assumption that one must adjust to a socially determined
reality. Firestone, on the other hand, questions the very fabric of this
society and demands that it be revised in quite a radical fashion. In short,
what she requires is an androgynous society in which the family is dis-
banded and women stop bearing children.

Her suggestion is based on the premise that women are enslaved by the
family—by childbearing and raising—and that the only way to free women
from this enslavement is to do away with it altogether. (Her ideas about
the family should be read in conjunction with those of Carl N. Degler in
*At Odds: Women and the Family in America from the Revolution to the
Present,* discussed above, in chapter one.) To make her point, she investigates some of the myths about women that abound in our culture—popular
and otherwise. In doing this, she equates the experiences of women with
those of children and blacks. Women and children share the common experience of being powerless, dependent, and physically different from men—
this final difference is confirmed by the fashions foisted upon women and
children who wear clothes that tend to exaggerate their differences from
men. As background to these assertions, Firestone—drawing on the work of

Philippe Ariès—provides a concise history of the family and the advent of the concept of childhood in the late Middle Ages. Racism she defines as an extension of sexism. Speaking metaphorically, she claims that the black man is forced to play the role of son in the American family and women are forced to remain the daughters.

Love she identifies as the "pivot of women's oppression today" (Firestone, 142). Sounding like Gilman, she says that it is for love that women sell themselves to men; it is on women's love that men have built their culture. The act of falling in love, according to Firestone, functions for women as a camouflage for their real status in society. The notion of romantic love she defines as corrupted by and contributing to the sex class-system. One of the consequences of this romanticism is the stereotyping of women, by which they are seen no longer as individuals but as a class. Another is the situation in which women see themselves as sex objects.

This occurs because women only see other women—and never men—in this role. The ultimate consequence of this corruption of love is the fact that women are left without valid representations of themselves; everywhere they look, they are seeing male images of women—false images that, nonetheless, have been given form and legitimacy. Confined to the paradigms of the patriarchal society, women are literally unable to see themselves as they really are or to objectify this reality in any meaningful way. What Firestone is saying here clearly has direct bearing on a study of popular culture since so much of popular culture is concerned with the image of women.

It also appears as though Firestone herself is having an influence on the production of popular culture, as much of the recent feminist science fiction, such as Marge Piercy's *Woman on the Edge of Time,* seems specifically intended to illustrate the revolution that Firestone calls for. In Piercy's novel, for example, all children are conceived and carried to term in vitro; a family is composed of three adults, and men can be injected with hormones so that they too might nurse the babies.

Another influential text is Adrienne Rich's *Of Woman Born: Motherhood as Experience and Institution.* In this book, as her title suggests, Rich distinguishes between two forms of motherhood: one, the open-ended personal experience; the other, the closed institutionalized stereotype promulgated by social mythology. As a social historian, Rich is most provocative when she discusses the alienation of women from their bodies. Sounding a lot like Phyllis Chesler in *Women and Madness* (see below), Rich claims that the daughters of Western culture are like motherless children, bereft of the mother love that all human beings require. Part of this lack she attributes to the fact that daughters are raised in a patriarchal society that assigns more value to its sons than its daughters. Another contributing factor is that daughters are raised to see themselves through the eyes of men, to judge themselves by male standards. Moreover, when mothers concede power and collaborate with patriarchal values, it is their daughters who suffer anger and humiliation. In order to overcome some of these problems, according to Rich, society itself must change the way it thinks.

In making this suggestion, Rich aligns herself with other radical feminists who find a reciprocal relationship between language and perception. When she claims that in the "interstices of language lie powerful secrets of the culture," Rich is acknowledging the source of male strength (Rich, 253, Bantam). What she is after is a transformation—of language, perception, behavior, and thinking. To achieve this transformation she argues that women must repossess their bodies, must experience the world through their bodies in an intensely personal and not a public way. Women, she claims, through the institution of motherhood, have become alienated from their bodies because they have been "incarcerated" in them (Rich, xv, Bantam). Another source of this alienation has been the Western insistence on dualities, such as Erik Erikson's insistence that women are marked, because of their womb, by an affinity to inner space—a theory Rich dismisses as preposterous since inner and outer space are "continuous, not polar" (Rich, 48, Bantam). Quoting Karl Stern (*The Flight from Woman*), she reminds us also that, to certain thinkers, the so-called feminine qualities of intuition and spirituality have been perceived as anathema to the mode of scientific inquiry (a simplistic notion at best; certainly an inaccurate one that ignores documented cases of "accidental" discoveries or those that appear in dreams, such as Friedrich Kekulé's dream of a snake with its tail in its mouth that in 1865 suggested to him the structure of the benzene molecule).

In her discussion of alienation, Rich attacks the recently popular concept of androgyny, finding fault not only with the concept but with the structure of the word itself. "In a truly postandrogynous society," she writes, "the term 'androgyne' would have no meaning" (Rich, 62, Bantam). If the transformation she calls for is to take place in our thinking, it will be necessary to eliminate these dualities, "to reintegrate what has been named the unconsciousness, the subjective, the emotional with the structural, the rational, the intellectual" (Rich, 67, Bantam). She concludes her brilliant analysis of the situation and its solution with the remarkable statement that she wants women "*to think through the body*," to convert women's "physicality into both knowledge and power" (Rich, 290, Bantam; Rich's italics). In delivering this challenge to women, she is echoing the theories of knowledge propounded by Michael Polanyi, who, after much investigation into perceptual experiments (set up and run by other scientists), became convinced of the bodily source of all knowledge (see, for example, his *Knowing and Being*). Her conclusions are best summed up by the evocative phrase "the corporeal ground of our intelligence," with which she opens her work (Rich, 21, Bantam). Intent on healing the division between our mind and our body, Rich would have us recapture the oneness of the universe that predominates in early matriarchal myths. (For a discussion of how these matriarchal myths inform women's literature, see Grace Stewart's *A New Mythos: The Novel of the Artist as Heroine, 1877-1977*, discussed above, in chapter two.)

A number of recent texts explore the relationship of women and social mythology. In what is probably the best known of these texts, *The Feminine Mystique*, Betty Friedan examines many of the myths that control women's behavior and self-perception. (Friedan's book is also discussed above, in the introduction and in chapter three.) The aggregate of these social myths Friedan labels the "feminine mystique." She defines the feminine mystique as that situation in which women believe that their purpose in life is to become as feminine as possible; in which women believe that their only natural state is one of femininity; and in which science claims that it can never hope to understand women because their intuitive qualities are beyond the ken of the rational pursuit of knowledge. Although Friedan finds the origins of the feminine mystique in the teachings and expectations of the patriarchy, she also, much like Simone de Beauvoir, blames women for participating in this mystique. Where de Beauvoir faults woman for accepting the role of the "other," Friedan claims that "the chains that bind her in her trap are chains in her own mind and spirit" (Friedan, 31). When Friedan published *The Feminine Mystique* in 1963, she set off a series of events that rapidly coalesced into the century's second women's rights movement. As the inspiration for this new wave of feminism, Friedan's book retains a special place in its brief history. In the memorable phrase, "feminine mystique," Friedan seems to have captured the essence of the problems that plague Western women; in attributing the origins of the concept to the mid-twentieth century, however, Friedan was somewhat shortsighted (on this point, see William Henry Chafe's *The American Woman*, discussed above, in chapter one).

Another feminist theoretician who examines the role of women in society is Elizabeth Janeway. In *Man's World, Woman's Place: A Study in Social Mythology*, Janeway demonstrates how social mythology functions not only to describe our world but, more importantly, prescribe how we experience it. Janeway has written this book, she says, in "an effort to understand how social mythology...evolves and operates, for not only our actions but even our perceptions are affected by the web of ideas in which we live" (Janeway, 295). The source of these ideas is, in large measure, our social mythology. And the source of mythology Janeway finds in "psychological drives" (Janeway, 26). That is to say, mythology is a projection of a person's—or a culture's—desires. In giving shape and form to desire, myths also give shape and form to fear; this occurs because with the desire is born the fear that the desire will be denied. What originates as an emotional need, therefore, takes on both prescriptive and proscriptive aspects. In other words, the social mythology insists on the thinking and behavior that will fulfill desire and, concomitantly, prohibits that which will deny it.

In attempting to understand the social mythology that teaches that women belong—quite naturally—at home, Janeway, much like Firestone, recounts the history of the family as recorded by Philippe Ariès in *Centuries of Childhood: A Social History of Family Life*. In his history, Ariès reports that the family was essentially a middle-class invention that originated in the Middle Ages to meet the needs of an emerging bourgeoisie. Over the course of time, because it has continued to meet particular social needs, an entire mythology has grown up around the family. This social mythology insists that when a woman wants to leave the home "she is acting to overthrow an eternal image and abandon relationships that have existed since time began" (Janeway, 15). The woman who wants to leave her home is, in other words, acting unnaturally.

But as irrational as this position might seem to feminist thinkers, social mythology, as John Stuart Mill and Elizabeth Janeway both point out, cannot be overthrown on the strength of logical argument alone. "Facts," Janeway remarks, "can be disproved....But myth has its own, furious, inherent reason-to-be because it is tied to desire" (Janeway, 28). Social mythology is also necessary to our culture for the simple fact that it holds us together by providing "a ground of shared belief" (Janeway, 299).

Mythology affects individuals, according to Janeway, by assigning them roles to play. As Peter Berger and Thomas Luckmann point out in *The Social Construction of Reality*, there is nothing inherently wrong with roles; roles are, in their ideal state, intended to be shorthand ways of dealing with the complexities of the world. Or, as Janeway puts it, roles are a form of communication through which one indicates "the meaning of the activity" in which one is engaged (Janeway, 79). The problem that Janeway finds in the roles assigned to women is that they have no unity; that is, a woman plays several roles that, in effect, never coalesce in a meaningful pattern. Unlike a man, a woman, to paraphrase Janeway, is expected to be and rewarded for being flexible and adaptable—qualities that have come to be associated with what psychologists identify as "feminine nature" (Janeway, 86-87). Not unexpectedly, the very qualities that women are expected to manifest are those that keep them outside the mainstream of American life, which genuinely values "individual freedom and individual responsibility" (Janeway, 99).

Like de Beauvoir and Friedan, Janeway is not unaware of the fact that women contribute to their own enslavement by internalizing what she calls the "voice of authority" (Janeway, 101). And she also recognizes that once women accept the terms of patriarchal mythology, they find themselves in a vicious circle from which there is no escape. That is, once they accept helplessness and passivity as their natural state of being, they no longer have the capacity to act. In brief, they become their own prison.

Other sobering studies of the effects of social mythology on women are found in Phyllis Chesler's *Women and Madness* and Mary Daly's *Gyn/ Ecology: The Metaethics of Radical Feminism*. Chesler's book, which is an exposé of the myths and realities of female madness, is based on extensive scholarship—including the work of Freud, Jung, and Reich—and personal interviews that Chesler conducted with women who had been diagnosed as insane. One of her most frightening conclusions is that society has used and continues to use madness—mental illness, depression—as a way to control women, to keep them from expressing their own identity and anger. Because Chesler documents her findings so carefully, her book is especially useful in helping to explain how some women have become helpless, passive victims of a patriarchal society. Mary Daly's *Gyn/Ecology* is also valuable as a history of the mistreatment of women. To her task of unearthing the deep cultural misogyny that pervades all societies—past and present, foreign and near—Daly brings a razor-sharp mind and a keen eye. She misses nothing, and has the scholarship to back up her conclusions, most of which condemn the practices, mythology, and attitudes of patriarchal society. Daly brings to light, for example, research on Chinese foot-binding, Indian suttee, and genital mutilation; these passages make for painful reading, but they are, after all, central to an understanding of women's history and social mythology. Daly also provides historical data on the fifteenth-century *Malleus Maleficarum* ("The Hammer of Witches") which taught that " 'all witchcraft comes from carnal lust which is in women insatiable' " (quoted in Daly, 180). If she condemns the practices listed here, she is no less willing to damn American gynecology, which she accuses of torturing women. Daly is bold and radical not only in her assumptions and conclusions, but in her use of language. In an attempt to make her readers see what they heretofore have been blind to, throughout her text she reminds us of the real (root) meaning of words. Her method takes some getting used to, but it functions as a constant reminder of the words we have lost (like "glamour") and the words that hold us in tyranny (like the terms that denigrate women by identifying a woman with portions of her anatomy). Daly also invents a whole new vocabulary that is extensive enough to require a glossary at the end of her book. The book itself is thoroughly documented with copious, informative footnotes. Like Chesler's *Women and Madness*, its theories and content are central to an understanding of women and popular culture.

Other books that look into the effects of mythology on women are *The Curse: A Cultural History of Menstruation* by Janice Delaney, Mary Jane Lupton, and Emily Toth and *Black Rage* by William H. Grier and Price M. Cobbs (*Black Rage* is discussed above, in chapter one). As the title suggests, *The Curse* is a study of social attitudes toward menstruation, as they have been expressed in mythology, legend, literature, and advertising. Still other approaches to sexual mythology are Ashley Montagu's *The Natural Superiority of Women*, in which he uses scientific facts to prove his theory that women are better adapted than men for survival; and Hoffman Reynolds Hays's *The Dangerous Sex: The Myth of Feminine Evil*, in which he uses anthropological and literary evidence to examine male attitudes toward women. Robert Jay Lifton's *The Woman in America* reprints Erik H. Erikson's infamous essay "Inner and Outer Space: Reflections on Womanhood," in which Erikson claims that women are by nature introspective and intuitive because they have a womb.

A lighthearted footnote to these studies of mythology is Carol Wald's *Myth America: Picturing Women, 1865-1945* (text by Judith Papachriston). This book is a collection of art that includes advertising cards, decorative prints, display advertisements, package inserts, postcards, and rotogravures—all intended to illustrate how women have been pictured in our popular culture. The photographs are accompanied by a text and selections from contemporary poems, popular songs, and so forth.

Although the following works are grounded primarily in literary theory, their authors do, for the most part, attempt to relate critical theory to women's cultural experience. In "The New Feminist Criticism," for example, Annis Pratt suggests that the critic's first task is to identify feminine and feminist literature. To do this properly, the critic will have to perform what she identifies as two discrete tasks: that of judging whether or not the work is "novelistically successful," which would amount to a textual analysis; and that of assigning its relevance to women, which would amount to a contextual analysis (Pratt, 873). In her essay, Pratt challenges Leslie Fiedler's *Love and Death in the American Novel* and Josephine Lurie Jessup's *The Faith of Our Feminists* because Fiedler and Jessup, in her opinion, do not understand feminism. In conclusion, Pratt calls for studies that would reveal what she calls a " 'myth of the heroine,' " suggesting that the psychological development of heroines occurs in phases that are identifiably different from those of the hero (Pratt, 877). (For a rebuttal to her critical divisions, see Lillian Robinson's "Dwelling in Decencies," discussed below.)

Because of their emphasis on class—and their desire for social change— the work of the Marxist critics is particularly appropriate to a study of women and popular culture. One such critic is Lillian S. Robinson, whose *Sex, Class, and Culture* is a compilation of twelve of her critical essays that were written between 1968 and 1977. In the five essays that constitute part one, Robinson establishes her critical methodology and philosophy; in part two, she applies this method to literature and television.

Perhaps the most important contribution that Robinson and other feminist critics have made to the field of literary theory is to demonstrate that criticism, while purporting to be both objective and disinterested, has been instead both implicitly and explicitly male-oriented (see also, Doris Schumacher's "Subjectivities: A Theory of the Critical Process," discussed below). In their view, literary criticism has been heretofore almost exclusively the tool of the (white) male ruling class, the members of which have invoked its values and assumptions in order to invalidate the work of all women—white or nonwhite. In order to combat this situation, Robinson argues, feminist criticism must revolutionize the thinking and behavior of society. Unfortunately, it is at this point that Robinson and the other Marxists fall short of their own expectations. As Robinson herself ruefully acknowledges, it is very difficult to translate her Marxist ideas into social change. Although the structure of her book suggests her desire to make real this transformation, there remains, finally, a disjunction between its form and content. This is by no means to denigrate what Robinson has accomplished in this collection. She is an incisive thinker who provokes her readers into concluding that, however idealistic her ideas, they are of considerable merit.

In "Dwelling in Decencies: Radical Criticism and the Feminist Perspective," Robinson takes to task several critics who, in her judgment, have betrayed the feminist goals of social revolution. One such critic who earns her contempt is Fred Patte, whose study of the 1850s, *The Feminine Fifties*, she identifies as "dangerous" for its antifeminist bent (Robinson, 13). Another work that Robinson judges to be antifeminist and reactionary is *The Faith of Our Feminists* by Josephine Lurie Jessup. A more recent critic, Annis Pratt, comes under attack for her suggestions that textual criteria are, in Robinson's words, "somehow independent of ideology" (Robinson, 17). (Here Robinson is referring to Annis Pratt's "The New Feminist Criticism," a paper originally presented along with "Dwelling in Decencies" as part of the MLA Workshop on Feminist Literature and Feminine Consciousness, 27 December 1970; Pratt's essay is discussed above.) Having outlined her quarrels with these thinkers, Robinson forwards her own requirements for feminist criticism. Her major contention is that if it is to be effective, feminist criticism must be "ideological and moral . . . it must be revolutionary" (Robinson, 3). Observing that Kate Millet's *Sexual Politics* is not the last word in feminist criticism, Robinson argues that feminist analysis must go beyond the "political implications of the language and themes of literature" (Robinson, 15). Feminist criticism, in short, must transform the world.

The second essay in her collection is "Modernism and History," which she wrote with Lise Vogel. In this essay, which covers much of the same ground as "Dwelling in Decencies," Robinson and Vogel attack modernism because its effect is to "detach culture from history" (Robinson, 23).

In "The Critical Task" Robinson takes as her premise the notion of Marx and Engels that "The ruling class is materially sustained and reinforced by the circulation of certain ideas" (Robinson, 49). This concept, when taken in conjunction with the Marxist argument that "real life determines consciousness," has clear-cut implications for a study of women and popular culture (Robinson, 51). A companion to this essay is "Criticism—and Self-Criticism,"

in which Robinson defines the relationship between the proletarian struggle
and literary study. For her, the relationship can be summed up as a willingness to take "mass culture seriously," and in so doing investigate its intentions, forms, and myths (Robinson, 67). She continues this idea in "Criticism:
Who Needs It?," where she attempts to bridge the gap between theory
and practice. Calling once more for a study of mass culture and its effects
on the masses, she chides students of popular culture for obviating the
differences between culture created by the masses and that created for
the masses. Her goal, as she explains it, is to use criticism to demonstrate
how the ruling class uses popular culture to obstruct the revolution of the
working class. She wants to demonstrate this, she says, in a way that will
be meaningful to the working class itself.

Although all of the essays in the second section of Robinson's book
are worthy of consideration, the one most pertinent to a study of women
and popular culture is "What's My Line?" Taking as her premise that
television, as no other art form, "has evolved a series of conventions for
the portrayal of the work experience," Robinson explores the implications
this holds for women (Robinson, 311). According to her, television has
created the myth that even among working women their sex is more important than the work they do; women who work on television, therefore, are
seen as simply playing a role. Of the women professionals on prime time
television, Robinson observes that they are "equally and dramatically unfeminine," and that they appear in greater numbers than in the real world
(Robinson, 335). The jobs that most women really hold—as secretaries,
typists, waitresses, or saleswomen—are by and large neglected on television.
And the housewife, except in commercials, "does not have very much
to do" (Robinson, 335). The commercials come under particular attack from
Robinson because she sees them as degrading women and as reinforcing
the mythology that housework is woman's "*natural* function" (Robinson,
339; Robinson's italics). Robinson closes her perceptive essay with the
remark that television "not only defines woman and work but at its most
nihilistic, as with Mary Hartman, tells her just how crazy she is to turn
on TV for meaning" (Robinson, 341).

Another attack on formalism appears in Fraya Katz-Stoker's "The Other
Criticism: Feminism vs. Formalism." Although this essay does not address
the question of popular culture directly, it does raise some issues about
the politics of literary criticism that could be applied to popular literature. For example, much like Robinson, Katz-Stoker calls for a revival
of sociological (Marxist) criticism that would reconnect life and art and
in so doing point out the social problems that need so desperately to
be corrected.

A useful collection of critical essays is *Feminist Literary Criticism: Explorations in Theory*, edited by Josephine Donovan. Of particular interest
is Cheri Register's "American Feminist Literary Criticism: A Bibliographical

Introduction." In this essay, Register reviews major critical texts according to three categories of feminist criticism that she sets up. These categories are the following: criticism that analyzes the image of women; criticism that examines the negative criticism of women writers; and criticism that establishes feminist literary standards. In the first category Register discusses Leslie Fiedler's *Love and Death in the American Novel*, which she identifies as not feminist; Kate Millet's *Sexual Politics*, for which she has high praise; Mary Ellmann's *Thinking About Women*; Katherine M. Rogers's *The Troublesome Helpmate*; and Shulamith Firestone's *The Dialectic of Sex* (for discussion of the final two books, see chapter two and above in this chapter). Besides offering a helpful overview of these approaches, Register makes the important point that idealized female stereotypes are just as dangerous and misleading as negative images of women in literature, as they condition women to "seek consolation in myths rather than work for social change" (Donovan, 6). In the second part of her essay, Register attacks what she calls "phallic criticism," which judges women writers by whether or not they accede to the traditional view of femininity. In the third part of her essay, Register addresses what is perhaps the most difficult question facing feminist critics—what the relationship is between critical and political theory. She also offers her own tantalizing theory that women write mainly popular literature as a sort of self-fulfilling prophecy because they have been taught that critics won't take them seriously.

The position taken by Register on behalf of feminist critics that literature, to be acceptable as feminist, must speak to women's experience coincides nicely with Doris Schumacher's "Subjectivities: A Theory of the Critical Process." Like Lillian Robinson, Schumacher argues that all criticism is value-laden and sex-linked; she also believes that what feminist critics have contributed to the field of literary theory is an awareness of this fact (see above). For her, feminist criticism is fully as conservative as other criticism because its methodology is the same as that of other schools. The difference is that for feminists the self is woman and the other (using Simone de Beauvoir's terms) is man. What Schumacher hopes will eventuate as a result of this perceptual switch is the notion that sex is paradigmatic; or, as she puts it, "an *idea* in the mind of the writer" (Donovan, 36; Schumacher's italics). Hers is a valuable and thought-provoking essay.

Sounding a bit outdated because of recent feminist displeasure with androgyny, Marcia Holly invokes this concept to define realistic literature in her essay "Consciousness and Authenticity: Toward a Feminist Aesthetic." Although there are additional essays in Donovan's collection, none except her own "Afterword: Critical Re-Vision" really speaks to the subject of women in popular culture. In this short essay, Donovan comments on the notion of perceptual paradigms, reminding her readers that everyone sees the world—and literature—through a "filter of concerns and awareness" (Donovan, 76).

BIBLIOGRAPHY

Beauvoir, Simone de. *The Second Sex.* Translated and edited by H. M. Parshley. 1952. Reprint. New York: Alfred A. Knopf, 1968.

Berger, Peter L., and Thomas Luckmann. *The Social Construction of Reality: A Treatise in the Sociology of Knowledge.* Garden City, N.Y.: Doubleday & Co., 1966.

Chafe, William Henry. *The American Woman: Her Changing Social, Economic, and Political Roles, 1920-1970.* New York: Oxford University Press, 1972.

Chesler, Phyllis. *Women and Madness.* Garden City, N.Y.: Doubleday & Co., 1972.

Cornillon, Susan Koppelman, ed. *Images of Women in Fiction: Feminist Perspectives.* Bowling Green, Ohio: Bowling Green University Popular Press, 1972.

Daly, Mary. *Gyn/Ecology: The Metaethics of Radical Feminism.* Boston: Beacon Press, 1978.

Degler, Carl N. *At Odds: Women and the Family in America from the Revolution to the Present.* New York: Oxford University Press, 1980.

Delaney, Janice, Mary Jane Lupton, and Emily Toth. *The Curse: A Cultural History of Menstruation.* New York: Mentor Books, 1976.

Donovan, Josephine. "Afterword: Critical Re-Vision." In *Feminist Literary Criticism: Explorations in Theory,* edited by Josephine Donovan, pp. 76-81. Lexington, Ky.: University of Kentucky Press, 1975.

———, ed. *Feminist Literary Criticism: Explorations in Theory.* Lexington, Ky.: University of Kentucky Press, 1975.

Firestone, Shulamith. *The Dialectic of Sex: The Case for Feminist Revolution.* New York: William Morrow and Co., 1970.

Friedan, Betty. *The Feminine Mystique.* New York: W. W. Norton & Co., 1963.

Gilman, Charlotte Perkins. *Women and Economics: A Study of the Economic Relation between Men and Women as a Factor in Social Evolution.* Edited with an introduction by Carl N. Degler. 1898. Reprint. New York: Harper & Row/ Harper Torchbooks, 1966.

Grier, William H., and Price M. Cobbs. *Black Rage.* New York: Basic Books, 1968.

Hays, H|offman| R|eynolds|. *The Dangerous Sex: The Myth of Feminine Evil.* New York: G. P. Putnam's Sons, 1964.

Holly, Marcia. "Consciousness and Authenticity: Toward a Feminist Aesthetic." In *Feminist Literary Criticism: Explorations in Theory,* edited by Josephine Donovan, pp. 38-47. Lexington, Ky.: University of Kentucky Press, 1975.

Janeway, Elizabeth. *Man's World, Woman's Place: A Study in Social Mythology.* New York: William Morrow and Co., 1971.

Katz-Stoker, Fraya. "The Other Criticism: Feminism vs. Formalism." In *Images of Women in Fiction: Feminist Perspectives,* edited by Susan Koppelman Cornillon, pp. 315-37. Bowling Green, Ohio: Bowling Green University Popular Press, 1972.

Lifton, Robert Jay, ed. *The Woman in America.* Boston: Houghton Mifflin Co., 1965.

Mill, John Stuart. *The Subjection of Women.* Edited by Sue Mansfield. 1869. Reprint. A Crofts Classic. Arlington Heights, Ill.: AHM Publishing Co., 1980.

Montagu, Ashley. *The Natural Superiority of Women.* Rev. ed. New York: Collier Books, 1968.

Polanyi, Michael. *Knowing and Being.* Edited by Marjorie Grene. Chicago: University of Chicago Press, 1969.

Pratt, Annis. "The New Feminist Criticism." *College English* 32, no. 8 (May 1971): 872-78.

Register, Cheri. "American Feminist Literary Criticism: A Bibliographical Introduction." In *Feminist Literary Criticism: Explorations in Theory,* edited by Josephine Donovan, pp. 1-28. Lexington, Ky.: University of Kentucky Press, 1975.

Rich, Adrienne. *Of Woman Born: Motherhood as Experience and Institution.* New York: W. W. Norton & Co., 1976. (Paperback edition. New York: Bantam Books, 1977.)

Robinson, Lillian S. "The Critical Task." In her *Sex, Class, and Culture,* pp. 47-52. Bloomington, Ind., and London: Indiana University Press, 1978.

————. "Criticism—and Self-Criticism." In her *Sex, Class, and Culture,* pp. 53-68. Bloomington, Ind., and London: Indiana University Press, 1978.

————. "Criticism: Who Needs It?" In her *Sex, Class, and Culture,* pp. 69-94. Bloomington, Ind., and London: Indiana University Press, 1978.

————. "Dwelling in Decencies: Radical Criticism and the Feminist Perspective." In her *Sex, Class, and Culture,* pp. 3-21. Bloomington, Ind., and London: Indiana University Press, 1978.

————. *Sex, Class, and Culture.* Bloomington, Ind., and London: Indiana University Press, 1978.

————. "What's My Line?" In her *Sex, Class, and Culture,* pp. 310-42. Bloomington, Ind., and London: Indiana University Press, 1978.

————, and Lise Vogel. "Modernism and History." In *Sex, Class, and Culture,* edited by Lillian S. Robinson, pp. 22-46. Bloomington, Ind., and London: Indiana University Press, 1978.

Schumacher, Doris. "Subjectivities: A Theory of the Critical Process." In *Feminist Literary Criticism: Explorations in Theory,* edited by Josephine Donovan, pp. 29-37. Lexington, Ky.: University of Kentucky Press, 1975.

Stewart, Grace. *A New Mythos: The Novel of the Artist as Heroine, 1877-1977.* St. Albans, Vt.: Eden Press Women's Publications, 1979.

Veblen, Thorstein. "The Economic Theory of Women's Dress." *Popular Science Monthly* 46 (November 1894): 198-205.

————. *The Theory of the Leisure Class: An Economic Study of Institutions.* 1899. Reprint. New York: Modern Library, 1934.

Wald, Carol. *Myth America: Picturing Women, 1865-1945.* Text by Judith Papachriston. New York: Pantheon, 1975.

Wollstonecraft, Mary. *A Vindication of the Rights of Woman.* Edited by Carol H. Poston. 1792. Reprint. A Norton Critical Edition. New York: W. W. Norton & Co., 1975.

APPENDIX I

Selected Periodicals

Abstracts of Popular Culture: A Quarterly Publication of International Popular Phenomenon. Bowling Green State University Popular Press. Bowling Green, Ohio 43403. 1976-.

Aphra: The Feminist Literary Magazine. Box 893, Ansonia Station, New York, New York 10023. 1969-.

Aurora. c/o SF³, Box 1624, Madison, Wisconsin 53701. (Continues *Janus.*)

Black Women's Voice. National Council of Negro Women, Inc., 1346 Connecticut Ave., N.W., Washington, D.C. 20036.

Calyx: A Journal of Art and Literature by Women. Calyx, Inc., Box 118, Route 2, Corvalis, Oregon 97330. 1976-.

Chrysalis: A Magazine of Women's Culture. Chrysalis, Inc., Women's Building, 1727 North Spring Street, Los Angeles, California 90012. 1977-1981.

Coaching: Women's Athletics. Intercommunications, Inc., P.O. Box 867, 50 South Main Street, Wallingford, Connecticut 06492. (Former titles: *Coach: Women's Athletics* and *Woman Coach.*) 1975-.

Essence: The Magazine for Today's Black Woman. Essence Communications, Inc., 1500 Broadway, New York, New York 10036. 1970-.

Feminist Studies. Feminist Studies, Inc., c/o Women's Studies Program, University of Maryland, College Park, Maryland 20742. 1972-.

Journal of American Culture. Popular Culture Center, Bowling Green State University, Bowling Green, Ohio 43403. 1978-.

Journal of Popular Culture. Popular Culture Center, Bowling Green State University, Bowling Green, Ohio 43403. 1967-.

Journal of Popular Film and Television. Popular Culture Center, Bowling Green State University, Bowling Green, Ohio 43403. (Former title: *Journal of Popular Film.*) 1971-.

Journal of Reprints Affecting Women's Rights and Opportunities. Today Publications & News Service, Inc., 621 National Press Building, Washington, D.C. 20045. 1975-.

Journal of Women's Studies in Literature. Eden Press Women's Publications, 1538 Sherbrooke Street W., Suite 201, Montreal, Quebec, Canada H3G 1L5. 1979-.

Ms. Magazine. Ms. Foundation for Education and Communication, Inc., 119 West 40 Street, New York, New York 10018. 1972-.

New Moon. Box 2056, Madison, Wisconsin 53701. 1981-.

New Woman: First Magazine for the Thinking Woman. Allied Publications, Inc., 2900 N.E. 12th Terrace, Fort Lauderdale, Florida 33307. 1971-.

Quest: A Feminist Quarterly. P.O. Box 8834, Washington, D.C. 20003. 1974-.

Regionalism and the Female Imagination. Department of English, Pennsylvania State University, University Park, Pennsylvania 16802. (Continues: *Kate Chopin Newsletter.*) 1975-.

Signs: Journal of Women in Culture and Society. University of Chicago Press, 11030 Langley Avenue, Chicago, Illinois 60628. 1975-.

Sportswoman. Finefrock Publishing, Inc., 3732 Mount Diablo Boulevard, Lafayette, California 94549. 1973-.

Standard Periodical Directory. Oxbridge Communications, Inc., New York, New York 10016. S.v. "Women's Liberation"; "Women's Fashions."

Ulrich's International Periodicals Directory, 18th ed., 1979-80. R. R. Bowker Company, New York, New York 10036. S.v. "Women's Interests," pp. 1684-93.

University of Michigan Papers in Women's Studies. Women's Studies Program, 1058 LSA Building, University of Michigan, Ann Arbor, Michigan 48104. 1974-.

The Witch and the Chameleon. Apartment 6, 2 Paisley Avenue, Hamilton, Ontario, Canada. (Subtitle, issues 5 and 6: "A Feminist View of Science Fiction.") 1974-.

Women and Film. Berkeley, California 90404. 1972-1976. (Available in microfilm from University Microfilms International, Ann Arbor, Michigan.)

Women & Literature. Department of English, Douglass College, Rutgers University, New Brunswick, New Jersey 08903. 1973-. (Beginning with volume 8, published as annual volume by Homes & Meier Publishers, Inc., 30 Irving Place, New York, New York 10003.)

Women's Coaching Clinic. Prentice-Hall, Inc., Box 500, Englewood Cliffs, New Jersey 07632. 1977-.

WomenSports. WomenSports Publishing Company, 230 Park Avenue, New York, New York 10017. 1974-.

Women's Studies: An Interdisciplinary Journal. Gordon and Breach Science Publishers, Ltd., 41-42 William IV Street, London W.C. 2 England. 1972-.

Women's Studies Newsletter. Publication of the Feminist Press and the National Women's Studies Association. Feminist Press's Clearinghouse on Women's Studies, Box 334, Old Westbury, New York 11568. 1972-.

Women Studies Abstracts. P.O. Box 1, Rush, New York 14543. 1972-.

Special Issues and Sections of Periodicals

Chicago Journalism Review 4, no. 7 (July 1971). Special issue, "Women and the Media."

College English 32, no. 8 (May 1971). Special issue on women's literature and criticism.

Daedelus 93 (Spring 1964): 577-803. Special issue, "The Woman in America."

Ebony 21 (August 1966). Special issue on "The Negro Woman."

Film Library Quarterly 5, no. 1 (Winter 1971-1972). Special issue, "Women in Film."

Futures 7, no. 5 (October 1975). Special issue, "Women and the Future."

Journal of American Folklore 88, no. 347 (January-March 1975). Special issue, "Women and Folklore."

Journal of Communication 24, no. 2 (Spring 1974). Special issue on women.

_____. 26, no. 4 (Autumn 1976); 160-200. Special section on women and blacks, "Equality in Advertising."

_____. 25, no. 2 (Spring 1975); 98-119. Special section on "Women in Detective Fiction."

Life, 1976. Special report, "Remarkable American Women, 1776-1976."

Take One 3, no. 2 (January 1972). Special issue, "Women and Film."

The Velvet Light Trap, no. 6 (Fall 1972). Special issue, "Sexual Politics and Film."

APPENDIX 3

A Selected List of Bibliographies, Biographies, and Information Guides Relevant to Women in Popular Culture

Arthur and Elizabeth Schlesinger Library on the History of Women in America. *The Manuscripts Inventories and the Catalogs of the Manuscripts, Books and Pictures.* Boston: G. K. Hall & Co., 1973.

Ballou, Patricia K. "Bibliographies for Research on Women." *Signs: Journal of Women in Culture and Society* 3, no. 2 (Winter 1977): 436-50.

————. *Women: A Bibliography of Bibliographies.* Boston: G. K. Hall Reference Books, 1980.

Berkowitz, Tamar, ed. *Who's Who and Where in Women's Studies.* Old Westbury, N.Y.: Feminist Press, 1974.

Bibliographic Index: A Cumulative Bibliography of Bibliographies, Vol. 20. New York: H. W. Wilson Co., 1980. (1937-present; yearly since 1969.)

"The Black Family and the Black Woman: A Bibliography." Mimeographed. Bloomington, Ind. Prepared by Library Staff and the Afro-American Studies Department, Indiana University, 1972.

Brignano, Russell C. *Black Americans in Autobiography: An Annotated Bibliography of Autobiographies and Autobiographical Books Written since the Civil War.* Durham: Duke University Press, 1974.

Butler, Matilda, and William Paisley, eds. *Women and the Mass Media: Sourcebook for Research and Action.* New York: Human Sciences Press, 1979.

Cardinale, Susan. *Special Issues of Serials About Women, 1965-1975.* Monticello, Ill.: Council of Planning Librarians, 1976.

Cole, Johnneta B. "Black Women in America: An Annotated Bibliography." *Black Scholar* 3, no. 4 (December 1971): 42-53.

Dannett, Sylvia G. L. *Profiles of Negro Womanhood.* Negro Heritage Library. Vol. 1. *1619-1900.* Chicago: Educational Heritage, 1964.

Davis, Lenwood G. *The Black Woman in American Society: A Selected Annotated Bibliography.* Boston: G. K. Hall & Co.: 1975.

Eichler, Margrit. *An Annotated Selected Bibliography of Bibliographies on Women.* Waterloo: University of Waterloo, Department of Sociology, 1973. Printed by the AUCL Committee on the Status of Women.

Fairbanks, Carol. *More Women in Literature: Criticism of the Seventies.* Metuchen, N.J., and London: Scarecrow Press, 1979.

Franzwa, Helen. "The Image of Women in Television: An Annotated Bibliography." In *Hearth and Home: Images of Women in the Mass Media,* edited by Gaye

Tuchman, Arlene Kaplan Daniels, and James Benet, pp. 273-99. New York: Oxford University Press, 1978.

Friedman, Barbara, et al., eds. *Women's Work and Women's Studies, 1973-1974: A Bibliography.* New York: Barnard College Women's Center, 1975. Distributed by the Feminist Press.

Gherman, Dawn Lander. "Frontier and Wilderness: American Women Authors." *University of Michigan Papers in Women's Studies* 2, no. 2: 7-38.

Haber, Barbara. *Women in America: A Guide to Books, 1963-1975.* Boston: G. K. Hall & Co., 1978.

Harrison, Cynthia Ellen. *Women's Movement Media: A Source Guide.* New York: R. R. Bowker Co., 1975.

Klotman, Phyllis Rauch. *Frame by Frame—A Black Filmography.* Bloomington, Ind.: Indiana University Press, 1979.

Kowalski, Rosemary Ribich. *Women and Film: A Bibliography.* Metuchen, N.J.: Scarecrow Press, 1976.

Krichmar, Albert. *The Women's Movement in the Seventies: An International English-Language Bibliography.* Metuchen, N.J.: Scarecrow Press, 1977.

_____. *The Women's Rights Movement in the United States, 1848-1970: A Bibliography and Sourcebook.* Metuchen, N.J.: Scarecrow Press, 1972.

Leonard, Eugenie Andruss, et al. *The American Woman in Colonial and Revolutionary Times, 1565-1800: A Syllabus with Bibliography.* Philadelphia: University of Pennsylvania Press, 1962.

Loader, Jayne. "Women in the Left, 1906-1941: A Bibliography of Primary Sources." *University of Michigan Papers in Women's Studies* 2, no. 1 (September 1975): 9-82.

Lynn, Naomi B., Ann B. Matasar, and Marie Barovic Rosenberg. *Research Guide in Women's Studies.* Morristown, N.J.: General Learning Press, 1974.

Mainiero, Lina, ed. *American Women Writers: A Critical Reference Guide From Colonial Times to the Present.* 2 vols. [vol. 1, A-E; vol. 2, F-Le.] New York: Frederick Ungar Publishing Co., 1979-1980.

Michigan Department of State. *Bibliography of Sources Relating to Women.* Lansing, Mich.: Michigan History Division, Michigan Department of State, 1975.

Miller, Wayne Charles. *A Comprehensive Bibliography for the Study of American Minorities.* 2 vols. New York: New York University Press, 1976.

Myers, Carol Fairbanks. *Women in Literature: Criticism of the Seventies.* Metuchen, N.J.: Scarecrow Press, 1976.

New York Times Cumulative Subject and Personal Name Index—Women 1965-1975. Glen Rock, N.J.: Microfilming Corporation of America, 1978.

"1974 Bibliography of Women in British and American Literature, 1660-1900." *Women and Literature* 3 (Fall 1975): 33-64.

Notable American Women, 1607-1950: A Biographical Dictionary. Cambridge, Mass.: Harvard University Press, Belknap Press, 1971.

Powers, Anne. *Blacks in American Movies: A Selected Bibliography.* Metuchen, N.J.: Scarecrow Press, 1974.

Rush, Theressa Gunnels, Carol Fairbanks Myers, and Esther Spring Arata. *Black American Writers, Past and Present: A Biographical and Bibliographical Dictionary.* 2 vols. Metuchen, N.J.: Scarecrow Press, 1975.

Schlobin, Roger C. *Andre Norton: A Primary and Secondary Bibliography.* Masters of Science Fiction and Fantasy, edited by L. W. Currey. Boston: G. K. Hall Reference Books, 1980.

Schockley, Ann Allen, and Sue P. Chandler. *Living Black American Authors: A Biographical Directory.* New York: R. W. Bowker Co., 1973.

Sense and Sensibility Collective. *Women and Literature: An Annotated Bibliography of Women Writers.* 2d ed., rev. and enl. Cambridge, Mass.: Sense and Sensibility Collective, 1973.

Sims, Janet L., comp. *The Progress of Afro-American Women: A Selected Bibliography and Resource Guide.* Foreword by Bettye Thomas. Westport, Conn.: Greenwood Press, 1980.

Smith College Library. *Catalog of the Sophia Smith Collection.* 2d ed. Northampton, Mass.: Smith College, 1976.

Sullivan, Kaye. *Films For, By and About Women.* Metuchen, N.J.: Scarecrow Press, 1980.

Terris, Virginia R. *Women in America: A Guide to Information Sources.* Vol. 7. American Studies Information Guide Series. Detroit: Gale Research Company, 1980.

Wheeler, Helen [Rippier]. *Womanhood Media: Current Resources about Women.* Metuchen, N.J.: Scarecrow Press, 1972.

_____. *Womanhood Media Supplement: Additional Current Resources about Women.* Metuchen, N.J.: Scarecrow Press, 1975.

White, Barbara A. *American Women Writers: An Annotated Bibliography of Criticism.* New York: Garland Publishing, 1977.

Who's Who among Black Americans, 1980-81. 3d ed. Edited by William C. Matney. Northbrook, Ill.: Who's Who Among Black Americans Publishing Company, 1981.

Who's Who in Colored America: An Illustrated Biographical Directory of Notable Living Persons of African Descent in the United States. 7th ed. Edited by G. James Fleming and Christian E. Burkel. Yonkers-on-Hudson, N.Y.: Christian E. Burkel & Associates, 1950.

Who's Who of American Women: A Biographical Dictionary of Notable Living American Women. Chicago: A. N. Marquise, 1978.

Willard, Frances E., and Mary A. Livermore. *American Women: Fifteen Hundred Biographies with over 1,400 Portraits.* 2 vols. Rev. ed. New York: Mast, Crowell & Kirkpatrick, 1897.

_____, eds. *A Woman of the Century. Fourteen Hundred-Seventy Biographical Sketches Accompanied by Portraits of Leading American Women in All Walks of Life.* 1893. Reprint. New introduction by Leslie Shepard. Detroit: Gale Research Co., 1967.

Williams, Ora. *American Black Women in the Arts and Social Sciences: A Bibliographic Survey,* Rev. and enl. ed. Metuchen, N.J.: Scarecrow Press, 1978.

_____. "A Bibliography of Works Written by American Black Women." *CLA Journal* 15, no. 3 (March 1972): 354-77.

Women's History Research Center. *Films by and/or about Women: Directory of Filmmakers, Films, and Distributors Internationally, Past and Present.* Berkeley: Women's History Research Center, 1972.

Women's History Sources: A Guide to Archives and Manuscript Collections in the United States. New York and London: R. R. Bowker Co., 1979. Vol. 1, *Collections,* edited by Andrea Hinding. Vol. 2, *Index,* edited by Suzanna Moody.

APPENDIX 4

Chronology of Important Dates

1637 Trial of Anne Hutchinson for antinomianism
1650 Anne Bradstreet, *The Tenth Muse Lately Sprung Up in America*
1676 Mrs. Mary Rowlandson captured by Indians during King Philip's War
1678 Anne Bradstreet, *Several Poems*
1682 Mrs. Mary Rowlandson, *The Soveraignty and Goodness of God...Being a Narrative of the Captivity of Mrs. Mary Rowlandson*
1692 Salem witchcraft trials
1704 Sarah Kemble Knight journeys by horseback from Boston to New York
1759 Phillis Wheatley sold at slave auction in Boston
1773 Phillis Wheatley, *Poems on Various Subjects, Religious and Moral*
1791 Susanna Rowson, *Charlotte Temple: A Tale of Truth*
1792 Mary Wollstonecraft, *A Vindication of the Rights of Women*
     Lady's Pocket Library
1793 Catherine Ferguson (an ex-slave) opened "Katy Ferguson's Schools for the Poor" in New York City
1798 Charles Brockden Brown, *Alcuin*
1801 Tabith Tenney, *Female Quixotism*
1808 Slave trade officially abolished
1818 Hannah Mather Crocker, *Observations on the Real Rights of Women*
1819 Emma Willard, *Plan for Improving Female Education*
1820 Maria Becraft established first boarding school for young black women in Washington, D.C.
1821 Troy Female Seminary founded by Emma Willard
1822 Catharine Maria Sedgwick, *A New England Tale*
1824 Hartford Female Seminary founded by Catharine E. Beecher
1827 Slave Isabella (Sojourner Truth) freed
     Sarah Josepha Hale, *Northwood*
     Human ovum discovered
1828 The *Ladies' Magazine* founded by Sarah Josepha Hale
1830 The *Lady's Book* founded by Louis Antoine Godey
1831 Nat Turner's rebellion
     The *Liberator* founded by William Lloyd Garrison
1832 Female Anti-Slavery Society founded in Boston
     Charles Knowlton, *Fruits of Philosophy*

1833   American Anti-Slavery Society founded in Philadelphia
      Prudence Crandall admits black girl to her school in Canterbury, Conn.
         (public pressure forces her to close school the next year)
      Oberlin College established (admitted blacks and women)
1834   American Female Moral Reform Association founded
      Millworkers strike in Lowell, Mass.
1835   Harriot K. Hunt begins to practice medicine
1837   National Convention of the Female Anti-Slavery Society
      Godey's Lady's Book established by Louis Antoine Godey; Sarah Josepha
         Hale hired as editor
      Mount Holyoke established as seminary by Mary Lyon (became college in
         1893)
1838   Sarah M. Grimké, *Letters on the Equality of the Sexes and the Condition
      of Women*
1840   World Anti-Slavery Convention (London)
      Lowell Offering founded in Lowell, Mass.
1841   Catharine E. Beecher, *Treatise on Domestic Economy*
      Operatives' Magazine founded in Lowell, Mass.
1842   The *Factory Girl* founded in New Market, N.H.
1843   Former slave Isabella adopts name "Sojourner Truth"
1844   *Factory Girl's Garland* founded in Exeter, N.H.
1845   Lowell Female Labor Reform Association founded; Sarah G. Bagley, president
      Sarah G. Bagley testifies at legislative hearing for ten-hour work day (Massa-
         chusetts House of Representatives)
      Margaret Fuller, *Woman in the Nineteenth Century*
      Rubber nipple for baby bottles patented
1846   Sarah G. Bagley becomes first woman to operate telegraph in America
      Margaret Coxe, *The Young Lady's Companion*
1847   Elizabeth Blackwell enters Geneva Medical College (New York)
1848   Seneca Falls Convention organized in Seneca Falls, N.Y., by Lucretia Mott
         and Elizabeth Cady Stanton
      Maria Mitchell, astronomer, elected to American Academy of Arts and
         Sciences
      Charles Meigs, *Females and Their Diseases*
      Boston Female Medical College founded by Samuel Gregory
1849   Harriet Tubman escapes from slavery
      Elizabeth Blackwell graduates from Geneva Medical College, first in her class
      Mrs. E. D. E. N. Southworth, *Retribution*
1850   Maria Mitchell elected to Association for the Advancement of Science
      Fugitive Slave Law passed
      Susan Warner (under pen name Elizabeth Wetherell), *The Wide, Wide World*
1851   Isaac M. Singer patented sewing machine with foot treadle
      Mary Sharp College founded
      Harriet Beecher Stowe, *Uncle Tom's Cabin*
      Amelia Jenks Bloomer advocates loose trousers (introduced by Elizabeth
         Smith Miller) in *The Lily*; soon known as the Bloomer costume
      Sojourner Truth addresses women's rights convention in Akron, Ohio
      Myrtilla Miner founds first teacher-training school for black girls in Wash-
         ington, D.C.

1852 American Women's Educational Association founded by Catharine Beecher
Susan Warner, *Queechy*
1854 Maria Cummins, *The Lamplighter*
Marion Harland (pen name of Mary Virginia Hawes), *Alone*
1855 Catharine Beecher, *Letters to the People on Health and Happiness*
1857 New York Infirmary for Women and Children founded by Drs. Elizabeth
Blackwell, Emily Blackwell, and Marie Zackrzewska
1859 Mrs. E. D. E. N. Southworth, *Capitola; or, The Hidden Hand*
1862 Harriet Tubman serves as scout in Union Army
1863 Thanksgiving reinstituted as national holiday by Abraham Lincoln, at urging
of Sarah Josepha Hale
New York City Draft Riots
1864 Swarthmore College founded
Rebecca Lee becomes first black woman to earn medical degree in America
1865 Vassar Female College opens (chartered 1861 by Matthew Vassar; 1867 renamed Vassar College)
1866 First official Young Women's Christian Association founded in Boston
Augusta Jane Evans, *St. Elmo*
1867 *Harper's Bazaar* founded as *Harper's Bazar*
Martha Finley, *Elsie Dinsmore*, volume one; 1868, volume two
1868 Sorosis founded by Jennie Cunningham Croly
The Revolution founded by Elizabeth Cady Stanton and Susan B. Anthony
1869 Wyoming Territory enacts country's first woman suffrage bill
National Woman Suffrage Association (NWSA) founded by Susan B. Anthony
and Elizabeth Cady Stanton
American Woman Suffrage Association (AWSA) founded
1870 *Woman's Journal* founded as voice of AWSA
1871 Victoria Woodhull publicly declares her support of free love (Steinway Hall,
New York)
Marion Harland, *Common Sense in the Household*
1873 *The Queen* founded (renamed *McCall's Magazine*, 1897)
The Comstock Law passed by Congress
Dr. Edward H. Clarke, *Sex in Education*
Association for the Advancement of Women founded
1874 Woman's Christian Temperance Union (WCTU) founded
Typewriter developed by Remington
1875 Lydia E. Pinkham's Vegetable Compound first marketed
Smith College opened (chartered 1871; bequest of Sophia Smith)
Wellesley College opened (chartered 1870)
Mount Herman Seminary (Mississippi) founded by Sarah Dickey for black girls
1877 Dr. Mary Putnam Jacobi, *The Question of Rest for Women During Men-
struation*
1878 *The Narrative of Sojourner Truth*, as told to Olive Gilbert
Silas Weir Mitchell, *Fat and Blood*
1879 Radcliffe College established as adjunct to Harvard University
Frances Willard elected president of WCTU
Belva Lockwood admitted to practice law before the bar of the Supreme
Court

1882   Association of Collegiate Alumnae (ACA) founded by Marion Talbot; later
      to become American Association of University Women (AAUW)
1883   *Ladies' Home Journal* founded by Cyrus H. K. Curtis
1885   *Good Housekeeping* founded by Clark W. Bryan
      Bryn Mawr College opened by the Society of Friends
1886   *Cosmopolitan* founded by Paul J. Schlicht
1887   Silas Weir Mitchell, *Doctor and Patient*
      College Settlement Association founded
1889   Hull House established by Jane Addams
      Business Woman's Journal founded by Mary F. Seymour
      Edward A. Bok becomes editor of *Ladies' Home Journal*
1890   General Federation of Women's Clubs (GFWC) founded
      National American Woman's Suffrage Association (NAWSA) founded
      Daughters of the American Revolution (DAR) founded
1892   Frances E. W. Harper, *Iola Leroy; or, Shadows Uplifted*
1894   M. Carey Thomas named president of Bryn Mawr
1895   Elizabeth Cady Stanton, *The Woman's Bible*
      National Colored Women's Congress, Atlanta, Georgia
1898   Charlotte Perkins Gilman, *Women and Economics*
1902   Kosher meat riot in Brooklyn and other cities
1903   Women's Trade Union League (WTUL) founded
      Charlotte Perkins Gilman, *The Home*
1906   Permanent waves invented by Charles Nestlé
1907   Anna Jarvis campaigns for observance of Mother's Day
1909   "Uprising of the Twenty Thousand" (female garment-workers strike)
1910   Triangle Shirtwaist fire
      National Association for the Advancement of Colored People (NAACP)
      founded
1911   *Motion Picture World* founded
      National Federation of Settlements founded
1912   *Photoplay* founded
1913   Eleanor Hodgman Porter, *Pollyanna*
1914   Mother's Day instituted by joint resolution of Congress
1915   *The Birth of a Nation* (Lillian Gish)
      A Fool There Was (Theda Bara)
1919   Nineteenth Amendment approved by Congress
      League of Women Voters founded
1920   Nineteenth Amendment ratified
      Women's Council of the Commission on Interracial Cooperation founded
      Margaret Sanger, *Family Limitation*
1921   Sheppard-Towner Act
      "Miss America" Beauty Pageant inaugurated in Atlantic City, N.J.
      Kotex sanitary napkins introduced through advertisement
1922   Anti-Lynching Crusaders founded by black women
1923   Equal Rights Amendment proposed by National Women's Party
1924   National Congress of Mothers renamed the Parent-Teacher Association
      School of Euthenics established at Vassar College
1925   Institute to Coordinate Women's Interests established at Smith College

1926 Margaret Sanger, *Happiness in Marriage*
1927 Clara Bow stars in movie based on Elinor Glyn's *It*
1928 800-meter race for women in Olympics
     Margaret Sanger, *Motherhood in Bondage*
     Viña Delmar, *Bad Girl*
1930 Association of Southern Women for the Prevention of Lynching formed
     by white women
1931 Jane Addams awarded Nobel Peace Prize
     Pearl S. Buck, *The Good Earth*
1932 Mildred ("Babe") Didrikson wins gold medals in javelin, hurdles, and high
     jump at Los Angeles Olympics
1934 Catholic Legion of Decency founded
     Production Code Administration instituted to implement film industry's Pro-
     duction Code
1935 *The Littlest Rebel* (Shirley Temple)
1936 Margaret Mitchell, *Gone with the Wind*
     Marjorie Hillis, *Live Alone and Like It*
     Tampax (invented by Dr. Earle Haas) marketed
1937 Zora Neale Hurston, *Their Eyes Were Watching God*
1938 Fair Labor Standards Act
1939 *Gone with the Wind* (Vivien Leigh)
     Hattie McDaniel wins Academy Award for Best Actress in a Supporting
     Role in *Gone with the Wind*
1941 *Woman of the Year*
1942 Philip Wylie, *Generation of Vipers*
1943 Betty Smith, *A Tree Grows in Brooklyn*
1946 *The Outlaw* (Jane Russell)
     Babe Didrikson Zaharias wins U.S. Golf Association amateur competition
1947 Ferdinand Lundberg and Marynia Farnham, *Modern Woman: The Lost Sex*
1949 Ladies Professional Golf Association (LPGA) founded
     "I Remember Mama" premieres
1950 Gwendolyn Brooks's *Annie Allen* wins Pulitzer Prize for Poetry
1951 "I Love Lucy" premieres
     "Search for Tomorrow" premieres
1952 Charlotta A. Bass, vice-presidential nominee of the Progressive Party, be-
     comes first black woman on national ticket
1953 Tenley Albright wins world championship in figure skating
     Playboy founded by Hugh Hefner
     Alfred Kinsey, *Report on Sexual Behavior in the Human Female*
1955 Rosa Parks arrested in Montgomery, Alabama, for refusing to move to
     seat in back of the bus
     "Gunsmoke" premieres
     "Queen for a Day" premieres
     "Does she...or doesn't she?" Clairol advertising campaign
1959 Barbie doll introduced
1961 Citizen's Advisory Council on the Status of Women set up by Kennedy
     administration
1962 Helen Gurley Brown, *Sex and the Single Girl*

1963   Betty Friedan, *The Feminine Mystique*
       Mary McCarthy, *The Group*
1964   "Bewitched" premieres
       Title VII of the Civil Rights Act passed by Congress
1965   "I Dream of Jeannie" premieres
       Daniel P. Moynihan, "The Negro Family: The Case for National Action"
           (The Moynihan Report)
1966   National Organization for Women (NOW) founded by Betty Friedan
       Helen Gurley Brown named editor of *Cosmopolitan*
1967   Sue Kaufman, *Diary of a Mad Housewife*
1968   Gwendolyn Brooks appointed poet laureate of Illinois
       "Julia" premieres
       Shirley Chisholm elected to Congress
1969   Ursula K. Le Guin, *The Left Hand of Darkness*
1970   Kate Millet, *Sexual Politics*
       Shulamith Firestone, *The Dialectic of Sex: The Case for Feminist Revo-
           lution*
       The Left Hand of Darkness wins Hugo Award and Nebula Award
       "The Mary Tyler Moore Show" premieres
       It Ain't Me, Babe (first feminist underground comic)
1971   Association for Intercollegiate Athletics for Women (AIAW) founded
1972   Title IX of the Education Amendments Act
       Marge Piercy, *Small Changes*
       Alix Kates Shulman, *Memoirs of an Ex-Prom Queen*
       Dr. Mary Jane Sherfey, *The Nature and Evolution of Female Sexuality*
       Lady Sings the Blues (Diana Ross)
       Sounder (Cicely Tyson)
       Barbara Jordan elected to Congress
       Preview issue of *Ms.* magazine
       Shirley Chisholm becomes first black woman to run for president of the
           United States
1973   Billie Jean King vs. Bobby Riggs tennis match
       Viva founded
       Erica Jong, *Fear of Flying*
1974   U.S. Congress revises Little League charter to allow females to play baseball
       National Collegiate Athletic Association (NCAA) no longer bans women
           from membership
       Shirley Polykoff Advertising, Inc., founded
       "Police Woman" premieres
1975   Joanna Russ, *The Female Man*
1976   Marge Piercy, *Woman on the Edge of Time*
       "The Bionic Woman" premieres
       "Charlie's Angels" premieres
       "Mary Hartman, Mary Hartman" premieres
1977   National Women's Conference, Houston
       Patricia Roberts Harris appointed Director of HUD (first black woman to
           serve in cabinet)
       Chris Evert named *Sports Illustrated's* Athlete of the Year

Janet Guthrie races in Indianapolis 500
Bowie Kuhn refuses to admit women reporters to locker rooms during World Series

1978 Judge Carl Rubin rules that girls cannot be forbidden to participate in contact sports
Le Anne Schreiber appointed head of sports department at *New York Times*
Nancy Kassebaum elected to United States Senate
The Ann Landers Encyclopedia A to Z

1979 Black Fashion Museum opens in New York City
National Archives for Black Women's History founded
Susan B. Anthony dollar introduced

1980 Andrea Jaeger becomes, at 15, youngest seeded player at Wimbledon
Nancy Lieberman drafted by the Women's Professional Basketball League (WBL)
NCAA votes to sponsor women's championships
Nine to Five (Dolly Parton, Jane Fonda, Lily Tomlin)
The Women's Room shown on television, starring Lee Remick
"It's a Living" premieres

1981 Sandra Day O'Connor named to the United States Supreme Court
Betty Friedan, *The Second Stage*

APPENDIX 5

Important Research
Centers and Institutions

Boston Public Library
    Galatea Collection
    Antislavery papers
Brooklyn Public Library
    Material on clothing, design, fashion
Carnegie Library of Pittsburgh
    Charles Chauncey Mellon Collection
Drexel Institute of Technology Libraries, Philadelphia
    Material on clothing, design, fashion
Duke University Library, Durham, N.C.
    William Perkins Library
    Southern women
Elmira College, Elmira, N.Y.
    Hamilton Library
    Genteel women's reading
Fisk University Library, Nashville, Tenn.
    Black women
Franklin D. Roosevelt Library, Hyde Park, N.Y.
    Democratic National Committe, Women's Division Papers
    Frances Perkins Papers
Harvard University, Cambridge, Mass.
    Houghton Library
    Lydia Maria Child correspondence
    Elizabeth Palmer Peabody Papers
    Louisa May Alcott manuscripts
Howard University, Washington, D.C.
    Moorland-Spingarn Research Center
    Black women and black women's organizations
Library of Congress, Washington, D.C.
    League of Women Voters of the United States Papers
    National Women's Trade Union League Papers
    Women's Joint Congressional Committee Papers
    National Association for the Advancement of Colored People Papers
    Elizabeth Cady Stanton Papers

Mary Church Terrell Papers
Booker T. Washington papers
Louisiana State University, Baton Rouge
    Department of Archives and Manuscripts
    Southern women
    Papers on women planters
Massachusetts Historical Society, Boston
    Papers of late eighteenth-century families
Michigan State University, East Lansing
    Russel B. Nye Popular Culture Collection
    Dime novels
    Comic books
    Harlequin romances
    Confession and movie magazines
National Archives, Washington, D.C.
    Official documents and records
Newberry Library, Chicago
    Ayer Collection
    Indian captivities
New York Public Library
    Schomburg Collection
    Schwemmer-Lloyd Collection
    The Ellis Gray Loring Collection, Child Correspondence
    Peabody Correspondence, Berg Collection
Northwestern University Library, Evanston, Ill.
    Biblioteca Femina
    Special Collections—Women's Collection
Pennsylvania Historical Society, Philadelphia
    Antislavery materials
Radcliffe College, Cambridge, Mass.
    Arthur and Elizabeth Schlesinger Library on the History of Women in America
    American Association of University Women Papers
    Child Care Parents Association Papers
    International Federation of Working Women Papers
    Frances Perkins Papers
    Blackwell Family Papers
    Charlotte Hawkins Brown Papers
    Black Women Oral History Project
    Pinkham Collection
Smith College Library, Northampton, Mass.
    Sophia Smith Collection
    Mary Beard Papers
    Carrie Chapman Catt Papers
University of California, Los Angeles
    Pulp Magazine Collection from 1895 to present
University of Michigan, Ann Arbor
    William L. Clements Library
    Theodore Dwight Weld Collection

University of North Carolina, Chapel Hill
　Southern Historical Collection
Women's History Research Center, Berkeley, Calif.
　Literature on the woman's movement
　Films

Additional information regarding research centers and institutions is available in the following:

Arthur and Elizabeth Schlesinger Library on the History of Women in America. *The Manuscripts Inventories and the Catalogs of the Manuscripts, Books and Pictures.* Boston: G. K. Hall & Co., 1973.

Ash, Lee. *Subject Collections: A Guide to Special Book Collections and Subject Emphases as Reported by University, College, Public and Special Libraries, and Museums in the United States and Canada.* 4th ed. New York: R. R. Bowker Co., 1974.

Davis, Lenwood G. *The Black Woman in American Society: A Selected Annotated Bibliography.* Boston: G. K. Hall & Co., 1975.

Harrison, Cynthia Ellen. *Women's Movement Media: A Source Guide.* New York: R. R. Bowker Co., 1975.

Lynn, Naomi B., Ann B. Matasar, and Marie Barovic Rosenberg. *Research Guide in Women's Studies.* Morristown, N.J.: General Learning Press, 1974.

Michigan Department of State. *Bibliography of Sources Relating to Women.* Lansing, Mich.: Michigan History Division, Michigan Department of State, 1975.

National Union Catalog of Manuscript Collections, 1959-. Washington, D.C.: Library of Congress, 1959-.

Smith College Library. *Catalog of the Sophia Smith Collection.* 2d ed. Northampton, Mass.: Smith College, 1976.

Williams, Ora. *American Black Women in the Arts and Social Sciences: A Bibliographic Survey.* Rev. and enl. ed. Metuchen, N.J.: Scarecrow Press, 1978.

Women's History Sources: A Guide to Archives and Manuscript Collections in the United States. New York and London: R. R. Bowker Company, 1979. Vol. 1, *Collections,* edited by Andrea Hinding. Vol. 2, *Index,* edited by Suzanna Moody.

Index

AAUW, 41
abolition. *See* reform movements
abolitionist novels, 107-8
abortion, 29, 162; opposition to, 24
"The Abuse of Eve by the New World Adam" (L. R. Pratt), 103, 122
"Achievement-Related Motives and the Woman Athlete" (Birrell), 181-82, 192
"Active Women in Ads" (A. Poe), 167, 190
"Actress Archetypes in the 1950s" (Welsch), 141, 153
Adams, Abigail, 8, 59
Adams, Henry, 105
Adams, John, 8
Adams, John Quincy, 8
Adams, Louisa Catherine, 73
Adam's Rib, 19
Addams, Jane, 41, 59, 67; Nobel Peace Prize won by, 19
Adventure, Mystery and Romance (Cawelti), 57
advertising: agencies, 167-68; histories of, 164; in magazines, 165-66; manuals, 162-63; of menstrual products, 176; of patent medicine, 56; rise of magazine, 164; role of, in feminine mystique, 28; studies of women in, 162-68, 189-90; of swimming suits, 175; on television, 166-67; in women's magazines, 58
Advertising Age, 166
advertising industry, rise of, 17
"Advertising Portraying or Directed to Women," 166-67, 189
Advertising to Women (Naether), 162-63, 189
Advertising to Women, Inc., 167
"Advising and Ordering" (Turow), 156, 160
affected mythology, 4

African writers, 109
The Afro-American Woman (Harley and Terborg-Penn), 74, 80
"Afterword: Critical Re-Vision" (Dovovan), 208-9
"Ain't I a Woman?" (Truth), 16
Albright, Tenley, 21, 179
Alcott, Louisa May, 105; *Jo's Boys*, 96; *Little Women*, 92, 116
Alcuin (C. B. Brown), 104
Alice Doesn't Live Here Anymore, 141
alienation, 26, 28, 97-98. *See also* bodies: alienation of women from their
Allen, Henry Wilson [pseud. Clay Fisher; Will Henry], 96
Allen, Hervey, *Anthony Adverse*, 117
Allen, Mary, *The Necessary Blankness*, 106, 117
Allen, Woody, 24
"All in the Family," 58
All the Happy Endings (Papashvily), 89-91, 122, 143, 152
Alone (Terhune), 15, 91
Alyx (Russ), 115
A.M.A., 52, 56
"The Amazon Legacy" (Chesler), 187, 194
American Black Women in Arts and Social Sciences (O. Williams), 77, 85, 110, 124
American Costume, 1840-1920 (Worrell), 168, 192
"American Dream, Nightmare Underside" (McKnight), 97, 121
The American Eve in Fact and Fiction (Earnest), 58-59, 78
"American Feminist Literary Criticism" (Register), 207-8, 210
"The American Galatea" (J. Montgomery),

97, 121
An American Girl, 148
American Magazine, 9, 126
The American Movie Goddess (McCreadie),
    140, 152
"American SF and the Other" (Le Guin),
    114, 120
The American Woman (Chafe), 42-43, 78,
    128, 133, 202, 209
The American Woman's Home (Beecher
    and Stowe), 13
"The American Woman's Pre-World War I
    Freedom in Manners and Morals"
    (McGovern), 72, 82
America Through Women's Eyes (Beard),
    63, 77
The Anatomy of American Popular Culture
    (Bode), 88, 118
Anderson, Madeline, 149
Anderson, Sherwood, 97
Andre Norton (Schlobin), 115, 123
Andrews, Deborah D., and William D.
    Andrews, "Technology and the
    Housewife . . . ," 46-47, 77
"The Androgynous Advantage" (Duquin),
    181, 192
androgyny, 19; call for, by feminists, 199, 208;
    as goal of sports, 181; in literature, 106,
    112-13; rejection of, by feminists, 201
"Androgyny, Ambivalence, and Assimilation
    in *The Left Hand of Darkness*" (Hayles),
    113, 120
Angelou, Maya, 108-9; *I Know Why the
    Caged Bird Sings*, 59
Annas, Pamela, "New Worlds, New Words,"
    112, 117
Annie Allen (G. Brooks), 21
anorexia nervosa, 179
Anspach, Karlene, *The Why of Fashion*,
    168, 190
Anthony, Susan B., 16, 59; as editor of *The
    Revolution*, 132; in the suffrage movement,
    15
Anthony Adverse (Hervey Allen), 117
antifeminists, at National Women's
    Conference, 28
anti-intellectualism, 33-34, 76
"Anti-Intellectualism and the American
    Woman" (Welter), 76, 84
Anti-Lynching Crusaders, 19
antinomianism, 7, 66, 71-72, 103
Antioch College, 34
anti-suffragists, 40-41, 67

The Apex Treasury of Underground Comics
    (Donahue and Goodrick), 186, 194
"The Apologetic and Women in Sport"
    (P. Del Rey), 181, 192
"Appearance and the Self" (Stone), 168
Archer, Isabel, 97
archetypes, distortion of, in science fiction,
    112. *See also* heroines; mythology;
    stereotypes
"Are Athletics Making Girls Masculine?"
    (D. A. Sargent), 183, 194
"Are You Being Two-Faced?" (Gilbert and
    Williamson), 184, 193
Ariès, Philippe, 200; *Centuries of
    Childhood*, 203
Armitage, Susan H., "Women's Literature
    and the American Frontier," 96-97, 117
Arthur, Jean, 19
Arthur, T. S., 90
artist, woman as, in fiction, 98-99
"The Art of Convention" (Falke), 96, 119
The Art of Swimming (J. A. Bennett), 175
Arzner, Dorothy, 140-41, 145
Association of Alumnae, 41
Association of Southern Women for the
    Prevention of Lynching, 19
Atherton, Gertrude, 97
Atkins, Thomas R., ed., *Sexuality in the
    Movies*, 144-45, 150
At Odds (Degler), 28-30, 40, 42, 46, 78
Atwan, Robert, *Edsels, Luckies, and Frigi-
    daires* (with McQuade and Wright),
    164, 189
"At War with Herself" (M. Kelley), 73, 81
Atwood, Margaret, *Surfacing*, 99
Austin, Mary, 88
"The Autobiography of Miss Jane Pittman"
    (Gaines), 157
The Awakening (Chopin), 96
"The Awful Fate of the Sex Goddess"
    (Tyler), 144

Bacall, Lauren, 148
Bacon, Mary, 185
Badami, Mary Kenny, "A Feminist Critique
    of Science Fiction," 111-12, 117
Bad Girl (Delmar), 117
Bambara, Toni Cade, 108, 109. *See also*
    Cade, Toni
Banner, Lois, ed., *Clio's Consciousness
    Raised* (with Hartman), 47, 67-71, 76, 80
Banta, Martha, "They Shall Have Faces,
    Minds, and (One Day) Flesh," 105, 117

Bara, Theda. *See* Goodman, Theodosia
Baraka, Imamu, 60
"The Barbarian" (Russ), 115
Barbie doll, 21
Bardot, Brigitte, 141
Bargainnier, Earl F., "I Disagree," 110, 118
Barker-Benfield, George James, *The Horrors of the Half-Known Life*, 51, 77
Barnett, Evelyn Brooks, "Nannie Burroughs and the Education of Black Women," 74, 77
Barnett, Rosalind, *Beyond Sugar and Spice* (with Rivers and Baruch), 185, 193
Barr, Amelia, *Between Two Loves*, 96
Barth, John, 107
Bartlett, Irving H., "The History and Psychodynamics of Southern Womanhood" (with Cambor), 38-39, 77
Baruch, Grace, *Beyond Sugar and Spice* (with Rivers and Barnett), 185, 193
Basinger, Jeanine, "Ten That Got Away," 141, 150
Bass, Charlotta A., 21, 74
Batson, Susan, 146
"The Battle of the Sexes" (Lauer and Lauer), 171-72, 191
Batty, Linda, *Retrospective Index to Film Periodicals, 1930-1971*, 150
Baym, Nina, 196; "Portrayal of Women in American Literature, 1790-1870," 104-5, 118; *Woman's Fiction*, 57, 77, 89, 91-94, 118, 143, 150; "The Women of Cooper's *Leatherstocking Tales*," *103, 118*
Beard, Mary R., ed., *America Through Women's Eyes*, 63, 77
"Beautiful and Damned" (Mussell), 101, 122
beauty. *See* cosmetics; feminine mystique; lady; mythology; myths; social mythology
beauty contests, 177
Beauvoir, Simone de, 169, 202-03; on Brigitte Bardot, 141; concept of other in, 208; on narcissism, 177; *The Second Sex*, 145, 170, 177, 190, 198-99, 209
Beavers, Louise, 146
Beecher, Catharine E., 34; *The American Woman's Home* (with H. B. Stowe), 13; development of calisthenics program by, 184; "Female Health in America," 66; Hartford Female Seminary founded by, 13; *Letters to the People on Health and Happiness*, 12-13; as proponent of domestic science, 46-47; "Statistics of Female Health," 67; on status of women, 13; *A Treatise on Domestic Economy*, 13, 47; *Woman Suffrage and Woman's Profession*, 67; on women's domestic education, 13-14
"Before *Godey's*" (Stearns), 130, 135
Belgrave, Cynthia, 146
"Beliefs About Success and Failure" (McHugh et al.), 182, 193
Bell, Roseann P., ed., *Sturdy Black Bridges* (with Parker and Guy-Sheftall), 109-10, 118
"Belles, Sirens, Sisters" (Gerard), 148-49, 151
The Bell Jar (Plath), 99
Bellow, Saul, 105
Benet, James, ed., *Hearth and Home* (with Tuchman and Daniels), 130-31, 135, 154-55, 160
Bennett, James Arlington, *The Art of Swimming*, 175
Bennett, Rex, "Selling Women, Selling Blacks," (with Culley), 167, 189
Berch, Bettina, "Scientific Management in the Home," 47, 77
Berger, Arthur Asa: "Rhoda's Marriage," 158; *The TV-Guided American*, 158
Berger, Peter, 166; *The Social Construction of Reality* (with Luckmann), 203, 209
Bergler, Edmund, *Fashion and the Unconscious*, 168
Berkshire Conference of Women Historians, 68
best-sellers, studies of, 116-17
Betancourt, Jeanne, *Women in Focus*, 149-50
Between Two Loves (Barr), 96
Beuf, Ann, "Doctor, Lawyer, Household Drudge," 156, 158
"Bewitched," 22
Beyond Her Sphere (Harris), 42, 47-49, 80
Beyond Sugar and Spice (Rivers et al.), 185, 193
Beyond the Forest, 141
Bickman, Martin, "Le Guin's *The Left Hand of Darkness*," 113-14, 118
bicycle: advertisements of the, 164; effects of, on dress, 161-62
The Big Sleep, 145
Bildungsroman, 103
Birrell, Susan, "Achievement-Related Motives and the Woman Athlete," 181-82, 192
birth control, 12, 59, 69-70; as male province, 46; as topic of comics, 162. *See also* contraception
Birth of a Nation, 18
bitch, 18; in film, 148; as stereotype in literature, 97, 105

Index

Bittner, James W., "A Survey of Le Guin Criticism," 113, 118

Blache, Alice Guy, 141

Black, J. Anderson, *A History of Fashion* (with Garland), 168, 190

"Black Ads Are Getting Blacker" (Chapko), 167, 189

Black Americans in Autobiography (Brignano), 110, 118

"Black and White Women in Interaction and Confrontation" (Lerner), 75, 81

Black-Eyed Susans (Washington), 108-9, 124

The Black Family and the Black Woman (Indiana University), 76-77, 110, 118

Black Film as Genre (Cripps), 146, 151

Black Films and Filmmakers (Patterson), 145, 152

Black Film Stars (Landay), 146, 151

Black Hollywood (Null), 146-47, 152

Black Images in Films . . ., 146, 150

black literature: authors of, 99, 107-8; images of women in, 105-10; loss of, to modern readers, 86-87; as popular literature, 87, 105-6; studies of, 99, 105-10

Black Macho and the Myth of the Superwoman (Wallace), 60-61, 84

"Black Male Perspectives on the Nineteenth-Century Woman" (Terborg-Penn), 74, 84

black matriarch, 28, 60, 64; image of, on television, 157

Black Matriarchy (Bracey et al.), 39, 77

Black Power Movement, 59-60, 162

Black Rage (Grier and Cobbs), 61, 79, 204, 209

Blacks in American Films (Mapp), 146, 152

Blacks in American Movies (Powers), 147, 152

Blacks in Films (Pines), 147, 152

Blackwell, Elizabeth, 50, 59; "Sexual Passion in Men and Women," 66

black whore, image of, on television, 157

The Black Woman (Cade), 61, 77

The Black Woman in American Society (L. Davis), 77-78, 110, 119, 133

"The Black Woman's Struggle for Equality in the South, 1895-1925" (Neverdon-Morton), 74, 82

black women: absence of, in advertising, 163, 167; bibliographies of, 133; as chattel, 161; documentaries of, 63-65; economics of, 7; effects of idealized image of beauty on, 162; in the eighteenth century, 30; employment of, 74; in film, 136, 145-47; founding of Anti-Lynching Crusaders by, 19; founding of National Federation of Afro-American Women by, 16; histories of, 27, 59-65, 73-74; images of, on television, 155-57; impact of World War II on, 43; invisibility of, 64; in literature, 59, 61; as matriarchs, 28, 60, 64; myths of, 10, 59-62; National Colored Women's Congress convened by, 16; in the nineteenth century, 64; in politics, 21; in reform movements, 16; regarded as less evolved, 53; in the south, 39; stereotypes of, 146; in suffrage movement, 40; in the west, 36

"Black Women Image Makers" (Washington), 108, 124

"Black Women in America" (Cole), 77-78

Black Women in American Life (Loewenberg and Bogin), 64-65, 82

"Black Women in Films" (Mapp), 145, 152

"Black Women in the Blues Tradition" (Harrison), 74, 80

"Black Women in the United States" (Lerner), 75, 81

Black Women in White America (Lerner), 63-65, 81

Black Women Novelists (B. Christian), 39, 78, 107-8, 118, 145, 151

Blassingame, John, 72

Bloomer, Amelia: as editor of *The Lily*, 172; as popularizer of the Bloomer costume, 15; in reform movement in fashion, 15

Bloomer costume, 161, 172

Bloomquist, Linda Edwards, "Women and Blacks on TV" (with O'Kelley), 167, 189

blue-collar. *See* class; class differences; factory workers; immigrants; industry; lower class; working class

Blue Lagoon, 24

The Bluest Eye (Morrison), 109, 148

bluestockings, 34

Bobbsey Twins, 110

Bode, Carl: *The Anatomy of American Popular Culture*, 88, 118; "The Scribbling Women," 88, 118; "The Sentimental Muse," 88, 118

bodies: alienation of women from their, 10, 12, 23, 55, 161, 179, 200-202; control of women's, 23; effects of exercise on women's, 179, 183; as icons, 101; relationship of women to their, 99-102, 107-8, 178; right of women to their, 70, 161-62; role of women's, 198-99; women identified with their, 53; women's, as guinea pigs, 51; women's

perception of their, 180-81. *See also* sex; sex organs; sexuality; sports
"Body Image and Sex Stereotyping" (Mathes), 180, 193
Bogin, Ruth, *Black Women in American Life* (with Loewenberg), 64-65, 82
Bogle, Donald, *Toms, Coons, Mulattoes, Mammies, and Bucks*, 146, 150
Bok, Edward, 56, 164; as editor of *Ladies' Home Journal*, 126-27; as social reformer, 127
Bond, Jean Carey, "Reader's Forum," 108, 118, 157-58
bonding between women, 30-31
The Bonds of Womanhood (Cott), 31, 78
Books for Pleasure (Greene), 116-17, 120
Boston Female Medical College, 50
The Bostonians (James), 103
Boston Women's Health Book Collective, 162; *Our Bodies, Ourselves*, 23
Botkin, B. A., ed., *Lay My Burden Down*, 59
Bow, Clara, 18, 144
Bracey, John H., ed., *Black Matriarchy* (with Meier and Rudwick) 39, 77
Brackett, Leigh, 116
Bradley, Marion Zimmer, 112, 115; *The Keeper's Price*, 113, 115, 118
Bradstreet, Anne, 67, 103
Braun, Eric, "Where Have All the Stylists Gone?" 148, 150
"Breaking Out" (It Ain't Me Babe Basement Collective), 22-23
Breen, Walter, *Darkover Concordance*, 115, 118
Bretnor, Reginald, ed., *Science Fiction Today and Tomorrow*, 112, 118
Brignano, Russell C., *Black Americans in Autobiography*, 110, 118
Broner, Esther M., *Her Mothers*, 99
Brooks, Gwendolyn, 108; *Annie Allen*, 21; *Maud Martha*, 109; Pulitzer Prize won by, 21
Brooks, Louise, 141
Brooks, Robert D., "The Playmate of the Month" (with Kallan), 130, 134
Brown, Charles Brockden: *Alcuin*, 104; *Ormond*, 104; *Wieland*, 104
Brown, Helen Gurley: as editor of *Cosmopolitan*, 22, 129-30; *Sex and the Single Girl*, 22
Brown, Herbert Ross, *The Sentimental Novel in America, 1789-1860*, 87, 118
Brown, William Hill, *The Power of Sympathy*, 87, 104

Browne, Ray B., ed., *Icons of America* (with Fishwick), 177-78, 190
Buckley, Robert B., "Therapy of Fashion" (with Miller and Carpenter), 169-70, 191
Buckskin Belle, 188
Buffalo Belle, 188
Burgher, Mary, 109
Burke, James Henry, *80 Years of Best-Sellers, 1895-1975* (with Hackett), 117, 120
Burney, Fanny, 92
business, women in, 8
Butch Cassidy and the Sundance Kid, 22
Butler, Matilda: "A Scale for Sexism" (with Pingree et al.), 167, 190; ed., *Women and the Mass Media* (with Paisley), 130-31, 133

Cade, Toni: ed., *The Black Woman*, 61, 77; "On the Issue of Roles," 61, 77; "The Pill," 61, 77. *See also* Bambara, Toni Cade
Calvert, Catherine, "Five Women Filmmakers," 149, 151
Calvinism, 67; decline of, 32. *See also* Puritans
Cambor, C. Glenn, "The History and Psychodynamics of Southern Womanhood" (with Bartlett), 38-39, 77
Cameron, Ian, and Elizbeth Cameron, *Dames*, 150-51
"The Campaign for Woman's Rights in the 1920's" (Chambers), 72, 78
Cantor, Muriel S., "Where Are the Women in Public Broadcasting?" 155, 159
Capitola (Southworth), 15, 91
"A Cap Maker's Story" (Schneiderman), 65
captivity tales, 6, 36, 103
Cardinale, Susan, *Special Issues of Serials About Women, 1965-1975*, 133
careers. *See* Dexter, Elisabeth; education; factory workers; Harris, Barbara J.; industry; legal profession; medical profession; professions; Walsh, Mary Roth
Career Women of America, 1776-1840 (Dexter), 49, 78
Caribbean writers, 109
Carmichael, Stokely, 60
Carnal Knowledge, 145, 148
Carnes, Valerie, 196; "Icons of Popular Fashion," 177-78, 190
Carpenter, Lewis G., "Therapy of Fashion" (with Miller and Buckley), 169-70, 191
Carrell, Kimberley W., "The Industrial Revolution Comes to the Home," 47, 77
Carroll, Diahann, 146

Carson, Josephine, *Silent Voices*, 59
cartoons, studies of, 188-89
"A Case for Violet Strange" (J. Cornillon),
  103, 119
"The Case of the American Jezebels"
  (Koehler), 71-72, 81
"A Case Study of Technological and Social
  Change" (Cowan), 47, 70-71, 78
Cather, Willa, 88
Catholic Legion of Decency, 19, 144
Catt, Carrie Chapman, 41
Cavalcade of the American Novel
  (Wagenknecht), 88, 124
Cawelti, John G.: *Adventure, Mystery and
  Romance*, 57; *The Six-Gun Mystique*,
  96, 118
"The Celebrity Magazines" (Honey), 128, 134
censorship. *See* Catholic Legion of Decency;
  Production Code
Centuries of Childhood (Ariès), 203
Century of Struggle (Flexner), 8, 39-40, 79
Chafe, William Henry, *The American
  Woman*, 42-43, 78, 128, 133, 202, 209
"The Challenge of Women's History"
  (Lerner), 75, 81
Chambers, Clarke A., "The Campaign for
  Women's Rights in the 1920's," 72, 78
Chanel, Coco, 169
Chapko, Michael K., "Black Ads Are Getting
  Blacker," 167, 189
Charles of the Ritz, 168
Charlotte Temple (Rowson), 8-9, 33-34, 57,
  86, 90, 97, 102, 104
Charnas, Suzy McKee: *Motherlines*, 23
Chase, A. W., *Dr. Chase's Recipes*, 12
"A Checklist of SF Novels with Female
  Protagonists," (Fergus), 111, 119
Chesbro', Caroline, 93
Chesler, Phyllis: "The Amazon Legacy," 187,
  194; *Women and Madness*, 98, 118, 170,
  190, 204, 209
Chevli, Lyn, 187; *Tits & Clits Comix* (with
  Sutton), 23
Child, Lydia Maria, 67; *History of Women in
  All Ages and Nations*, 34
childbirth, 19, 38, 45, 65; alternative methods
  of, 23, 199-200; history of, 54-55
childhood. *See* Ariès, Philippe
childraising, as a political issue, 28-29
Chisholm, Shirley, 63
Chopin, Kate, 59; *The Awakening*, 96
Christian, Barbara, 196; *Black Women
  Novelists*, 39, 78, 107-8, 118, 145, 151

Christina, R. W., *Psychology of Motor
  Behavior and Sport* (with Landers), 181
Christman, Margaret C., *Suiting Everyone*
  (with Kidwell), 168-69, 191
churches, role of women in, 6-7, 27, 30, 70.
  See also church societies; religion
church societies, 37
"Cinderella vs. Statistics" (Higashi), 73, 80
cinema. *See* film
"Circumstance as Policy" (Malzberg), 113,
  121
Citizen's Advisory Council on the Status of
  Women, 22
Civil Rights Act, Title VII of the, 22
Civil Rights legislation, 182
Civil Rights Movement, 60, 63; effects of,
  on women, 37, 48; role of black women
  during the, 16
Civil War: effects of, on dress reform, 173;
  effects of, on fiction, 95; effects of, on
  women, 92, 95; property rights of women
  before the, 161
Claflin, Tennessee, 59; *Constitutional Equal-
  ity a Right of Woman*, 173, 190
Clairol, 168
Clareson, Thomas D.: ed., *Many Futures,
  Many Worlds*, 112, 119; *Science Fiction
  Criticism*, 115-16, 119; ed., *Voices for the
  Future*, 114, 119
Clarissa (Richardson), 57
Clarke, Edward H., *Sex in Education*, 13
Clarke, Shirley, 149
class, women as a, 5, 170, 176, 199-200. *See
  also* class differences; Firestone, Shula-
  mith; leisure class; lower class; Marxism;
  middle class; Robinson, Lillian S., working
  class
class differences, 44-45, 48, 52-53, 66
Cleaver, Eldridge, 60
Clio's Consciousness Raised (Hartman and
  Banner), 47, 67-71, 76, 80
clitoridectomies, 11, 69, 204
"Clothes and Government" (Langner),
  170, 191
clothing. *See* fashion
Coaching the Female Athlete (D. M. Miller),
  183-84, 193
Cobbs, Price M., 62-63; *Black Rage* (with
  Grier), 61, 79, 204, 209
Code of the Comics Magazine Association,
  186
The Code of the West (Grey), 96
Cole, Johnneta B., "Black Women in Amer-

ica," 77-78

colleges, establishment of women's 34, 50.
See also education

Collins, Roy, 186

Colonial period, 4, 7, 67, 71, 73; attitude
toward recreation in, 180; literature of the,
103; role of women in the, 26, 30, 48, 63, 66

" 'Combat in the Erogenous Zone' "
(Tuttleton), 105, 123

"Comes the Revolution" (Phillips), 185, 193

comics, 67, 188; histories of, 186-89, 194-95.
See also underground comics

"Comics as Culture" (Inge), 188

"Coming of Age in America" (Welter), 76, 84

Comix Book, 188

commercials, as degrading to women, 207.
See also advertising

"Community Work of Black Club Women"
(Lerner), 75, 81

*The Complete Encyclopedia of Television
Programs, 1947-1979* (Terrace), 155, 160

Comstock Law, 12-13

conflict, 3, 5, 17, 24

conjure woman, in literature, 107-8

Conrad, Susan Phinney, *Perish the Thought*,
33-35, 78

"Consciousness and Authenticity" (Holly),
208-9

conservatism, 3, 24, 28, 187; women opposed
to, 38

consolation literature, 33

conspicuous consumption, 27, 58, 173, 177,
198. *See also* consumers; leisure class

Constitutional Equality a Right of Woman
(Claflin), 173, 190

consumers: relationship of, to women's magazines, 58, 129-30; women as, 17, 27-28, 44,
73, 162-63. *See also* advertising; conspicuous consumption; consumer society;
Industrial Revolution

consumer society, 178. *See also* advertising;
conspicuous consumption; consumers; Industrial Revolution

"Contemporary Feminism" (Friedman),
73, 79

contraception, 54; effects of, on role of wom-
en, 38; state laws regarding, 162. *See also*
birth control

Conway, Jill, "Women Reformers and American Culture, 1870-1930," 72, 78

Cooper, Anna J., 74

Cooper, James Fenimore, *Leatherstocking
Tales*, 103-4

The Coquette (Foster), 90

Corbett, Katharine T., "Louisa Catherine
Adams," 73, 78

Cornillon, John, "A Case for Violet Strange,"
103, 119

Cornillon, Susan Koppelman: "The Fiction
of Fiction," 102, 119; ed., *Images of Women
in Fiction*, 102-3, 111, 119

Cornish, Ellen, 184

Cornwell, Regina, "Maya Deren and
Germaine Dulac," 149, 151

"Correspondence..." (G. Smith and
Stanton), 172-73, 191-92

corsets, 54, 173-74

cosmetics, 169-70, 177-78

"Cosmetics and Attitudes Toward Women
in the Seventeenth Century" (Drew-Bear),
178, 190

Cosmopolitan, 22, 164, 167; cartoons in, 188;
studies of, 125, 129-30

costume. *See* fashion

Cott, Nancy F., 29; *The Bonds of Womanhood*, 31, 78; ed., *Root of Bitterness*,
66, 78

counterculture. *See* conflict; science fiction;
underground comics

A Country Doctor (Jewett), 50, 96

Courant, 104

Courtney, Alice E., "Women in TV Commercials" (with Whipple), 156, 159, 166, 189

The Covered Wagon, 145

Cowan, Ruth Schwartz, "A Case Study of
Technological and Social Change," 47,
70-71, 78

Cowie, Alexander, *The Rise of the American
Novel*, 88

Craft, Ellen, 64

Crain, Jane Larkin, "Feminist Fiction,"
100, 119

Crawford, Janie, 108

Crawford, Joan, 139-40

Crawley, Ernest, "The Sexual Background of
Dress," 170, 190

"Creating a Feminist Alliance" (Dye), 72, 78

Cries and Whispers, 145

crime shows, 58

Cripps, Thomas, *Black Film as Genre*,
146, 151

"The Critical Task" (L. S. Robinson),
206, 210

"Criticism—and Self-Criticism" (L. S. Robinson), 206-7, 210

"Criticism: Who Needs It?" (L. S. Robinson),

207, 210

Culley, James D., "Selling Women, Selling Blacks" (with Bennett), 167, 189

cult of domesticity, 9, 66; effects of, on black women, 107-8; effects of, on southern women, 36-39; effects of, on western women, 35; height of, 21; modern version of, 21; in nineteenth-century fiction, 92; as repressive, 31; response to, by intellectuals, 33-34; rise of, 17, 27, 48; sentimentalism of, 15. *See also* mythology; myths; social mythology; Victorian period; woman's sphere

cult of the lady, 161. *See also* cult of domesticity

cult of true womanhood, 5, 76, *See also* cult of domesticity

"The Cult of True Womanhood, 1820-1860" (Welter), 76, 84

cultural mythology, studies of, 29, 60-61. *See also* mythology; myths; social mythology

Cummins, Maria, *The Lamplighter*, 15, 91

Currey, L. W., 115; *A Research Guide to Science Fiction Studies* (with Tymn and Schlobin), 116, 124

The Curse (Delaney et al.), 204, 209

Curtis, Cyrus H. K., as founder of *Ladies' Home Journal*, 127

Dall, Caroline Healey, 34

Daly, Mary, *Gyn/Ecology*, 44, 52, 55, 78, 106, 119, 177, 190, 204, 209

Dames (Cameron and Cameron), 150-51

Dandridge, Dorothy, 146

The Dangerous Sex (Hays), 205, 209

Daniels, Arlene Kaplan, ed., *Hearth and Home* (with Tuchman and Benet), 130-31, 135, 154-55, 160

Darkover, 113

Darkover Concordance (Breen), 115, 118

Darkover Newsletter, 115, 119

Darwin, Charles, 48, 51

Darwinism, 197

David, Jay, ed., *To Be a Black Woman* (with Watkins), 59-60, 84, 110, 124

Davidson, Sara, 99

Davis, Angela, 61

Davis, Bette, 139-41

Davis, Lenwood G., *The Black Woman in American Society*, 77-78, 110, 119, 133

Davis, Paulina Wright, 34

Davis, Sarah, 109

Day, Doris, 141, 144

"Daytime Television" (Lopate), 157, 159

death, sentimental view of, 33

DeBolt, Joe, ed., *Ursula K. Le Guin*, 113, 119

Dee, Ruby, 146

Deep Throat, 145

"Defenders of the Faith" (Welter), 76, 84

Degler, Carl N.: *At Odds*, 28-30, 40, 42, 46, 78, 199, 209; on Charlotte Perkins Gilman, 198

Deland, Margaret, 76

Delaney, Janice, *The Curse* (with Lupton and Toth), 204, 209

Delany, Samuel R.: Introduction to *Alyx*, 115, 119; *Tales of Nevèrÿon*, 115

Delineator, 128-29

Deliverance (Dickey), 106

Delmar, Viña, *Bad Girl*, 117

del Rey, Lester, "Helen O'Loy," 112

Del Rey, Patricia, "The Apologetic and Women in Sport," 181, 192

Demeter, myth of, 98

Demos, John, "Husbands and Wives," 71, 78

Deren, Maya, 149

The Descendant (Glasgow), 96

"Desegregating Sexist Sport" (Edwards), 183, 193

The Deserted Wife (Southworth), 91

detective fiction, 57, 76, 110

de Varona, Donna, 186

Dexter, Elisabeth, 50; *Career Women of America, 1776-1840*, 49, 78

dialectical materialism, 199. *See also* Firestone, Shulamith; Marxism; Robinson, Lillian S.

The Dialectic of Sex (Firestone), 22, 42, 79, 199-200, 208-9

"Diaries of Frontier Women" (Schlissel), 73, 83

Diary of a Mad Housewife (Kaufman), 100

Dickens, Charles, 106

Dickey, James, *Deliverance*, 106

Dickinson, Emily, 105

Didion, Joan, 105; *Play It As It Lays*, 99

Didrikson, Mildred ("Babe"), 19

Dietrich, Marlene, 19, 138-39, 141, 144

Dimity Convictions (Welter), 70, 75-76, 84

Dinsmore, Elsie, 92

Dior, Christian, 169

"Discovering Worlds" (S. Wood), 114, 124

discrimination. *See* racial oppression; racial prejudice; racism; sexism

"Discrimination Against Afro-American Women in the Women's Movement, 1830-

1920" (Terborg-Penn), 74, 84
disestablishment: of the clergy, 31-33; of women, 32
The Dispossessed (Le Guin), 112, 114, 116
"The Divided Woman" (Giddis), 141, 151
Doctor and Patient (Mitchell), 45
Dr. Chase's Recipes (Chase), 12
"Doctor, Lawyer, Household Drudge" (Beuf), 156, 158
Doctors Wanted (Walsh), 49-50, 84
Dr. Zay (Phelps), 50
documentary histories, 63-67
Does She... or Doesn't She? (Polykoff), 168, 190
"Domestic Experience and Feminist Theory" (Grant), 73, 79
"Domestic Mythology" (Gilman), 67
domestic novel: authors of, 89-90, 94-95; as compensation for reality, 88; decline of, 91; as forms of rebellion, 89-91; messages of, 33; as reassurance to women, 88-89; rise of, 90; as soap opera, 88. *See also* sentimental fiction; sentimental heroine; woman's fiction
domestic responsibilities of women, 197. *See also* homemaking; housewives
domestic science, 46-47. *See also* Beecher, Catharine E.
"Dominant or Dominated?" (Lemon), 155, 159
Donahue, Don, *The Apex Treasury of Underground Comics* (with Goodrick), 186, 194
Donovan, Josephine: "Afterword: Critical Re-Vision," 208-9; ed., *Feminist Literary Criticism*, 207-9
"Dorothy Arzner's *Dance, Girl, Dance*" (Kay and Peary), 140-41, 151
Douglas, Ann, 196; *The Feminization of American Culture*, 31-33, 78, 94, 127-28, 133. *See also* Wood, Ann Douglas
Downing, Mildred, "Heroine of the Daytime Serial," 156, 159
Dred Scott decision, 161
Dreiser, Theodore, 105
dress. *See* fashion.
Dress, Adornment, and the Social Order (Roach and Eicher), 169-71, 191
"Dress of Women" (S. Grimké), 172
dress reform, 174; feminist response to, 161
"Dress Reform as Antifeminism" (Kunzle), 174, 191
Drew, Nancy, 110

Drew-Bear, Annette, "Cosmetics and Attitudes Toward Women in the Seventeenth Century," 178, 190
Duggan, Cathy, 185
Dulac, Germaine, 141, 149
Duniway, Abigail Scott, as editor of *New Northwest*, 133
Dunkel, Margaret, "What Constitutes Equality for Women in Sport?" 182, 192
Dunn, Theresa, 102
Duquin, Mary E., 196; "The Androgynous Advantage," 181, 192; "Beliefs About Success and Failure" (with McHugh and Frieze), 182, 193
"Dwelling in Decencies" (L. S. Robinson), 97, 122, 205-6, 210
Dyar, Mary, 66
Dye, Nancy Schrom, "Creating a Feminist Alliance," 72, 78
Dyer, Mary, 66
"The Dynamics of Cultural Resistance" (Gerbner), 154-55, 159

Earle, Alice Morse, *Two Centuries of Costume in America, 1620-1820*, 168, 190
The Early American Novel (Loshe), 87, 121
Earnest, Ernest, *The American Eve in Fact and Fiction*, 58-59, 78
The Earthsea Trilogy (Le Guin), 113
East, Elizabeth R., "Federal Civil Rights Legislation and Sport," 182, 192
Ebony, 167
economic role of women, 7
economics. *See* Gilman, Charlotte Perkins; Veblen, Thorstein
economic status of women, 6, 71; effects of war on, 43, 48; in the eighteenth century, 30; in the nineteenth century, 26-27, 52; in the seventeenth century, 26, 30, 48; in the twentieth century, 52. *See also* Gilman, Charlotte Perkins
"The Economic Theory of Women's Dress" (Veblen), 173-74, 192
Eden, Barbara, 22
Edgeworth, Maria, 92
Edmondson, Madeleine: *From Mary Noble to Mary Hartman* (with Rounds), 156, 159; *The Soaps* (with Rounds), 156, 159
Edsels, Luckies, and Frigidaires (Atwan et al.), 164, 189
education: attitudes toward, 34, 53; of black women, 74; domestic, 13; effects of, on women, 13; improvements in women's, 34,

41; inadequate, for women, 33, 42, 45; need
for domestic, 31; role of, in feminine
mystique, 47; role of magazines in, 126;
role of, in medicine, 52; role of mothers in,
30, 44, 46; schools for women's, founded,
13-14; sex, 53-54; studies of, 73-74
Education Amendments Act, Title IX of, 22,
182-83, 185
Edwards, Harry, "Desegregating Sexist
Sport," 183, 193
Ehrenreich, Barbara, *For Her Own Good*
(with English), 44, 51-53, 79
Eicher, Joanne Bubolz, ed., *Dress, Adorn-
ment, and the Social Order* (with Roach),
169-71, 191
80 Years of Best-Sellers, 1895-1975 (Hackett
and Burke), 117, 120
Eldredge, Charles, 94
"Elizabeth Cady Stanton on Marriage and
Divorce" (E. Griffith), 73, 79-80
"Elizabeth Stuart Phelps and the Gates Ajar
Novels" (Suderman), 94, 123
Ellet, Elizabeth, *The Woman of the Amer-
ican Revolution*, 34
Ellmann, Mary, *Thinking About Women*, 208
Elmira College, 34
Emancipation Proclamation, 161
Emerson, Ralph Waldo, 104
English, Deirdre, *For Her Own Good* (with
Ehrenreich) 44, 51-53, 79
Entrikin, Isabelle Webb, *Sarah Josepha Hale
and Godey's Lady's Book*, 127, 133
"Equality in Advertising" (*Journal of
Communication*), 167, 189
ERA, 43, 67; opposition to, 24; and sport,
182; support for, 22
"The ERA and Women's Sport" (Rose), 182,
193-94
Erikson, Erik, 94, 201; "Inner and Outer
Space," 205
Ernest Linwood (Hentz), 15, 34
Ernst, Lois Geraci, 167
Essays in Feminism (Gornick), 76, 79, 182,
193
Essence, 130
Estren, Mark James, *A History of Under-
ground Comics*, 194
Evans, Augusta, 38, 105; heroines of, 93;
St. Elmo, 15, 91
Evans, Mari, 59, 109
Eve, 89
The Evening and the Morning (Sorensen), 97
Evert, Chris, 23

Everyone Was Brave (O'Neill), 40-42, 45, 82
"Everywoman's Jewelry" (E. Gordon and
Nerenberg), 176, 190
exercise: benefits of, 179; bicycling as form
of, 161-62; dangers in, 53, 183; effects of,
185; need for, 45; programs, 45, 184. *See
also* sports; swimming
existentialism, 198-99
"The Exquisite Slave" (H. Roberts), 174, 191

The Faces of Eve (Fryer), 89, 120
factory workers, 26, 43, 72, 75. *See also*
immigrants; working class
Fairbanks, Carol, *More Women in Literature*,
117, 119. *See also* Myers, Carol Fairbanks
The Faith of Our Feminists (Jessup), 205-6
Falke, Anne, "The Art of Convention," 96,
119
Falling Bodies (Kaufman), 100
family: the black, 60, 62-63, 72; courses in
the, 47; mythology of the, 203; as political
issue, 28-29, 40-41, 49; relationship of woman to the, 46; role of television in promoting
the, 157; role of women in the, 199-200.
See also childbirth; childraising; marriage
Family Circle, 131
Farnham, Marynia, *Modern Woman* (with
Lundberg), 20, 43
Farrington, Samuel, 94
fashion: histories of women in, 168-78, 190-
92; iconology of, 177-78; image of women
in, 58; production of, 168-69; and psycho-
therapy, 169-70; reform movement in,
171-74; as symbol of authority, 170; and
technology, 175-76. *See also* cosmetics;
jewelry
" 'The Fashionable Diseases' " (A. D. Wood),
68, 85
Fashion and the Unconscious (Bergler), 168
Fashion for Everyone (Ley), 168, 191
fashion magazines, study of, 129
"Fashion Magazines Mirror Changing Role
of Women" (Tortora), 129, 135
Fat and Blood (Mitchell), 45
Faulkner, William, 105
Fauset, Jessie Redmon, 108
Fear of Flying (Jong), 86, 99-102
"Federal Civil Rights Legislation and Sport"
(East), 182, 192
federal laws, 182
" 'The Female Appendage' " (Hogeland), 72,
80
Female Complaints (Stage), 55-57, 84, 127,

135
"Female Complaints" (Welter), 76, 84
The Female Experience (Lerner), 65-66, 81
"Female Health in America" (Beecher), 66
The Female Man (Russ), 111-12, 116
Female Quixotism (Tenney), 90
Females and Their Diseases (Meigs), 11
The Feminine Fifties (Patte), 206
"Feminine Hygiene, Fashion, and the Emancipation of American Women" (Schroeder), 176, 191
feminine mystique, 202; in advertising manuals, 163; characteristics of, 28; in fiction, 100-101; literature of, 9; sources of, 43. *See also* archetypes; *The Feminine Mystique*; heroines; mythology; sentimental fiction; sentimental heroine; social mythology; stereotypes
The Feminine Mystique (Friedan), 18, 21, 28, 41, 79, 128, 134, 143, 151, 202, 209
"The Feminine Plastique" (Reisig), 130, 134
femininity, 179-81, 202. *See also* feminine mystique; lady
feminism: early examples of, 17, 46; histories of, 28, 40-43, 49, 67, 73, 75; of late twentieth century, 22, 24, 187. *See also* ERA; feminist revolution; social feminism; suffrage; suffrage movement; women's movement; women's rights
"Feminism for a Sporting Future" (Heide), 182, 193
"A Feminist Critique of Science Fiction" (Badami), 111-12, 117
"Feminist Fiction" (Crain), 100, 119
Feminist Literary Criticism (Donovan), 207-9
Feminist Perspectives on Housework and Childcare (Swerdlow), 75
feminist revolution, 23; call for, 24. *See also* feminism; women's movement
"The Feminists" (Lerner), 75, 81
Feminist Studies, 75
The Feminization of American Culture (Douglas), 31-33, 78, 94, 127-28, 133
"The Feminization of American Religion, 1800-1860" (Welter), 70, 76, 84-85
Fergus, George, "A Checklist of SF Novels with Female Protagonists," 111, 119
Ferguson, Marjorie, "Imagery and Ideology," 131, 134
Fern, Fanny. *See* Willis, Sara
fertility, 29
Fetterley, Judith, *The Resisting Reader*, 106, 119

fiction, 8; woman's (*see* woman's fiction). *See also* best-sellers; domestic novel; science fiction; sentimental fiction
"Fictional Feminists in *The Bostonians* and *The Odd Women*" (Maglin), 103, 121
"The Fiction of Fiction" (Cornillon), 102, 119
Fiedler, Leslie, *Love and Death in the American Novel*, 205, 208
"Fighting Sexism on the Airwaves" (Mills), 156, 159
film: absence of women in, 22, 58; decline of women in, 139-40; influence of World War II on, 139; lesbianism in, 140; myths of women in, 137-38, 142-43; portrayal of women in, 137-48; as protest, 143-44; psychological study of women in, 145; sex goddesses in, 138-40, 144; and society, 136-37; studies of women in, 58, 72-73, 136-53; women in production of, 140-41, 145
Film Library Quarterly, 148, 153
Films and Filming, 147-48
"Films by and about Women," 149, 151
Films by and/or about Women, 150, 153
Films for, by and about Women (Sullivan), 149, 153
Final Analysis (Gould), 100
Finley, Ruth, *The Lady of Godey's*, 127, 134
Firestone, Shulamith, 203; *The Dialectic of Sex*, 22, 42, 79, 199-200, 208-9
First International Festival of Women's Films, 149
Fisher, Clay. *See* Allen, Henry Wilson
Fishwick, Marshall, ed., *Icons of America* (with Browne), 177-78, 190
Fitzgerald, F. Scott, 97, 105-6
Five Centuries of American Costume (Wilcox), 168, 192
"Five Women Filmmakers" (Calvert), 149, 151
flapper, 20; image of, in film, 142-43
Fleming, Peggy, 179
Flexner, Eleanor, 48; *Century of Struggle*, 8, 39-40, 79
The Flight from Woman (Stern), 201
Flora, Cornelia Butler, "The Passive Female," 128, 134
"Focus on the Actress as a Person and a Profession," 146
"Folk Linguistics" (Kramer), 188-89, 194
folklore, 35-36
Fonda, Jane, 141
Fontenot, Chester J., 109
A Fool There Was, 18

foot-binding, 204
For Her Own Good (Ehrenreich and English), 44, 51-53, 79
Forrey, Carolyn, "The New Woman Revisited," 95-96, 119
Foster, Hannah Webster, *The Coquette*, 90
Fourteenth Amendment, 16
Fox, William, 144
Frame by Frame (Klotman), 147, 151
"Frankie Mae" (J. W. Smith), 109
Franklin, Benjamin, 175
Franzwa, Helen: "The Image of Women in Television," 155, 159; "Working Women in Fact and Fiction," 129, 134
Fratianne, Linda, 179
Frazier, E. Franklin, *The Negro Family in the United States*, 62
" 'Free in Fact and at Last' " (Schultz), 105-6 123
free love, 59
free love movement, 15
French, Brandon, *On the Verge of Revolt*, 139, 143-44, 151
French, Marilyn, 99; *The Women's Room*, 86, 100
Freud, Sigmund, 101, 199, 204; use of theories of, in analyzing film, 142
Friedan, Betty, 196, 203; *The Feminine Mystique*, 18, 20-21, 28, 41, 79, 128, 134, 143, 151, 202, 209; founding of NOW by, 22; on role of women's magazines, 128-29
Friedman, Barbara, ed., *Women's Work and Women's Studies* (et al.), 76, 79
Friedman, Jean E.: "Contemporary Feminism," 73, 79; ed., *Our American Sisters* (with Shade), 71-73, 79
Friend, Beverly, "Virgin Territory," 112, 119
The Friendship Wreath, 90
Friends of Darkover: *Darkover Newsletter*, 115, 119; *Starstone 1*, 115, 123
Frieze, Irene Hanson, "Beliefs About Success and Failure" (with McHugh and Duquin), 182, 193
"From Maidenhood to Menopause" (Haller), 53-54, 80
From Mary Noble to Mary Hartman (Edmondson and Rounds), 156, 159
"From Olive Oyl to Sweet Polly Purebread" (Levinson), 158-59, 189, 194
From Reverence to Rape (Haskell), 136-40, 151
From Sambo to Superspade (Leab), 146, 151
From Sundown to Sunup (Rawick), 39, 83

"Frontier and Wilderness" (Gherman), 36, 79
frontier women, 35, 73. *See also* pioneer women
Frontier Women (Jeffrey), 35, 80
"Fruits of Passion" (Jordan), 72, 80
Fryer, Judith, *The Faces of Eve*, 89, 120
Fuller, Henry B., 89
Fuller, Margaret, 33, 76; *Woman in the Nineteenth Century*, 34, 105
Futures, 111

Gaines, Ernest, "The Autobiography of Miss Jane Pittman" (TV movie), 157
Garbo, Greta, 19, 141, 144, 148
Garland, Hamlin, 97
Garland, Madge, *A History of Fashion* (with Black), 168, 190
The Garland, 90
Gates Ajar novels (Phelps), 94
gay. *See* homosexuality; lesbianism
Gayle, Addison, 109
Gelman, Judith S., *Women in Television News*, 158-59
Gender Advertisements (Goffman), 165-66, 189
General Federation of Women's Clubs, 41-42
General Magazine and Historical Chronicle, 164
Generation of Vipers (Wylie), 20, 144, 153
genital mutilation, 11, 69, 204
Genly, Ai, 114
genuine mythology, 4
Georgia, University of, 36
Georgia Female College, 34
Gerard, Lillian, "Belles, Sirens, Sisters," 148-49, 151
Gerbner, George, 165, 196; "The Dynamics of Cultural Resistance," 154-55, 159
"Get Christy Love," 157
Gherman, Dawn Lander, "Frontier and Wilderness," 36, 79
Gibson, Althea, 183
Giddis, Diane, "The Divided Woman," 141, 151
Gilbert, Bill: "Are You Being Two-Faced?" (with Williamson), 184, 193; "Programmed to Be Losers" (with Williamson), 184, 193; "Women Are Getting a Raw Deal" (with Williamson), 184, 193; "Women in Sport" (with Williamson), 184
Gilda, 145
Gill, Gerald R., 74
Gilman, Charlotte Perkins, 41, 200; "Domes-

tic Mythology," 67; on dress reform, 171; *Herland*, 23; *The Home*, 67; *Women and Economics*, 42, 65, 72, 79, 177, 190, 197-98; "Women's Evolution from Economic Dependence," 66; "The Yellow Wallpaper," 11-12, 67, 198

Giovanni, Nikki, 61, 109

girl, as term for female, 126. *See also* lady

Girl Fight Comics (Robbins), 23

"The Girls in the Cartoons" (Streicher), 156, 158-59, 189, 195

The Girl Sleuth (Mason), 110, 121

Gish, Dorothy, 18

Gish, Lillian, 18, 138, 143

Gissing, George, *The Odd Women*, 103

Glasgow, Ellen, 38, 59, 88; *The Descendant*, 96

Glimpses of Fifty Years (F. Willard), 65

Glyn, Elinor, *It*, 18

Godey, Louis Antoine, as founder of *Godey's Lady's Book*, 127

Godey's Lady's Book, 14; art in, 128; influence of, on readers, 127-28; predecessors of, 130; as proponent of woman's sphere, 27; studies of, 125, 127-29

Godwin, Gail, 99

Goffman, Erving, 196; *Gender Advertisements*, 165-66, 189

Golden Multitudes (Mott), 116, 122

The Golden Notebook (Lessing), 99

Gone With the Wind (movie), 146

Gone With the Wind (Mitchell), 116

"The Good-Bad Girl" (Wolfenstein and Leites), 145, 148, 153

Good Housekeeping, 168; fiction in, 128-29

Goodman, Theodosia [Theda Bara], 18, 143-44

Goodrick, Susan, *The Apex Treasury of Undeground Comics* (with Donahue), 186, 194

"Good Times," 157

Gordon, Eleanor, "Everywoman's Jewelry" (with Nerenberg), 176, 190

Gordon, Linda: "Voluntary Motherhood," 69-70, 79; *Woman's Body, Woman's Right*, 70, 79

Gornick, Vivian: *Essays in Feminism*, 76, 79, 182, 193; "Female Narcissism as a Metaphor in Literature," 76, 79; Introduction to *Gender Advertisements*, 165-66, 189; "Why Do These Men Hate Women?" 76, 79; "Why Radcliffe Women Are Afraid of Success," 76, 79; "Why Women Fear Suc-

cess," 76, 79; ed., *Woman in Sexist Society* (with Moran), 176-77, 189-90

gothic romances, modern, 86, 92, 100-101

Gough-Yates, Kevin, "The Heroine," 147-48, 151

Gould, Lois, 99; *Final Analysis*, 100; *A Sea-Change*, 100; *Such Good Friends*, 100

government, 26, 170; control of birth control, 12; propaganda, 4, 132; role of, in civil rights, 22; role of, in education, 46. *See also* federal laws

Grable, Betty, 141

Graham, George, *Lady's and Gentleman's Magazine*, 126-27

Grant, Mary, H., "Domestic Experience and Feminist Theory," 73, 79

"The Great American Bitch" (D. B. Schmidt), 97, 123

great depression, 20

Green, Anna Katharine, 76

Green, Joyce, 61

Greenberg, Martin Harry, *Ursula K. Le Guin* (with Olander), 113, 122

Greendorfer, Susan L., "Socialization into Sport," 181, 193

Greene, Suzanne Ellery, *Books for Pleasure*, 116-17, 120

Greenspan, Bud, 186

Gregory, Samuel, 50

Grey, Zane, *The Code of the West*, 96

Grier, William H., 62-63; *Black Rage* (with Cobbs), 61, 79, 204, 209

Griffith, David Wark, 18, 138

Griffith, Elisabeth, "Elizabeth Cady Stanton on Marriage and Divorce," 73, 79-80

Grimké, Angelina, 38, 50. *See also* Weld, Angelina Grimké

Grimké, Charlotte Forten, 63

Grimké, Sarah M., 38, 59, 67; "Dress of Women," 172; and fashion reform, 171; *Letters on the Equality of the Sexes*, 66; "Marriage," 65

"Growing Sophistication of Film Content" (Jacobs), 145

Growing Up Female, 148

Guthrie, Janet, 23, 186

Gutman, Herbert G., 29, 72

Guy-Sheftall, Beverly, ed., *Sturdy Black Bridges* (with Bell and Parker), 109-10, 118

gynecology, 11, 51, 66, 68, 204. *See also* Daly, Mary

Gyn/Ecology (Daly), 44, 52, 55, 78, 106, 119, 177, 190, 204, 209

Haber, Barbara, *Women in America,* 77, 80

Hackett, Alice Payne, *80 Years of Best-Sellers, 1895-1975* (with Burke), 117, 120

Hale, Sarah Josepha, 59, 90; criticism of, 128; as editor of *Godey's Lady's Book,* 14, 127-29; as formulator of popular taste, 128; as founder of *Ladies' Magazine,* 14; influence on education of, 14; influence on magazine publishing of, 14; studies of, 127-28

Half a Century (Swisshelm), 65

Hallelujah, 146

Haller, John S., Jr.: "From Maidenhood to Menopause," 53-54, 80; *The Physician and Sexuality in Victorian America* (with R. Haller), 54, 80

Haller, Robin M., *The Physician and Sexuality in Victorian America* (with J. Haller), 54, 80

Hallinan, Vincent, 74

Hamill, Dorothy, 179

Hanna, Delphine, 184

Hansberry, Lorraine, 109; *A Raisin in the Sun,* 59

Happiness in Marriage (Sanger), 18

Hardy Boys, 110

Harland, Marion. *See* Terhune, Mary Virginia Hawes

Harlem Renaissance, 108

Harley, Sharon: ed., *The Afro-American Woman* (with Terborg-Penn), 74, 80; "Northern Black Female Workers," 74, 80

Harlow, Jean, 19, 138, 144

Harper, Frances E. W., 59; *Iola Leroy,* 16

Harper's Bazaar, studies of, 127, 129-30

Harper's Bazaar (Trahey), 130, 135

Harper's Bazar. See Harper's Bazaar

Harris, Barbara J., *Beyond Her Sphere,* 42, 47-49, 80

Harris, Elizabeth Forsling, 22

Harrison, Daphne Duval, "Black Women in the Blues Tradition," 74, 80

Hart, James D., *The Popular Book,* 116, 120

Hartford Female Seminary, 13, 34, 184

Hartman, Mary, 156

Hartman, Mary S., ed., *Clio's Consciousness Raised* (with Banner), 47, 67-71, 76, 80

Harvard, 45

Haskell, Molly, 196; essay on Liv Ullman, 141; *From Reverence to Rape,* 136-40, 151

Hawkins, Robert Parker, "A Scale for Sexism" (with Pingree et al.), 167, 190

Hawks, Howard, 141

Hawthorne, Nathaniel, 14, 89-90, 94, 97, 104-5

Hayles, N. B., "Androgyny, Ambivalence, and Assimilation in *The Left Hand of Darkness,"* 113, 120

Haymes, Howard, "Movies in the 1950s," 145, 151

Hays, Hoffman Reynolds, *The Dangerous Sex,* 205, 209

health, 68. *See also* Beecher, Catharine E.; corsets; " 'The Fashionable Diseases' "; medical profession; physicians

Hearth and Home (Tuchman et al.), 130-31, 135, 154-55, 160

Hefner, Hugh, 21

Heide, Wilma Scott, "Feminism for a Sporting Future," 182, 193

Heilbrun, Carolyn G.: "The Masculine Wilderness of the American Novel," 106, 120; *Toward a Recognition of Androgyny,* 106, 120

Heinlein, Robert, 111, 116

Heiress of All the Ages (Wasserstrom), 89, 124

"Helen O'Loy" (L. del Rey), 112

" 'A Helpmate for Man Indeed' " (Stoeltje), 35-36, 84

Helva, 112

Hemingway, Ernest, 97, 105-6

Hemingway, Mariel, 24

Henderson, Zenna, 116

Henry, Will. *See* Allen, Henry Wilson

Hentz, Caroline Lee, 90, 93; *Ernest Linwood,* 15, 34

Hepburn, Audrey, 141

Hepburn, Katharine, 19, 140

Herman, Sondra R., "Loving Courtship or the Marriage Market?" 72, 80

Her Mothers (Broner), 99

Hernton, Calvin C.: "The Negro Woman," 59; *Sex and Racism in America,* 59

heroic medicine, 52, 69

"The Heroine" (Gough-Yates), 147-48, 151

"Heroine of the Daytime Serial" (Downing), 156, 159

heroines: black, 107-8; in gothic fiction, 100-101; limitations on, 101-2; types of, in literature, 94, 96-97, 104-5, *See also* film: myths of women in; film: sex goddesses in; Gough-Yates, Kevin; Higashi, Sumiko; images of women; sentimental fiction; sentimental heroine

Herrick, Robert, 89

"Hidden Riches" (J. H. Wilson), 73, 85

Higashi, Sumiko, 196; "Cinderella vs. Statistics," 73, 80; *Virgins, Vamps, and Flappers,* 73, 80, 142-43, 151
histories of women, 25-85
The History and Development of Advertising (Presbrey), 164, 190
"The History and Psychodynamics of Southern Womanhood" (Bartlett and Cambor), 38-39, 77
A History of American Magazines (Mott), 126, 134, 164, 189
A History of Fashion (Black and M. Garland), 168, 190
A History of Underground Comics (Estren), 186, 194
History of Women in All Ages and Nations (Child), 34
Hoekstra, Ellen, "The Pedestal Myth Reinforced," 128, 134
Hoffman, Arnold R., "Social History and the Crime Fiction of Mary Roberts Rinehart," 110, 120
Hogeland, Ronald W., " 'The Female Appendage,' " 72, 80
Hogue, Miki King, 186
Holiday, Billie, *Lady Sings the Blues,* 59
Hollander, Anne, *Seeing Through Clothes,* 168, 191
Holly, Marcia, "Consciousness and Authenticity," 208-9
Hollywood. *See* film
"Hollywood Heroines Under the Influence" (Maslin), 141, 152
Holmes, Mary Jane, 91, 93
Holmes, Oliver Wendell, *Puerperal Fever As A Private Pestilence,* 55
Holt, Victoria, 101
The Home (Gilman), 67
homemaking, 42, 71, 128. *See also* Beecher, Catharine E.; cult of domesticity; domestic responsibilities of women; domestic science; housewives
"A Home of One's Own" (Regan), 101-2, 122
homosexuality, 144, 162. *See also* lesbianism
homosocial bonding, 27, 29-31
Honey, Maureen: "The Celebrity Magazines," 128, 134; "Recruiting Women for War Work," 132, 134
Horn, Maurice: *Women in the Comics,* 187, 194; *The World Encyclopedia of Comics,* 186, 194
Horne, Lena, 146
Horner, Matina, 182

The Horrors of the Half-Known Life (Barker-Benfield), 51, 77
"Housewifery and Motherhood" (Jenkins), 73, 80
housewives, 20-21, 29, 40, 73, 75; in advertising, 164, 166-67; in fiction, 88-91, 95, 100-101, 104; in magazines, 128-30; women as professional, 27; work of, 47. *See also* cult of domesticity; homemaking
Howe, Julia Ward, 73
Howells, William Dean, 89, 105
"How I Learned to Ride the Bicycle" (F. Willard), 73, 85, 183, 194
" 'How to Be a Woman' " (Nowak), 47, 82
How to Save Your Own Life (Jong), 99
Hudson, Jackie, "Physical Parameters Used for Female Exclusion from Law Enforcement and Athletics," 180, 193
Hull, Gloria T., 109
"Humanbecoming" (Morgan), 102-3, 121
humor. *See* cartoons; underground comics
Hunt, Harriot K., 50
Hurlock, Elizabeth B., "Sumptuary Law," 170-71, 191
Hurston, Zora Neale, 109; *Their Eyes Were Watching God,* 108
"Husbands and Wives" (Demos), 71, 78
Hutchinson, Anne, 7, 66, 71-72, 103

I Am Curious Yellow, 145
I Am Somebody, 149
icons: of fashion, 177-78; use of, to counter mythology, 142; of women in magazines, 130; of women in movies, 136-37. *See also* images of women
Icons of America (Browne and Fishwick), 177-78, 190
"Icons of Popular Fashion" (Carnes), 177-78, 190
ideal woman, 9; Mary Pickford as, 137; role of magazines in creating image of, 128. *See also* cult of domesticity; lady
Ideas of the Woman Suffrage Movement, 1890-1920 (Kraditor), 37, 40, 67, 81
identity, 31, 73; cultural, 5; difficulty in defining, 43, 53; loss of individual, 10; quest for, 98-99; woman's right to her own, 24
"I Disagree" (Bargainnier), 110, 118
"I Dream of Jeannie," 22
"I Gave Her Sack and Sherry" (Russ), 115
I Know Why the Caged Bird Sings (Angelou), 59
illness, 12-13, 44-45; examinations of women

for, 55; medicines for, 57; politics of, 52-53; as sex-oriented, 53. *See also* health; neurasthenia; physicians; rest cure

"I Love Lucy," 21

"The Image of Woman in Advertising" (Komisar), 166, 189

"The Image of Women in Science Fiction" (Russ), 102, 111, 122

"The Image of Women in Television" (Franzwa), 155, 159

"Imagery and Ideology" (Ferguson), 131, 134

"Images of Black Women in Afro-American Poetry" (Rushing), 74, 83

images of femininity, 62

images of women, 3-4; in advertising, 156, 165-67; as beautiful, 61; in film, 141-46; in magazines, 129-31; male, 200; role of magazines in creating ideal, 128; on television, 154-58; *See also* archetypes; icons; roles; social mythology; stereotypes; Weibel, Kathryn

Images of Women (Millum), 166, 189

"Images of Women in Early American Literature" (Stanford), 103-4, 123

Images of Women in Fiction (Cornillon), 102-3, 111, 119

immigrants, 40, 65; regarded as less evolved, 53; role of, 27. *See also* lower class; working class

Indian captivity tales, 6, 36, 103

individualism, 29

industrialization, 66. *See also* Industrial Revolution; science; technology

Industrial Revolution, 9; effects of, on advertising, 164; effects of, on women, 26, 47, 51-53, 89-90, 92. *See also* industrialization; science; technology

"The Industrial Revolution Comes to the Home" (Carrell), 47, 77

industry, women in, 42, 66. *See also* industrialization; Industrial Revolution; technology

inequality: sexual, 42; as woman's natural state, 51; in work force, 28, 43. *See also* racism, sexism

Inge, M. Thomas, ed., "Comics as Culture," 188

Ingraham, J. H., 90

"In Search of Our Mothers' Gardens" (Walker), 8

intellectuals, 33-35

interdisciplinary studies, 57-60, 67-74, 76

"An Interview with Madeline Anderson . . . ," 149, 151

"In the Beginning" (O'Neill), 72, 82-83

Introduction to *Wonder Woman* (Steinem), 187, 195

Iola Leroy (Harper), 16

Irving, Washington, 104

Ishmael (Southworth), 15, 91, 116

"Is There a Female Film Aesthetic?" (Eleanor Perry), 149, 152

It (Glyn), 18

It Ain't Me, Babe, 22, 188

It Ain't Me Babe Basement Collective, "Breaking Out," 22-23

"I Thought She Was Afeared . . ." (Russ), 115

"It's Not So Much . . ." (C. T. Williams), 157-58, 160

"Jackie!" (Lopate), 131-32, 134

Jackson, Andrew, 90

Jacobi, Mary Putnam: *The Question of Rest for Women During Menstruation,* 45

Jacobs, Lewis: "Growing Sophistication of Film Content," 145; *The Rise of the American Film,* 145, 151

James, Henry, 89, 97, 105; *The Bostonians,* 103

"James Michener's America" (Michener), 186, 193

Janeway, Elizabeth, *Man's World, Woman's Place,* 5, 112, 120, 202-3, 209

Jarvis, Anna, 18

Jeffrey, Julie Roy, *Frontier Women,* 35, 80

Jenkins, William D., "Housewifery and Motherhood," 73, 80

Jessup, Josephine Lurie, *The Faith of Our Feminists,* 205-6

jewelry, 176

Jewett, Sarah Orne, 88; *A Country Doctor,* 50, 96

Johnston, Claire: "Myths of Women in the Cinema," 142, 151; "Women's Cinema as Countercinema," 142

Johnston. Mary, 88

Jones, Gayl, 109

Jones, James P., "Nancy Drew, WASP Super Girl of the 1930s," 110, 120

Jones, Marie M., *Woman's Dress,* 173, 191

Jones, Mary Jane, "The Spinster Detective," 110, 120

Jong, Erica: *Fear of Flying,* 86, 99-102; *How to Save Your Own Life,* 99

Jordan, June, 109

Jordan, Winthrop, "Fruits of Passion," 72, 80

Jo's Boys (Alcott), 96

Julia, 24

Jung, Carl, 88, 204

"Just a Housewife" (Lerner), 75, 81

"Kali on Main Street" (Schechter), 18

Kallan, Richard A., "The Playmate of the Month" (with Brooks), 130, 134

Kaplan, Janice, *Women and Sports,* 178-80, 193

Katz-Stoker, Fraya, "The Other Criticism," 103, 120, 207, 209

Kaufman, Sue, 105; *Diary of a Mad Housewife,* 100; *Falling Bodies,* 100

Kay, Karyn: "Dorothy Arzner's *Dance, Girl, Dance"* (with Peary), 140-41, 151; ed., *Women and the Cinema* (with Peary), 140-42, 151

The Keeper's Price (Bradley), 113, 115, 118

Kekulé, Friedrich, 201

Kelley, Florence, 41

Kelley, Mary: "At War With Herself," 73, 81; ed., *Woman's Being, Woman's Place,* 73-74, 81

Kenealy, Arabella, "Woman as Athlete," 183, 193

Kent, George E., 109

Kern, Donna Rose Casella, "Sentimental Short Fiction by Women Writers in *Leslie's Popular Monthly,"* 132, 134

Kesey, Ken, 106

Kidwell, Claudia B.: *Suiting Everyone* (with Christman), 168-69, 191; *Women's Bathing and Swimming Costume . . . ,* 174-75, 191

Killers of the Dream (L. Smith), 38, 83

King, Billie Jean, 185

King, Martin Luther, 21

Kinsey, Alfred, *Report on Sexual Behavior in the Human Female,* 21

kinship systems, 30, 39

"The Kitchen Crisis" (Smart-Grosvenor), 61, 83

kitchens, 47, 61

Klotman, Phyllis Rauch, *Frame by Frame,* 147, 151

Klute, 141

Knight, Sarah Kemble, 103

Knowing and Being (Polanyi), 201, 210

Koehler, Lyle, "The Case of the American Jezebels," 71-72, 81

Komisar, Lucy, "The Image of Woman in Advertising," 166, 189

Kowalski, Rosemary Ribich, *Women and Film,* 149, 151

Kraditor, Aileen: *Ideas of the Woman Suffrage Movement, 1890-1920,* 37, 40, 67; ed., *Up From the Pedestal,* 67, 81, 172-73, 191

Kramer, Cheris: "Folk Linguistics," 188-89, 194; "Stereotypes of Women's Speech," 188, 194

Krichmar, Albert: *The Women's Movement in the Seventies,* 76, 81; *The Women's Rights Movement in the United States, 1848-1970,* 76, 81

Krouse, Agate Nesaule, "Why Women Kill" (with Peters), 110, 120

Kuhn, Bowie, 24

Künstlerromanen, 98

Kunzle, David, "Dress Reform as Anti-feminism," 174-191

Kuscsik, Nina, 185

labor force, 20, 42, 49, 71, 132

labor unions, 42, 72

The Lace Ghetto (Nunes and White), 67, 82

Ladies' Home Journal, 56, 164, 167; cartoons in, 188; fiction in, 128-29; history of, 127; studies of, 125, 127-28

Ladies' Magazine and Repository of Entertaining Knowledge, 9

ladies' magazines, 101, 130; role of, in establishing myth of the lady, 10. *See also* fashion magazines; women's magazines

Ladies' Monitor, 9

Ladner, Joyce A., *Tomorrow's Tomorrow,* 61-63, 81

lady, 4, 9, 26; myth of, in south, 36-38; origins of concept of, 26-27; as term for female, 126. *See also* cult of domesticity; girl; woman's sphere

"The Lady and Her Physician" (Morantz), 69, 82

"The Lady and the Mill Girl" (Lerner), 72, 75, 81

The Lady of Godey's (Finley), 127, 134

The Lady Persuaders (Woodward), 125-26, 135

Lady's and Gentleman's Magazine, 126-27

Lady Sings the Blues (Holiday), 59

LaGuardia, Robert, *The Wonderful World of TV Soap Operas,* 155-56, 159

The Lamplighter (Cummins), 15, 91

Landay, Eileen, *Black Film Stars,* 146,151

Landers, D. M., *Psychology of Motor Behavior and Sport* (with Christina), 181

Langer, Susanne K., 166

Langner, Lawrence, "Clothes and Government," 170, 191
language: changes in, 100, 126, 201; fear of obscene, 18; film as, 142; and perception, 201; use of, to denigrate women, 17, 31, 188, 204
Lanyi, Ronald Levitt, "Trina, Queen of the Underground Cartoonists," 188, 194
Larsen, Nella, 108-9
"The Last American Massacre" (Alexander Walker), 144
Last Tango in Paris, 145
Lauer, Jeanette C., and Robert H. Lauer, "The Battle of the Sexes," 171-72, 191
Lawrence of Arabia, 22
Lay My Burden Down (Botkin), 59
Leab, Daniel J., *From Sambo to Superspade,* 146, 151
Leatherstocking Tales, 103-4
Lee, Don L., *We Walk the Way of the New World,* 61-62
Lee, Hannah F. S., 90
Lee, Lawrence L., ed., *Women, Women Writers, and the West* (with Lewis), 36, 81, 96-97, 120
Lee, Stan, *The Superhero Women,* 186, 194
Lee, Sylvia B., "The Mormon Novel," 97, 120
The Left Hand of Darkness (Le Guin), 112-14, 116
legal profession, obstacles to women entering the, 48
legal subordination of women, 6
Legion of Decency, Catholic, 19, 144
Le Guin, Ursula K.: "American SF and the Other," 114, 120; *The Dispossessed,* 111-12, 114, 116; *The Earthsea Trilogy,* 113; *The Left Hand of Darkness,* 112-14, 116; "Science Fiction and Mrs. Brown," 114, 121; "Surveying the Battlefield," 114, 121; *The Wind's Twelve Quarters,* 114, 121; "Winter's King," 114; works on, 111-16
"Le Guin's *The Left Hand of Darkness*" (Bickman), 113-14, 118
Leigh, Vivien, 139
leisure class, 52, 173-74, 198. *See also* middle class
Leites, Nathan: "The Good-Bad Girl" (with Wolfenstein), 145, 148, 153; *Movies* (with Wolfenstein), 145, 153
Lemon, Judith, "Dominant or Dominated?" 155, 159
Lerner, Gerda, 50, 196; "Black and White Women in Interaction and Confrontation,"

75, 81; "Black Women in the United States," 75, 81; *Black Women in White America,* 63-65, 81; "The Challenge of Women's History," 75, 81; "Community Work of Black Club Women," 75, 81; *The Female Experience,* 65-66, 81; "The Feminists," 75, 81; "Just a Housewife," 75, 81; "The Lady and the Mill Girl," 72, 75, 81; "The Majority Finds Its Past," 75, 81; *The Majority Finds Its Past,* 75, 82; "New Approaches to the Study of Women in American History," 75, 82; "Placing Women in History," 75, 82; "The Political Activities of Antislavery Women," 75, 82; "Women's Rights and American Feminism," 75, 82
lesbianism, 66, 100, 140. *See also* homosexuality
Leslie's Popular Monthly, 132
Lessing, Doris, *The Golden Notebook,* 99
Letters on the Equality of the Sexes (S. Grimké), 66
Letters to Country Girls (Swisshelm), 65
Letters to the People on Health and Happiness (Beecher), 12-13
Levinson, Richard M., "From Olive Oyl to Sweet Polly Purebread," 158-59, 189, 194
Lewis, Merrill, ed., *Women, Women Writers, and the West* (with Lee), 36, 81, 96-97, 120
Lewis, Sinclair, 97, 106
Ley, Sandra, *Fashion for Everyone,* 168, 191
"The Liberation of Black Women" (P. Murray), 63, 73, 82
Liberty's Daughters, 7, 29-31
Liberty's Daughters (Norton), 29-31, 48, 82
Library of Congress, *New Serial Titles,* 133-34
Life, 164
Lifton, Robert Jay, ed., *The Woman in America,* 205, 209
L'il Lulu, 23
The Lily, 172
Lincoln, Melissa Ludke, 186
Lindsey, Kay, 61
literary criticism: feminist, 205-8; male orientation of, 205-6, 208; and theory, 205
literature, women in popular, 86-124. *See also* best-sellers; domestic novel; heroines; poetry; science fiction; sentimental fiction; woman's fiction
"The Literature of Impoverishment" (A. D. Wood), 95, 124
Little League, 22
The Littlest Rebel, 146

Little Women (Alcott), 92, 116
Lloyd, Chris Evert, 186
Local Colorists, 95
Loewenberg, Bert James, *Black Women in American Life* (with Bogin), 64-65, 82
Looking for Mr. Goodbar (Rossner), 101-2
Loos, Anita, 145
Lopate, Carol: "Daytime Television," 157, 159; "Jackie!" 131-32, 134
Lopez, Nancy, 186
Lorde, Audre, 61, 109
Loren, Sophia, 148
Loshe, Lillie Deming, *The Early American Novel,* 87, 121
"Louisa Catherine Adams" (Corbett), 73, 78
love. *See* romantic love
Love and Death in the American Novel (Fiedler), 205
"Loving Courtship or the Marriage Market?" (Herman), 72, 80
Lowell, Amy, 20
Lowell, Josephine Shaw, 41
lower class, 45-46, 53-54; black women of the, 62; use of corsets by, 174; use of jewelry by, 176. *See also* working class
Lucinda, the Mountain Mourner (Manvill), 90
Luckmann, Thomas, 166; *The Social Construction of Reality* (with Berger), 203, 209
Lundberg, Ferdinand, *Modern Woman* (with Fernham), 20, 43
Lundwell, Sam J., *Science Fiction,* 116, 121
Lupino, Ida, 141
Lupton, Mary Jane, *The Curse* (with Delaney and Toth), 204, 209
Lydia E. Pinkham's Vegetable Compound, 56-57
Lying In (Wertz and Wertz), 52, 54-55, 85
Lynn, Janet, 179
Lyon, Mary, 13, 34
Lyra the Femizon, 186

McCabe and Mrs. Miller, 148
McCaffrey, Anne: "Hitch Your Dragon to a Star," 112-13; *The Ship Who Sang,* 112; works on, 112, 116
McCall's: fiction in, 129; studies of, 125, 127, 129; "Togetherness" campaign of, 21
MacCann, Richard Dyer, *The New Film Index* (with Perry), 150, 152
McCreadie, Marsha, ed., *The American Movie Goddess,* 140, 152
McDaniel, Hattie, 146

McGovern, James R., "The American Woman's Pre-World War I Freedom in Manners and Morals," 72, 82
McGrath, Ellie, "The Weaker Sex? Hah!" 185, 193
McGrath, Kathleen Conway, "Popular Literature as Social Reinforcement," 102, 121
McHugh, Maureen C., "Beliefs About Success and Failure" (with Duquin and Frieze), 182, 193
McKinney, Nina Mae, 146
McKnight, Jeannie, "American Dream, Nightmare Underside," 97, 121
McLuhan, Marshall, 178
McQuade, Donald, *Edsels, Luckies, and Frigidaires* (with Atwan and Wright), 164, 189
McQueen, Butterfly, 146
Mademoiselle, 164
"Magazine Heroines" (Phillips), 131, 134
magazines: British, 166; directories of, 133; histories of, 9, 125-27, 164; history of advertising in, 164; images of women in popular, 129-32; studies of women in, 125-35; use of, for government propaganda, 132. *See also* ladies' magazines; men's magazines; women's magazines
Magazines in the Twentieth Century (Peterson), 127, 134, 164, 189
Magazines in the United States (Wood), 126-27, 135
Magazine War Guide, 132
Maglin, Nan Bauer, "Fictional Feminists in *The Bostonians* and *The Odd Women*," 103, 121
Mailer, Norman, 105
"The Majority Finds Its Past" (Lerner), 75, 81
The Majority Finds Its Past (Lerner), 75, 82
makeup. *See* cosmetics
Malleus Maleficarum, 204
Malzberg, Barry N., "Circumstance as Policy," 113, 121
mammy, image of, 17, 107, 146
Mann, Carol, 185
Mansfield, Jayne, 22
Man's World, Woman's Place (Janeway), 5, 112, 120, 202-3, 209
Manvill, P. D., *Lucinda, the Mountain Mourner,* 90
Many Futures, Many Worlds (Clareson), 112, 119
Mapp, Edward: *Blacks in American Films.*

146, 152; "Black Women in Films," 145, 152
"Marlene Dietrich" (Alexander Walker), 153
marriage, 65, 73; debate over, 72; as
  institution, 30, 40; as repressive, 96;
  restructuring of, 198; sanctity of, 19, 69-70.
  See also cult of domesticity; family; free
  love movement; Gilman, Charlotte Perkins
"Marriage" (S. Grimké), 65
Marshall, Paule, 107-9
Marston, William Moulton, 187
Martin, Wendy: "Profile: Susanna
  Rowson . . . , " 94, 121; "Seduced and
  Abandoned in the New World," 97-98, 121
Martineau, Barbara, "Thoughts about the
  Objectification of Women," 149, 152
Marvel comics, 186
Marxism: and literary theory, 205-8; as
  method, 199
Marxist critics. *See* Firestone, Shulamith;
  Robinson, Lillian S.
Mary Hartman, 156
Mary Noble, 156
Mary Olivier (M. Sinclair), 99
"The Mary Tyler Moore Show," 58, 157-58
"The Masculine Wilderness of the American
  Novel" (Heilbrun), 106, 120
masculinity, 28, 177, 180-81
"The Masculinity/Femininity Game"
  (Oglesby), 180-81, 193
Masel-Walters, Lynne, "To Hustle with the
  Rowdies," 132, 134
Masinton, Charles G., and Martha Masinton:
  "Second-class Citizenship," 105, 121
"The Mask of Beauty" (Stannard), 170, 176-
  77, 192
Maslin, Janet, "Hollywood Heroines Under
  the Influence," 141, 152
Mason, Bobbi Ann, *The Girl Sleuth,* 110, 121
Mass Culture (Rosenberg and White), 145,
  152
masturbation, 53-54, 76
Mathes, Sharon, 196; "Body Images and Sex
  Stereotyping," 180, 193
Mathis, June, 145
matriarchate, 62
matriarchy, 39, 60, 62-64
Maud Martha (G. Brooks), 109
"Maya Deren and Germaine Dulac"
  (Cornwell), 149, 151
media: black women in, 155, 157; as
  conservative force, 154-55; images of
  women in mass, 154; use of, as propaganda,
  132; women in mass, 130-31. *See also*

suffrage press
medical profession, 44-46; as against
  feminism, 54; attitudes of, toward women,
  51-55; barriers to women in, 49-50; drop
  in women entering, 48, 50; effects of rise
  of, on women, 54-55; rise of, 49-52, 54-56,
  69; role of education in, 52. *See also* heroic
  medicine; medicine; physicians; science
medicine, 137. *See also* health; heroic
  medicine; medical profession; physicians;
  science
Medusa (Marvel comics), 186
Meier, August, ed., *Black Matriarchy* (with
  Bracey and Rudwick), 39, 77
Meigs, Charles, *Females and Their Diseases,*
  11
Mellen, Joan, *Women and Their Sexuality in
  the New Film,* 140, 152
Melville, Herman, 33, 89, 104
Memoirs of an Ex-Prom Queen (Shulman),
  86, 103
Men and Steel (Vorse), 63
menarche, 23, 68. *See also* menopause;
  menstruation
Mencken, H. L., 106
menopause, 68-69. *See also* menarche,
  menstruation
men's magazines: descriptions of, 125-26;
  images of women in, 130
menstrual pain, 45
menstruation, 23, 45, 76; effects of sports on,
  179, 185; introduction of sanitary napkins
  and tampons for, 19, 176; misinformation
  about, 12; as subject of women's underground comics, 23, 162. *See also* menarche;
  menopause
mental illness, 204
"The Merchant's Daughter" (Welter), 76, 85
Michener, James A.: "James Michener's
  America," 186, 193; *Sports in America,*
  185, 193
Michigan, University of, 65
Mickelson, Anne Z., *Reaching Out,* 99-100,
  121
middle class, 35; the black, 17; and the cult
  of domesticity, 48; kitchens of the, 47;
  limitations on the, 45-46, 62; norms in
  advertising, 166; prejudices of the, 40;
  reformers of the, 45-46; rise of the, 9; role
  of the, in suffrage movement, 39; sexual
  habits of the, 53-54; use of corsets by the,
  174; writers of the, 89. *See also* cult of
  domesticity; leisure class

Midnight Cowboy, 22, 145
midwives, 12, 50; as victims of profession-
  alization, 52, 54
Mill, John Stuart, 198, 203; *The Subjection
  of Women,* 197, 209
Miller, Aurelia Toyer, 166
Miller, Donna Mae, *Coaching the Female
  Athlete,* 183-84, 193
Miller, Elizabeth Smith, "On the Bloomer
  Costume," 172, 191
Miller, Theo K., "Therapy of Fashion" (with
  Carpenter and Buckley), 169-70, 191
Millet, Kate, *Sexual Politics,* 22, 206, 208
Mills, Kay, "Fighting Sexism on the Air-
  waves," 156, 159
Millum, Trevor, 165; *Images of Women,* 166,
  189
ministers, relationship of, to women, 31-33
Mirror Mirror (Weibel), 57-58, 84, 129-30,
  135, 140, 153, 158, 160, 169, 192
miscegenation, 72
misogyny, 48, 144, 204; in film, 136; in
  literature, 106
"Miss America" Beauty Pageant, 18
Mitchel, Delores, "Women Libeled," 187-88,
  195
Mitchell, Margaret, *Gone With the Wind*
  (novel), 116
Mitchell, Silas Weir, 11, 69; *Doctor and
  Patient,* 45; *Fat and Blood,* 45; as inventor
  of rest cure, 68, 198
"Modernism and History" (L. S. Robinson
  and Vogel), 103, 122, 206, 210
Modern Screen, 129
Modern Woman (Lundberg and Farnham),
  20, 43
momism, 20, 43
Monroe, Marilyn, 22; downfall of, 144; as
  image of ultra-feminine woman, 139-40
Montagu, Ashley, *The Natural Superiority of
  Women,* 204-5, 209
Montgomery, Elizabeth, 22
Montgomery, Judith H., "The American
  Galatea," 97, 121
Montgomery Bus Boycott, 21
Moore, Catherine L., 115
Moran, Barbara K., ed., *Woman in Sexist
  Society* (with Gornick), 176-77, 189-90
Morantz, Regina, 70; "The Lady and Her
  Physician," 69, 82
More Women in Literature (Fairbanks), 117,
  119
Morgan, Edmund S., "The Puritans and

Sex," 71, 82
Morgan, Ellen, "Humanbecoming," 102-3,
  121
Morgan, Marabel, *The Total Woman,* 53
Mormon fiction, 97
"The Mormon Novel" (S. B. Lee), 97, 120
Mormons, 35
Morrison, Toni, 99, 107; *The Bluest Eye,*
  109; *Sula,* 100
Morton, Sarah Wentworth, 87
mother: images of good, 98, 105; images of
  terrible, 18, 98, 106. *See also* motherhood
motherhood, 67, 70; institution of, 200-201;
  veneration of, 27, 31, 41, 43; voluntary,
  69-70. *See also* birth control; contra-
  ception; mother
Motherlines (Charnas), 23
mothers and daughters, relationship of, 200-
  201
Mother's Day, 18
Motion Picture Almanac, 150, 152
Mott, Frank Luther: *Golden Multitudes,*
  116, 122; *A History of American
  Magazines,* 126, 134, 164, 189
Mott, Lucretia, 16, 59, 65; and the Seneca
  Falls Convention, 15
Mount Holyoke College, 13, 34
movies. *See* film
"Movies in the 1950s" (Haymes), 145, 151
Moynihan, Daniel P.: Moynihan Report, 60,
  62; *The Negro Family,* 62
Moynihan Report, 60, 62
"Mrs. Sigourney and the Sensibility of the
  Inner Space" (A. D. Wood), 94, 124
Ms., 186-87; founding of, 22; images of
  women in, 131; studies of, 130-31
mulatta, 10; image of, in literature, 107-8
Mullen, Richard D., ed., *Science-Fiction
  Studies* (with Suvin), 114-15, 122
Mulvey, Laura, "Visual Pleasure and Nar-
  rative Cinema," 142, 152
"Murder Most Genteel" (Welter), 76, 85
Murray, James P., *To Find an Image,* 146,
  152
Murray, Pauli, "The Liberation of Black
  Women," 63, 73, 82
Mussell, Kay J., "Beautiful and Damned,"
  101, 122
Myers, Carol Fairbanks, *Women in
  Literature,* 117, 122. *See also* Fairbanks,
  Carol
"Mystical Feminist" (Welter), 76, 85
Myth America (Wald), 205, 210

mythology: of American west, 96-97; of black
women in literature, 108-9; and literature,
97-98, 102, 105; need for female, 98-101;
sexual, of black and white women, 107-8;
social (*see* social mythology). *See also*
affected mythology; archetypes; feminine
mystique; heroines; myths; social
mythology; stereotypes
myths: of black women, 59-62; of femininity,
25, 45; of a heroine, 205; of ideal woman,
4; of the lady, 9; matriarchal, 202; of
motherhood, 41; patriarchal, 203; of
southern women, 36-39; of western women,
35; of woman's sphere, 27; of women and
sport, 179-83, 186; of women on television,
207. *See also* affected mythology; archetypes, feminine mystique; heroines; images
of women; mythology; social mythology;
stereotypes
"Myths of Women in the Cinema" (Johnston),
142, 151

Naether, Carl A.: *Advertising to Women*, 162-
63, 189
"Nancy Drew, Ballbuster" (Zacharias), 110,
124
"Nancy Drew, WASP Super Girl of the 1930s"
(J. P. Jones), 110, 120
"Nannie Burroughs and the Education of
Black Women" (E. B. Barnett), 74, 77
narcissism, 61, 102, 177, 199; play on
women's, in advertising, 163; role of, in
fashion, 177
The Narrative of Sojourner Truth (Truth), 16
National Advertising Review Board, 166-67
National American Woman Suffrage
Association, 15, 42
National Association of Colored Women, 74
National Consumers' League, 41
National Federation of Afro-American
Women, 16
National Federation of Settlements, 41
National Velvet, 141
National Women's Conference, 22, 28
National Women's Party, proposal of ERA by
the, 19
The Natural Superiority of Women
(Montagu), 204-5, 209
*The Nature and Evolution of Female
Sexuality* (Sherfey), 23
The Necessary Blankness (M. Allen), 106, 117
The Negro Family (Moynihan), 62
The Negro Family in the United States

(Frazier), 62
The Negro in Films (Noble), 146, 152
"The Negro Woman" (Hernton), 59
neofeminism, 102-3
neoromanticism, 53
Nerenberg, Jean, "Everywoman's Jewelry"
(with Gordon), 176, 190
neurasthenia, 54. *See also* Mitchell, Silas
Weir
Neverdon-Morton, Cynthia, "The Black
Woman's Struggle for Equality in the
South, 1895-1925," 74, 82
"New Approaches to the Study of Women in
American History" (Lerner), 75, 82
Newcomb, Horace, 58; *TV: The Most
Popular Art,* 155, 159
New Dimensions in Popular Culture (Nye),
128-29, 134
New England Hospital for Women and
Children, 50
A New-England Tale (Sedgwick), 15
"The New Feminist Criticism" (A. Pratt), 205,
210
The New Film Index (MacCann and E. S.
Perry), 150, 152
A New Mythos (Stewart), 98-99, 123, 202, 210
New Northwest, 133
New Serial Titles, 133-34
New Woman, 95-96, 99
"The 'New Woman' in the New South" (A. F.
Scott), 72, 83
"The New Woman Revisited" (Forrey), 95-96,
119
"New Worlds, New Words" (Annas), 112, 117
New Yorker, 164, 188
Nicholls, Peter, *Science Fiction at Large,*
114, 122
1950s: fiction of the, 91; films of the, 139-41,
143-44; political developments of the, 21;
popular culture of the, 21, 188; view of
women in the, 44, 47
1940s: best-sellers of the, 116-17; films of the,
58, 139-41, 148; popular culture of the, 20,
187-88; social changes of the, 20, 43
1970s: fiction of the, 112-16, 148-49; films of
the, 58, 140-41; political developments of
the, 22-23; popular culture of the, 22-24,
156, 187-88; sports in the, 182, 184-86
1960s: films of the, 58, 101, 140, 147-48;
political developments of the, 22; popular
culture of the, 22
Nineteenth Amendment, 22. *See also*
suffrage; suffrage movement

nineteenth century: role of women in, 17.
  See also Victorian period
1930s: changes in the south in the, 38;
  fiction of the, 110, 117; films of the, 19,
  138-39; political developments of the, 19,
  42; technology in the, 47
1920s: best-sellers of the, 116-17; films of the,
  138, 142-43; political developments of the,
  19, 42, 97; sexuality in the, 18-19; social
  changes in the, 20; technology in the, 47;
  view of women in the, 42, 97
Noble, Mary, 156
Noble, Peter, *The Negro in Films,* 146, 152
Norma Rae, 24
Norris, Frank, 105
North, Andrew. *See* Norton, Alice Mary
North American Review, 34
North Carolina, University of, 36
"Northern Black Female Workers" (Harley),
  74, 80
Norton, Alice Mary [pseud. Andre Norton;
  Andrew North], 115-16
Norton, Andre. *See* Norton, Alice Mary
Norton, Mary Beth: *Liberty's Daughters,* 29-
  31, 48, 82
Novak, Kim, 22, 148
NOW, 22, 67
Nowak, Marion, " 'How to Be a Woman,' "
  47, 82
Now Voyager, 147
Null, Gary, *Black Hollywood,* 146-47, 152
Nunes, Maxine, ed., *The Lace Ghetto* (with
  D. White), 67, 82
nursing, 48-49
Nye, Russel B.: ed., *New Dimensions in
  Popular Culture,* 128-29, 134; *The
  Unembarrassed Muse,* 88-89, 122

Oates, Joyce Carol, 99, 105-6; *them,* 102
Oberlin College, 34, 184
objectification of women, 10
O'Brien, Sharon, "Tomboyism and
  Adolescent Conflict," 73, 82
obstetrics, 12, 54-55
The Odd Women (Gissing), 103
Office of War Information, Magazine Bureau
  of the, 132
Of Woman Born (Rich), 70, 83, 200-202, 210
Oglesby, Carole A., 196; "The Masculinity/
  Femininity Game," 180-81, 193; ed.,
  Women and Sport, 180-83, 193; "Women
  and the Sport Governance System," 182, 193
O'Hara, Scarlett, 139

O'Kelley, Charlotte G., "Women and Blacks
  on TV" (with Bloomquist), 167, 189
Olander, Joseph D., *Ursula K. Le Guin* (with
  Greenberg), 113, 122
Olive Oyl, 158
O'Loy, Helen, 112
Onassis, Jackie Kennedy, image of, in
  women's magazines, 131-32
O'Neill, William L.: *Everyone Was Brave,*
  40-42, 45, 82; "In the Beginning," 72, 82-83
"On the Bloomer Costume" (E. S. Miller),
  172, 191
On the Verge of Revolt (B. French), 139,
  143-44, 151
orgasms, 28, 54
Orlando (Woolf), 99
Ormond (C. B. Brown), 104
Osgood, Frances, sentimental literature of,
  127
"The Other Criticism" (Katz-Stoker), 103,
  120, 207, 209
Oui, images of women in, 130
Our American Sisters (Friedman and Shade),
  71-73, 79
Our Bodies, Ourselves (Boston Women's
  Health Book Collective), 23
Out of the Bleachers (Twin), 73, 183, 194
The Oven Birds (G. Parker), 66-67, 82
"Ozzie and Harriet," 58

Pace, Judy, 146
Paisley, William: "A Scale for Sexism" (with
  Pingree et al.), 167, 190; ed., *Women and
  the Mass Media* (with Butler), 130-31, 133
Paley, Grace, 99
Pamela (Richardson), 57
Papachriston, Judith, 205
Papashvily, Helen Waite, *All the Happy
  Endings,* 89-91, 122, 143, 152
"Parables of De-Alienation" (Suvin), 115, 123
Parker, Bettye J., ed., *Sturdy Black Bridges*
  (with Bell and Guy-Sheftall), 109-10, 118
Parker, Gail, ed., *The Oven Birds,* 66-67, 82
Parks, Rosa, 21
"Participation in Public Affairs" (Spruill), 71,
  84
Parton, James, 94
"The Passive Female" (Flora), 128, 134
patent medicine, 56-57
Patte, Fred, *The Feminine Fifties,* 206
"Patterns in Prime Time" (Tedesco), 156, 159
Patterson, Lindsay, ed., *Black Films and
  Filmmakers,* 145, 152

Patton, Gwen, 61
Paul, Alice, 41
Peabody, Elizabeth Palmer, 35
Pearl Harbor, 43
Peary, Gerald: "Dorothy Arzner's *Dance,
Girl, Dance*" (with Kay), 140-41, 151;
Women and the Cinema (with Kay), 140-
42, 151
"The Pedestal Myth Reinforced" (Hoekstra),
128, 134
Penthouse, 164; images of women in, 130
perception: psychology of, in advertising,
165-66; role of language in determining,
201; role of social mythology in determin-
ing, 202. *See also* perceptual paradigms
perceptual paradigms, 208. *See also*
perception
Perebinossoff, Philippe, "What Does a Kiss
Mean . . . , " 187, 195
Perish the Thought (Conrad), 33-35, 78
Perry, Edward S., *The New Film Index* (with
MacCann), 150, 152
Perry, Eleanor, "Is There a Female Film
Aesthetic?" 149, 152
Persephone, myth of, 98
Peters, Margot, "Why Women Kill" (with
Krouse), 110, 120
Peterson, Theodore, *Magazines in the
Twentieth Century,* 127, 134, 164, 189
Peterson's, 129
Petry, Ann, 109
Petunia Pig, 23
Phelps, Elizabeth Stuart, 76; *Dr. Zay,* 50;
Gates Ajar novels of, 94; *The Story of
Avis,* 99
Phillips, B. J., "Comes the Revolution,"
185, 193
Phillips, E. Barbara, "Magazine Heroines,"
131, 134
Photoplay, 129
"Physical Parameters Used for Female
Exclusion from Law Enforcement and
Athletics" (Hudson), 180, 193
*The Physician and Sexuality in Victorian
America* (Haller and Haller), 54, 80
physicians: attitudes of, toward patent
medicine, 56; attitudes of male, to women,
45, 50-52, 54, 68; professionalization of,
49-52, 54-56, 69; role of, in treating women,
11-12. *See also* medical profession; science
Pickford, Mary, 18, 137, 143
Picnic, 143
Picnic on Paradise (Russ), 115

Piercy, Marge, 99, 105; *Small Changes,* 23,
100; *Woman on the Edge of Time,* 23, 86,
200
Pines, Jim, *Blacks in Films,* 147, 152
Pingree, Suzanne, "A Scale for Sexism" (et
al.), 167, 190
Pinkham, Lydia E., 55-57
pioneer women, 35-36. *See also* frontier
women
"Placing Women in History" (Lerner), 75, 82
Plath, Sylvia, 106; *The Bell Jar,* 99
Playboy, 21, 23, 164; cartoons in, 188; images
of women in, 130
Play It As It Lays (Didion), 99
"The Playmate of the Month" (Kallan and
R. D. Brooks), 130, 134
Poe, Alison, "Active Women in Ads," 167,
190
Poe, Edgar Allan, 104
poetry, 74. *See also* Brooks, Gwendolyn;
poets; Sigourney, Lydia Huntley; Walker,
Margaret; Wheatley, Phillis
poets, 8, 21, 94, 103, 105, 109. *See also* poetry
Polanyi, Michael: *Knowing and Being,* 201,
210; on perception, 201; on role of body,
201
political activism, 130
"The Political Activities of Antislavery
Women" (Lerner), 75, 82
political: activities of women, 26, 75;
advancement, 24; changes, 136-37;
conflict, 3-4; divisions, 65; loss of influence,
27, 32, 41, 49; organizations, 73; problems,
71; process, 40; roles, 42; southern women,
37-38; theory, 208; women, 17, 37-38, 61
political writing, 22-24, 86; black, 61;
nineteenth-century, 94-95; twentieth-
century, 102-3, 105, 112. *See also* science
fiction; underground comics
politics: absence of, in *Godey's,* 14; anti-
racial, 19, 21; exclusion of women from,
70; of illness, 52-53; of literary criticism,
205-8; of popular culture, 3-4, 131-32; role
of women in, 42, 66-67, 74-75. *See also*
sexual politics
Polykoff, Shirley: *Does She . . . or Doesn't
She?* 168, 190; founding by, of advertising
agency, 21; role of, in Clairol, Inc., 21
Popcorn Venus (Rosen), 136-38, 152
"Popular Art in *Godey's Lady's Book"*
(Ricciotti), 128, 134
The Popular Book (Hart), 116, 120
popular culture, use of, as propaganda, 4, 20,

132
"Popular Literature as Social Reinforcement"
   (K. C. McGrath), 102, 121
pornography, 130; in film, 24
"Portrayal of Women in American Literature,
   1790-1870" (Baym), 104-5, 118
The Power of Sympathy (W. H. Brown), 87,
   104
Powers, Anne, *Blacks in American Movies,*
   147, 152
Prairie Kate, 188
Pratt, Annis, 206; "The New Feminist
   Criticism," 205-6, 210
Pratt, Linda Ray, "The Abuse of Eve by the
   New World Adam," 103, 122
pregnancy. *See* birth control; childbirth;
   contraception
Presbrey, Frank S., *The History and
   Development of Advertising,* 164, 190
Pretty Baby, 24
printing, developments in, 90
Proctor, Jenny, 59
Production Code: description of, 18-19;
   effects of, on women, 19, 138, 144; location
   of, 150; role of Mae West in creation of, 18
professionalization: effects of, on women,
   49-55, 75; of medicine, 49-52, 54-56
professions: decline of women in, 48-50;
   male-dominated, 44-45, 49-50; novels about
   women in the, 50; women in, 42, 47-52
"Profile: Susanna Rowson . . . " (Martin), 94,
   121
"Programmed to Be Losers" (Gilbert and
   Williamson), 184, 193
Progressive Era, 41, 44, 71, 73
Progressive Party, 74
progressivism, 41, 44, 197
The Progress of Afro-American Women (J. L.
   Sims), 77, 83, 110, 123, 133, 135
"The Projection of a New Womanhood"
   (Ryan), 72-73, 83, 143, 153
Project on the Status and Education of
   Women, 182
"Prologue: The Myth" (Spears), 180, 194
propaganda, 4, 132
property rights: lack of, for women, 26, 30;
   of women, 161
prostitution, 19, 59
Protestantism, 31-32, 70. *See also* Calvinism;
   churches; disestablishment; ministers;
   religion
Protestant Nuns, 45
protest literature. *See* political writing

protest movements. *See* reform movements
Prynne, Hester, 97
psychological studies of women, 20, 43, 60-63,
   76, 168-70, 181-82, 204
psychologists, role of, in feminine mystique,
   28, 43
psychology, role of, in popular culture, 20
Psychology of Motor Behavior and Sport
   (Landers and Christina), 181
"Puberty to Menopause" (Smith-Rosenberg),
   68-69, 83
public broadcasting, 155
public policy, 44-46
puerperal fever, 54-55
Puerperal Fever As a Private Pestilence
   (O. W. Holmes), 55
Purdy, James, 106
Puritans: 6, 71; morality of, 97, 103
"The Puritans and Sex" (E. S. Morgan), 71, 82
Pygmalion myth, 97
Pynchon, Thomas, 106

Quakers, 67
Queechy (S. Warner), 91
Queen Christina, 147
"Queen for a Day," 21
quest, pattern of the, in women's literature,
   98-99
*The Question of Rest for Women During
   Menstruation* (Jacobi), 45

Rabkin, Eric S., *Science Fiction* (with
   Scholes), 116, 123
races, 39, 48, 59, 107, 167. *See also* black
   women; Civil Rights Movement; racial
   oppression; racial prejudice; racism;
   reform movements; slavery
racial differences, 66
racial oppression, 63, 74. *See also* black
   women; Civil Rights Movement; races;
   racial prejudice; racism; reform movements; slavery
racial prejudice, 37, 40, 74. *See also* black
   women; Civil Rights Movement; races;
   racial oppression; racism; reform movements; slavery
racial themes in film, 146-47
racism, 61, 64, 146, 200. *See also* black
   women; Civil Rights Movement; races;
   racial oppression; racial prejudice; slavery
Radcliffe, 36, 57
"A Radical Ethic for Sports" (J. Scott), 183,
   194

radical feminists, 41, 201
radicalism, 22, 24, 53, 198-99, 204; black, 60;
    in dress reform, 171-72; fear of, 41; of the
    1970s, 42
radical life style, 72
A Raisin in the Sun (Hansberry), 59
Ramsaye, Terry, ed., *International Motion
    Picture Almanac,* 152
Rawick, George P., *From Sundown to Sunup,*
    39, 83
Reaching Out (Mickelson), 99-100, 121
"Reader's Forum" (Bond), 108, 118, 157-58
Reconstruction, 41
"Recruiting Women for War Work" (Honey),
    132, 134
Redmond, Sarah Parker, 64
Red Sonja, 186
reflection hypothesis, 154
Reform Dress, 15, 173
reform movements, 15-16; abolition as part
    of, 15; in fashion, 15, 171; free love, 15;
    in the nineteenth century, 27, 72;
    preconditions for, 43; temperance as part
    of, 15-16
Regan, Nancy, "A Home of One's Own,"
    101-2, 122
Reginald, Robert, *Science Fiction and
    Fantasy Literature,* 116, 122
Register, Cheri, "American Feminist Literary
    Criticism," 207-8, 210
Reich, Wilhelm, 204
Reichert, Julia, 149
Reisig, Robin, "The Feminine Plastique,"
    130, 134
"Relicts of the New World" (K. L. Rogers),
    73, 83
religion: feminization of, 70, 76; in literature,
    91; role of, in black culture, 64-65; role of,
    in cult of domesticity, 31, 70; television as,
    154-55. *See also* antinomianism; churches;
    disestablishment; ministers; Protestantism;
    Puritans
*Report on Sexual Behavior in the Human
    Female* (Kinsey), 21
A Research Guide to Science Fiction Studies
    (Tymn et al.), 116, 124
The Resisting Reader (Fetterley), 106, 119
rest cure, 11, 68; effects of, on Charlotte
    Perkins Gilman, 198. *See also* Mitchell,
    Silas Weir
*Retrospective Index to Film Periodicals,
    1930-1971* (Batty), 150
"Revealing Herself" (Sternburg), 148, 153

The Revolution, 132
Revolutionary War, 7, 58; effects of, on
    religion, 70; effects of, on women, 29-30;
    role of women during, 30. *See also* Ellet,
    Elizabeth
"Revolution in Women's Sports"
    (*WomenSports*), 185, 193
Reynolds, Debbie, 148
"Rhoda," 158
"Rhoda's Marriage" (A. A. Berger), 158
Rhoda Trail, 188
Ricciotti, Dominic, "Popular Art in *Godey's
    Lady's Book,*" 128, 134
Rich, Adrienne: on language and perception,
    201; *Of Woman Born,* 70, 83, 200-202,
    210; on subject of woman's body, 101; on
    women's alienation, 200-202
Richards, Beah, 146
Richardson, Samuel, 8, 92; *Clarissa,* 57;
    Pamela, 57
Richter, Conrad, 97
Riegel, Robert E., "Women's Clothes and
    Women's Rights," 171-72, 191
Riley, Glenda, "Women in the West," 36, 83
Rinehart, Mary Roberts, 110
Ringgan, Fleda, 91
The Rise of the American Film (Jacobs), 145,
    151
The Rise of the American Novel (Cowie), 88
Rivers, Caryl, *Beyond Sugar and Spice* (with
    Barnett and Baruch), 185, 193
Roach, Mary Ellen, ed., *Dress, Adornment,
    and the Social Order* (with Eicher), 169-71,
    191
Robbins, Trina, 22, 186-88; *Girl Fight
    Comics,* 23; *It Ain't Me, Babe,* 188; *Wet
    Satin,* 188
Roberts, Helene, "The Exquisite Slave," 174,
    191
Robins, Margaret Dreier, 41
Robinson, Bill "Bojangles," 146
Robinson, Lillian S.: "The Critical Task,"
    206, 219; "Criticism—and Self-Criticism,"
    206-7, 210; "Criticism: Who Needs It," 207,
    210; "Dwelling in Decencies," 97, 122,
    205-6, 210; "Modernism and History" (with
    Vogel), 103, 122, 206, 210; *Sex, Class, and
    Culture,* 205-7, 210; "What's My Line?" 157,
    159, 207, 210
Robinson, Pat, 61
Rogers, Katherine, *The Troublesome
    Helpmate,* 106, 122, 208
Rogers, Kim Lacy, "Relicts of the New

World," 73, 83

roles: of black women in film, 145-46; decline of women's, in film, 139-40; fragmentation of women's, 28; played by women, 203; of women after the Civil War, 37; of women in film, 137-48. *See also* Berger, Peter; icons: Janeway, Elizabeth

Rølvaag, O. E., 97

romance, as genre, 57

The Roman Spring of Mrs. Stone, 148

Romanticism, 32, 67; and black pride, 61; effects of, on women, 53; as in love, 200

romantic love, as instrument of oppression, 200. *See also* Firestone, Shulamith; Perebinossoff, Philippe

Romantic period, 33

Root, Waverly, "Women are Intellectually Inferior," 20

Root of Bitterness (Cott), 66, 78

Rose, Carol L., "The ERA and Women's Sport," 182, 193-94

Rosen, Marjorie, 196; *Popcorn Venus,* 136-38, 142, 152; "Women, Their Films, and Their Festival," 149, 153

Rosenberg, Bernard, *Mass Culture* (with White), 145, 152

Ross, Diana, 146

Ross, Ida, 91

Rossi, Lee D.: "The Whore vs. the Girl-Next-Door," 130, 134

Rossner, Judith, *Looking for Mr. Goodbar,* 101-2

Roth, Philip, 106

Rothman, Sheila, 48, 66, 196; *Woman's Proper Place,* 43-46, 83

Rothman, Stephanie, 141

Rothschild, Amalie, 149

Roughly Speaking, 141

Rounds, David: *From Mary Noble to Mary Hartman* (with Edmondson), 156, 159; *The Soaps* (with Edmondson), 156, 159

Rowlandson, Mary, 8, 103; *The Soveraignty and Goodness of God,* 6

Rowson, Susanna Haswell, 8-9; *Charlotte Temple,* 8-9, 33-34, 57, 86, 90, 97, 104; profile of, 94, 102

Rubin, Carl, 22

Rudwick, Elliott, ed., *Black Matriarchy* (with Bracey and Meier), 39, 77

Rushing, Andrea Benton, "Images of Black Women in Afro-American Poetry," 74, 83

Russ, Joanna, 196; "The Barbarian," 115; *The Female Man,* 23, 86, 111-12, 116; "I Gave Her Sack and Sherry," 115; "The Image of Women in Science Fiction," 102, 111, 122; "I Thought She Was Afeared . . . , " 115; *Picnic on Paradise,* 115; "The Second Inquisition," 115; "Somebody's Trying to Kill Me . . . , " 100, 122; "Towards an Aesthetic of Science Fiction," 114, 122; "What Can a Heroine Do?" 101-2, 123; works on, 112, 115-16

Russell, Rosalind, 139, 141

Rutgers University, 68

Ryan, Mary P.: "The Projection of a New Womanhood," 72-73, 83, 143, 153; *Womanhood in America,* 25-29, 83

St. Cloud Visiter [sic], 65

St. Elmo (A. J. Evans), 15, 91

Salem witchcraft trials, 26

Sands, Diana, 146

Sanger, Margaret, 46; *Happiness in Marriage,* 18

sanitary napkins, 19

"Sapphire," 62

Sappho, 117

Sarah Josepha Hale and Godey's Lady's Book (Entrikin), 127, 133

Sargent, Dudley A., "Are Athletics Making Girls Masculine?" 183, 194

Sargent, Pamela: "Women in Science Fiction," 111, 123; *Women of Wonder,* 111

satire. *See* underground comics

Saturday Evening Post, 9, 167; appeal to women of the, 126-27

Sayer, Lydia, 171

"A Scale for Sexism" (Pingree et al.), 167, 190

Schechter, Harold, "Kali on Main Street," 18

Schlesinger Library, 36, 57

Schlissel, Lillian, "Diaries of Frontier Women," 73, 83

Schlobin, Roger C.: *Andre Norton,* 115, 123; *A Research Guide to Science Fiction Studies* (with Tymn and Currey), 116, 124; *The Year's Scholarship in Science Fiction and Fantasy, 1972-1975,* 115-16, 123

Schmidt, Dolores Barracano, "The Great American Bitch," 97, 123

Schmidt, Dorey, 132

Schneider, Rosalind, 149

Schneiderman, Rose, "A Cap Maker's Story," 65

Scholes, Robert, *Science Fiction* (with

Rabkin), 116, 123
Schreiber, Le Anne, 186
Schreiner, Olive, 52
Schroeder, Fred E. H., "Feminine Hygiene, Fashion, and the Emancipation of American Women," 176, 191
Schuetz, Stephen, "Spot Messages Appearing within Saturday Morning Television Programs" (with Sprafkin), 155, 159
Schultz, Elizabeth, " 'Free in Fact and at Last,' " 105-6, 123
Schumacher, Doris, "Subjectivities," 205, 208, 210
Schweninger, Loren, "A Slave Family in the Ante Bellum South," 72, 83
science, role of, in women's subordination, 20, 48, 51-54. *See also* industrialization; Industrial Revolution; medical profession; technology
science fiction: alternatives to childbirth in, 200; anti-technological attitudes in feminist, 52; concept of family in, 200; image of women in, 102, 111-12; studies of, 111-16; women's, 23, 113-16
Science Fiction (Lundwell), 116, 121
Science Fiction (Scholes and Rabkin), 116, 123
Science Fiction and Fantasy Literature (Reginald), 116, 122
"Science Fiction and Mrs. Brown" (Le Guin), 114, 121
Science Fiction at Large (Nicholls), 114, 122
Science Fiction Criticism (Clareson), 115-16, 119
Science-Fiction Studies (Mullen and Suvin), 114-15, 122
Science Fiction Today and Tomorrow (Bretnor), 112, 118
"Scientific Management in the Home" (Berch), 47, 77
scopophilia, 142
Scott, Anne Firor, 29, 48; "The 'New Woman' in the New South," 72, 83; *The Southern Lady,* 36-38, 83
Scott, Hazel, 146
Scott, Jack, "A Radical Ethic for Sports," 183, 194
"The Scribbling Women" (Bode), 88, 118
"The 'Scribbling Women' and Fanny Fern" (A. D. Wood), 94-95, 124
Scudder, Vida, 41
A Sea-Change (Gould), 100
"Search for Tomorrow," 21

"Second-class Citizenship" (Masinton and Masinton), 105, 121
"The Second Inquisition" (Russ), 115
The Second Sex (Beauvoir), 170, 177, 190
Sedgwick, Catharine Maria, 90, 93; *A New-England Tale,* 15
"Seduced and Abandoned in the New World" (Martin), 97-98, 121
Seeing Through Clothes (Hollander), 168, 191
Self-Raised (Southworth), 15
"Selling the Self-Made Woman" (Walsh), 50, 84
"Selling Women, Selling Blacks" (Culley and R. Bennett), 167, 189
seminaries, establishment of women's, 34
Seneca Falls Convention, 11, 21, 42, 67
Sense and Sensibility Collective, *Women and Literature,* 103, 123
sentimental fiction, 8-9; British influence on, 89-90, 92; characteristics of, 88-89, 104; history of, 87-88; in magazines, 127-28, 132; as precursor to modern popular fiction, 57. *See also* domestic novel; sentimental heroine; woman's fiction
sentimental heroine: in contrast to author, 94-95; description of, 87-91; as stereotype, 94. *See also* domestic novel; sentimental fiction; woman's fiction
sentimentalism, 67; effects on women of, 32-34
sentimental literature, as source of popular culture, 32. *See also* sentimental fiction
"The Sentimental Muse" (Bode), 88, 118
The Sentimental Novel in America, 1789-1860 (H. R. Brown), 87, 118
"Sentimental Short Fiction by Women Writers in *Leslie's Popular Monthly*" (Kern), 132, 134
settlement houses, 27
sewing machine, 90
sex, 18, 23, 59; in film, 138-39, 142; in Freud, 199; identification of women by their, 53, 66, 68-69; interracial, 72; Puritan's view of, 71; as subject of magazines, 130-31. *See also* bodies; homosexuality, lesbianism; sex manuals; sex organs; sexuality; sexual mythology; sexual stereotypes
Sex (West), 18
Sex and Racism in America (Hernton), 59
Sex and the Single Girl (H. G. Brown), 22
Sex, Class, and Culture (L. S. Robinson), 205-7, 210

"Sex Differences in Sports" (P. S. Wood), 185, 194
sex goddesses, 19, 22, 138-40, 144
Sex in Education (E. H. Clarke), 13
Sex in the Movies (Alexander Walker), 144, 153
sexism, 131, 142, 145; in advertising, 166-67; in cosmetics, 177; in sport, 182-85. *See also* racism, sexual discrimination; sexual exploitation; sexual mythology; sexual stereotypes
sex manuals, 11, 53-54
sex objects, women as, in advertising, 164, 166
sex organs, women identified with their, 53, 66, 68-69
Sex Psyche Etcetera in the Film (Tyler), 144, 153
"The Sexual Background of Dress" (Crawley), 170, 190
sexual discrimination, illegality of, 22. *See also* racism; sexism
sexual exploitation, 66. *See also* sex; sexism; sexual discrimination
sexuality, 18, 66-67; attitudes toward women's, 27, 29, 39, 51, 54, 66, 68-69, 76, 138; black women's, 10-11, 107; evidence of, 18; as form of self-perception, 181; lack of, in film, 19; Puritan's attitudes toward, 71; role of, in feminism, 40-42; as slavery, 66; white women's, 11; of women in film, 140-45. *See also* Kinsey, Alfred; sex; sexual mythology; Sherfey, Mary Jane
Sexuality in the Movies (Atkins), 144-45, 150
sexual mythology, effects of, on black women, 60-61. *See also* Johnston, Claire; sex; sexuality; sexual stereotypes
"Sexual Passion in Men and Women" (Blackwell), 66
sexual politics, 22, 149, 206
Sexual Politics (Millet), 22, 206
"Sexual Politics and Film" (*Velvet Light Trap*), 149, 153
sexual stereotypes, 4. *See also* sex; sexuality
Shade, William G., ed., *Our American Sisters* (with Friedman), 71-73, 79
Shadoian, Jack, "Yuh Got Pecos . . . ," 188, 195
Shane, 143
Shanna the She-Devil, 186
Shaw, Anna Howard, 41; *The Story of a Pioneer,* 63
She Done Him Wrong, 146
"she-merchants," 48

Sheppard-Towner Act, 18
Sherfey, Mary Jane, *The Nature and Evolution of Female Sexuality,* 23
The Ship Who Sang (McCaffrey), 112
Shirley Polykoff Advertising, Inc., 168
The Shocking Miss Pilgrim, 141
Shulman, Alix Kates, 105; *Memoirs of an Ex-Prom Queen,* 86, 103
The Sibyl, 171
Sigourney, Lydia Huntley, 34, 67, 88, 94; sentimentalism in, 15; sentimental literature of, 127
Silent Voices (Carson), 59
Sims, Janet L., *The Progress of Afro-American Women,* 77, 83, 110, 123, 133, 135
Sims, J. Marion, 11, 51, 68-69
Sinclair, May, *Mary Olivier,* 99
sitcoms, images of women in, 157-58
The Six-Gun Mystique (Cawelti), 96, 118
"A Slave Family in the Ante Bellum South" (Schweninger), 72, 83
slave narratives, 36, 39, 60, 66; image of black women in, 108
slavery, 7-8, 63, 66; attitudes of women toward, 37; effects of, on families, 39, 72; effects of, on women, 38, 61-62. *See also* black women; races; racism
Slote, Bernice, "Willa Cather and the Sense of History," 97, 123
Small Changes (Piercy), 23, 100
Smart-Grosvenor, Verta Mae, "The Kitchen Crisis," 61, 83
Smith, Amanda Berry, 64
Smith, Betty, *A Tree Grows in Brooklyn,* 116
Smith, Elizabeth Oakes, *Woman and Her Needs,* 34
Smith, Gerrit, "Correspondence . . . ," 172-73, 191
Smith, Jean Wheeler, "Frankie Mae," 109
Smith, Lillian, *Killers of the Dream,* 38, 83
Smith, Robyn, 185
Smith, Sharon, *Women Who Make Movies,* 149, 153
Smith, Sydney, 90
Smith College, 13
Smith-Rosenberg, Carroll, 29, 70; "Puberty to Menopause," 68-69, 83
SNCC, 60
The Soap Opera Book (Soares), 155-56, 159
soap operas: images of women in, 156; origins of, in sentimental novel, 58; studies of, 155-

56
The Soaps (Edmondson and Rounds), 156, 159
Soares, Manuela, *The Soap Opera Book,* 155-56, 159
The Social Construction of Reality (Berger and Luckmann), 203, 209
social feminism, 41-42
"Social History and the Crime Fiction of Mary Roberts Rinehart" (Hoffman), 110, 120
social inequities: causes of, 196, 199; results of, 196; role of education in effecting, 197. *See also* inequality
socialism, 197
socialization: of black women, 62; and sports, 179-81; of women by popular culture, 4, 9-10, 20, 31, 37, 51, 128, 187-88
"Socialization into Sport" (Greendorfer), 181, 193
social legislation, 44-45
social mythology, 3-5; and desire, 202-3; desire to transform, 24; as determined by television, 157; effects of, on nineteenth-century fiction, 89, 94; effects of, on women, 204; of the family, 203; movies as, 136, 141-43; negative and positive manifestations of, 202; negative stereotypes of women in, 17-18; reaction to, 17; as related to athletics, 179, 183; role of, in determining perception, 202; role of movies in creating, 137-38; similar role of women and blacks in, 199-200. *See also* archetypes; cultural mythology; heroines; icons; mythology; myths; stereotypes
Society of Friends, 67
"Somebody's Trying to Kill Me . . . " (Russ), 100, 122
Some Like It Hot, 143
Sorenson, Virginia, *The Evening and the Morning,* 97
Sorosis, 41
southern belle, 38
Southern Ladies Companion, 38
The Southern Lady (A. F. Scott), 36-38, 83
"The Southern Lady" (Wolfe), 38, 85
Southern Literary Messenger, 38
Southern Quarterly Review, 38
southern women, studies of, 36-39. *See also* black women
Southworth, Mrs. E. D. E. N., 90-91, 93; *Capitola,* 15, 91; *The Deserted Wife,* 91; *Ishmael,* 15, 91, 116; *Self-Raised,* 15

The Soveraignty and Goodness of God (Rowlandson), 6
Speaking of Science Fiction (P. Walker), 116, 124
Spears, Betty, "Prologue: The Myth," 180, 194
Special Issues of Serials About Women, 1967-1975 (Cardinale), 133
speech patterns, studies of, in cartoons, 188-89
Spillane, Mickey, 57
"The Spinster Detective" (M. J. Jones), 110, 120
Sport (Weiss), 183, 194
sports: effect of, on women's bodies, 179, 183, 185; effects of Title IX on, 182-83, 185; history of women in, 180, 184; legislation of, 182, 185; myths of women in, 179-83, 186; sexism in, 184; socialization of women and, 180-82, 184; studies of women in, 178-86, 192-94; women's championships in, 180
Sports Illustrated, 23; Athlete of the Year as picked by, 23-24
Sports in America (Michener), 184, 193
"Sportswomanlike Conduct," 185, 194
"Spot Messages Appearing within Saturday Morning Television Programs" (Schuetz and Sprafkin), 155, 159
Sprafkin, Joyce N., "Spot Messages Appearing within Saturday Morning Television Programs" (with Schuetz), 155, 159
Springer, Marlene, ed., *What Manner of Woman,* 103-6, 123
Spruill, Julia Cherry, "Participation in Public Affairs," 71, 84
Stage, Sarah, *Female Complaints,* 55-57, 84, 127, 135
Standard Directory of Advertising Agencies, 167, 190
Standard Periodical Directory, 133, 135
Stanford, Ann, "Images of Women in Early American Literature," 103-4, 123
Stannard, Una, "The Mask of Beauty," 170, 176-77, 192
Stanton, Elizabeth Cady, 16, 34, 59; as convenor of Seneca Falls Convention, 15; "Correspondence . . . ," 172-73, 192; as editor of *The Revolution,* 132; and fashion reform, 171-73; role of, in suffrage movement, 15; 40; studies of, 73; *The Woman's Bible,* 15, 67
Starstone 1, 115, 123

"Star Trek," 113
"A Statistical Survey of American Fiction,
1774-1850" (L. Wright), 117, 124
"Statistics of Female Health" (Beecher), 67
Stearns, Bertha-Monica: "Before *Godey's*,"
130, 135
Steinem, Gloria: founding of *Ms.* by, 22;
Introduction to *Wonder Woman*, 187, 195
Stephens, Ann, sentimental literature of, 127
stereotypes: of the bitch, 97; of black women,
62; of black women in film, 146; of black
women in literature, 107-8; in cartoons,
189; dangers of, 208; sexual, of women in
film, 145, 147-48; of southern lady, 38-39;
of women in advertising, 163; of women in
contemporary literature, 105; of women in
eighteenth-century literature, 104; of
women in nineteenth-century literature,
94, 96-97, 105. *See also* archetypes;
heroines; icons; images of women;
mythology; myths; roles; sentimental
heroine; social mythology
"Stereotypes of Women's Speech" (Kramer),
188, 194
Stern, Karl, *The Flight from Woman*, 201
Sternburg, Janet, "Revealing Herself," 148,
153
Stewart, Grace, *A New Mythos*, 98-99, 123,
202, 210
Stockwell, Georgianna, 96
Stoeltje, Beverly J., " 'A Helpmate for Man
Indeed,' " 35-36, 84
Stone, Gregory, "Appearance and Self," 168
Storm, Sue, 186
The Story of a Pioneer (Shaw), 63
The Story of Avis (Phelps), 99
Stowe, Harriet Beecher, 46, 59, 67, 93; *The
American Woman's Home* (with Beecher),
13; as sentimental novelist, 88; studies of,
73; *Uncle Tom's Cabin*, 90, 116
Strange, Violet, 103
The Strange Love of Martha Jones, 145
Stratemeyer Syndicate, 110
Streicher, Helen White, "The Girls in the
Cartoons," 156, 158-59, 189, 195
Sturdy Black Bridges (Bell et al.), 109-10, 118
Sturgeon, Theodore, *Venus Plus X*, 112
style, women with, in film, 148. *See also*
fashion
The Subjection of Women (Mill), 197, 209
"Subjectivities" (Schumacher), 205, 208, 210
subscription libraries, 90
suburban living, 20-21. *See also* feminine

mystique; industrialization
Such Good Friends (Gould), 100
"A Sudden Trip Home in the Spring" (Alice
Walker), 109
Suderman, Elmer J., "Elizabeth Stuart Phelps
and the Gates Ajar Novels," 94, 123
suffrage, 29, 67; consequences of, 27, 48-49;
documents of, 67; drive for, in south, 37;
histories of, 39-42. *See also* feminism;
suffrage movement; suffrage press;
suffragists; women's movement; women's
rights
suffrage movement, 15-16, 70; organs of, 132-
33. *See also* feminism; suffrage press;
suffragists; women's movement; women's
rights
suffrage press, 132-33
suffragette, 17. *See also* suffragists
suffragists, 40-41; biographies of, 40; and
social issues, 96. *See also* feminism;
suffrage; suffrage movement; suffrage
press; women's movement; women's rights
Suiting Everyone (Kidwell and Christman),
168-69, 191
Sula (Morrison), 100
Sullivan, Kay, *Films for, by and about
Women*, 149, 153
"Sumptuary Law" (Hurlock), 170-71, 191
sumptuary laws, 170-71
Sunday, Bloody Sunday, 148
The Superhero Women (S. Lee), 186, 194
Surfacing (Atwood), 99
"Surveying the Battlefield" (Le Guin), 114,
121
"A Survey of Le Guin Criticism" (Bittner),
113, 118
suttee, 204
Sutton, Joyce, 187; *Tits & Clits Comix* (with
Chevli), 23
Suvin, Darko: "Parables of De-Alienation,"
115, 123; ed., *Science-Fiction Studies* (with
Mullen), 114-15, 122
Swarthmore, 13
Sweet Polly Purebread, 158
Swerdlow, Amy, ed., *Feminist Perspectives
on Housework and Childcare*, 75
swimming: as sport, 174-75; suits, history of,
174-75
Swisshelm, Jane: *Half a Century*, 65; *Letters
to Country Girls*, 65; *St. Cloud Visiter*
[sic], 65
Switzer, Kathy V., 186
symbolic annihilation, 131, 154

"The Symbolic Annihilation of Women by
the Mass Media" (Tuchman), 131, 135, 154,
160

Take One, 149, 153
tampons, 19, 176. See also menstruation
Taylor, Elizabeth, 141, 144, 148
teaching profession, 49
technology, effect of, on women, 44, 46-47,
70-71. See also industrialization;
Industrial Revolution; science
"Technology and the Housewife . . . "
(Andrews and Andrews), 46-47, 77
Tedesco, Nancy S., "Patterns in Prime Time,"
156, 159
television: black women on, 155, 157;
cartoons, 158; commercials, 156; as
conservative force, 154-55; as contributing
to social mythology, 157; daytime, 155-58;
images of women on, 155-58; as "new
religion," 154-55; news, 158; role of women
in, 58; studies of women in, 154-60
temperance. See reform movements; WCTU
Temple, Charlotte, 97
Temple, Shirley, 19, 138-39
Tenney, Tabitha, Female Quixotism, 90
"Ten That Got Away" (Basinger), 141, 150
Terborg-Penn, Rosalyn: ed., The Afro-
American Woman (with Harley), 74, 80;
"Black Male Perspectives on the
Nineteenth-Century Woman," 74, 84;
"Discrimination Against Afro-American
Women in the Women's Movement, 1830-
1920," 74, 84
Terhune, Mary Virginia Hawes [pseud.
Marion Harland], Alone, 15, 91
Terrace, Vincent, The Complete Encyclo-
pedia of Television Programs, 1947-1979,
155, 160
Terrell, Mary Church, 63, 74
terrible mother, 4, 98-99
Terris, Virginia R., Woman in America, 76,
84, 133, 135
Tess, 24
"That's My Mama?" 157
Their Eyes Were Watching God (Hurston),
108
them (Oates), 102
"Themes in Cosmetics and Grooming"
(Wax), 169, 192
theoretical studies, 196-210; sources of
modern, 196-99
Theory of the Leisure Class (Veblen), 72, 84,

173-74, 192
therapy. See psychologists; psychology; rest
cure; "Therapy of Fashion"
"Therapy of Fashion" (T. Miller et al.), 169-
70, 191
"They Shall Have Faces, Minds, and (One
Day) Flesh" (Banta), 105, 117
Thinking About Women (Ellman), 208
Thirteenth Amendment, 16, 161
Thomas, M. Carey, 41, 59
Thoreau, Henry David, 104
"Thoughts About the Objectification of
Women" (Martineau), 149, 152
Till the End of Time, 145
Title IX, 22, 182-83, 185
Tits & Clits Comix (Chevli and Sutton), 23
To Be a Black Woman (Watkins and David),
59-60, 84, 110, 124
Tocqueville, Alexis de, 13
To Find an Image (J. Murray), 146, 152
"To Hustle with the Rowdies" (Masel-
Walters), 132, 134
"Tomboyism and Adolescent Conflict"
(O'Brien), 73, 82
Tomorrow's Tomorrow (Ladner), 61-63, 81
Toms, Coons, Mulattoes, Mammies, and
Bucks (Bogle), 146-150
Tortora, Phyllis, "Fashion Magazines Mirror
Changing Role of Women," 129, 135
The Total Woman (Morgan), 53
Toth, Emily, The Curse (with Delaney and
Lupton), 204, 209
Toward a Recognition of Androgyny
(Heilbrun), 106, 120
"Towards an Aesthetic of Science Fiction"
(Russ), 114, 122
Tracy, Spencer, 19
tragic mulatto, 107-8, 146
Trahey, Jane, ed., Harper's Bazaar: 100 Years
of the American Female, 130, 135
Train, George Francis, 132
Trapp, Adeline, 175
A Treatise on Domestic Economy (Beecher),
13, 47
A Tree Grows in Brooklyn (B. Smith), 116
"Trina" (Ward), 188, 195
"Trina, Queen of the Underground
Cartoonists" (Lanyi), 188, 194
The Troublesome Helpmate (K. Rogers),
106, 122, 208
Troy Female Seminary, 13, 34
Truth, Sojourner, 60, 63-64; "Ain't I a
Woman?" 16; The Narrative of Sojourner

Truth, 16

Tubman, Harriet, 16, 60, 63-64

Tuchman, Gaye: ed., *Hearth and Home* (with Daniels and Benet), 130-31, 135, 154-55, 160; "The Symbolic Annihilation of Women by the Mass Media," 131, 135, 154, 160

Tulane, 36

The Turning Point, 24

Turow, Joseph, "Advising and Ordering," 156, 160

Tuttleton, James W., " 'Combat in the Erogenous Zone,' " 105, 123

The TV-Guided American (A. A. Berger), 158

TV: The Most Popular Art (Newcomb), 155, 159

Twain, Mark, 105

Twin, Stephanie, ed., *Out of the Bleachers,* 73, 183, 194

Two Centuries of Costume in America, 1620-1820 (Earle), 168, 190

Tyler, Parker: "The Awful Fate of the Sex Goddess," 144; *Sex Psyche Etcetera in the Film,* 144, 153

Tymn, Marshall B., 113; *A Research Guide to Science Fiction Studies* (with Schlobin and Currey), 116, 124; *The Year's Scholarship in Science Fiction and Fantasy, 1972-1975* (with Schlobin), 115-16, 123

Tyson, Cicely, 146

Tyus, Wyomia, 185-86

Ullman, Liv, 141

Ulrich's International Periodicals Directory, 133, 135

Una, 34

Uncle Tom's Cabin (Stowe), 90, 116

underground comics, 22-23, 186-88

The Unembarrassed Muse (Nye), 88-89, 122

An Unmarried Woman, 24

Updike, John, 105-6

Up From the Pedestal (Kraditor), 67, 81, 172-73, 191

upper-class, 52. *See also* leisure class; middle class

Up the Sandbox, 148

Ursula K. Le Guin (De Bolt), 113, 119

Ursula K. Le Guin (Olander and Greenberg), 113, 122

utopias, 66

vamp, 18; image of, in film, 138, 142-43, 145, 148

Vassar, 13-14; health program of, 45

Veblen, Thorstein, 52, 58, 169, 196, 199; "The Economic Theory of Women's Dress," 173-74, 192, 198, 210; *The Theory of the Leisure Class,* 72, 84, 173-74, 192, 198, 210

Velvet Light Trap, 149, 153

venereal disease, 54

Venus Plus X (Sturgeon), 112

Victorian period, 71-72; attitude of, toward sex, 53-54; concept of self in, 92; image of women in, 137-38, 143; role of women in, 32-33, 41

Vietnam, 18

Village Voice, 150

A Vindication of the Rights of Woman (Wollstonecraft), 196-97, 210

virgin, image of, in film, 138, 142-43

Virgins, Vamps, and Flappers (Higashi), 73, 80, 142-43, 151

"Virgin Territory" (Friend), 112, 119

"Visual Pleasure and Narrative Cinema" (Mulvey), 142, 152

Viva, 23

Vogel, Lise, "Modernism and History" (with L. S. Robinson), 103, 122, 206, 210

Vogue, 64; studies of, 127, 129

Voices for the Future (Clareson), 114, 119

"Voluntary Motherhood" (L. Gordon), 69-70, 79

voodoo, 109

Vorse, Mary Heaton, *Men and Steel,* 63

Wagenknecht, Edward, *Cavalcade of the American Novel,* 88, 124

Wald, Carol, *Myth America,* 205, 210

Walker, Alexander: "The Last American Massacre," 144; "Marlene Dietrich," 141, 153; *Sex in the Movies,* 144, 153

Walker, Alice, 61, 99, 107-9; "In Search of Our Mothers' Gardens," 8; "A Sudden Trip Home in the Spring," 109

Walker, Margaret, 109

Walker, Mary E., 171

Walker, Paul, *Speaking of Science Fiction,* 116, 124

Walking Papers, 148

Wallace, Michele, 62, 73; *Black Macho and the Myth of the Superwoman,* 60-61, 84

Walsh, Mary Roth, 51-52; *Doctors Wanted,* 49-50, 84; "Selling the Self-Made Woman," 50, 84

Ward, Ed, "Trina," 188, 195

Warner, Anna, 93
Warner, Susan, 93, 105; *Queechy,* 91; *The Wide, Wide World,* 15, 34, 57, 88-89
Warren, Mercy, 59
Warwick, Dionne, 146
Washington, Mary Helen, 109; ed., *Black-Eyed Susans,* 108-9, 124; "Black Women Image Makers," 108, 124
Wasserstrom, William, *Heiress of All the Ages,* 89, 124
Waterman, Jessie, 100
Waters, Ethel, 146
Watkins, Mel, ed., *To Be a Black Woman* (with David), 59-60, 84, 110, 124
Wax, Murray, "Themes in Cosmetics and Grooming," 169, 192
WCTU, 15-16, 37
"The Weaker Sex? Hah!" (E. McGrath), 185, 193
Weber, Lois, 141
Webster, Noah, 9; *American Magazine,* 127
Weekly Visitor or Ladies' Miscellany, 9
Weibel, Kathryn: on images of women in magazines, 129-30; *Mirror Mirror,* 57-58, 84, 129-30, 135, 140, 153, 158, 160, 169, 192
Weil, Claudia, 149
Weiss, Paul: *Sport,* 183; "Women Athletes," 183, 194
Weisskopf, Walter, 178
Weld, Angelina Grimké, 67. *See also* Grimké, Angelina
Wellesley College, 13
Wells-Barnett, Ida, 64
Welsch, Janice, "Actress Archetypes in the 1950s," 141, 153
Welter, Barbara, 5; "Anti-Intellectualism and the American Woman," 76, 84; "Coming of Age in America," 76, 84; "The Cult of True Womanhood, 1820-1860," 76, 84; "Defenders of the Faith," 76, 84; *Dimity Convictions,* 70, 75-76, 84; "Female Complaints," 76, 84; "The Feminization of American Religion, 1800-1860," 70, 76, 84-85; "The Merchant's Daughter," 76, 85; "Murder Most Genteel," 76, 85; "Mystical Feminist," 76, 85
Wertmuller, Lina, 141
Wertz, Dorothy C., and Richard W. Wertz, *Lying In,* 52, 54-55, 85
West, Mae: as androgynous, 138-39; critique of, 142; effects of Production Code on, 19; feminist interpretation of, 140, 144; role of, in creation of Production Code, 18, 139;

Sex, 18; as stylist, 148. *See also* Young, Stark
West, women in literature of the, 96-97
westerns (TV), 58
Wet Satin (Robbins), 188
We Walk the Way of the New World (D. Lee), 61-62
Wharton, Edith, 59, 88, 89
"What Can a Heroine Do?" (Russ), 101-2, 123
"What Constitutes Equality for Women in Sport?" (Dunkel), 182, 192
"What Does a Kiss Mean . . ." (Perebinossoff), 187, 195
"What Maisie Knows" (Young), 153
What Makes Women Buy (Wolff), 163, 190
What Manner of Woman (Springer), 103-6, 123
"What's My Line?" (L. S. Robinson), 157, 159, 207, 210
Wheatley, Phillis, 8, 109
"Where Are the Women in Public Broadcasting?" (Cantor), 155, 159
"Where Have All the Stylists Gone?" (Braun), 148, 150
Whipple, Thomas W., "Women in TV Commercials" (with Courtney), 156, 159, 166, 189
White, Cynthia L., *Women's Magazines, 1693-1968,* 125, 135
White, David Manning, ed., *Mass Culture* (with Rosenberg), 145, 152
White, Deanna, ed., *The Lace Ghetto* (with Nunes), 67, 82
White, Willye B., 183
Whitman, Walt, 104
Whitney, Phyllis A., 101
"The Whore vs. The-Girl-Next-Door" (Rossi), 130, 134
"Why Aren't We Writing About Ourselves?" (Yee), 103, 124
"Why Do These Men Hate Women?" (Gornick), 76, 79
The Why of Fashion (Anspach), 168, 190
"Why Radcliffe Women Are Afraid of Success" (Gornick), 76, 79
"Why Women Fear Success" (Gornick), 76, 79
"Why Women Kill" (Krouse and Peters), 110, 120
The Wide, Wide World (S. Warner), 15, 34, 57, 88-89
Wieland, Joyce, 141
Wieland (C. B. Brown), 104

Wilcox, R. Turner, *Five Centuries of American Costume,* 168, 192
"Willa Cather and the Sense of History" (Slote), 97, 123
Willard, Emma, 13, 34, 59
Willard, Francis E.: *Glimpses of Fifty Years,* 65; "How I Learned to Ride the Bicycle," 73, 85, 183, 194; role of, in WCTU, 15-16
William L. Clements Library, 65
Williams, Carol Traynor, "It's Not So Much . . . ," 157-58, 160
Williams, Ora, *American Black Women in the Arts and Social Sciences,* 77, 85, 110, 124
Williamson, Nancy: "Are You Being Two-Faced?" (with Gilbert), 184, 193; "Programmed to Be Losers" (with Gilbert), 184, 193; "Women Are Getting A Raw Deal" (with Gilbert), 184, 193; "Women in Sport" (with Gilbert), 184
Willis, Sara [pseud. Fanny Fern], *Ruth Hall,* 94-95
Wilson, August Evans. *See* Evans, Augusta
Wilson, Joan Hoff, "Hidden Riches," 73, 85
Wilson, Lois, 143
The Wind's Twelve Quarters (Le Guin), 114, 121
Wing, Isadora, 102
"Winter's King" (Le Guin), 114
Winthrop, John, 66-67
witchcraft trials, Salem, 7
witches: as described in the *Malleus Maleficarum,* 204; women accused as, 204
Witch Hazel, 23
witch hunts, of Middle Ages, 52
wives. *See* housewives
Wolfe, Margaret Ripley, "The Southern Lady," 38, 85
Wolfenstein, Martha: "The Good-Bad Girl" (with Leites), 145, 148, 153; *Movies* (with Leites), 145, 153
Wolff, Janet L., *What Makes Women Buy,* 163, 190
Wolheim, Donald A., 113
Wollstonecraft, Mary, *A Vindication of the Rights of Woman,* 196-97, 210
Woman and Her Needs (E. O. Smith), 34
"Woman as Athlete" (Kenealy), 183, 193
Woman Citizen, 132-33
Womanhood in America (Ryan), 25-29, 83
The Woman in America (Lifton), 205, 209
Woman in America (Terris), 76, 84, 133, 135
Woman in Sexist Society (Gornick and

Moran), 176-77, 189-90
Woman in the Nineteenth Century (Fuller), 34
The Woman of the American Revolution (Ellet), 34
"Woman of the Year," 20
Woman on the Edge of Time (Piercy), 23, 86, 112, 200
Woman's Being, Woman's Place (M. Kelley), 73-74, 81
The Woman's Bible (Stanton), 15
"The Woman's Bible" (Stanton), 67
Woman's Body, Woman's Right (L. Gordon), 70, 79
Woman's Dress (M. M. Jones), 173, 191
Womans Exchanges, 45-46
woman's fiction: authors of, 92-93; decline of, 92; heroines of, 92-93; plot of, 91-92; role of, in cult of domesticity, 14; as term, 91. *See also* domestic novel; sentimental fiction; sentimental heroine
Woman's Fiction (Baym), 57, 77, 89, 91-94, 118, 143, 150
woman's film, changes in the, 139. *See also* film; women's films
Woman's Home Companion, fiction in, 128. *See also* Woodward, Helen
Woman's Journal, 132-33
Woman's Proper Place (Sheila Rothman), 43-44, 83
woman's sphere, 42, 67; development of concept of, 27, 51-52; in the eighteenth century, 29-30; history of, 43-46; in New England, 31; in the nineteenth century, 50; paradoxes in, 31. *See also* cult of domesticity; Industrial Revolution; lady; social mythology; Victorian period
Woman Suffrage and Woman's Profession (Beecher), 67
A Woman Under the Influence, 141
women, on intelligence of, 20
"Women and Blacks on TV" (O'Kelley and Bloomquist), 167, 189
Women and Economics (Gilman), 42, 65, 72, 79, 177, 190, 197-98
Women and Film (Kowalski), 149, 151
"Women and Film" (*Take One*), 149, 153
Women and Literature (Sense and Sensibility Collective), 103, 123
Women and Madness (Chesler), 98, 118, 170, 190, 204, 209
"Women and Science Fiction" (S. Wood), 112, 124

Women and Sport (Oglesby), 180-83, 193
Women and Sports (Kaplan), 178-80, 193
Women and Their Sexuality in the New Film (Mellen), 140, 152
Women and the Mass Media (Butler and Paisley), 130-31, 133
"Women and the Sport Governance System" (Oglesby), 182, 193
"Women Are Getting a Raw Deal" (Gilbert and Williamson), 184, 193
"Women Are Intellectually Inferior" (Root), 20
"Women Athletes" (Weiss), 183, 194
Women in America (Haber), 77, 80
"Women in Detective Fiction" (*Journal of Communication*), 110, 124
"Women in Film," 148, 153
Women in Focus (Betancourt), 149-50
Women in Literature (Myers), 117, 122
"Women in Science Fiction" (P. Sargent), 111, 123
"Women in Sport" (Gilbert and Williamson), 184
Women in Television News (Gelman), 158-59
Women in the Comics (Horn), 187, 194
"Women in the West" (Riley), 36, 83
"Women in TV Commercials" (Courtney and Whipple), 156, 159, 166, 189
"Women Libeled" (Mitchel), 187-88, 195
"The Women of Cooper's *Leatherstocking Tales*" (Baym), 103, 118
Women of Wonder, 111
"Women on Women in Films," 149, 153
"Women Reformers and American Culture, 1870-1930" (Conway), 72, 78
Women's Bathing and Swimming Costume... (Kidwell), 174-75, 191
"Women's Cinema as Counterculture" (Johnston), 142
"Women's Clothes and Women's Rights" (Riegel), 171-172, 191
women's clubs, 37, 41-42, 66, 74
women's colleges, 36, 44
Women's Council of the Commission on Interracial Cooperation, 19
"Women's Evolution from Economic Dependence" (Gilman), 66
Women's Film Co-Op, 149-50
women's films, 22. *See also* film; woman's film
Women's Gymnasium and Field Association, 184
Women's History Research Center, 150, 153
"Women's Literature and the American Frontier," 96-97, 117
women's magazines, 9; and advertising, 58, 126-27, 129-30; decline of, 126; fiction in, 128-29; images of women in, 129-31; as instruments of socialization, 128; as pornographic, 130; role of, in feminine mystique, 43, 128-29; role of, in rise of single woman, 53; role of Sarah Josepha Hale in designing, 14; satires of, in underground comics, 188; studies of, 125-30. *See also* ladies' magazines
Women's Magazines, 1693-1968 (White), 125, 135
women's movement: attitudes of medical profession toward, 54; bibliographies of, 76; discrimination in, 74; extent of first, 17; failure of, 40-42; histories of, 39-43, 49, 72; potential of, for blacks, 59; role of Betty Friedan in, 202; second, 21-22, 202. *See also* ERA; feminism; feminist revolution; suffrage; suffrage movement; women's rights
The Women's Movement in the Seventies (Krichmar), 76, 81
WomenSports, 185
women's rights, role of government in guaranteeing, 22. *See also* feminism; suffrage; suffrage movement; women's movement
"Women's Rights and American Feminism" (Lerner), 75, 82
The Women's Rights Movement in the United States, 1848-1970 (Krichmar), 76, 81
The Women's Room (M. French), 86, 100
Women's Work and Women's Studies (B. Friedman et al.), 76, 79
"Women, Their Films, and Their Festival" (Rosen), 149, 153
Women Who Make Movies (Sharon Smith), 149, 153
Women, Women Writers, and the West (L. Lee and Lewis), 36, 81, 96-97, 120
women writers. *See* writers, women as
The Wonderful World of TV Soap Operas (La Guardia), 155-56, 159
Wonder Woman, 187, 195
Wood, Ann Douglas, 31, 69-70; " 'The Fashionable Diseases,' " 68, 85; "The Literature of Impoverishment," 95, 124; "Mrs. Sigourney and the Sensibility of the Inner Space," 94, 124; "The 'Scribbling Women' and Fanny Fern," 94-95, 124. *See also* Douglas, Ann
Wood, James Playsted, *Magazines in the United States,* 126-27, 135
Wood, P. S., "Sex Difference in Sports," 185, 194

Wood, Susan: "Discovering Worlds," 114, 124; "Women and Science Fiction," 112, 124

Woodhull, Victoria Claflin, 59; role of, in free love movement, 15

Woodward, Helen, 63; *The Lady Persuaders*, 125-26, 135

Woolf, Virginia, *Orlando*, 99

working class, 40, 207. *See also* class; class differences; factory workers; immigrants; industry; lower class; races

"Working Women in Fact and Fiction" (Franzwa), 129, 134

The World Encyclopedia of Comics (Horn), 186, 194

World War I, 58-59; effects of, on women, 41-42, 48; popular literature of, 117

World War II: effects of, on women, 20, 43, 48-49; popular literature of, 117

Worrell, Estelle Ansley, *American Costume, 1840-1920*, 168, 192

Wright, John W., *Edsels, Luckies, and Frigidaires* (with Atwan and McQuade), 164, 189

Wright, Lyle H., "A Statistical Survey of American Fiction, 1774-1850," 117, 124

Wright, Martha Coffin, 65

Wright, Richard, 60

Wright, Sarah E., 99

writers, women as, 86-117; black, 8, 16, 21, 61, 74, 99-100, 106-10; in the eighteenth century, 8, 86-88, 103-4; limitations on, 98, 101-2; 112; in the nineteenth century, 8-9, 13-16, 32, 57, 88-100, 102, 105; in the seventeenth century, 6-7, 103; in the twentieth century, 21-24, 61, 86, 88, 98-103, 105, 107-17. *See also* domestic novels; sentimental fiction

Wyeth, Maria, 99

Wylie, Philip, 43, 106; *Generation of Vipers*, 20, 144, 153

X-chromosome, 20

Yale, 45

The Year's Scholarship in Science Fiction and Fantasy, 1972-1975 (Tymn and Schlobin), 115-16, 123

Yee, Carole Zonis, "Why Aren't We Writing About Ourselves?" 103, 124

"The Yellow Wallpaper" (Gilman), 11-12, 67, 198

Young, Sheila, 185

Young, Stark, 141, 153

"Yuh Got Pecos..." (Shadoian), 188, 195

Zacharias, Lee, "Nancy Drew, Ballbuster," 110, 124

Zaharias, Babe Didrikson. *See* Didrikson, Mildred ("Babe")

Zakrzewska, Marie, 50

ABOUT THE AUTHOR

Katherine Fishburn is Associate Professor of English at Michigan State University. She is the author of *Richard Wright's Hero* as well as numerous articles on women's literature and women's studies.